DISCOVERING
the
BIBLE

Contributors

Robert D. Branson, Ph.D. (Boston University)
Professor of Biblical Literature
Chair of the Division of Religion and Philosophy
Olivet Nazarene University
Bourbonnais, Illinois

Jim Edlin, Ph.D. (Southern Baptist Theological Seminary)
Professor of Biblical Literature and Languages
Chair of the Division of Religion and Philosophy
MidAmerica Nazarene University
Olathe, Kansas

Tim M. Green, Ph.D. (Vanderbilt University)
Professor of Old Testament
Dean of the School of Religion
Trevecca Nazarene University
Nashville, Tennessee

Roger Hahn, Ph.D. (Duke University)
Dean of the Faculty and Professor of New Testament
Nazarene Theological Seminary
Kansas City, Missouri

David Neale, Ph.D. (Sheffield University)
Vice President for Academic Affairs, Academic Dean, and Professor of New Testament
Canadian Nazarene University College
Alberta, Canada

Jeanne Orjala Serrão, Ph.D. (Claremont Graduate University)
Dean of the School of Theology and Philosophy and Associate Professor of Biblical Literature
Mount Vernon Nazarene University
Mount Vernon, Ohio

Dan Spross, Ph.D. (Southern Baptist Theological Seminary)
Professor of Biblical Theology and Literature
Trevecca Nazarene University
Nashville, Tennessee

Jirair Tashjian, Ph.D. (Claremont Graduate University)
Professor of New Testament
Southern Nazarene University
Bethany, Oklahoma

Alex Varughese, Ph.D. (Drew University)
Professor of Biblical Literature
Mount Vernon Nazarene University
Mount Vernon, Ohio

DISCOVERING

◆ the ◆

BIBLE

Story and Faith of the Biblical Communities

Alex Varughese, Editor

Robert D. Branson ◆ Jim Edlin ◆ Tim M. Green
Roger Hahn ◆ David Neale ◆ Jeanne Orjala Serrão
Dan Spross ◆ Jirair Tashjian

Copyright 2006
Beacon Hill Press of Kansas City

ISBN-10: 0-8341-2247-2
ISBN-13: 978-0-8341-2247-5

Printed in China

Cover Design: Chad Cherry
Cover Photo: Scala/Art Resource, NY. *The Return of the Prodigal Son,* by Rembrandt Harmensz van Rijn, 1606-69. From the Hermitage, St. Petersburg, Russia.
Interior Design: Sharon Page

10 9 8 7 6 5 4 3

Picture Credits
Illustrations
Keith Alexander: 193
Gustave Doré/Planet Art: 161, 163, 164, 169, 208, 212, 246, 404
Sharon Page: 85, 403
Photographs
Todd Bolen: 327, 329, 330, 336, 338, 341, 348, 412, 413, 419, 421, 431, 433 (bot.)
Diamar Interactive: 118, 190, 242
Digital Stock: 35, 46, 145, 150, 253
Getty Images: 184
Illustrated Bible Life/Brad Elsberg: 1, 3 (l. & r.), 11, 13, 15, 17, 18, 19, 24, 34, 36, 40, 50, 51, 55, 56, 61, 75, 80, 85, 86, 102, 103, 105, 106, 108, 112, 119, 124, 125 (top and bot.), 126, 127, 136 (top), 140, 162, 177, 178, 181, 189, 192, 199, 224, 228, 229, 232, 234, 238, 257, 265, 274, 280, 282, 287, 293, 294, 299, 301, 308, 321 (bot.), 328, 337, 340, 353, 354, 355, 357, 358, 386, 387, 389, 390, 397, 401, 408, 420, 422, 428, 429, 432, 433 (top), 441
Illustrated Bible Life/Rich Houseal: 3 (m.), 9, 16, 20, 26, 49, 79, 83, 89, 94, 99, 113, 202, 203, 204, 210, 217, 223, 252, 256, 260, 269, 276, 319, 399, 405, 409, 416, 447
Illustrated Bible Life/Greg Schneider: 5-8, 104, 151, 165, 188, 213, 230, 251, 268, 279, 283, 296, 298, 311, 314, 316, 344, 439, 446
Nazarene Publishing House/Don Pluff: 30, 132, 343
Sharon Page: 243, 249
PhotoDisc: 179
Photos.com: 392
Alex Varughese: 38, 60, 63, 72, 73, 78, 95, 133, 136 (bot.), 137, 139, 148, 153, 191, 194, 221, 226, 307, 315, 321 (top), 366, 367, 371, 372, 373, 374, 379, 380, 381, 398, 438
William Youngman: 170

Map List

Library of Congress Cataloging-in-Publication Data

Varughese, Alex, 1945-
    Discovering the Bible : story and faith of the biblical communities / Alex Varughese, editor.
    p. cm.
    Includes bibliographical references and index.
    ISBN 0-8341-2247-2 (hardback)
    1. Bible—Textbooks. 2. Bible—Study and teaching. I. Varughese, Alex, 1945- II. Title.

    BS605.3.V37 2005
    220.6'1—dc22

                                                                2005034694

Contents

UNIT I
INTRODUCTION
17

UNIT II
THE BEGINNING OF A COMMUNITY OF FAITH
49

Preface

The Bible plays an important role in the Christian faith and in Christian education. Virtually all Christians affirm the Bible to be inspired Scripture and the Word of God. At least one version of the Bible can be found in every Christian household. Most Christians are acquainted with the stories of Adam and Eve, Noah, Abraham, Joseph, Moses, Samuel, David, Jesus, Peter, Paul, and other well-known biblical personalities. Biblical stories are part of the Sunday School curriculum in most Christian churches. Preachers use the Bible as the source of their preaching and teaching every time Christian communities gather to worship God. Reading and studying the Bible is a regular part of the devotional life of devout Christians. Often Christians turn to the Bible for final answers to questions on morality and ethics. In spite of the popularity of the Bible and its sacred place in the Church and society, there is an alarming level of biblical illiteracy among Christians today. This is evident particularly among young people who enter Christian colleges and universities. One primary reason for this crisis is the lack of a disciplined approach for understanding and studying the Bible. Often personal and group Bible studies focus on the application of the Bible to contemporary issues without attempting to inquire into the setting, literary form, and meaning of the text to its original audience. An important objective of *Discovering the Bible* is to help its readers discover the world behind the biblical books and to provide them with the basic knowledge necessary to grasp the Bible's meaning and message.

Discovering the Bible is written primarily as an introductory level textbook for Bible survey courses in Christian colleges and universities that include the study of the Bible as an integral part of their liberal arts education program. The Bible requirement in the liberal arts curriculum presupposes the significant contributions of the Bible to humanity's heritage and civilization and its value as a masterpiece of literature. *Discovering the Bible* is an excellent resource that introduces its readers to the historical, literary, and theological features of the Bible. It is also intended to guide the students into having a meaningful encounter with the living and powerful Word of God in a life-transforming way during the formative years of their college and university education. However, this volume is not just a textbook for college and university level Bible courses; another important goal of this volume is to provide a readable and easy-to-understand resource for general readers and adults who desire to enhance their knowledge of the Bible.

There are not many single-volume introductory surveys of the Bible on the market today. We regard *Discovering the Bible* as an important contribution to meeting this critical need. A special feature of this volume is the historical, cultural, literary, archaeological, hermeneutical, and theological sidebars. These sidebars offer concise insights that take the reader into a deeper understanding of the Bible as God's Word. The books of the Bible are introduced in this volume with sufficient introductory information given on authorship, date, setting, and other relevant data necessary to understand their contents. Each chapter features learning objectives, vocabulary lists, guiding questions, summary statements, questions for further reflection and application, and key resources for further study. In addition, at the end of most chapters is a Bible study assignment designed to guide the readers toward developing a systematic approach to studying Scripture. *Dis-*

covering the Bible also shows a deep concern for highlighting the theological concerns of the Bible. Though this volume is not intended to cover all the various aspects of biblical theology, every chapter demonstrates the conviction of the authors that God was at work in the history of the biblical communities. Wesleyan perspectives on sin, salvation, grace, faith, holiness, and the hope of the believer undergird each chapter and are summarized in the theological sidebars.

All the authors of this volume have taught freshman level Bible survey courses at Christian liberal arts colleges and universities; several of them have been engaged in teaching for more than a quarter of a century. Each author is qualified as a specialist in biblical studies at the doctoral level. *Discovering the Bible* demonstrates the combined wisdom and expertise of these Christian scholars who have committed their lives to Christian higher education. They have been successful in communicating a clear understanding of Scripture and promoting a lively and informed faith through this volume.

Both students and teachers will find *Discovering the Bible* inviting them into the message of the Bible. It is my prayer that your love for Scripture and your relationship with God will deepen through the study of this book.

—Roger L. Hahn
General Textbook Editor
Beacon Hill Press of Kansas City

Editor's Note to the Student

Welcome to a journey that will lead you to discover the Bible in new and refreshing ways. As a reader and student of the Christian Scriptures, you will find this journey a challenging as well as an exciting adventure. The purpose of this book is to provide you with a clear and strategically designed road map that will make this journey an incredible learning experience.

In this journey, you will come across various major crossroads in the story and faith development of the people of God—Israel in the Old Testament and the early Christian community in the New Testament. The various chapters in this book are designed to help you understand the significance of these historical events and religious traditions, not only to the ancient faith communities, but also to the people of God in our present day. Each chapter is carefully laid out not only with descriptions of these events and religious ideas, but also with "markers and signposts" that will help you navigate through the chapter without much difficulty. We invite you to take some time at the outset to get acquainted with these "markers and signposts" before you embark on your adventure of discovering the Bible.

Objectives

At the beginning of each chapter you will find a list of objectives. These objectives explain what you should be able to do as a result of your study of each chapter. As you read and study each chapter, we suggest that you keep these objectives in mind. Underline or highlight the sections in the chapter where you find descriptions of topics that would help you accomplish the objectives.

Key Words to Understand

Each chapter contains explanations or definitions of terms, and identification of key people and places. These terms are placed at the beginning of each chapter and identified in boldface type where they appear in the text of each chapter. Your understanding of these terms and ability to identify or describe them is essential to your successful journey through the Bible.

Questions to Consider as You Read

At the beginning of each chapter you will also find several questions. These questions are aimed at setting the stage for your reading and study of the subject matter in each chapter. Before you start reading the chapter, write down your answers to these questions. This exercise will help you to think ahead and be prepared for the historical and theological issues presented in the chapter.

Summary Statements

It is natural for every reader of a book or a chapter in a book to ask the question, "What's the main point?" We have provided you with some significant statements at the end of each chapter that summarize the main points in the chapter. Use these summary statements to review what you have learned and return to the sections you may have overlooked.

Questions for Reflection

Each chapter also ends with some questions. These questions will help you think further about the issues, events, and religious ideas that you have learned. The goal of these questions is to guide you not only to process what you have learned but also to challenge you to apply the lessons in your own life situation.

Bible Study Assignment

At the end of each chapter, starting with chapter 3, you will find a Bible study assignment. This assignment, if faithfully carried out, will help you to develop a systematic method of reading and interpreting the biblical text.

Resources for Further Study

We do not presume that this textbook will answer all the questions you have about the Bible. Though much work has gone into the production of this book, we also acknowledge the providence of God's grace through other scholars who contribute to our understanding of His Word. Each chapter ends with a list of two or more Bible commentaries or resources that we hope would help you in your continued study of the Bible.

Sidebars

Throughout each chapter we have included color-coded sidebars with brief but useful information on topics related to biblical interpretation, theology, history, culture of the biblical times, literary features, and archaeology. The symbols and color coding of these sidebars are given below.

(I) Interpretive/hermeneutical sidebars deal with interpretive issues or explanations related to specific biblical texts.

(T) Theological sidebars deal with significant theological issues we encounter in the biblical books.

(H) Historical sidebars give insight into the development of religious concepts, ideas, or other historically relevant matters related to particular topics.

(C) Cultural sidebars illustrate cultural customs and religious ideas of the biblical times.

(L) Literary sidebars explain unique literary features of the biblical text.

(A) Archaeological sidebars explain significant archaeological discoveries that shed light on selected biblical texts.

Visual Aids

We have provided in this book pictures, maps, and illustrations that will be of help to you as you study this book. It is our hope that a "picture is worth a thousand words!" We also encourage you to study the maps and attempt to bridge the geographical distance between you and the actual location of the biblical events.

Finally, our prayer is that you will find these "markers and signposts" immensely useful as you begin your adventure of discovering the Bible.

Editor's Note
to the Instructor

The primary purpose of this volume is to present a clear, concise, easy-to-read, and pedagogically sound textbook for introductory level Bible survey courses that are an important part of the general education curriculum at Christian colleges and universities. Each chapter of the book addresses pedagogical concerns that are crucial to the mastery of the content as well as its evaluation and application. The pedagogical method includes learning objectives; vocabulary lists; questions for the students to get them oriented to the materials in each chapter; surveys of the content of the biblical books; summary statements; questions for further reflection, evaluation, and application of lessons learned; a Bible study assignment; and two or more key resources for further reading and study.

We have also included in each chapter numerous sidebars that address a variety of topics and issues. These color-coded sidebars—categorized as interpretive, theological, historical, cultural, literary, and archaeological—are placed at strategic places throughout the chapter. Interpretive sidebars deal with interpretive issues or explanations related to specific biblical texts. Theological sidebars focus on in-depth analysis of key theological issues and their relevance and application to the contemporary readers of the Bible. Historical, cultural, literary, and archaeological sidebars give supplemental information that will enhance the reader's understanding of the Bible. It is our hope that you will find these sidebars to be a valuable resource for your students' deeper understanding of God's Word. In addition to the sidebars, this volume also includes a Bible Study Assignment at the end of each chapter, starting with chapter 3. Our goal is to introduce the students to a proper method of reading and studying the Bible. We hope you will encourage your students to complete these assignments as part of the requirements for your course.

The contributors of this book bring with them unique perspectives and specialized training in different parts of the Bible. Each chapter reflects the writer's scholarly interest, academic preparation, and teaching expertise. The book contains materials and methods of instruction we have tested and tried in our Bible survey classes. Our long years of experience in teaching introductory Bible courses has guided us in making decisions about the structure, format, and content of this book. We present this book as a scholarly work, yet written at the level of college freshmen, in an easy-to-understand language. We have attempted to deal with critical issues with profound clarity, without shortchanging scholarship for a superficial treatment of the subject matter.

Finally, we have dealt with the Bible as Christian Scriptures, keeping in mind the essential unity and continuity of the Old and New Testaments. Wherever it is appropriate, the writers have sought to make points of contact between the story and faith of Israel and that of the Church. Unity of the Bible, the continuity between the two Testaments, and God's redemptive plan for all humanity that He accomplished through the death and resurrection of Jesus Christ are primary convictions of the writers of this volume. It is our hope that the reader of this volume will gain a basic understanding of not only the history of the biblical communities but also the foundational themes of biblical theology.

May you find this book to be an important tool in your hands as you teach your students God's eternal and faithful Word, and minister to them His grace in your classroom!

Acknowledgments

This single volume *Discovering the Bible* is a condensed and abridged edition of *Discovering the Old Testament* (Beacon Hill Press of Kansas City, 2003) and *Discovering the New Testament* (Beacon Hill Press of Kansas City, 2005). I wish to express my gratitude to my colleagues for allowing me to edit their materials in these two previously published volumes to produce *Discovering the Bible*. The following list shows where the work of these scholars can be found in this volume:

Robert Branson—chapters 11, 12

Jim Edlin—chapters 10, 16, 17

Tim Green—chapters 7, 8, 9

Roger Hahn—chapters 1, 2, 23

David Neale—chapters 21, 22

Dan Spross—chapters 24, 25, 26, 27, 28

Jirair Tashjian—chapters 19, 20, 21

Jeanne Orjala Serrão—chapters 29, 30, 31, 32

Alex Varughese—chapters 1, 3, 4, 5, 6, 13, 14, 15, 16, 18, 23, 24, 25, 26, 27, 28, and Epilogue

Roger Hahn, the Centennial Initiative general editor for the Church of the Nazarene, and Bonnie Perry, managing editor of Beacon Hill Press of Kansas City, have been faithful supporters of this project. This volume reflects the strong commitment of Beacon Hill Press to provide quality academic resources to Christian colleges and universities as well as to pastors and laity. I also express my gratitude to Richard Buckner, ministry resources product line editor at Beacon Hill Press, for his editorial assistance and oversight of this project, and Sharon Page for her skillful design and layout of this book.

I present this volume to my wife, Marcia, as an expression of my gratitude for her faithful support of my writing activities. My prayer is that the faithful presence of God we have discovered in our life together will be the gift of God to the readers of this volume. Thanks be to God.

Alex Varughese, Editor

UNIT I

INTRODUCTION

Your study of this unit will help you to:

- Discuss the formation of the Bible and the canonization of the biblical books
- Describe the literary structure of the Bible
- Summarize the history of Bible translation
- Establish guidelines for reading and interpreting the Bible

■ One Story, Many Books

■ How Should One Read the Bible?

1

One Story, Many Books

bjectives:

Your study of this chapter should help you to:
- Summarize the process of the formation of the biblical books and the canonization of the Old and the New Testament
- Describe the various major literary sections of the Bible and the books that are part of each of these sections
- Discuss the unity and continuity of the bibli cal story in the Old and the New Testament
- Summarize the history of the Bible's translation

ey Words to Understand

Revelation
Incarnation
Inspiration
Dictation theory of inspiration
Dynamical theory of inspiration
Canon
Theology
Salvation history
Torah
Nebi'im
The Dead Sea Scrolls
Kethubim
Canonization
Gospels
Letters
Apocalyptic literature
Targums
Septuagint
Vulgate
Apocrypha

Questions to consider as you read:

1. What is the relationship of revelation and inspiration to the making of the Bible?

2. How do the biblical books demonstrate the unity and continuity of the biblical story?

3. How do you relate the concept of the covenant community to the formation of the Bible?

What Is the Bible All About?

God's Revelation in History

The story of the Bible is often called "the greatest story ever told." This is an appropriate way to characterize the Bible because it is the story of a relationship in which God reveals and expresses His love toward humanity. This story reveals to the reader who God is. It is the story of divine **revelation,** the account of God's self-disclosure to humanity through His words and actions. Thus, this story is more than a mere "story," rather it is history, because historical events serve as the setting of divine revelation recorded in the Bible.

Historical events, beginning with God's creation of the universe and humanity, the rise of human civilization, and the emergence of world political powers, are all part of the story of the Bible. The biblical story that begins in the Book of Genesis with the account of God's creation of the universe and humanity ends in the Book of Revelation with the expectation of the consummation of history and the creation of a new heaven and a new earth. The focal point of the biblical story is the revelation of God in and through the person of Jesus of Nazareth. God took the flesh-and-blood form of a human being in the person of Jesus **(Incarnation)** and thus He revealed himself totally and completely to the world. Historical events in the Old Testa-

God reveals himself to us through His creation; a sunset over the Sea of Galilee.

ment constitute the setting of this ultimate reality of God's self-disclosure. The New Testament gives us the record of God's actions in history through the establishment of the Christian community and the growth of the Church throughout the Roman world. Human history continues to serve as the arena of God's actions through Christ and His Holy Spirit. We need to consider this essential relationship between revelation and history as we embark upon a journey with the communities of faith in the Bible.

Inspiration

Divine **inspiration** played an active part in the receiving and recording of revelation by ancient biblical writers. Though we cannot adequately explain the method and process of inspiration, the Scriptures testify that God played an active part in the writing of the Bible (2 Timothy 3:16-17; 2 Peter 1:20-21). Some Christians view inspiration as God's dictation of His speech to the writers of the Bible **(dictation theory of inspiration).** Wesleyan evangelical theologians recognize the active involvement of the Holy Spirit in the writing of the Scriptures **(dynamical theory of inspiration).** The Holy Spirit prepared the biblical writers to receive and communicate revelation. These writers received special understanding of God's activities in history, which they interpreted through the eye of their faith traditions, and communicated through the activity of writing. Dynamical theory focuses on the actual involvement of God's Spirit in the life and work of the biblical writers. Since the Holy Spirit is the active Agent in

communicating revelation through the Scriptures, we need to submit ourselves to the authority and guidance of the Spirit for our correct understanding of the Word of God.

The Bible as Canon

Revelation and inspiration give the Bible the distinctive place in the Christian Church as its **canon.** In a popular sense, the term *canon* refers to a collection of writings accepted by a religious body as authoritative and normative for faith and practice. The Bible as canon reflects the authority of the Scriptures in the Christian tradition. The Bible has authority because it is the record of God's self-disclosure. The Bible sets the standard (literally, the word *canon* in Greek means a rod, standard, or something straight) for faith and practice.

Biblical History

Various biblical stories relate to us what God has done in the past, what God is doing in the present, and what God will do in the future. Biblical writers have not only collected and arranged historical materials but also interpreted events to show the meaning and purpose of God's activities in human history. Biblical history is thus theological history, something quite distinct from secular history in content and orientation **(theology** properly is a "science" or the study of God and His attributes). It is distinct from secular history because it focuses on the activities of God and assumes a direct relationship between God and various historical events.

Biblical writers view the salvation of humanity as the ultimate purpose of God's actions in history. New Testament writers claim that God fulfilled the salvation plan through Christ who came into our world "according to the definite plan and foreknowledge of God" (Acts 2:23, NRSV). The apostle Paul speaks of the coming of Jesus Christ as God's "plan for the fullness of time, to gather up all things in him, things in heaven and things on earth" (Ephesians 1:10, NRSV). This "fullness of time" (*kairos* in Greek) is the time or the season set by God to fulfill His plans and purposes, the focal point of which is the coming of Jesus into the world to bring salvation to sinful humanity. Scholars often describe biblical history as **salvation history** (*heilsgeschichte* in German) because of its emphasis on humanity's redemption from sin.

Biblical history has continuity and unity. This is evident in the stories of both the Old and the New Testaments. The following major events constitute the framework of the Old Testament story:

> *Creation and humanity's sin (Genesis 1—11)*
> *God's covenant with Abraham and his descendants (Genesis 12—50)*
> *Israel's exodus from Egypt and the Sinai covenant (Exodus 1—40)*
> *Israel's wilderness journey and the conquest of Canaan (Books of Numbers, Deuteronomy, Joshua)*
> *Israel under the leadership of charismatic leaders (Book of Judges and 1 Samuel 1—9)*
> *The beginning of monarchy (1 Samuel 10—1 Kings 11)*
> *The divided kingdoms of Israel (1 Kings 12—2 Kings 25)*
> *The exile and restoration (Books of Ezra and Nehemiah)*

During the divided kingdom period the people of Israel came under the political control of Assyria, which brought an end to the Northern Kingdom. When the Assyrian domination came to an end, Babylon gained control of the Southern Kingdom, which resulted in the exile of its population to Babylon. During the Persian period, the exiles returned to their homeland. The later story of Israel (the Jews), though not recorded in the Old Testament, is well known. After the Persians, the Greek rulers controlled Palestine for nearly 170 years. Following the Greek rule, the Jews established an independent Jewish kingdom that lasted for about 100 years. The Jewish independence came to an end when Rome gained political control of Palestine. The story of the New Testament is set in this larger historical context of the story of Israel. The New Testament history shows how the hopes and expectations of Israel concerning the coming of the Davidic Messiah were fulfilled in the person of Jesus of Nazareth. An essential part of this history is the coming of the Gentiles into the Church, an evident display of God's faithfulness to His promise to bring a blessing to all the families of the earth through the family of Abraham.

Historical narratives in the New Testament primarily focus on the following two categories:

> *Birth, life, ministry, death, and resurrection of Jesus (Gospels of Matthew, Mark, Luke, John)*
> *The beginning and the expansion of the Church in the Roman world (the Book of Acts)*

The New Testament history does not end with the Book of Acts, but rather it continues even to the present day and will continue until the Second Advent of Jesus Christ. Biblical history in a real sense is our history, because we not only have inherited this story from the men and women of the Bible but also are participants in the ongoing drama of redemption that continues to be played out on the stage of human history. We cannot remain on the sidelines of biblical history as spectators, but we must enter into this "story" and thus experience a living and dynamic relationship with God.

The Making of the Bible

The Old Testament

The Old Testament (also known as the Hebrew Scriptures) is the Bible of Judaism and part of the Christian Scriptures. Except for a few passages in the Aramaic language (such as Ezra 4:8—6:18; 7:12-26; Daniel 2:4*b*—7:28), the books of the Old Testament are written in the Hebrew language. There are 39 books in the Protestant edition of the Old Testament. The Roman Catholic Old Testament has 7 additional books, commonly known as deuterocanonical books or the Apocrypha.

The Jewish tradition divides the Hebrew Scriptures into three sections: Torah (the Law), Nebi'im (the Prophets), and Kethubim (the Writings). The books that belong to the **Torah** or the Law (Genesis, Exodus, Leviticus, Numbers, and Deuteronomy) contain the earliest records of human history, and the earliest history of Israel. The stories of Israel include the stories of

the ancestors of that nation, their establishment as a people by God, the rules and regulations established by God for Israel's faith and life in the world, and the story of their journey into the land of Canaan. Except for Genesis 1—11, these books cover the history of Israel from about 1900 B.C. to 1240 B.C.

The section **Nebi'im** (the Prophets) has two subdivisions. The first section, also known as the Former Prophets (Joshua, Judges, 1 and 2 Samuel, and 1 and 2 Kings), deals with the history of the people of Israel, from their entrance into the land of Canaan to the beginning of their captivity in Babylon (1240 B.C. to 587 B.C.). These books are known as the historical books in the Christian tradition. The second section, the Latter Prophets, contains the books of Israel's great prophets Isaiah, Jeremiah, and Ezekiel, and the Twelve (Hosea, Joel, Amos, Obadiah, Jonah, Micah, Nahum, Habakkuk, Zephaniah, Haggai, Zechariah, and Malachi).

Dead Sea Scrolls

The oldest Hebrew manuscripts we have today come from a period around 100 B.C. These manuscripts, found at Qumran, in the northwest area of the Dead Sea, shed some light onto our understanding of the history of the manuscripts of the Old Testament. **The Dead Sea Scrolls,** discovered between 1947 and 1956, include two copies of the Book of Isaiah (one in its complete form), a commentary on the Book of Habakkuk, a number of psalms, and fragments of all the books of the Old Testament, except Esther. In addition, the caves at Qumran also yielded a large number of nonbiblical materials.

The section **Kethubim** (the Writings) contains the following books: Psalms, Job, Proverbs, Ruth, Song of Songs, Ecclesiastes, Lamentations, Esther, Daniel, Ezra, Nehemiah, 1 Chronicles, and 2 Chronicles.

Formation of the Old Testament

The Old Testament in its present form is the result of a long and complex process that included the writing and development of manuscripts and the acceptance of selected manuscripts as recognized Scripture by Judaism. The stories in the Book of Genesis were part of Israel's faith traditions during the days of Moses (13th century B.C.). Beginning with the Book of Exodus, the bib-

lical events focus on the life and ministry of Moses. The stories of Exodus, Leviticus, Numbers, and Deuteronomy belong to the Mosaic period. Perhaps a substantial part of these stories remained as Israel's oral tradition (orally transmitted stories from one generation to another) for another three or more centuries before they were fixed in a written form. It is also possible that large portions of the Books of Joshua, Judges, 1 and 2 Samuel, and 1 and 2 Kings existed in the form of oral tradition for a considerable period of time. Books of the Prophets belong to a period between the 8th and the 5th century B.C. Most of the Writings also could be dated to this period. It is likely that most of the Old Testa-

Qumran Cave IV, which contained a nearly complete copy of the Greek translation of the 12 minor prophets.

ment books received their final form between 800 and 400 B.C.

The locations where the writing of the books of the Old Testament took place are not clearly known to us. Palestine and Babylon are the likely locations of the writing activity. We do not have the original manuscripts (autographs) of the Old Testament books. Later copies or manuscripts of the Old Testament books are the products of scribes who made careful and accurate copies of existing manuscripts. The wear and tear and the decay of the scrolls would have prompted the making of new copies of older manuscripts.

Qumran discoveries confirmed the scholarly opinion that a variety of manuscript traditions existed during the pre-Christian times. Though not much is known about the history and growth of Old Testament manuscripts, we believe that around 100 B.C. Jewish authorities in Palestine began the process of examining the various manuscript traditions in order to establish the standard and official Scriptures of Judaism. This meant that a large number of manuscripts did not receive recognition as Scripture. This process was completed by A.D. 100.

Since the establishment of a standard and authoritative manuscript tradition, Judaism took special care in copying and preserving the manuscripts of the Old Testament books. By about A.D. 500, the scribes introduced a system of vowels and marginal notes *(masorah)* to the text of the Old Testament. The Masoretic Text (MT), which is the textual source for the Hebrew Bible today, is traced to the completed work of these scribes.

Canonization of the Old Testament

At various stages in the history of the growth and transmission of the books of the Old Testament, Judaism took steps to recognize these books as authoritative and normative for faith and practice. The precise history of this process (**canonization**) is not known.

Scholars believe that the books of the Law (Torah) were the authoritative scriptures (canon) of Judaism by about 400 B.C. It is possible that these books became authoritative under the influence of Ezra the priest, who influenced the Jewish life in the fifth century B.C. Judaism accepted the Former and Latter Prophets as canon around 200 B.C. Some of the Kethubim (the Writings) were part of the sacred Scriptures of Judaism in the early part of the first century A.D. The references to the Law and the Prophets and the Psalms in the New Testament (see, for example, Luke 24:44) indicate the nature of the Jewish canon in the first century A.D. Official acceptance of the Kethubim as canon took place during the Council of Jamnia around A.D. 95. During this council, the rabbis gave their official endorsement to all the 39 Old Testament books.

The New Testament

Twenty-seven different pieces of ancient Christian literature form the New Testament. The arrangement of the New Testament shows some striking similarity to that of the Old Testament. Like the Old Testament the New Testament begins with a narrative collection followed by a collection of occasional writings written within that narrated his-

The earliest copies of the New Testament manuscripts were written on papyrus made from the reedlike stalks of papyrus plants.

tory. The New Testament, like the Old, concludes with a prophetic view to the future.

The Books of Matthew, Mark, Luke, and John are called **Gospels** and are named after the person traditionally thought to have written or collected the material in them. Though some events and words of Jesus are common to two or three or even all four of the Gospels, each Gospel writer created a unique portrait of the life and the meaning of Jesus. Each of the Gospels devotes almost a third of the book to the final week, death, and resurrection of Jesus.

The fifth narrative book is the Book of Acts, which is clearly a second volume by the author of the Gospel of Luke. The prologues of both Luke and Acts make it clear that Luke intended these two volumes to be understood as part of the ancient genre of history.

Following the Gospels and Acts the New Testament contains two collections of early Christian **letters.** The first collection contains letters written by the apostle Paul to various churches or individuals (Romans, 1 and 2 Corinthians, Galatians, Ephesians, Philippians, Colossians, 1 and 2 Thessalonians, 1 and 2 Timothy, Titus, Philemon). The second collection of letters is often called the General or Catholic Letters. The term *Catholic* comes from the fact that many (though not all) of these letters were written to churches rather than to individuals (Hebrews, James, 1 and 2 Peter, 1, 2, and 3 John, Jude). All the letters address specific concerns—usually problems or potential problems—which the author was trying to correct by the letter.

The final book of the New Testament is Revelation, an **apocalyptic literature** that contains prophetic visions of the end time. Like the Old Testament, the New Testament concludes with a word of hope for the future.

Formation of the New Testament

With one or two probable exceptions, all the authors of the New Testament books were Jewish in both nationality and religion. The common language of the Jews who lived in Palestine at Jesus' time was Aramaic. However, it is almost certain that each of the books of the New Testament were written in the common Greek dialect called koine (Greek for "common") that was used throughout the eastern half of the Roman Empire at that time. Koine Greek was not the language of the classical authors but the language of business and international relations during the time of Jesus.

The books of the New Testament were written between A.D. 50 and 100. As far as we know, only a single copy of each book existed and that copy was at the church to which or for which the book had been written. Second-century documents suggest that these writings were read aloud in the church along with the Old Testament readings. In the course of time other churches would have requested copies of these books, which in turn led to the process of copying the New Testament.

The earliest surviving copies of books of the New Testament are written on papyrus. While it is possible that some books of the New Testament were written on parchment (such as Luke and Acts, which may have been prepared for general publication), it is most likely the majority of the New Testament was first written and then copied on papyrus.

The oldest known copy of a New Testament book is a small piece of papyrus found in Egypt that contains a few verses from John 18. Specialists believe it was written about A.D. 125, within a single generation of the time the fourth Gospel was first written. Several partial papyrus copies of the Gospels, Acts, and Paul's letters that were copied between A.D. 180 and 220 have been found in the last century. Complete copies of the New Testament written on parchment around A.D. 325 have also been found in the past two centuries. New Testament textual critics now have more than 5,000 whole or partial manuscripts (handwritten copies) of the Greek New Testament, most of them discovered in the past 200 years.

Canonization of the New Testament

It is likely that the first collection of New Testament books by the Early Church was a collection of the Pauline letters. This collection was completed most likely in the first 25 years of the 2nd century. Sometime between A.D. 100 and 150 the four Gospels were collected and bound together for publication. Marcion (mid-2nd century A.D.), who rejected the Old Testament, seems to have

Minuscules and Uncials

Some of the early manuscripts from the 3rd to 6th century are in formal letters, similar to capital letters. These manuscripts are called uncials. Cursive style of writing that connects one letter to another became the dominant method of copying at a later period. Manuscripts in cursive style follow a smaller script known as minuscule. There are thousands of New Testament manuscripts in the minuscule form. However, scholars regard uncials as the earliest and the most reliable sources of the New Testament.

The following are the key uncials, all on leather parchments in codex form:

Codex Sinaiticus, dated to the 4th century, contains all the 27 books.

Codex Vaticanus, also dated to the 4th century, is missing the section after Hebrews 9:13.

Codex Alexandrinus, dated to the 5th century, is missing the Gospel of Matthew.

History of the Printed New Testament

Erasmus of Rotterdam is the first scholar to publish a copy of the New Testament in Greek (1516). Later he published four more editions (1519, 1522, 1527, 1535) of this New Testament. Several other editions appeared between 1546 and 1604 (four editions by Robert Stephanus, nine editions by Theodore Beza). All of these editions of the New Testament were based on a 4th-century manuscript, often called Lucianic, also known as Byzantine, Antiochian, Syrian, Ecclesiastical, Koine, or Common text. This text tradition remained as the standard text of the New Testament in Greek until the end of the 19th century. Following the publications of Codex Sinaiticus and Vaticanus in the mid-19th century, B. F. Westcott and F. J. A. Hort published a critical edition of the Greek New Testament in 1881. Their study of thousands of manuscripts and New Testament quotations in the writings of the Church Fathers led them to conclude that Codex Sinaiticus and Codex Vaticanus contain the most reliable text of the New Testament. The Greek New Testament published by the United Bible societies in 1966 is based on the work of Westcott and Hort. This critical edition gives us an "eclectic" text based on the best witness of New Testament passages found in ancient manuscripts and early Christian writings. The United Bible Society edition has become an important source for modern English translations.

been the first to produce a canonical list of the New Testament books, which consisted of the Gospel of Luke (with the first two chapters edited out) and 10 of the letters of Paul (all but 1 and 2 Timothy and Titus). It is likely that the Christian Church initiated the development of the New Testament canon to respond to the heretical teaching of Marcion. The Muratorian fragment (written between A.D. 180 and 200 and discovered in 1740) contains the oldest list of New Testament books. This document, not available to us in its complete form, lists Luke, John, Acts, the 13 letters of Paul, the letter of Jude, two letters of John, the Wisdom of Solomon, the Revelation of John, and the Revelation of Peter. It is believed that the part that was destroyed contained reference to Matthew and Mark.

From the early part of the 3rd century comes the list of Origen (A.D. 184-254), which includes the four Gospels, Acts, the 13 letters of Paul, 1 Peter, 1 John, and the Revelation of John as books accepted by all the churches. He also listed Hebrews, 2 Peter, 2 and 3 John, James, and Jude among the disputed books, and a number of other books that were clearly rejected by the traditional Christian faith. It seems that the Early Church lived with the three categories of Origen (accepted, disputed, rejected books) for over a century. We find for the first time the present canonical list of 27 books in the annual Easter letter of Athanasius (A.D. 367), bishop of Alexandria. In this letter to his churches he listed the 27 books as authoritative or canonical and as Scripture that should be read in the worship of the Church. It appears the Synod of Hippo in North Africa officially recognized the 27 books of the New Testament as canonical Scripture in A.D. 393. The actions of that council were read again and accepted by the Synod of Carthage in A.D. 397. The notes from this council clearly identify the 27 books of the New Testament as canonical Scripture.

Translation of the Bible

The first attempt to translate the Bible is traced to the synagogue custom of giving an extemporaneous rendering of the Hebrew Scriptures in the Aramaic language. This custom existed during the days of Ezra and Nehemiah in the middle of the 5th century B.C. (see Nehemiah 8:8) and continued through the first 400 years of the Christian era. The Jewish scribes began to put these oral paraphrases into writing before the time of Christ. These writings are known as **Targums** (which means "translation").

Translation of a portion of the Old Testament from Hebrew into Greek was the first actual event in the history of Bible translation. This was done in Alexandria, Egypt, for the benefit of the Greek-speaking Jews who lived in Egypt. By about 250 B.C., the translators produced the Torah in the Greek language. Within the next 200 years the entire Old Testament was available in the Greek language. This translation is known as the **Septuagint** (LXX).

The Bible in the Latin language was the second major event in the history of Bible translation. Scholars believe that a version of the Bible in the Latin language existed as early as A.D. 180. In the fourth century A.D., Bishop Jerome began the task of translating the Bible into Latin, using existing Latin versions and the Septuagint. In A.D. 385 he moved to Bethlehem, where he spent the next 14 years translating the Hebrew Bible into Latin. During the sixth and seventh centuries, the Church Fathers gave priority to Jerome's work over other existing Latin versions. Though the word *vulgata* (meaning "common") was previously a term applied to the earlier Latin versions, eventually Jerome's translation came to be known as the **Vulgate.** Gradually, the Latin Vulgate became the official Bible of Western Europe during the Middle Ages.

The Apocrypha

The Septuagint translators included in their work other religious writings that did not receive official recognition as inspired and authoritative Scriptures of Judaism. These writings are known to the Protestant tradition as the **Apocrypha,** which means books that are "hidden." The following 15 books make up the traditional list of the apocryphal books: 1 and 2 Esdras, the Prayer of Manasseh, Wisdom of Solomon, Ecclesiasticus, Judith, Tobit, Additions to Esther, Baruch, Epistle of Jeremiah, the Song of the Three Children, Susanna, Bel and the Dragon, and 1 and 2 Maccabees. The Septuagint in the first century A.D. contained all the apocryphal books, except 2 Esdras. Later these books became part of the Bible in the Latin language, and they received canonical status during the Middle Ages in the Roman Catholic Church. During the Protestant Reformation, the Reformers questioned the authority of the apocryphal books. Martin Luther expressed the view that these books lacked inspiration, though they have value as historical or devotional writings. The Roman Catholic tradition continues to view these books as inspired and refers to them as deuterocanon (canon of a lesser authority). Protestant churches in general follow Luther's view. Bibles produced by ecumenical scholars include the Apocrypha in their work.

John Wycliffe (1330-84) made the first systematic attempt to translate the Bible into the English language. The goal of Wycliffe's work was to fight against the corruption in the Church by making the Bible available to the common people. His complete New Testament appeared in 1380. Two years later, he and his friends completed the whole Bible. After his death in 1384, his friends revised the first edition. The church authorities condemned Wycliffe's writings and ordered his bones to be dug out of his grave and burned.

Page from 1611 edition of the King James Version.

Matthias chosen.   Chap.ij.   The fiery tongues.

William Tyndale (1494—1536) was the first scholar to translate a portion of the Bible from the original languages. Fearing reprisals from the Church authorities, Tyndale moved to Germany in 1524 and published the first edition of the New Testament in 1526. This was the first printed edition of the English Bible. The Church authorities condemned his work, charged him with heresy, and in 1536 he was condemned to death.

Since the work of Tyndale, the following translations appeared in English in the 16th century:

Miles Coverdale, an associate of Tyndale, published the first complete Bible in English in 1535. John Rogers, under the pen name Thomas Matthew, published Matthew's Bible in 1537. Sir Thomas Cromwell, secretary to King Henry VIII, commissioned the production of the Great Bible in 1539, which was the first authorized English version. The Geneva Bible produced in 1560 was the first English Bible to use numbered verses. In 1568, the Bishops' Bible appeared as a revision of the Great Bible.

In 1604 King James I commissioned a translation of the whole Bible, as close as it can be to the original languages, to be used in all churches of England during worship. About 54 scholars worked in six groups. The translation work was started in 1607 and was completed in 1611. The New Testament portion of this new version was mostly an adaptation of Tyndale's work. The King James Version remained as the most popular Bible in English for nearly two and a half centuries since its original publication. The first revision of the King James Version (the Revised Version) was completed in 1885, followed by the *American Standard Version* in 1901. The *Revised Standard Version,* a revision of the *American Standard Version,* was completed in 1952. More recent attempts in Bible translation include the *New American Standard Bible* (1960), *The Jerusalem Bible* (1966), the *New International Version* (1978), the *New King James Version* (1982), *The New Jerusalem Bible* (1985), the *New Revised Standard Version* (1990), and the *New Living Translation* (1996).

Two theories of translation guide the work of translators who aim to produce English translations of the Bible in our day. The first theory calls for a word-for-word (literal) translation that preserves as much as possible the original word order and sentence structure. This *formal equivalence* method, though it is the more desirable way for the average reader to get closer to the original texts of the Bible, is often difficult to accomplish. Since thought forms and sentence structure vary from language to language, it is very difficult to maintain a strict adherence to this theory. Even the most faithful literal translations to a certain extent must modify sentence structure and arrive at the meaning of words that seems most appropriate to the context. The *New American Standard Bible* is the closest example of a literal translation. The second method calls for *dynamic equivalence* or thought-for-thought translation, which requires the use of modern idioms and thought forms to convey the message most authentically and accurately to the modern readers. The *New Living Translation* utilizes this method through-

out the translation process, in which even the cultural expressions are translated into modern idioms. The *New International Version,* the *New Revised Standard Version,* and the *New King James Version* represent translations that utilize elements of both word-for-word and thought-for-thought methods of translation.

The Covenant Community

It is a serious mistake to assume that one can understand the Bible simply by studying its literary characteristics and its historical background. The books of the Bible were not written to inform people; they were written to transform people. Though the Bible is full of fascinating historical, literary, and even theological details that are worthy of study, as God's Word, its purpose is to form people into a community of fully devoted followers of Jesus Christ. The Bible continues to be a primary source of influence in the world today through the theological truths it proclaims and through its vision of a transformed human society.

The process of canonization of the Bible makes it clear that it is the product of a community of faith. Not only did the people of God in ancient times discern as a community of faith which books belonged in the Old and the New Testaments and which books would not be included, but they also recognized the truth that these books were written to and for their life and faith as covenant communities. Every book of the Bible portrays in some way a picture of what the covenant people of God should look like. What the people of God believe, how they live their lives in community, and how they witness their faith to the world—these are fundamental questions addressed by the Bible.

The faith, life in community, and prophetic witness in the world of the Church is neither generic nor formless. The community of faith is a specific, intentional, and structured community. Specifically the Church that gave form to the New Testament and was formed by the New Testament understood itself to be in continuity with the Old Testament people of God, the covenant community of Israel. The authors of the New Testament believed that God's saving activity in the Old Testament was part of the story and preparation for God's saving activity in Christ. The covenant that God made with Israel was not rejected or laid aside with the coming of Christ. It was renewed and through the Holy Spirit internalized into human hearts. Thus the community of faith that forms in and through the New Testament does not regard itself as a completely new thing. Rather, it is the logical outcome of what God had been doing through salvation history in response to both human rejection and acceptance of His grace.

Old Testament Israel understood herself to be bound to God by the covenant of Mount Sinai. That covenant came into being because of God's saving works for Israel. The covenant envisioned a people whose life together and whose lives individually would reflect the holiness of the God to whom they were bound. This vision created expectations for the people of God, and the covenant laid out the consequences of living up to those expectations or failing to accomplish them.

In a similar fashion the Church of the New Testament understood that they were part of a covenant community in continuity with Israel. The renewal of that covenant came into being because of God's saving work for them in Christ. The New Testament envisions a people whose life together and whose lives individually reflect the holiness and the love of the God who revealed himself in Christ. That vision creates expectations for the covenant community, and the New Testament, especially the letters and Revelation, describes the consequences of the Church's living up to or failing to live up to God's vision for them.

Central to this concept of covenant is the community of faith. Neither the Old nor the New Testament envisions faith as a purely private matter. Though an individual's relationship with God is intensely personal, it is always lived out in community. Individual believers recognize their life together in worship, instruction, and ministry as the context for their personal relationship with God. There are many places in the New Testament where the word *Christ* refers to Jesus as a historical individual who was crucified and raised from the dead. There are many other places where the word *Christ* means the Church, the Body of Christ, the community expression of Christ. This community is a nurturing community that invites and challenges its members to become like Christ. The Bible is the road map to that covenant way of life, and it invites anyone who encounters God's Word to enter into that covenant community.

Summary Statements

- Revelation and inspiration played a key role in the making of the Bible.
- Biblical books show the unity and continuity of the history of salvation.
- The Bible came into being through a long and complex process of manuscript development.
- Biblical books are arranged under various major sections, such as Law, Prophets, Writings, Gospels, letters, and prophecy.
- The process of canonization helped establish the authenticity and authority of the biblical books.
- Bible translation has been an ongoing part of the history of the people of God in the Old and New Testament times.
- Biblical books inform the people of God how to live the covenant way of life.

Questions for Reflection

1. How does the structure of the New Testament reflect its "real-to-life" character and its applicability?
2. To what degree do you see the direction of God in the process of canonization? What conclusions do you make about the nature of the canon?
3. In what ways have you experienced life in a covenant community like that which produced and was produced by the New Testament? In what ways has your life in the church lacked elements of a covenant community?

Resources for Further Study

Ewert, David. *From Ancient Tablets to Modern Translations: A General Introduction to the Bible.* Grand Rapids: Zondervan, 1983.

Metzger, Bruce M. *The Canon of the New Testament: Its Origin, Development, and Significance.* Oxford: Clarendon, 1987.

Wegner, Paul D. *The Journey from Texts to Translations: The Origin and Development of the Bible.* Grand Rapids: Baker, 1999.

Willimon, William H. *Shaped by the Bible.* Nashville: Abingdon, 1990.

2 How Should One Read the Bible?

O bjectives:

Your study of this chapter should help you to:

- Describe the relationship of exegesis and hermeneutics to the process of understanding the Bible
- Identify the three worlds of biblical interpretation
- Evaluate the significance of the historical and cultural context of the Bible for biblical interpretation
- Describe the ways in which the literary genres of the Bible provide keys for understanding
- Describe the role of the reader and theological presuppositions in understanding biblical texts

K ey Words to Understand

Hermeneutics
Exegesis
Narrative
Laws
Poetry
Prophetic speeches
Wisdom sayings
Apocalyptic
Parable
Letter
Interpretive framework

Q uestions to consider as you read:

1. Why is a careful method of reading and interpreting the Bible necessary?

2. How does knowledge of the historical context of a biblical text enable a reader to discover the meaning of that biblical text?

3. How do the literary features of the text, such as genre and form, influence one's understanding of the text?

4. How does one arrive at an appropriate theological understanding from the biblical texts?

People often assume that it is easy to read and understand the Bible. While this may seem to be true, often we find a variety of interpretations when people read the Bible. It is not unusual for two people to read the Bible and come to different conclusions about its meaning for the Christian life today.

The process of canonization described in chapter 1 assumed a role or an authority for the Bible as the Word of God. While Christians may differ in how God made the Bible a Divine Word, almost all Christians agree that the Bible has such scriptural authority. This means that the Bible is attempting to communicate a message from God. Since we discover that not everyone reads and understands the same message, we must give attention to how to read the Bible.

The study of how to read and interpret the Bible is called **hermeneutics.** It includes patterns to study to determine how a text was understood when it was first written and how it can be applied to Christian life today. The study of a text to determine its meaning either in its historical context (when it was first written and read) or in its literary context (as the text now stands) is often called **exegesis.** Much of the work of people usually described as Bible scholars is devoted to the work of exegesis.

Recent decades have witnessed a wide variety of opinions about the best methods of exegesis and hermeneutics. Some of the strongest debates in theological colleges and seminaries, as well as in denominations, are debates about exegesis and hermeneutics. This chapter will present one widely accepted approach to reading and interpreting the Bible. It is not the only approach that is influential in circles of Christian biblical scholarship today, but it incorporates many of the current ideas about how to organize the study and interpretation of the Bible.

This approach recognizes three major perspectives from which a reader may gain useful understanding of the Bible. These three perspectives "create a world" in which the Bible is studied. The perspective of *the world behind the text* studies the historical and cultural background of the biblical books. This perspective attempts to re-create the political, economic, social, and religious world in which the author and the original audience lived. The perspective of *the world within the text* studies the language and literary characteristics found in the Bible. This perspective creates the literary world of the text and focuses on the means by which communication of biblical materials takes place. The perspective of *the world in front of the text* studies how we read the Bible today and how we apply it both to our own lives and to the life of the

Jewish reader wearing tefillin containing Scripture on his forehead.

Christian Church. This perspective attempts to understand the world in which the Bible is read, studied, and preached as the Word of God to people of Christian faith. This is the world of the contemporary reader.

The World Behind the Text

For several centuries now, Bible scholars have considered the historical background an essential part of the study of the Bible. The importance of the historical background can be understood by an analogy between understanding another person and understanding the Bible. We believe we understand other persons better when we know something of their life story. We try to discover where they come from, the major events of their lives, and the various influences that seemed to shape them. In a similar fashion, Bible scholars believe we can understand the Bible better if we know its historical and cultural setting and various events that have shaped the content of the Bible.

We outline below some of significant historical and cultural developments that constitute the "world behind the text" of the Bible. Later in this volume, we will deal in detail with the historical and cultural background of both the Old and the New Testament.

The World from Which the Old Testament Came

The world behind Genesis 1—11 cannot be reconstructed with certainty. Most Bible scholars view these chapters as theological documents that convey Israel's understanding of the earliest history of humanity. Though historical details are lacking, these chapters nonetheless throw some light on humanity's earliest cultural and social developments as well as religious practices. The stories of Genesis 12—50 are set in the context of the Amorite culture that dominated the Syria-Palestine region in the early part of the second millennium B.C. The early part of the New Kingdom period in Egypt (13th century B.C.) provides the setting of the stories of Exodus. The 13th century B.C. also serves as the context of the wilderness stories of Numbers. One should look into the political, cultural, and religious context of Canaan for a better understanding of the materials in both Joshua and Judges (13th to 11th centuries B.C.).

The growing influence and control of Canaan by the Philistines is the world in which the stories of 1 and 2 Samuel take place. Second Samuel portrays political stability and the emergence of a united kingdom under King David, which was continued during the reign of Solomon (1 Kings 1—11). The rest of the stories of 1 and 2 Kings reflect the unstable political conditions resulting from the division of the kingdom of Solomon into two kingdoms and the empire-building activities of Assyria and Babylon in the 8th to 6th centuries B.C. During this period, the Canaanite culture and religion continued to dominate the religion of Israel. In addition, Israel also came under the influence of the Assyrian and Babylonian religious symbols and forms of worship. The Assyrian destruction of the Northern Kingdom in 722 B.C. and the Babylonian exile of Judah in 587 B.C. are crucial not only for our understanding of the history narrated in 1 and 2 Kings but also for our reading of the books of Israel's prophets. Amos, Hosea, Isaiah, Jeremiah, and Ezekiel vividly remind us of the deteriorating political, social, and religious conditions of Israel in the 8th to 6th centuries B.C. The emergence of Persia as a world power provided hope for the nation's return and rebuilding; however, the restoration work failed to accomplish its goal of creating a faithful community that would be obedient to God's saving purpose. The Books of Haggai, Zechariah, Malachi, Ezra, Nehemiah, and Esther reflect the conditions of the restoration period.

The World from Which the New Testament Came

The New Testament entered history at a period that was extremely formative for Western civilization. This period witnessed the demise of the Persian Empire, the rise and fall of the Greek Empire, and the establishment of the Roman Empire. The most pivotal event in Jewish history between the Testaments was the attempt of Antiochus IV (Epiphanes) to destroy Judaism in the first third of the second century B.C. The Maccabean Revolt that began in 167 B.C. was a battle both to preserve Jewish identity and to set Israel free from the ongoing power struggles of the remaining factions of Alexander the Great's Hellenistic Empire.

The issues at stake in the Jewish struggle to maintain their religious and national identity were intertwined with the great political movements in the Greco-Roman world. These events include the short-lived independence of the Jewish nation under the Hasmonean rulers, the incorporation of Judea as a part of the Roman Empire, and the ascension of Herod as King of Judea.

The New Testament authors who narrate Jesus' birth set that birth in the context of both the Roman Empire at center stage and Herod the Great on the margin. Herod maintained political stability through extremely cruel measures, which included the murder of anyone he considered a threat to his kingship. His death marked the beginning of a period of gradual destabilization in Judea and Galilee, with the kingdom now divided among his three sons Archelaus, Antipas, and Philip. Eventually Rome placed Judea and Galilee under Roman procurators who ruled with cruelty and decreasing regard for Jewish religious sensitivities. Jewish unrest increased and came to a head in the latter part of the 60s, fueled by Roman oppression, Jewish apocalyptic expectations, and the rising antagonism of the Zealots against foreign domination. The outcome was the tragic destruction of Jerusalem by the Roman army in A.D. 70.

As a result of Roman victory,

An Israelite storehouse at Hazor, probably dated to the period of King Ahab.

the Jewish sects of the Sadducees and the Essenes and the party of the Zealots were destroyed. Only the Pharisees and the Jewish followers of Jesus remained. In the following decades the Pharisees attempted to reestablish Jewish identity and pride by emphasis on observance of the Law with continued attention to circumcision, Sabbath observance, and dietary laws. Since the followers of Jesus were increasingly engaged in a mission to Gentiles, this had the effect of excluding the followers of Jesus from the new form of Judaism. Most New Testament scholars believe Matthew's Gospel was written to urge Jewish believers in Jesus to remain true to both their Jewish heritage and the Gentile mission.

Because the destruction of the Temple and Jerusalem in A.D. 70 was such a traumatic experience for Jews, scholars seek to understand how a number of New Testament books, including all four Gospels, Hebrews, and James, fit into the chronology of Jewish history leading up to and following that destruction. Christian preachers and missionaries promoted the Christian faith in a world that was fertile ground for various other religious movements and ideas. Judaism, the mystery religions, the fertility religions, and several Greek or Roman philosophies were all attractive options for Christian converts. The many competing religious voices caused confusion among Christian converts. A number of New Testament books —including Romans; 1 and 2 Corinthians; Galatians; Colossians; 1 and 2 Thessalonians; 1 and 2 Timothy; Titus; James; 1, 2, and 3 John; 2 Peter; and Jude—were written to clear up theological confusion that arose in churches where the earliest believers listened to many religious voices seeking to persuade them of the truth.

The religious confusion was a problem also for the empire, and some local civic leaders thought it harmful to social order and security. In a number of locations either the empire or local officials or both began trying to reduce the religious confusion by limiting or eliminating the spread of religions from the eastern part of the empire. These religions included the mystery religions, the fertility religions, and early Christianity. Several New Testament books, including Hebrews, 1 Peter, and Revelation, were written to encourage early believers to remain faithful to Christ in the face of actual or threatened persecution that was attempting to reduce the religious confusion of the time.

It is clear that an understanding of the historical context of the biblical books is very helpful in providing a perspective from which to understand the message of the Bible. For this reason the careful study of the historical context of the biblical books has been an important part of biblical studies for more than two centuries. Scholars seek to determine the date and authorship of each of the biblical books, the audience(s) to which they were written, and the purpose those books hoped to accomplish. With such information scholars attempt to place each book in the historical context described above and thus to understand the way that historical context shapes a proper understanding of the book.

The World Within the Text

The study of the world within the text is the study of the literary character of the Bible. Of particular interest is the way in which the literary art of the text creates a world into which the reader or listener can enter. Further, the literary character of the text may enable the reader or listener to discover new insights and truths by entering that world created by the text. Certainly from an evangelical perspective one would hope the reader or listener would be empowered by the new truths and insights to bring them into the reality of the so-called real world.

It is clear that different kinds of literature have different ways and different abilities to create a world into which a reader or listener can enter. For that reason the study of the literary genre of the Bible is extremely important.

Literary Genre of the Bible

Substantial sections of Genesis, Exodus, Numbers, Joshua, Judges, 1 and 2 Samuel, 1 and 2 Kings, Ruth, 1 and 2 Chronicles, Ezra, Nehemiah, and Esther in the Old Testament contain **narrative** materials. Narratives may be simple accounts that deal with historical events *(historical narratives)* or *biographical accounts* or *autobiographical accounts* or accounts that explain the origin of the name of a place or a custom *(etiological narratives)* or *family* or *tribal history*. Narratives follow a plot, which usually involves a crisis in a human situation or relationship. Narratives aim to show how the crisis came to be and how it was resolved or not resolved. The Books of Exodus, Leviticus, Numbers, and Deuteronomy contain a large amount of **laws** or legal materials. These laws may be *casuistic laws* that illustrate a specific action and its consequence or penalty, *prohibitions, prescriptions, instructions,* or *commands* for proper living within the covenant community of Israel.

Approximately one-third of the Old Testament is in **poetry.** Psalms, Proverbs, Song of Songs, and Lamentations are some of the Old

Roman theater at Caesarea Maritima. This theater provided entertainment for Herod's guests.

Testament books that are completely in poetry. Within the Psalms, we find different types of psalms, such as *hymns, laments, thanksgiving psalms, psalms of confidence, liturgical psalms, royal psalms, wisdom psalms,* and *historical* and *prophetic psalms.* These psalms were used in Israel in various contexts of worship, and they provided the people with appropriate language for their worship of God.

The books of the Prophets contain **prophetic speeches** given by Israel's prophets. Prophetic speeches usually follow a messenger style form. *Messenger style speeches* conveyed a message of salvation and/or judgment. We also find within the prophetic books other forms such as *legal disputes, narratives, prayers, confessions, parables, vision accounts, instructions, wisdom sayings, funeral songs,* and so forth, that the prophets created to communicate a word from God. **Wisdom sayings** aimed to impart wisdom instructions through *discourses* and *dialogues* (Job and Ecclesiastes) and *proverbial statements* (Proverbs). Discourses and dialogues focus on complex issues of life and existential questions for which there are no clear answers. Proverbial statements seek to help the untrained person to become a productive and responsible individual in society. The Book of Daniel contains **apocalyptic** visions about God's sovereignty over human history and the establishment of His kingdom. These visions give hope to the faithful in the midst of their suffering for the sake of their faith in God.

The New Testament makes use of three major literary genres; they are narrative, letter, and apocalyptic. Gospels belong to the narrative genre. Within this genre, the Gospel writers utilize a variety of literary forms to communicate their message. *Sayings* are short, usually one-line statements that can stand alone or could be spoken in several different contexts. The *proverbs* or *wisdom sayings* are open-ended. They require the listener to think through the fact that they can be applied in either a universal way or in many ways. *Legal sayings* are sayings that pronounce the law of the kingdom or describe ministry principles.

Prophetic sayings are sayings that announce the coming of either salvation or judgment. Some of the sayings of Jesus are so embedded in stories about Jesus that the story is necessary to get the point of the saying. These stories are often called *pronouncement stories.* The saying usually comes at or near the end of the story. To correctly interpret the story one must focus on the saying rather than on the details of the story.

Many of the teachings of Jesus found in the Gospels are found in one of the **parable** forms. Jesus' parables are expansions of a central figure of speech, usually either a simile or a metaphor. Scholars usually describe Jesus' parables using four categories.

The *similitude* is an extended simile. Most of the similitudes are Kingdom parables that begin with the phrase, "The kingdom of God is like . . ." They appeal to a common truth and once the listener is willing to consider the comparison the teaching point has been successfully made. A second type of parable is often called a *parable proper.* It usually begins with a phrase like, "A certain person . . ." A parable proper gives a specific person for a point of comparison and tells a

Biblical "Criticism"

For some people the use of the word *criticism* to describe methods of studying the Bible seems inappropriate. The use of that word arose from the German term *Kritik* used to describe various methods of analyzing documents and texts. Thus the various biblical criticisms are methods of analyzing aspects of the Bible and its background. Following are some of the more common forms of biblical criticism:

Historical Criticism: the analysis of the historical background and historical accuracy of the Bible.

Textual Criticism: the analysis of manuscripts of either the Old or New Testaments to determine the most likely reading of the original.

Source Criticism: the analysis of biblical books seeking to determine possible sources used by the biblical author.

Form Criticism: the analysis of the literary forms of individual paragraphs of the biblical text. Form criticism was severely criticized (in the normal sense of the word) when it tried to establish historical authenticity on the basis of literary forms.

Redaction Criticism: the analysis of the way biblical authors edited (redacted) the sources available to them in the writing of the biblical books.

Tradition Criticism: the analysis of the way Old Testament authors made use of historical "traditions" from an earlier period of the Old Testament.

Composition Criticism: the analysis of the way biblical authors composed their books by studying the beginning, the structure and flow of materials, and conclusion of the book.

Social-Scientific Criticism: the analysis of the biblical world and biblical text from the perspective of the social sciences, especially sociology and cultural anthropology.

Rhetorical Criticism: the analysis of the rhetorical strategies used by the biblical authors.

Canonical Criticism: the analysis of the way the various parts of the biblical canon are to be related to each other or the analysis of the forces that led to the particular shape of the biblical canon that now exists.

Narrative Criticism: the analysis of the way narrative texts are shaped and the way they shape readers.

Reader-Response Criticism: the analysis of the way readers participate with a text in creating meaning for that text.

story. Often the parable proper begins in a very real-to-life way, but just as the listener has entered into the story and identified with the main character Jesus would introduce a very unusual twist to the story. This often drove home the point He was trying to teach.

An *example story* is a parable that clearly focuses on an expected response from the listeners. The best-known example story is the parable of the Good Samaritan found in Luke 10:29-37. The Samaritan of the parable was the one whose behavior they should emulate. A fourth type of parable is the *allegory*. Allegories are extended metaphors with several points of comparison. An allegory is a message in code about another subject, usually a theological truth. Allegories have been used very effectively for centuries to teach basic moral and doctrinal truths.

The parables illustrate the power of the world within the text. Parables appeal to the listener's imagination and enable the listener to enter a world created by the parable. There the listener is able to see truths and to make responses that he or she might not make if left to simply consider the matter from the standpoint of logic or argument. The world within the text is a place that allows the reader or listener to participate in the story without understanding or even thinking about the world behind the text, the historical background.

Letter writers also have certain flexibility that they can use within the constraints or conventions of letters. Unlike narratives, letters do not have freedom to change the basic structure of the beginning of each letter. The New Testament letters all follow the basic conventions of the typical Greco-Roman letter: salutation consisting of author's name, recipients' name(s), and greeting; thanksgiving; body of the letter; closing conventions.

Because letters are direct communication and dialogical rather than indirect like narratives, letters often will use different forms than those found in narratives.

One of the common forms found in letters is a *list*. Some lists are lists of virtues or vices. The lists of virtues and vices were a common form for moral and ethical teaching in the Greco-Roman world. Another particular form is sometimes called a list of rules for behavior. These lists are also called *household codes*. These codes describe the expected behaviors of husbands and wives, parents and children, and masters and slaves. Such household codes were also common teaching tools in the Greco-Roman world.

In some ways *word chains* are similar to lists. However, word chains are lists of concepts linked together in order to produce a movement toward a climax. These word chains are created for rhetorical effect to persuade the reader or listener.

The *diatribe* is a common form used in Paul's letters. Diatribes are rhetorical questions that anticipate objections of the reader or listener and give voice to those objections. This enables the author to answer the objection. *Hymns* are a literary form found in both letters and narratives of the New Testament. The opening two chapters of Luke are the primary locations in the Gospel narratives where hymns are used. In the letters a hymn is simply quoted by the author as a message already shared by both author and audience. In this way the author of the letter invites the readers or listeners into a shared world within the text, the world created by a hymn already known and loved.

Most scholars believe the basic genre of Revelation is *apocalyptic*. Apocalyptic literature made use of visions, symbols, and journeys through heaven to paint a picture of either God's coming judgment on the enemies of God's people or of God's coming salvation of His people. Some apocalyptic literature portrays both judgment and salvation. It is easy to observe the characteristics of Revelation that suggest its genre is apocalyptic.

However, the author of Revelation also describes the book as *prophecy* and has constructed it so that it has many of the structures of a *letter*. Thus the author of Revelation has freely adapted three different genres in constructing the book. In terms of understanding Revelation, we need to keep all three genres in mind and note the ways in which the author both follows and departs from the basic structures of each genre.

The World in Front of the Text

The study of the world in front of the text is the study of the way readers create meaning from the text. It deals with the ways in which the message of the text is recognized and appropriated by contemporary readers. Thus the world in front of the text focuses on the role of the reader and on the theological and practical applications that contemporary readers draw from the text.

The Role of the Reader

The process of hermeneutics has long recognized the role of the author in creating the meaning he or she intended to invest in a text. The role of the text as the vehicle by which meaning is carried and communicated has also long been recognized. The role of the reader has not received equal attention in hermeneutics though that lack has been somewhat remedied in recent decades. Authors may produce texts, but the text produced by authors never communicates without readers or listeners. An author may send a message through a text, but unless a reader or listener receives the message from the text, no communication takes place. The world of the author and the world of the reader meet in the text to produce meaning.

This does not mean that the reader can create any meaning he or she desires from the text. The way in which the author shapes the text clearly rejects many meanings a reader might like to impose on a text. However, a wise author recognizes that the process of communication will not be complete until the reader or listener has encountered the text and taken meaning from it. The wise author writes in such a way as to influence the meaning the reader will encounter in and take from the text.

One of the realities of communication is that the sender (author or speaker) can never completely control the meaning that the receiver (reader or listener) will receive. Language itself and texts in particular will always have certain "gaps" in meaning. For example, when Paul writes of "the love of God" being poured into our hearts in Romans 5:5, are we to understand "the love of God" to mean the love we have for God or the love God has for us? This is an example of a *grammatical gap*. In instances like this, a reader will fill in the gap by determining which way to understand the ambiguous phrase. That action of the reader may happen instinctively or it may require conscious thought. The author may try to control the result by the context or may instinctively trust the reader to arrive at the correct understanding.

Grammatical gaps are usually easily resolved. Literary or poetic gaps may be quite easy or more difficult for the reader or listener to resolve. James 1:13 states, "For God cannot be tempted by evil and he himself tempts no one" (NRSV). Should the reader add the words "with evil" to the final phrase? This is a *poetic* or *literary gap*. The author may have purposely created this gap to engage the reader in thinking about the role of God and temptation. The use of literary devices such as simile, hyperbole, and metaphor create literary gaps. The reader must determine the point of comparison for the communication to be successful. When Matthew quotes Jesus' saying, "You are the salt of the earth, . . . you are the light of the world" (Matthew 5:13-14), he requires the reader to determine the significance of the metaphors salt and light.

It should be clear that the closer the world of the author and the world of the reader are to each other, the more likely the reader will be to successfully close the gaps in the text. Likewise, it should be clear that the reader's *presuppositions* will play an important role in determining the way in which he or she closes the gaps in the text. The presuppositions or assumptions that a reader brings to a text become filters that allow some meanings to pass through the text into the understanding of the reader and cause other meanings to be filtered out. It is possible for a reader to become aware of at least some of his or her presuppositions. When this takes place the reader may then examine, reflect upon, and perhaps modify those presuppositions.

The reader's presuppositions are often held subconsciously. In contrast, one's beliefs are usually conscious. Those beliefs will also function as filters of meaning when reading a text. A person's presuppositions, beliefs, and attitudes constitute an **interpretive framework** that shapes the way a person reads the Bible.

Every reader brings to the Bible certain theological presuppositions. These theological presuppositions may include a commitment to certain theological conclusions that the reader will find in a text. However, the theological presuppositions of a reader most often function

tion to shape what the reader believes the Bible to be. Thus when readers believe the Bible to be the inspired Word of God revealing the will of God for all things necessary to salvation, they will read given texts in the Bible different from those who do not share that presupposition. Though some academic teachers of the Bible believe such theological presuppositions about the Bible should be removed when studying the Bible academically, it is better to simply recognize one's presuppositions. An academic reading of the Bible should cause the reader to reflect on his or her theological presuppositions about the text rather than to reject those presuppositions. Reflection on one's theological presuppositions offers the opportunity for new insights that may lead one to modify those theological presuppositions and beliefs. Obviously such modification might reject the presuppositions and beliefs previously held, or it might affirm and strengthen the beliefs and presuppositions with deeper understanding.

Theological and Practical Applications of the Text

Theological presuppositions about the Bible also shape the way readers interpret biblical text and find their application. The reader who presupposes that the Bible is the Word of God will interpret it in ways that are theological and practical for Christian living. How is this world in front of the text created?

First, those who believe that the Bible is the Word of God will usually conclude that the theological message communicated by the text is true. Thus they will seek theological meaning through both the world behind the text and the world within the text. Particularly, they will view the literary strategies used by the author of the text as sources of theological understanding. Thus, for example, the reader will recognize in the genre of gospel the message of good news from God. If the text is a prophecy of salvation in the Old Testament, they will recognize in the text a message of hope and salvation. If the text is a proclamation story in the Gospels, the reader will conclude that the particular saying that is the point of that proclamation story is the theological truth that should be understood from the text. If the text is a hymn of praise to Christ, the reader will take the message of that hymn to be the theological truth that is to be understood from the text.

In some instances the text will make direct theological affirmations. First John 4:16 declares that God is love. Leviticus 19 and Isaiah 6 (as well as many other passages) declare that God is holy. Certain

A prayerful attitude is important when we read the Bible.

texts declare that Jesus is the Messiah, the Son of God, and Lord. Other texts state that the Church is chosen by God to be holy. Once a reader presupposes that the Bible is the inspired Word from God, it is not difficult to derive theological truth from such direct affirmations.

In other instances, particularly in narrative sections, the text creates a world into which the reader imaginatively enters. The understanding that emerges from that encounter with the text will be regarded as theological truth for a reader who believes the Bible to be the Word of God. For example, Jesus' statement that the kingdom of God is like a mustard seed does not make a direct affirmation about the Kingdom (other than the affirmation that it is like a mustard seed). However, once the reader grasps the point of the similitude that the kingdom of God may have a small beginning and a great conclusion, that insight grasped by imagination is taken as theological truth. Narrative sections of Scripture yield theological understanding by such imaginative acts of reading much more often than by direct affirmation.

In some instances a text will give instructions to the original readers in a way that seems clearly bound by the culture of the author and audience. For example, in 1 Corinthians 11:2-16 Paul carefully argues that a woman should have a veil over her head when she prays and prophesies publicly in the church. Likewise a man should not cover his head when speaking in church. Though a few Christian groups understand this to be a direct affirmation of appropriate dress for men and women in church today, most understand

Paul's words to be conditioned by cultural assumptions of his time that are not shared by many modern cultures. In such cases a person who believes the New Testament to be the Word of God does not simply disregard the teaching of this passage. Rather, such a reader seeks to understand an underlying theological principle that led Paul to give the instructions he gave. In texts where cultural issues are evident, instead of following the literal instructions of the writers as that which express truth for today the readers will take the underlying principle as the theological truth that is applicable to their own cultural context.

Humility and Grace in Reading the Text

It is often easy for a reader who believes the Bible to be the inspired Word of God revealing God's will for people's salvation to assume that his or her theological reading of the text is as authoritative as the Scripture itself. The act of discovering theological truth in the text arises from theological presuppositions and beliefs that the reader brings to the text. Such theological interpretation should be done with humility and grace toward those who may not see the same truths in the text. If God is truly revealing himself and His will through the text, then one may trust God to accomplish that through the work of the Holy Spirit and the reading of each reader. God does not need one reader to coerce another reader to reveal truth to that second reader.

Conclusion

If one believes the Bible to be the Word of God or even a significant religious message, then the reader of the Bible needs to enter all three worlds discussed in this chapter. The world behind the text offers insight into the real-life circumstances in which the text first came into being. The world within the text provides the vehicle by which the meaning of the text can be discovered. There its energy and power was first known. The world in front of the text is where meaning ultimately connects to the reader; it cannot be ignored. Understanding each "world" and developing skill in working in each is essential to reading the Bible.

Summary Statements

- The diverse understandings at which people arrive when reading the Bible means we need a method by which we can read the Bible and agree on its meaning.
- The world behind the text provides an important framework in which to understand the biblical texts.
- The world behind the text helps us understand the Bible as a real-to-life book.
- The literary characteristics of the Bible help us understand the communication strategies of the biblical writers.
- Partnership of the readers with the author and text is important to allow meaning to emerge from the text.
- The theological presuppositions of the reader shape the ways in which he or she finds theological truth in the Bible.

Questions for Reflection

1. How does study of the historical and cultural background help you see the real-world nature of the biblical world?

2. What are some literary forms of the present world that you are familiar with? How does understanding them help you understand the way biblical authors used literary forms?

3. What are your theological presuppositions about the nature of the Bible? How have those presuppositions influenced the way you have understood the Bible?

Resources for Further Study

Dyck, Elmer, ed. *The Act of Bible Reading: A Multi-disciplinary Approach to Biblical Interpretation.* Downers Grove, Ill.: InterVarsity Press, 1996.

Fee, Gordon D., and Douglas Stuart. *How to Read the Bible for All Its Worth,* 2nd ed. Grand Rapids: Zondervan Publishing House, 1993.

Hauer, Christian E., and William A. Young. *An Introduction to the Bible: A Journey into Three Worlds,* 3rd ed. Englewood Cliffs, N.J.: Prentice Hall, 1993.

Tate, W. Randolph. *Biblical Interpretation: An Integrated Approach,* rev. ed. Peabody, Mass.: Hendrickson Publishers, 1996.

UNIT II

THE BEGINNING OF A COMMUNITY OF FAITH

Your study of this unit will help you to:

- Describe the world in which Israel's history and faith originated
- Discuss Israel's faith traditions about the origin of the world and humanity
- Summarize the story of the origin of Israel as a covenant people of God

- ■ The World of Israel's Origin
- ■ Israel Looks at the Beginning: Genesis
- ■ Israel Becomes a Covenant Community: Exodus
- ■ Road to the Promised Land: Leviticus, Numbers, and Deuteronomy

3   The World of Israel's Origin

O bjectives:

Your study of this chapter should help you to:
- Describe the general geographical setting of the Old Testament
- Identify the various cultures of the ancient Near East
- Recognize and locate key Old Testament sites on a map of Palestine

Q uestions to consider as you read:

1. Discuss how your particular geographic origin and culture may have shaped or influenced your religious perceptions.
2. What is the end result of studying history without the knowledge of geography?

K ey Words to Understand

Fertile Crescent
Sumerians
Cuneiform
Akkadians
Amorites
Hittites
Hurrians
Assyrians
Babylonians
Persians
Hyksos
Philistines
Pentapolis
Canaanites
Phoenicians
Arameans
Ammonites
Moabites
Edomites
Midianites
Amalekites
Palestine
Coastal plain
Hill country
Jordan valley
Transjordan
Negev
Shephelah

In chapter 2 we discussed the importance of understanding *the world behind the text* to gain a proper understanding of the biblical text. In this chapter we will briefly survey the geographical and cultural setting in which the development of Israel's history and faith traditions took place. This world includes not only the land called Canaan in the Old Testament, which became the home of the people of Israel, but also the neighboring countries and peoples in the ancient Near East.

The Ancient Near East

The world of the Old Testament—which includes modern countries such as Iraq, Syria, Lebanon, Jordan, Israel, and the northern part of Egypt—is mostly made up of dry and barren desert, with some fertile river valleys and numerous high and rugged mountains. Civilizations and cultural groups emerged in this region near the fertile valleys and river systems. Conflict and struggle for power was a way of life in this ancient world. Various powerful ethnic groups dominated this region at different times and controlled its

Ancient Near East—the Fertile Crescent.

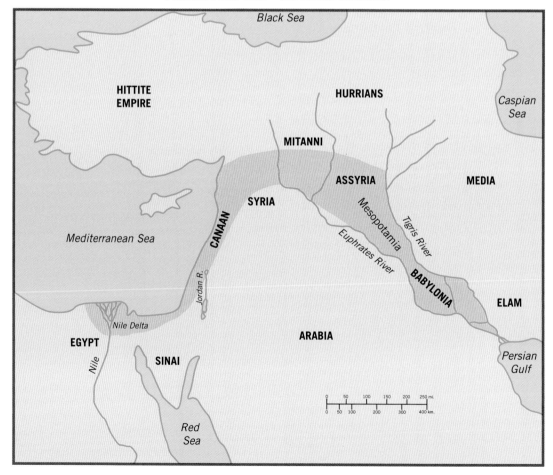

fertile land and trade routes. This region was also frequently the target of drought, famine, flood, locust attack, and other natural disasters. Life in this region, in short, was far from safe and secure.

The fertile and watered land area within the ancient Near East is made up of the Mesopotamian valley, the Nile delta, and Syria-Palestine. These three regions together have roughly the shape of a crescent (the **Fertile Crescent**). The Syria-Palestine region serves as the land bridge that connects the continents of Africa and Asia. In the ancient times various political powers made attempts to control this region because of its strategic importance to transportation and trade in the ancient world.

The Mesopotamian Valley

Mesopotamia, the land between the Euphrates and the Tigris rivers, in biblical times was made up of Assyria in the north and Babylon in the south. Various ethnic groups controlled the Mesopotamian region in the ancient times. We will briefly mention here some of the most significant cultures that dominated this region from 3000 B.C. to 330 B.C.

The **Sumerians** established their culture and civilization in the southern part of the Mesopotamian valley in the early part of the third millennium B.C. Scholars regard the Sumerian civilization as the first significant civilization in the history of humanity. They invented the wedge-shaped writing **(cuneiform)** and built cities such as Sumer, Eridu, Ur, Larsa, and Nippur. The Sumerians produced a number of religious myths and epics, including the earliest version of the Babylonian creation story *(Enuma Elish)*.

The **Akkadians,** a seminomadic Semitic group, gained control of the southern part of the Mesopotamian valley around 2300 B.C. and built an empire under the leadership of Sargon the Great. Though the Sumerian control of this area came to an end, their culture continued to have influence over this region. The Akkadians borrowed or adapted various elements of the Sumerian culture and religion. The Akkadian version of the creation epic *(Enuma Elish)* is believed to be an expansion of the Sumerian creation story.

The **Amorites** dominated virtually all parts of Mesopotamia and Syria-Palestine by the 18th century B.C. They were a Semitic group who established Mari and Babylon as centers of their political power. Mari discoveries include thousands of inscriptions that deal with legal, domestic, and business matters. Scholars believe that Israel's ancestors belonged to the Amorites.

The **Hittites** occupied the central part of Asia Minor between 2000 and 1700 B.C. The Hittite laws and treaty texts are important sources of our understanding of the ancient Near Eastern legal and political customs.

The **Hurrians** or Horites originally belonged to the mountains of Armenia. In the 17th and 16th centuries B.C., there was a tremendous influx of the Hurrians into all parts of the Fertile Crescent. In Mitanni, the Hurrians established a dynasty and an empire that controlled Syria and Upper Mesopotamia. This empire was later taken over by the Assyrians. Nuzi, in the East Tigris region, was a center of the Hurrian civi-

C Who Are the Semitic People?

The term *Semitic* has different connotations. Some scholars apply this term to those racial groups that have descended from Shem, one of the three sons of Noah. More broadly, this term applies to all who speak languages that belong to the Semitic family of languages (ancient languages such as Akkadian, Ugaritic, Canaanite, Phoenician, Hebrew, Aramaic, Ethiopic, Arabic, etc.). More narrowly, this term has been applied in modern times to the people of the Jewish ancestry. We use this term here in the broader sense to include all the ancient people that were related to each other by common cultural and linguistic characteristics.

lization. Nuzi tablets (dated to the 15th century B.C.) contain several parallels to the customs and culture of Israel's ancestors.

The **Assyrians** played a key role in the destiny of the nation Israel in the 8th and 7th centuries B.C. The northern part of Mesopotamia was the home of the Assyrians. Asshur and Nineveh were the chief cities of Assyria. The Assyrians launched an empire-building program in the 8th century B.C. under the leadership of Tiglath-pileser III and gained political control over Syria, Israel, and even Egypt. In the middle of the 7th century B.C., Assyria began to decline in power and lost control of its empire under the joint attack of Medes, Babylonians, and Scythians. The Babylonians destroyed Nineveh in 612 B.C. and with that the Assyrians ceased to exist as a nation.

The **Babylonians** became a major political power in the 7th century B.C. The southern part of Mesopotamia came to be known

as Babylon. The city of Babylon located on the Euphrates was the most influential city of the Babylonians. In 587 B.C. the Babylonians captured Jerusalem and forced the Jews to go into exile in Babylon. The Jewish exile lasted until 539 B.C. when Babylon was taken over by the Persian Empire. Cyrus the Persian king gave freedom to the Jews in exile, and he allowed them to return to their homeland. However, Jewish communities continued to exist in Babylon even after the Exile came to an end.

The **Persians** became a major political power in the 6th century B.C. under the leadership of Cyrus. Modern Iran was the home of the Persians. Cyrus incorporated the once powerful Medes and later the Babylonians into his empire. The empire extended westward to include Asia Minor, Syria, Palestine, and Egypt. The expansion eastward reached as far as India. Eventually the Persians declined in strength and their empire later became part of the world that Alexander the Great conquered around 335 B.C.

The Nile Delta Region (Lower Egypt)

The Old Testament mentions Egypt as the home of the people of Israel in the early part of her existence. Egypt of the Old Testament is the northern part of the land of Egypt (also known as Lower Egypt or the Delta region). Israel, in her later history, remembered Egypt as the land of her bondage. Egypt continued to exert political power over Israel at various times. Israel's kings often made alliances with Egypt, though the prophets condemned such actions as returning

Sphinx near the Pyramids of Giza.

to bondage and slavery. A substantial number of the Jews made Egypt their home during the Babylonian invasion of Judah in 587 B.C. Later Alexandria became a center of Jewish life in Egypt.

The Egyptian history is divided into the Old Kingdom period (2900-2300 B.C.), the Middle Kingdom period (2100-1710 B.C.), and the New Kingdom period (1550-330 B.C.). The two intermediate periods (2300-2100 B.C. and 1710-1550 B.C.) were marked by political and economic instability, and struggle for power among rival pharaohs. It is likely that Abraham made his journey to Egypt during the latter part of the Middle Kingdom period. During the second intermediate period, Egypt's rulers were **Hyksos**, a Semitic people who ruled Egypt for over 100 years. Joseph and the rest of Jacob's family settled down in Egypt during the early part of the Hyksos domination. The stories of Moses, Israel's bondage, and the exodus from Egypt belong to the early part of the New Kingdom period. By about 1000 B.C., Egypt lost its political strength, and it continued to deteriorate, as the world saw the rise of new emerging powers such as Assyria, Babylon, Persia, and Greece in the next several centuries.

Syria-Palestine Region

The Syria-Palestine area is the most frequently mentioned region in the Old Testament. This region is made up of countries such as Israel, Lebanon, Syria, and Jordan in the political map today. On the eastern coastal area of the Mediterranean Sea were the lands of the Philistines (Philistia),

Late Bronze Age gate at Megiddo.

most of which descended from Canaan, grandson of Noah. Cities like Jericho, Megiddo, Beth-Shan, Ai, Shechem, Gezer, and Lachish were centers of the Canaanite culture in the third millennium B.C. Toward the end the third millennium, the Amorites from the Mesopotamian valley invaded Canaan and destroyed many of the Canaanite cities. The Amorite invasion continued through the early part of the second millennium. Various Amorite groups settled down in Canaan and rebuilt the cities they destroyed. Abraham, who left his home Ur in southern Mesopotamia to settle down in Canaan, was most likely a part of the Amorite settlers (see Genesis 11:27—12:4). The inhabitants of this area included Girgashites, Perizzites, Jebusites, Hivites, and Hittites (see 15:19-20). It is likely that all of these people were subgroups within the Amorites.

the Cannanites (Canaan), and the Phoenicians (Phoenicia). Other ancient countries in this region included Syria (northeast), Ammon, Moab, Edom, and Midian (east and southeast). The southern Negev area was the home of the ancient Amalekites.

The **Philistines** were the primary inhabitants on the coastal plain southwest of Canaan, on the eastern shore of the Mediterranean Sea. They came to this region from Crete or some other islands in the Mediterranean Sea around 1200 B.C. Ashkelon, Ashdod, Gaza, Ekron, and Gath are among the key cities the Philistines established in this area (the Philistine **Pentapolis**). We know from biblical records that they were a constant threat to the Israelites. In the early years of Israel's history in Palestine, the Philistines exercised control over much of the coastal region and the lower hill country of Judah. The Philistine threat against Israel came to an end when David became king over Israel (1000 B.C.).

Prior to Israel's coming into the land of Canaan (Palestine), the primary inhabitants of this region were the **Canaanites,** a mixture of various ethnic and cultural groups,

The **Phoenicians,** who inhabited the northwest area on the eastern shores of the Mediterranean, were traders and seagoing people who had spread into Palestine and influenced the culture and religion of the Canaanites. Tyre was an important center of their trade and culture. They had made alliances with David and Solomon, kings of Israel, and helped design and build the Temple in Jerusalem during the days of Solomon.

The **Arameans** probably descended from the Amorite group and made Aram or Syria their home sometime during the second millennium B.C. The Bible makes several connections between the Israelites and the Arameans. The home of Abraham for a while was Haran, also known as Padan-Aram, the city of Nahor, and Aram Naharaim. The ancestors of Israel (Abraham, Isaac, and Jacob) maintained contact with this region. The earliest confessional creed of Israel (see Deuteronomy 26:5-10) refers to the father of Israel (most likely Jacob) as a "wandering Aramean." The center of the state of the Arameans was Damascus, which still remains as the capital of Syria. The people of Israel had frequent border struggles with the Syrians/Arameans from the 10th through the 8th centuries B.C.

The **Ammonites,** the **Moabites,** and the **Edomites** were the three primary groups of people who in-habited the area east and southeast of Canaan. The Book of Genesis describes the Ammonites and the Moabites as the descendants of Lot (19:30-38), and the Edomites as the descendants of Esau, Jacob's brother (chap. 36). The Ammonites lived directly east of the Jordan val-ley, with Rabbath-Ammon (modern Amman) as their capital. The Moabites, located south of the Am-monite territory, and the Am-monites maintained social and reli-gious contact, including marriage relationships with the Israelite pop-

Israel's neighboring kingdoms in the 13th century B.C.

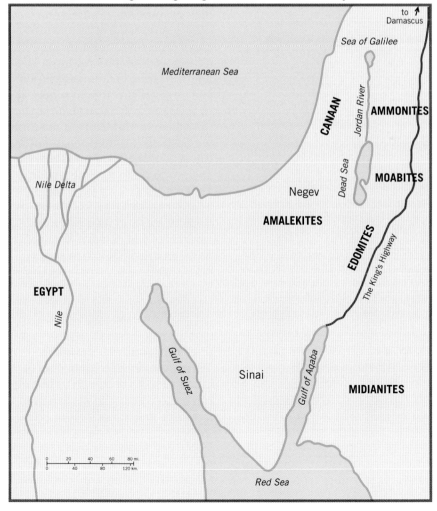

ulation. The Edomites, also related to the ancestors of Israel, kept a hostile attitude toward the Israelites. They were located directly south of Moab. The most important trade route of ancient times, "the King's Highway," going north to south went through Edom and Moab.

The **Midianites** and the **Amalekites** also played a role in the history of Israel. The Midianites occupied the land southeast of Edom. The Book of Genesis traces their origin to Abraham and Keturah (25:1-2). Moses' wife was the daughter of a Midianite priest. The Midianites oppressed Israel during the period of judges. The Amalekites were located directly south of Canaan, in the Negev area. These descendants of Esau (36:12) were the first nation that waged war against the people of Israel during Israel's journey to the Promised Land (see Exodus 17:8-16).

The people of Israel lived and attempted to maintain their religious identity as God's chosen people in the midst of a world that was for the most part hostile toward their existence. While there were military conflicts and struggles for survival and freedom, Israel also came under the powerful religious and cultural influence of these peoples around them. The Old Testament history narrates to us the tragic consequences of Israel's attempt to borrow cultural and religious ideas from these surrounding nations. The end result was the loss of their identity, and the freedom that God brought to them by saving them from their bondage to the Egyptians. To this story, we shall return later.

The Land of Palestine

The land God promised to give to the descendants of Abraham is described in Exodus as a "land flowing with milk and honey" (3:8). This land has various names, in addition to the common designations such as the Promised Land and the Holy Land. In the Bible, it is commonly called Canaan. The other common name is Palestine, which actually associates the land with the Philistines, who were once the greatest threat to Israel's existence in the Promised Land. This name comes from Herodotus, a Greek historian who lived in the fifth century B.C. Romans and others who came after used the name Palestine, and it remained in popular use until recently. The Land of Israel is the modern political term for the area that belongs to the Jewish state today.

Canaan or **Palestine** is the term we prefer to use for the land of the Old Testament Israel since it carries no political connotations. This land is located between the Mediterranean Sea (the Great Sea in the Bible) and the desert. It is relatively small in area, about 350 miles long from north to south and 60 miles wide from east to west. However, the biblical boundary "from Dan to Beer-sheba" was only 150 miles long. This land shows extreme variations in physical features and climate. Within this small region, one could be at a place such as Mount Hermon, which is 9,100 feet above sea level, and in a few hours reach the Dead Sea area, which is nearly 1,300 feet below sea level, the lowest spot on earth.

Palestine has four distinct geographical regions. The **coastal**

plain along the Mediterranean Sea stretches from Gaza in the south to Lebanon in the north. This area is a narrow strip of land with hills on the east and the sea on the west. The Mount Carmel range, which almost reaches the sea in the northern part of the land, divides the coastal plain into a northern and southern section. Acco in the northern part of the plain was an important harbor city in ancient times. The southern section includes the Plain of Sharon, a fertile area with a natural harbor Joppa (modern Jaffa). The Philistines controlled the southern part of the Plain of Sharon, the area south of Joppa, and hence this region is sometimes called the Plain of Philistia.

The central **hill country** is the second main geographical subdivision of the land of Palestine. This strip of land extends from Galilee in the north to the Negev in the south. It has three parts: the hills of Galilee, the hills of Samaria, and the hills of Judah. A valley that runs from east to west divides the hills of Galilee into Upper Galilee and Lower Galilee. The mountains of Upper Galilee are higher in elevation than those of the Lower Galilee. The Lower Galilee region has isolated mountains like Mount Tabor and broad valleys. The Plain of Jezreel (also known as the valley of Jezreel), which is about 50 miles long, connects the coastal region with the Jordan valley. It is about 20 miles wide from north to south and separates the Galilee region from the hills of Samaria. Important trade and military routes went through this region in the ancient times. Megiddo was an important fortified city located on the west-

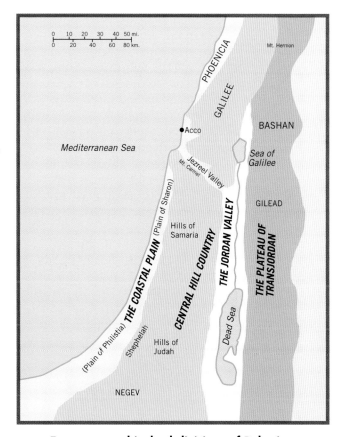

Four geographical subdivisions of Palestine.

ern edge of the Jezreel valley. The hills of Samaria include many hills and broad valleys that are very fertile and well known for agriculture. Mount Gerizim and Mount Ebal are located in this region. Two primary cities of this region in the ancient times were Samaria and Shechem. The hills of Judah are a continuation of the hills of Samaria. Jerusalem, located in this region, has an altitude of 2,600 feet above sea level. Hebron and Bethlehem also belong to this region.

The third distinctive geographical subdivision of Palestine is the **Jordan valley,** which is part of a geological depression that extends from the foothills of Mount

Hermon in the north to the Red Sea in the south. The Jordan River that originates in the north in the area of Dan runs through this valley. Between the Sea of Galilee and the Dead Sea, the Jordan River takes a twisting and winding path. The Sea of Galilee (also known as Chinnereth and Lake of Tiberius), a freshwater lake about 13 miles long and 8 miles wide, is well known for its plentiful fish and sudden storms. The Dead Sea (also known as the Salt Sea, at 1,296 feet below sea level), about 65 miles south of the Sea of Galilee, is approximately 50 miles long and 10 miles wide. Though the freshwaters of the Jordan River run into this sea, it has a high salt and other mineral content, because of constant water evaporation. The salt content (about 30 to 33 percent) makes it impossible to support any plant or animal life. The most important city in the Jordan valley, and perhaps the oldest city in Palestine, is Jericho, located 7 miles north of the Dead Sea.

The fourth major geographical subdivision of Palestine is the Plateau of **Transjordan,** located east of the Jordan River, and it makes up the modern country of Jordan. In the north is the region of Bashan, a fertile plateau, well known for its pastureland and cows and bulls. The Yarmuk River separates Bashan from the hills of Gilead in the south. The region of Gilead is also known for its fertile soil and agricultural products. The river Jabbok runs east to west through this region. The ancient kingdoms of Ammon, Moab, and Edom were located south of Gilead.

The geographical regions of Palestine also include the **Negev** area, which makes up the southern border of Palestine (see Genesis 12:9; 20:1). The Negev is a dry, hot, and barren region that did not have any economic significance in biblical times. Beer-sheba is an important place in the Negev region because of its association with the patriarchs of Israel (see 21:31-32; 26:17-33). Kadesh-barnea, where the people of Israel encamped during their wilderness journey, is about 50

Jerusalem is located in the northwest region of the Judean Desert.

One of the sources of the Jordan River near the Lebanon-Israel border.

miles south of Beer-sheba. In the southwest part of Palestine is the **Shephelah** region (the "lowlands") that separates the southern part of the coastal plain (the area of the Philistines) from the hill country of Judah. This region was the scene of many encounters between the Israelites and the Philistines. Lachish was an important fortified center in the Shephelah region.

This ancient world is the world in which God brought into existence a people called Israel. The Israelites developed their unique belief system within this general geographical region. Perhaps the most important element of Israel's faith is the belief that one true God, who is sovereign and majestic, created the universe. This belief stands in sharp contrast to the polytheistic beliefs of creation we find among Israel's neighboring cultures.

Genesis, the first book of the Bible, opens with Israel's faith in God as the Creator. This faith is found in Genesis as the theological foundation of Israel's narrative of her own beginning as a people, which begins with the traditions about Abraham, Isaac, and Jacob. We shall now turn to these theological and historical developments in the Book of Genesis.

Summary Statements

- Our knowledge of the geographical setting is essential to our understanding of the message of the Old Testament.
- The land of the Old Testament is a part of the ancient Near East.
- Palestine is the land bridge between Asia and Africa.
- Israel's ancestors belonged to the Amorite ethnic group.
- God brought Israel into existence as a nation in a world once dominated by the cultural, political, and religious influences of various polytheistic peoples.
- Egypt's history helps place some of the biblical stories in historical perspective.
- Palestine is a land characterized by distinct geographical regions, which include plains, hills, mountains, desert, and valleys.

Questions for Reflection

1. What impact does a knowledge of geography have on your understanding of the Bible?
2. What is the relationship between cultural customs and religious beliefs?
3. Why do you think Israel's religion often succumbed to the religious and cultural influences of its neighboring peoples?

Bible Study Assigment

Read Genesis 11:27—13:18 and locate all the places mentioned in this text on a map of the ancient Near East during the time of the patriarchs. Consult a Bible atlas that would provide you with different maps of the ancient Near East and Palestine.

Resources for Further Study

May, Herbert G., ed. *Oxford Bible Atlas.* New York: Oxford University Press, 1984.
Page, Charles R., II, and Carl A. Volz. *The Land and the Book: An Introduction to the World of the Bible.* Nashville: Abingdon, 1993.

4 Israel Looks at the Beginning: Genesis

Objectives:

Your study of this chapter should help you to:

- Explain the title, authorship, and the main content of the Book of Genesis
- Discuss Israel's theological ideas about creation and the earliest history of humanity
- Evaluate the theological significance of God's call of Abraham to the overall scheme of biblical history
- Discuss biblical concepts such as ancestral promises and fulfillment, covenant, election, and divine providence that are illustrated in the patriarchal narratives

Key Words to Understand

Primeval traditions
Patriarchal traditions
Enuma Elish
Image of God
Ziggurats
Gilgamesh Epic
Hapiru
Covenant
Circumcision
Election
Bethel
Peniel
Hyksos

Questions to consider as you read:

1. What are the theological claims of the creation stories in Genesis?

2. What is the portrait of the world revealed through the narratives in Genesis 3—11?

3. What is the overall purpose of God's covenant promises to Abraham?

4. How did Abraham's descendants respond to the covenant with God?

The opening book of the Bible is about the beginning. Readers of this book will recognize in this book two beginnings—the beginning of the universe and the beginning of the nation Israel. From the opening chapters, which deal with the origin of the universe and humanity, the narratives move on to the beginning of the nation Israel. The early chapters of this book provide resources for theological reflections on creation, humanity, sin, and God and His relation to the world. Stories in the later chapters trace Israel's history to her ancestors Abraham, Isaac, and Jacob. Though much of what we find in Genesis is the story of Israel's beginning, this story is not disconnected from the stories of creation and the earliest chapters of humanity's story. Israel's faith community has found in the stories of creation and humanity the proper historical and theological context in which God brought them into existence. The Christian faith also begins with the confession that God is the Creator of the heavens and the earth. In the Christian perspective, the early stories of Genesis set the stage for the unfolding of the redemptive drama in the Bible. The final scene of that drama is depicted in the Revelation, the last book of the Bible. The visionary writer of Revelation anticipates that just as there was a beginning for the world in which God brought heavens and earth into existence, there will be a new beginning—a new heaven and earth.

Composition of the Pentateuch

The Book of Genesis is the first book of the Torah or the Pentateuch. The composition of the entire Pentateuch in its final form continues to be a subject of debate among biblical scholars. Traditional Jews associate the materials in these books with Moses. Some evangelical Christians also maintain the Mosaic authorship of the Pentateuch. Modern critical study of the Pentateuch identifies the Pentateuch as a composite document made up of several literary and theological sources, dating from the mid-ninth century B.C. to the fifth century B.C.[1] However, the literary development and the shaping of the final form of the Pentateuch cannot be established with any certainty. Narrative and legal collections in these books most likely were transmitted through oral tradition for a considerable period of time from the days of Moses until steps were taken by Israel's scribes to fix them into writing. It is also possible that the present final form of the Pentateuch may include legal, literary, and theological traditions developed in the later history of Israel. Most likely the Pentateuch existed in the present form by mid-fifth century B.C. We will give attention to the final canonical form of the Pentateuch, which presents these books as a unified literary composition that contains the foundational sources of Israel's history and theology.

Content

The title Genesis (meaning "beginning" or "origin") comes from the Greek translation of the Bible (the Septuagint). The story of the Book of Genesis is told in 50 chapters. The first 11 chapters are known as the **primeval traditions**/narratives. These chapters contain narratives that set the stage for God's encounter with Abraham. Chapters 12—50 deal with the stories of Abraham, Isaac, and Jacob, the great patriarchs of Israel's faith and history (**patriarchal traditions**/narratives). The Book of Genesis contains several family stories that connect one generation with the next generation. Where there are gaps in these family stories, we find extended genealogies or family trees that trace groups of people or individuals to particular ancestors (see chaps. 5; 10; 11:10-32; 25:12-18; and 36). These genealogies seem to show the interrelationships and familial connections of various social and ethnic groups that existed in the ancient world.

Primeval Traditions

■ Two Creation Accounts (1:1—2:25)

Israel's faith claims that the God who encountered their ancestor with the call to become a source of blessing to all the peoples of the earth is the sovereign Creator of the universe. It is not surprising then that we find this claim as the beginning point of Israel's faith traditions in Genesis.

Two theological traditions about God as Creator affirm Israel's creation faith in the opening chapters of Genesis. We should note that these are not the only places where Israel's creation is found in the Old Testament. A number of psalms, the Book of Job, and the Book of Isaiah also contain extensive treatment of this theme. The two traditions about creation in Genesis (1:1—2:4a; 2:4b-25) present a balanced portrait of Israel's theological understanding about God, the universe, and humanity. The first account is a summary description of the creation of the world and everything in it. The second account is a more specific treatment of the making of humanity. It seems that these two traditions

existed side by side in Israel's history. The first account with its careful literary style and structure reflects a sophisticated theological formulation, a creedal statement that articulates Israel's faith in God as Creator. This account serves the dual purpose of affirming Israel's faith as well as rejecting the pagan claims of the origin of the world and the superiority of their gods. The simplicity of the language and the narrative structure of the second account have led some scholars to assign this story to a date earlier than the first creation account.

Careful reading of Genesis 1:1—2:4a shows that the focus of the text is on the Creator and what He made. Our usual questions of why, how, and when are not answered in this account. The subject of the action (God) is prominent (see the repeated phrase "And God said . . ."). The result of the action, namely, what God made, is also clear. The similarity of its language and other expressions to some of the hymns of praise in the Psalms (for example, see Psalm 104), leads us to think that perhaps this creation account serves as an invitation to the reader to worship and praise the creator God.

An Excerpt from the *Enuma Elish*

When Marduk hears the words of the gods,
his heart prompts (him) to fashion artful works.
Opening his mouth he addresses Ea
To impart the plan he had conceived in his heart:
Blood I will mass and cause bones to be.
I will establish a savage, "man" shall be his name.
Verily, savage-man I will create.
He shall be charged with the service of the gods
That they might be at ease![2]

Israel's Understanding of the Universe

The first account of creation reflects Israel's understanding of the structure of the universe (cosmology). Israel viewed the earth as flat and circular. Above the earth is a dome-shaped sky or the firmament that rests on the mountains around the edge of the earth. Water above the sky is the source of rain. The earth rests on pillars that float in the waters below the earth (Psalm 46:2). These waters supply the springs, streams, and rivers (Job 38:16). This prescientific Hebrew cosmology cautions us against a literal interpretation of the creation traditions.

The first account begins with the theological claim that *Elohim* (Hebrew for *God*) "created" the universe ("the heavens and the earth"). The verb *created* (*bara'* in Hebrew) signifies God's power to bring into existence things that do not exist. The apostle Paul claims that such was the faith of Israel's ancestor Abraham that he believed in the God "who gives life to the dead and calls into existence the things that do not exist" (Romans 4:17, NRSV).

The narrative of the first creation account moves from the condition of chaos to order, beauty, light, and life and finally to God's rest on the seventh day (the Sabbath).[3] The recurring phrase "And God said . . ." describes creation by the power of God's word or command. Though the account places the creation activities of God within the framework of the Jewish week in which the day begins in the evening, there is no satisfactory explanation to the meaning of *day* (*yom* in Hebrew). It is likely that the ancient tradition was not at all concerned with the questions we ask about the duration of the day.

The first creation story also portrays God's twofold activities of separation of what He created (see 1:3-10) and filling of the heavens and the earth and the seas with light and life (see vv. 11-26). The activity of separation signifies God's authority to set up boundaries to His creation. The activity of filling indicates God's desire and purpose to bring life and beauty to what He created. Moreover, the Creator bestows life-giving activity as His blessing to the creation (see vv. 22, 28). The climax of God's creation was humanity, which He made in His image and likeness. God made humanity as male and female, both genders with equality before God and with responsibility and relationship to the Creator. Israel's creation faith also affirms the truth that both humanity and animals are sustained and cared for by the gracious provisions of God (vv. 29-30). After completing His work of creation in six days, God rested (*shabat* in Hebrew means "to cease") from all His work on the seventh day. The Sabbath reminds the readers that the rhythm of work and rest is an essential part of God's creational order.

The second creation story (2:4*b*-25) also deals with the work of God as the Creator. However, in this second account, the emphasis is on the nature of the human individual and the divinely set agenda for human existence. The na-

Humanity in the Image of God

The **image of God** is a significant biblical idea. The words *image* and *likeness* mean the same. First of all, it is important to note that God created both male and female in His image. One gender does not have a better share of God's image. Moreover, the image is reflected in both individual and community existence (notice the language, "he created him . . . he created them" in 1:27). In the context of the Genesis account of creation, "the image" refers to humanity's function, place, and responsibility in the created world as God's representatives (v. 26). Just as God is love, His "image" also ought to be a reflection of divine love. Human individuals and the community reflect God's image when they love God with their whole being—heart, soul, and strength (Deuteronomy 6:4)—and love each other with unselfish love (Leviticus 19:18; Mark 12:29-31). Loving God with unreserved obedience and loving others in an unselfish manner are thus essential marks of being the "image of God."[4]

ture and destiny of humanity and the nature of human relationship with God and with each other are key issues addressed here.

This creation story begins with the relationship of the *man* (*'adam* in Hebrew) to the ground (*'adamah* in Hebrew). In most instances, the reference to the *man* in Genesis 1—4 (*'adam*) has the definite article, which conveys the idea of the man in a generic sense (humanity). What makes this earth creature a living being (*nephesh* in Hebrew) is the life-giving breath of God. Thus, humanity is dependent on God for life and vitality without which the human condition is the same as that of the ground.

The second account of creation makes it clear that work is the task for which God made humanity. Human freedom and divine prohibition are also key issues in this narrative. The story conveys the idea that the garden belongs to God and human freedom has its limit. The "tree of the knowledge of good and evil" (2:17) is a symbol of the boundary of human freedom and the authority of God

to set such boundaries. The story suggests that humanity's proper relation to God depended on their recognition of this boundary and their faithful adherence to the prohibition.

The narrative of the making of the woman from the man focuses on the equality and partnership between the man (*'ish* in Hebrew) and the woman (*'ishshah* in Hebrew). Just as there is solidarity between *'adam* and *'adamah,* there is solidarity and partnership between the man and the woman. The man recognized the woman as a part of his own being, of his own kind, the one with whom he was destined to become "one flesh." The narrative ends with the final statement that the man and the woman were "naked," but they were not ashamed. This reflects the state of innocence, truthfulness, and integrity of relationship that characterized the existence of humanity's first couple.

■ Humanity's Sin

The story of Genesis 3 is a continuation of the story that begins in 2:4*b*. The narrative begins with the serpent's question, which focuses on the prohibition in the garden. The woman's response also focuses on the prohibition and the warning of death (3:2-3). Humanity's desire for freedom and autonomy are central issues in this narrative. The serpent makes the claim that violating the prohibition will not lead to death and that humanity has the potential to become "like God" (v. 5). Lack of trust in God, desire for self-sovereignty, and misuse of freedom led humanity to violate the divine prohibition (v. 6). The narrative also shows the damaging consequences of sin that resulted in brokenness and dissonance at all levels of relationship (vv. 7-13). God's judgment of sin further made humanity's existence difficult and troublesome. The narrative traces the pain of childbirth, domination of the woman by the man, lack of productivity of the earth, and the prospect of death to humanity's sin (vv. 14-19).

The instruction we find in this narrative is that we must live in the experience of freedom that God graciously offers to us, but with the discernment and recognition that our freedom has limits. Misuse of freedom leaves open the door for evil to enter into our world. God calls us to trust Him and His words when we are faced with the anxieties of life. When we are tempted, our model is Jesus, who resisted the power of the tempter and his attempts to exploit the human anxieties and desires of life (see Matthew 4:1-11).

■ Cain and Abel

The world outside of the garden is the context of the story in Genesis 4. The narrative moves from stability and structure in human relationships to jealousy, anger, violence, and homelessness. The power of evil is already at work in human relationships. It is interesting to note that the first recorded murder takes place in the setting of worship, as a result of an apparent conflict over the question of what is the appropriate way of worship. Total contempt for God's instructions and warning and contempt for human life are also crucial issues in this story. Humanity takes yet another turn away from God, leading to violence of brother against brother. In this story, the one who acted in violence ultimately is the one who becomes a fugitive, living in fear and living as a wanderer without a home. The narrative ends with a powerful display of God's grace extended to a brother who refused to show grace to his brother. The fugitive's life is protected with a mark on his forehead. We are reminded here of Jesus' admonition to "go and be reconciled to your brother" before we offer our gifts to God (Matthew 5:23-24).

■ A Universal Judgment

The next segment in the primeval stories shows that the power of sin continued to exploit and dominate the human society. Violence became a way of life for the descendants of Cain (Genesis 4:17-24). Chapter 5 is a genealogy that traces the ancestry of Noah to Seth, a third son born to Adam. Genesis 6:1-8 shows that sin continued to dominate humanity. The biblical story of the Flood (chaps. 6—9) begins with the report that the widespread and malignant growth of sin brought grief and pain to God.

Noah, a righteous and blameless person who "found favor in

the eyes of the LORD" (6:8), and his family survived the judgment that destroyed the world (vv. 5-9). God thus spares a righteous person and opens the way for humanity to continue after the Flood. In this early tradition, we find at work the theological principle of salvation of the righteous and judgment of the wicked. This story also anticipates a new beginning for humanity, again a gracious act on the part of God. The narrative ends with an account of God making a covenant with Noah (8:21—9:17). The covenant contained the promise of a predictable and dependable world with seasons and cycles of nature. This covenant is eternal in nature. It is a solemn promise by the sovereign Creator who understands the frailties and sinfulness of humanity and treats them with patience, love, and compassion. The Flood account thus ends with a note of hope for the post-Flood humanity. This graciousness of God toward us, in the final analysis, is the hope for humanity's salvation.

The concluding statement of the Flood narrative establishes the three sons of Noah (Shem, Ham, and Japheth) as the ancestors of the post-Flood humanity (9:18-19). The genealogical record in chapter 10 gives the list of nations that descended from Shem, Ham, and Japheth.

■ A Scattered Humanity

There was a new beginning for humanity (11:1-2). The Tower of Babel narrative seems to place the origin of human civilization and sedentary life in the southern part of ancient Mesopotamia. This narrative also may be understood as Israel's indictment of the city of Babylon and its temple-towers known as **ziggurats.**

The post-Flood civilization undertook the task of city building in resistance to the divine mandate given to humanity to "fill the earth" (1:28; 9:1). Pride and arrogance are other issues we find in this narrative. When humanity resisted God's mandate, He came down and disrupted their plans

The *Gilgamesh Epic*

Other ancient cultures also maintained their own traditions of a universal flood that destroyed the earth in the ancient past. The most notable one is the Mesopotamian account preserved in the **Gilgamesh Epic.** This epic is the story of Gilgamesh, king of Erech, two-thirds god and one-third man, and his search for immortality. The fear of death drove the hero Gilgamesh to go on a journey to meet Utnapishtim who long ago survived a great flood and attained immortality. When the great gods planned to destroy humanity with a flood for no apparent reason, the god Ea warned Utnapishtim and instructed him to build a boat to escape the catastrophe. The story also includes reference to the sending of birds to see if the water was subsiding. In another version of the Flood story, the *Atrahasis Epic*, the hero is called Atrahasis, who also received warning about the Flood and built a boat to escape the Flood. Even though the Mesopotamian flood story has some external parallels to the Old Testament account, there are significant differences between the two in content and theology. Perhaps the most important difference is the lack of any moral or ethical reason for the acts of the deities in the Mesopotamian accounts.[5]

and confused their language (11:5-9). The result was the scattering of humanity abroad over the face of the earth. Through judgment God fulfilled His will for His creation that they multiply and fill the earth.

The rest of the biblical story informs us that the God who divides and scatters in judgment is also the God who gathers humanity. The next chapter in the Book of Genesis (12) focuses on the beginning of the gathering activity of God. God encountered and called Abraham, a member of this scattered humanity, to a trusting relationship with Him. Abraham's obedient faith would usher in for all families of the earth a blessing from God (vv. 1-3). The faith of Israel traces its history to this divine-human encounter. We shall now turn to this story.

■ Patriarchal Traditions

The patriarchal stories belong to the early part of the second millennium, when the Amorites controlled most of Mesopotamia and Syria-Palestine (1950-1700 B.C.). We may assign 1900-1800 B.C. as the approximate date for Abraham. Abraham was a descendant of Shem, one of the three sons of Noah (11:27). He was a native of Ur, an urban center in the southern part of Mesopotamia (v. 31). He belonged to the Amorite ethnic group (see Deuteronomy 26:5), among whom Hebrews perhaps existed as a subculture (Genesis 14:13). Some scholars think that the Hebrew people were part of a lower socioeconomic group in the ancient Near East known as **Hapiru.**

Israel's patriarchal traditions (chaps. 12—50) contain the summary accounts of the life events of Abraham, Isaac, and Jacob, the three great ancient ancestors of the nation Israel. This section contains the Abraham traditions in 12:1—25:18, and the Jacob traditions in 25:19—50:26. The Jacob traditions include the stories of Isaac, Jacob's father (chap. 26), and the stories of the sons of Jacob (chaps. 37—50).

■ Abraham: From Haran to Canaan

Genesis 11:29-32 serves as the connecting link between the primeval traditions and the patriarchal traditions. This narrative traces the journey of Terah, a descendant of Shem, and his family, which included Abraham and his wife, Sarah, from Ur in the southern part of Mesopotamia with Canaan as their destination. They stopped their journey at Haran, in the northwestern part of Mesopotamia, where they settled down and established their home.

The Abraham stories begin with God's command to Abraham to leave his home and set out on a journey to a destination that God would show him later. The command was followed by the divine promises that God would make Abraham a great nation and a blessing to all the families of the earth. The divine promise that Abraham would be a blessing to "all peoples on earth" meant that Abraham's obedience and trust in God would usher in a new reality of life for all the people of the world. The apostle Paul finds in this divine program "the gospel in advance," which invites all nations to share in the blessings of Abraham, by following his example of faith (Galatians 3:8-9). Abraham obeyed this command and departed Haran when he was 75 years of age. The journey took

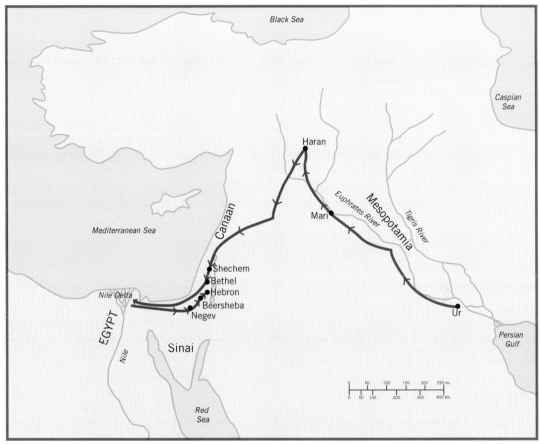

Abraham's journey from Ur to Canaan and his sojourn in Egypt.

Abraham and his family, including his nephew Lot, to the land of Canaan, the original destination of the family's journey when it left Ur. As Abraham traveled through the land, he set up altars at various places to worship God, who frequently appeared to him.

■ God's Covenant with Abraham

God's **covenant** with Abraham is a major event in the patriarchal traditions. Though Abraham expressed his doubt and fear due to the delay in the fulfillment of the promise concerning a son, God reassured him that he would indeed have numerous descendants.

God then ratified this promise with a ritual following the covenant-making custom of the ancient world (Genesis 15:7-17). The covenant making was concluded by an oath from God that He would give the land between the Nile River and the river Euphrates to Abraham's descendants.

"Abraham believed the LORD, and he credited it to him as righteousness" (v. 6). Abraham, by faith, trusted in God's promise, and in turn God granted righteousness to Abraham because of his trust in Him. Abraham not only heard the word of promise but also embraced it as a reality for himself and for his future generations.

■ Circumcision

In response to God's covenant promise, He required Abraham to establish the ritual of **circumcision** as a sign of the covenant for all the future generations. Abraham circumcised all the male members of his household, including himself, and Ishmael who was his son through Hagar, the servant of Sarah (17:1-27). On the part of Abraham, the act of circumcision was an act of obedience to God as well as faith in action through an external, visible, and ineradicable sign. This mark established Abraham and his descendants as the faithful and trusting recipients of God's covenant promises. Later in the biblical tradition, circumcision became a metaphor for the true commitment of faith that originates within one's heart.

■ The Offering of Isaac

The birth of Isaac (21:1-5) was the first event in the fulfillment of the divine promises to Abraham. However, God's unexpected command to offer Isaac as a burnt offering (22:1-19) posed a threat to the future of the promises that God made to Abraham. God's command to Abraham is reported as a test through which God would know if Abraham truly *feared* God. In the end this test would also prove the trustworthiness of God. In the biblical tradition, *the fear of the Lord* is one's submission to the sovereign authority of God. Trust and obedience are essential ingredients of one's fear of the Lord. There was obedience on the part of Abraham without hesitation or questions because he trusted God with His promises. The story ends with the report that God remained faithful to His promises (vv. 17-19).

■ Abraham's Final Years

The story of Abraham ends with the account of his death at the age of 175 (25:7-11). His sons Isaac and Ishmael buried their father in the cave of Machpelah. Ishmael, born through Hagar (16:1-16; 21:8-21), is seldom given any special attention in Jewish and Christian traditions, though in the Islamic tradition Ishmael occupies a central place. It is important to note that the Ishmael narrative is a major part of the patriarchal stories. Though Ishmael stands outside of the covenant promises in these stories, he and his descendants also received the promise of becoming a great nation. There is nothing in these narratives that indicates ongoing strife and conflict between the son of promise and the son who remains outside the promise. The fact that they both came together to bury their father is an indication that there was unity and reconciliation between them. These two ancestors—Isaac of the Jewish people and Ishmael of the Arab Muslims—model for their modern-day descendants the potentiality of

An ancient mud-brick gate dated to the middle Bronze Age (the period of Abraham) at Dan in northern Israel.

Covenant

Covenant is a formal and legally binding contract between two parties. Covenant ceremony consisted of oath-taking by both parties, sacrificial rituals, and eating a meal together to seal the terms of the covenant. The sacrificial ritual in some instances also included cutting animals into two halves. Biblical examples show different types of covenants. A covenant between two people of the same socioeconomic status is called a parity covenant (see Genesis 21:22-34; 26:17-33; 31:43-54). God's covenants that focus on the divine promises (God's covenant with Noah, Abraham, and David) may be called promissory covenants. God's covenant with Israel at Mount Sinai focuses on the conditions God set forth for His relationship with that nation. Conditional covenants require the beneficiaries of the covenant to show loyalty and allegiance to the covenant maker.

a life of peace and reconciliation. The Abraham narratives end with a summary description of Ishmael's descendants who occupied the Arabian Desert.

The rest of the patriarchal stories focus on the family history of Abraham's covenant children, and the struggle and conflict among them, though they were destined to be a source of blessing to the world. We will now turn to this story.

■ Jacob's Narratives

The second part of the patriarchal traditions contains the stories of Abraham's son Isaac, Isaac's son Jacob, and Jacob's 12 sons (Reuben, Simeon, Levi, Judah, Dan, Naphtali, Gad, Asher, Issachar, Zebulun, Joseph, and Benjamin). In these stories the narrator portrays history with remarkable honesty and with very little attempt to hide the negative characteristics and traits of the covenant family. These stories also show how God worked out His plans and purposes through the children of Abraham, though the covenant family was plagued with deception, conflict, and crisis in their everyday life.

The story of the birth of Esau (later called Edom) and Jacob, the two sons of Isaac and Rebekah (25:19-26), is a key event in the patriarchal narratives. Before the birth of her sons, God's word came to Rebekah: "Two nations are in your womb, . . . and the older will serve the younger" (v. 23). This divine word conveyed to her the destiny of her sons. Esau, the natural heir to the birthright privileges, will take a second place in the family. God's choice of Jacob over Esau is often described as the **election** of Jacob. Election here is not an arbitrary choice on the part of God, but rather a gracious act that conveys the idea

Dome of the Rock on the Temple Mount—the traditional site of Mount Moriah.

Patriarchal Customs and Religion

Israel's patriarchal traditions give us a glimpse of the way of life and worship in ancient times. The patriarchs lived a seminomadic life, wandering from place to place, seeking pasture and water supply. They lived in tents, raising sheep and other animals. They often entered into covenant relationship with their neighbors and lived in peace in the land that God had promised to give them (21:22-34; 26:26-31).

The patriarchal family included extended members and household servants. The head of the household was the leader of the family. Abraham's rescue of Lot shows that the servants of the house constituted an "army" that protected, defended, and even rescued the family in trouble (chap. 14). Marriage was arranged by the groom or by the family. Marriage custom included the payment of dowry by the groom or the family in the form of gold and silver or through labor (24:52-53; 29:16-30). A wife had the right to choose her maidservants as surrogates to conceive children for her husband (16:1-3; 30:1-21). In the absence of progeny, couples designated an adopted slave as their heir (15:2-3).

The patriarchs worshiped God by erecting an altar at the places where God appeared to them (Shechem, Bethel, Beersheba, and Hebron). They revisited these places to remember God's appearance. There was no priesthood or elaborate rituals. The patriarchs called God by various names. These names convey their understanding of the manifestation of the power of God in various ways. In Israel's later history, the places of patriarchal worship became important religious centers and places of spiritual pilgrimage.

that the promise belongs to God and does not have any human ownership. Jacob still was the second-born son. He simply received the promise of receiving something that was not a natural right to him by his birth order. The fact that Jacob asked his brother to sell him his birthright for a bowl of red stew shows that he, too, was unaware of his mysterious election by God.

Genesis 28:10-22 is an important narrative in the patriarchal traditions. God encountered Jacob, who was fleeing from home after deceiving both his father and his brother, in a dream at a certain place where he stopped to spend the night. Through this mysterious encounter God gave Jacob the covenant promises that He had made to Abraham. This encounter was an important turning point in Jacob's life. The dream made him aware of the role he was to play in the future of the covenant family, a future that is hidden in the unconditional promises of God. That future would become a reality, not through his deceptive and scheming ways of life, but rather through a trusting relationship with the God of his fathers. Jacob gave the name **Bethel** (which means "house of God") to that location to commemorate this life-changing religious experience that night.

Genesis 32 narrates another major turning point in Jacob's life. This is the story of his return to Canaan from Haran where he spent over 15 years as a servant in the house of his uncle Laban. He had with him his two wives, Rachel and Leah, and 11 children (his 12th son, Benjamin, was born later), and the property he accumulated while at Laban's house.

This chapter powerfully portrays the difficulty of homecoming for Jacob, who had left his home in conflict, fear, and broken relationship with his brother. The story narrates a struggle at the Jabbok River crossing between Jacob and a mysterious individual whom Jacob later came to recognize as God himself. The struggle ends with Jacob's acknowledgment that he is Jacob, meaning "a scheming, cunning heel grabber," and God's renaming of Jacob to Israel, meaning "God protects" or "God preserves." Jacob testified afterward that he had seen God face-to-face and he named the place of this encounter **Peniel,** meaning "the face of God." The continuing story in chapter 33 narrates the emotional reunion between the two brothers with weeping and hugging. Paul echoes this transformation when he writes: "If anyone is in Christ, he is a new creation; the old has gone, the new has come" (2 Corinthians 5:17)!

The last major segment of the patriarchal stories is the story of Jacob's children, in which Joseph, the 11th son, plays a prominent role (chaps. 37—50). Scholars place the accounts of Joseph in Egypt during the early part of the **Hyksos** rule in Egypt (about 1700 B.C.).

This section begins with a narrative about Jacob's special love for Joseph and Joseph's dreams, which caused his brothers to mistreat him and eventually to sell him to the Ishmaelite caravan traders, who sold him as a slave to the Egyptians. Conflict thus continues to plague the covenant family. The biblical narrative focuses on Joseph's rise to prominence in Egypt from humiliating circumstances, including a period of incarceration. Even in the midst of the most humiliating circumstances and days of uncertainty, Joseph lived a faithful life, with integrity, courage, and hope. The stories include the birth of his sons Manasseh and Ephraim, who later became two tribes among the 12 tribes of Israel (chaps. 39—41). The highlight of this section is the reunion of Joseph with his family, including his father. The very same brothers who mistreated him became the object of his favor and compassion, and through his kindness his family made Egypt their home.

Genesis 39—50 reiterate the theme that the Lord was with Joseph in all circumstances of life. In these stories there is no direct

Abraham, Isaac, and Jacob dug out wells to claim ownership of water in the places where they sojourned in Canaan.

divine-human encounter, which is a characteristic of the patriarchal stories. Joseph nonetheless experiences God's faithful presence and His providential care and guidance in strange and mysterious ways. Only in retrospect he recognizes the truth that his misfortunes were a path that God had prepared for a secure future for his family who had sent him into exile.

The final segment of the Genesis story focuses on the reconciliation between Joseph and his brothers (Genesis 50:15-26). After the death of their father, Joseph's brothers came to Joseph seeking his forgiveness for the wrong they had committed against him. Joseph reminded them that their harmful actions were indeed part of God's good plans to bring about the welfare they were enjoying in Egypt. Joseph's words and actions reflect God's intended plan for the children of Abraham. The covenant family's calling from God was to become mediators of God's blessings to all the families of the earth (12:3). In this story, we find that calling beginning its work in and through the life of Joseph.

The remainder of the Pentateuch (Exodus, Leviticus, Numbers, and Deuteronomy) is the story of the shaping of the children of Jacob, now known as Israel, to become the source of God's blessing to all the people of the world. In the Book of Exodus we encounter the events that set in motion this divine plan for Israel. We will now turn to the story of these God-Israel encounters narrated in Exodus.

Summary Statements

- God created humanity in His image.
- Humanity mistrusted God's word and abused their freedom.
- God brought His judgment upon sinful humanity.
- God called Abraham to become a source of blessing to all the families of the earth.
- Abraham responded to God's call and the covenant through obedience and trust.
- The Bethel and Peniel experiences were important turning points in the life of Jacob.
- God demonstrated His sovereignty and providence in and through the various life events of Joseph.

Questions for Reflection

1. What hope do you find in the truth that God has the power to bring into existence things that do not exist?
2. What should be the proper Christian response to gender inequality and sex discrimination, based on the biblical concept of both male and female being in the image of God?
3. Discuss how we can live a life that is a source of blessing to others in the world in which we live today (using illustrations from the life events of Abraham, Isaac, Jacob, and Joseph).

Bible Study Assignment

Read Genesis 21:8-21. Answer the following questions.

1. Read Genesis 12—20 and identify the previous stories in the patriarchal narratives that shed light on our understanding of 21:8-21.
2. What do you think is the main plot of this story?
3. What are the human issues that are important in this story?
4. How are the human issues/crises in this story resolved? How does God's intervention help resolve these crises?
5. What does this story teach you about proper human relationships and treatment of others who are outside of the faith community?
6. What does this narrative teach you about God?

Resources for Further Study

Brueggemann, Walter. *Genesis*, in *Interpretation: A Bible Commentary for Teaching and Preaching*. Atlanta: John Knox Press, 1982.

Fretheim, Terence E. *The Book of Genesis: Introduction, Commentary, and Reflections*, vol. 1 in *The New Interpreter's Bible*. Nashville: Abingdon Press, 1994. Pages 516-673.

5 Israel Becomes a Covenant Community: Exodus

bjectives:

Your study of this chapter should help you to:

- Summarize the historical and social setting of the exodus story
- Describe the goal and purpose of the Mount Sinai covenant
- Discuss the contemporary relevance of the Ten Commandments
- Relate the Exodus themes of the covenant and the Tabernacle with corresponding themes in the New Testament

Key Words to Understand

Exodos
Seti I
Raameses II
Theophany
Yahweh
Passover
Sea of Reeds
Sinai covenant
Covenant code
Tabernacle
Holy of holies
Ark of the covenant
Holy place

Questions to consider as you read:

1. What theological understanding do we gain from the Book of Exodus about God's character and attributes?

2. What is a covenant? What are the covenantal responsibilities?

3. What is the significance of the Tabernacle?

God's visitation of His people to bring salvation to them is a prominent theme in the Bible. As Joseph anticipated before his death (Genesis 50:24-25), God came to visit the children of Israel in Egypt. He set them free from their bondage. This redemption story is not an isolated event in biblical history. It is directly linked to God's call and covenant with Abraham, Isaac, and Jacob. Moreover, the Exodus story of redemption is also connected to Israel's creation faith. In biblical theology, redemption is the goal of creation. The Book of Exodus reveals God not only as the Redeemer but also as the God who enters into a covenant with those whom He redeemed. The goal of this chapter is to trace this story of God's visitation of Israel and the actions He took to enter into a covenant relationship with His redeemed people.

Setting

The title of the second book of the Torah comes from the Greek title *exodos* ("going out" or "departure") in the Septuagint translation. The stories of the Book of Exodus belong to the new kingdom period in Egypt. Scholars think that **Seti I** (1309-1290 B.C.) was the Pharaoh who imposed hard labor on the Israelite population and ordered the killing of the newborn male children of Israel. The descendants of Jacob most likely lived a normal life in the Goshen area of the Nile delta

The Nile valley is well-known for its rich soil.

until this royal policy was instituted. Israel's escape from Egypt took place during the reign of **Raameses II** (1290-1224 B.C.). A popular date given to the exodus event is 1280 B.C. Biblical tradition maintains that Israel was in Egypt for 430 years (see Exodus 12:40; Galatians 3:17).

Content

The Book of Exodus has two main parts:

Escape from Egypt　　1:1—18:27
Covenant Making at
　Sinai　　　　　　19:1—40:38

■ Escape from Egypt

The Book of Exodus begins with a theological claim that God fulfilled His covenant promise of making Abraham's descendants too numerous to count even in the land of Egypt (see 1:7 and Genesis 15:5). Concern for national security seems to have been the underlying reason for the Pharaoh's decision to put Israel under slavery and hardship. In the stories preserved in Exodus 1 and 2, we find, on the one hand, the oppressiveness of the power structures in the world against a marginalized people. On the other hand, we also find in these stories God coming to visit the poor and oppressed with His love and care for them, to bring freedom and life to the community being threatened with death by a royal decree. Chapter 2 narrates the birth of Moses as the son of an Israelite couple under these oppressive conditions. The narrative of the deliverance of infant Moses from the royal decree of death anticipates the escape of all Israel through God's supernatural intervention. This chapter also presents Moses as a person with a deep concern for justice for his people and loyalty to his heritage, though through strange and mysterious circumstances he grew up as the son of Pharaoh's daughter.

God's concern for a people who cry out in the midst of their suffering is central to the story of God's call of Moses (3:1—4:17). God's appearance to Moses in the burning bush, commonly called a **theophany** experience, makes it very clear that He is a God who is committed to fulfill His promises to the patriarchs. This story also portrays God's intense commitment to save the oppressed from their oppressors. The call of Moses also conveys to us the truth that He does not choose the powerful and the most influential in the world to accomplish His saving purpose. Moses was by no means the most qualified or most prepared to do this task for God, as indicated by Moses' own objection to this call. This account also conveys the truth that God is a God who is present with His people, both those who are in the midst of their suffering and the one being asked to go to lead them out of their bondage. This promise of the faithful presence of God is powerfully reflected in the divine name **Yahweh,** which Israel understood as the personal name of her God. Though Moses objected to this call, he finally consented to be a participant in God's plan for the future of His people.

The stories of Exodus (chaps. 5—11) indicate that Moses' task was not easy. Pharaoh was not easily convinced of the mission of Moses and his demand in the name of Yahweh. He also encountered opposition to his leadership from an angry and upset crowd of

God's Personal Name

The origin of God's personal name Yahweh (Jehovah in older English translations) is not clearly known to us. The divine name contains four Hebrew consonants transliterated as YHWH. We also do not know the exact pronunciation of the name. The later Jewish tradition supplied the vowels of *Adonai*, another epithet for God, to the four letters YHWH. In the Jewish tradition this divine name is not pronounced because of its sacredness. Most English Bibles translate the divine name as "the Lord."

The four letters of the divine name come from the root form of a Hebrew verb *hayah*, which means "to be." God's eternal existence, His continuing presence in His creation, and His power to cause things to happen are all ideas conveyed by this root verb form of the divine name. Yahweh is the God who was, who is, and who will be with His people in all of their history. The name signifies His *being-there with us* in all of life's circumstances. He is Immanuel—God with us (Isaiah 8:10). The phrase "I AM" essentially conveys this understanding of God (Exodus 3:14).

the Israelites who blamed him for their increased hardship. Pharaoh, who "hardened" his heart against Yahweh, ultimately consented to yield when Egypt came under a series of divine judgments, culminating in the death of the firstborn male children of the Egyptians. These calamities, called the plagues, revealed Yahweh's power not only over the political powers but also over the deities that the Egyptians believed were in control of the land of Egypt.

In the midst of the calamities that came upon Egypt, God protected the people of Israel. During the final plague of the death of the firstborn, Israel kept the **Passover** through the ritual of the smearing the blood of a lamb on the doorframes of their houses

The Passover

In Israel's faith, the Passover provides a context both to commemorate God's redemption of Egypt and to instill faith in a new generation. Through the reenactment and retelling of the Passover story, the people of Israel even today enter into their past history and find an identity with their ancestors who held on to the hope of entering the Promised Land in the midst of their struggle for life.

The crucial element in the Passover ritual was the blood of the sacrificial lamb that provided protection for the Israelites. In the New Testament, the sacrifice of Christ receives significance as the sacrifice of the Passover lamb (1 Corinthians 5:6-8), and Jesus as the Lamb slain to ransom men and women for God (Revelation 5). The Passover, both in the Old and the New Testament, deals with God's redemptive work that culminates in giving hope to the community of faith. The Old Testament Passover provides us with an initial contact and entry point into the redemptive work of God that is fully realized through our redemption in Jesus. The New Testament redemption is first and foremost freedom from sin and evil, which leads to a new life in Christ. The Passover meal for the Church is the Lord's Supper, which links and identifies the Christian life with the suffering, death, and resurrection of Jesus. This sacred fellowship also energizes us with the hope for our future life with Christ.

and eating its roasted meat with unleavened bread and bitter herbs in a hurried manner (12:1-13). The ritual is called the Passover *(pesach)* because on the day God passed through Egypt in judgment, He passed over (the verb *pasach* in Hebrew means "to have compassion/protect/skip over") the children of Israel (see vv. 11-13). We find specific instructions in Exodus 12 and 13 to keep the ritual of *pesach* and the feast of unleavened bread as annual events to evoke the memory of God's gracious protection.

The 10th plague prompted Pharaoh to let Israel leave Egypt. Israel's exodus began from Raameses and the journey took them down toward the **Sea of Reeds**. Scholars find it difficult to give a precise identification of the sea (*yam suph* in Hebrew is not the Red Sea, rather the Sea of Reeds). God went before Israel to lead them in this journey by manifesting His presence in a "pillar of cloud" by day and a "pillar of fire" by night (13:20-22). Pharaoh made one last-minute attempt to retake

The possible route of Israel's journey from Egypt to Mount Sinai.

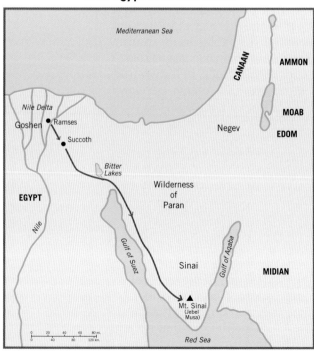

the Israelites under his control by pursuing them with his army. At the Sea of Reeds, God delivered His people by dividing the sea and by drowning the Egyptian army in the sea. Israel saw and witnessed the power of Yahweh, her God. The Lord "saved" Israel, and they "put their trust" in Him (14:30-31). The exodus and the crossing of the Sea of Reeds are central events in the faith traditions of Israel. Through these events Israel came to know God's faithfulness, justice, mercy, and salvation. The exodus event was yet another step toward the fulfillment of God's covenant promises to the patriarchs.[1]

■ Covenant Making at Sinai

Israel arrived at Mount Sinai three months to the day after leaving Egypt. The exact location of Mount Sinai is not known. The traditional site is Jebel Musa ("Mountain of Moses") in the southern part of the Sinai Peninsula where St. Catherine's Monastery is located. At Mount Sinai, God met with Moses and revealed to him His purpose for the people whom He redeemed from Egypt (19:3-6). God saved Israel from Egypt to bring them into a new relationship with himself (v. 4). The relationship is called a covenant *(berit),* and the future of the God-Israel relationship depended on Israel's willing-

ness to "obey" their God (literally "listen to my voice") and to "keep" the covenant with Him (v. 5). This covenant (known as the **Sinai covenant**) was a further development of God's covenant with Abraham. In return for Israel's faithfulness, God promised to treat them as a specially prized possession, a kingdom of priests, and a holy nation (vv. 5*b*-6).

Israel received from God the Ten Commandments at Mount Sinai as the 10 primary conditions of the Sinai covenant (20:1-17). The commands are generally divided into two groups or "two tablets" (see 24:12; 31:18; 34:1). The first 4 commandments deal with relations to God (20:3-11), and the last 6 commandments deal with relations to other individuals (vv. 12-17). Of the

Mountains in the vicinity of Sinai. St. Catherine's Monastery is in the valley.

T   Covenant and Holy Living

At Mount Sinai, Israel became an elect and holy nation by entering into a covenant relationship with God (19:3-8). God's election of Israel brought that nation to a specially privileged place in the world. Election also meant for Israel the responsibility to mediate God's blessings to the nations in the world. Likewise, God called her to be a holy nation, a nation "set apart" (*qadash* in Hebrew) for God's service. In biblical theology, the pursuit of holiness means an ongoing faithful and trusting relationship with the God who calls His people to be holy.

The Ten Commandments

The first commandment (20:3) calls for Israel's exclusive relation to Yahweh as her only God. Genuine love for God demands from us our complete loyalty and devotion to God. The second commandment (vv. 4-6) prohibits any attempt to give God a visible representation in any form. This commandment invites us to contemplate with wonder and amazement the awesome holiness of the Creator who fills the whole earth with His glory (Isaiah 6:3). The third commandment (Exodus 20:7) prohibits the misuse of God's holy name for self-serving and illegitimate purposes. The commandment calls us to carefully scrutinize our words and actions in the name of God, to see whether we are glorifying God or profaning His name. The fourth commandment (v. 8) calls for the experience of "rest" after the six days of labor. The Sabbath is holy—a time for rest *set apart* from the ordinary times of the day or the week.

The fifth commandment (v. 12) is the only commandment with a promise attached to it. The way we love God is best reflected in the way we treat our parents, who are our most immediate neighbors. The sixth commandment (v. 13) is a prohibition against violating human life, which is sacred. This commandment upholds the dignity and worth of every human being. The seventh commandment (v. 14) calls for faithfulness in the marital relationship. Fidelity in the marital relationship reflects fidelity to the covenant with God.

The eighth commandment (v. 15) prohibits the violation of the rights of others to hold and enjoy property. This commandment speaks against economic inequities, profit making at the expense of the poor and the disadvantaged, and all other forms of exploitation in our society. The ninth commandment (v. 16) prohibits lying in the court that would lead to the miscarriage of justice in the society. Our community life depends on our commitment to speak truthfully about our neighbor. The tenth commandment (v. 17) prohibits lustful ambition and desire to acquire what is not legitimately our own. Our covenant with God calls us to treat others and their property with love and care.

10, 8 are stated as negative commandments, but with positive implications. When an action or behavior is prohibited, the opposite of that action or behavior is elicited by these negative commandments.

Exodus 20:22—23:33 contains the specific laws related to the Sinai covenant. This section is often called the Book of the Covenant or the **covenant code.** This collection of laws has several parallels to the laws of the ancient Near East, particularly to the Code of Hammurabi (1792-1750 B.C.) and the Hittite laws of the 16th century B.C.[2] This section begins and ends with a call to loyalty demonstrated through proper worship and God's promise of blessings and protection (20:21-26; 23:20-33). The main body of the covenant code contains specific laws dealing with slaves, capital crimes, noncapital crimes, damage to property, social and religious duties, ethical duties, and religious festivals (21:1—23:19). The following is a list of some of the larger issues that receive attention in the covenant code: humane treatment of each other; punishment for crime that is equitable and sanctioned by the society; protection of the property rights of others; restitution for damages done to others; care, concern, and compassion for the economically disadvantaged; commitment to honesty and justice; and setting aside specific time to give thanks to God.[3]

At Mount Sinai, God instructed Israel to build a tentlike structure, known as the Tent or the **Tabernacle,** following the specific pattern and plan provided by Him (chaps. 25—31; 35—40). The function of the Tabernacle was to give Israel the visible and tangible evidence of the reality of God's abiding presence with His people in their daily journey.

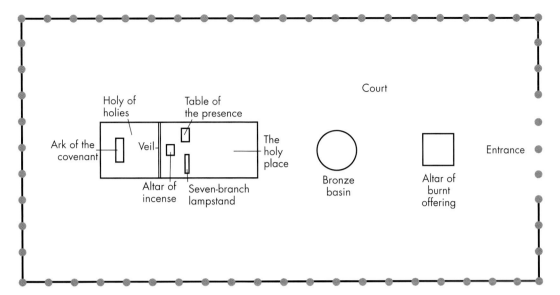

A diagram of the Tabernacle.

The Tabernacle was comprised of three areas: the court, the holy place, and the holy of holies. The **holy of holies,** the innermost area of the Tabernacle, was the most holy place, and it was separated from the holy place with a veil (26:31-33). The **ark of the covenant,** a wooden chest overlaid with pure gold, was located in this sacred space. The ark housed the testimonies or the two tablets of stone on which the commandments were written. In Israel's later history, the ark became the visible symbol of God's power and presence.

The **holy place** was the outer chamber of the Tabernacle. Only members of the priesthood had access to this place. This sacred space contained the table for "the bread of presence," a seven branched lampstand (menorah), and an altar of incense for the offering of fragrance.

The court was part of the enclosure of the Tabernacle that defined the boundary of the sacred area. The altar and the basin for washing were placed in the court. The

altar (also known as the altar of burnt offering or the altar of bronze) was for offering sacrifices on behalf of the worshiping community (see Leviticus 1—7).

In the Tabernacle narratives (Exodus 25—31; 35—40), we find not only the place of worship but also a proper pattern of worship. Doing God's work, giving to God, and receiving from God—all were to be done in faithfulness to the holy God who dwelt in the midst of Israel. The Tabernacle as a whole was a visible reminder not only of God's holiness but also of the possibility of meeting with this holy God.

The innermost sanctuary (holy of holies) at an Israelite temple at Arad in the southern part of Israel. Solomon may have built this temple for the soldiers stationed here during his reign.

An altar for sacrifice at the Israelite temple at Arad.

sor who pleads for God's mercy and forgiveness upon the sinful Israel. In the end, God granted Moses' appeal for mercy and manifested His glory to him as a sign of His continued favor toward His faithful servant.

The story of the Exodus ends with a postscript—a remembrance by a later faithful community that "the cloud of the LORD was over the tabernacle by day, and fire was in the cloud by night, in the sight of all the house of Israel during all their travels" (40:38). Israel's *exodus* from Egypt thus turned out to be a daily walk under the gracious and providential guidance of the God who saved them from their bondage. This faithful presence of God with His people in all "their travels," even in the midst of their rebellion and unfaithfulness, is a central theme in the rest of the biblical story.

The story of Israel's apostasy of making the golden calf is placed between the instructions concerning the building of the Tabernacle (chaps. 25—31) and the narrative that deals with its actual construction (chaps. 35—40). The golden calf story vividly portrays the idolatrous worship of Israel and the subsequent judgment of God that came upon the apostate nation. This story also portrays Moses as an unrelenting interces-

As for Israel at Mount Sinai, this was only the beginning of their journey with God.

T The Tabernacle in the New Testament

A number of New Testament writers have adopted the terminology of the Tabernacle in their writings. The Gospel writer John speaks of the ultimate reality of the presence of God with His people through Jesus of Nazareth in the Incarnation. "The Word became flesh and made his dwelling [or, *tabernacled*] among us" (John 1:14). John thus connects the place of the divine presence with the incarnate Christ. Perhaps the most detailed Christian interpretation of the Tabernacle is found in the Letter to the Hebrews. The writer of this letter refers to the earthly Tabernacle as a "copy and shadow of what is in heaven" (8:5). The writer further conveys that the furnishings and the rituals in the earthly Tabernacle reflected the truth that "the way into the Most Holy Place [that is, the real presence of God] had not yet been disclosed" (9:12). However, Christ who appeared as "high priest" "entered the Most Holy Place once for all by his own blood" not only for the "eternal redemption" but also to "cleanse our consciences from acts that lead to death," and to enable us to "serve the living God" (vv. 11-14). The Tabernacle in the Old Testament thus remains as the pledge and guarantee of God's promise to dwell with us through our Lord Jesus Christ. The apostle Paul further describes the Christian believer as "God's temple," the dwelling place of the Holy Spirit (1 Corinthians 3:16-17; 6:19-20).

Summary Statements

- Even in a foreign land, Israel multiplied and became great in number according to the covenant promises of God.
- God heard the cry of the people of Israel and appointed Moses to lead them out of Egypt.
- God revealed himself to Moses and Israel by His personal name Yahweh.
- God redeemed Israel from the Egyptians and led them out of Egypt under the leadership of Moses.
- God brought Israel to Mount Sinai and entered into a covenant relationship with them.
- God gave Israel the Ten Commandments as the basic guidelines for their life as God's people in the world.
- Israel sinned against God through idolatry, but God restored them through the intercessory prayers of Moses.
- God promised Israel His indwelling presence among them through the plan and pattern for the construction of the Tabernacle.

Questions for Reflection

1. What are some of the lessons we learn about promises in the Bible based on the story of Israel in Egypt?
2. Describe your experience of God as a God who is "there being with us."
3. How does God perform His act of deliverance today? Give illustrations from your personal life or the life of someone very close to you.
4. What does it mean to say that our relationship with God is a covenant relationship?

Bible Study Assignment

Read carefully Exodus 1:1-22 and answer the following questions.

1. What is the geographical, historical, cultural, and religious setting of this narrative?
2. Who are the key characters in this story? What is the role of each of these characters in this narrative?
3. Based on 1:1-7, what does this story say about God and the power of His blessing given to the patriarchs in Genesis?
4. What are the social and political realities described in verses 8-14?
5. Based on verse 12, how did God respond to the social and political oppression by the ruling class that is threatening to weaken and marginalize Israel?
6. How did the midwives who feared the Lord respond to the royal decree? What hope did they display for the future of their nation?

Bible Study Assignment, *cont.*

7. What narrative in the New Testament is a counterpart to this story? What are the parallels between these two stories?

8. What particular understanding of God is being conveyed through this Exodus story, even though He is not explicitly portrayed at the center of this narrative?

9. How should the church today hear and respond to this exodus narrative in the midst of similar social and political realities in our world today?

10. What hope do you find in this narrative for the poor and oppressed people of our day?

Resources for Further Study

Brueggemann, Walter. *The Book of Exodus: Introduction, Commentary, and Reflections,* vol. 1 in *The New Interpreter's Bible.* Nashville: Abingdon Press, 1994. Pages 690-981.

Childs, Brevard S. *The Book of Exodus: A Critical, Theological Commentary,* in *Old Testament Library.* Philadelphia: Westminster Press, 1974.

Fretheim, Terrence E. *Exodus,* in *Interpretation: A Bible Commentary for Teaching and Preaching.* Louisville: John Knox Press, 1991.

6 Road to the Promised Land:
Leviticus, Numbers, and Deuteronomy

bjectives:

Your study of this chapter should help you to:

- Describe the content of Leviticus, Numbers, and Deuteronomy
- Discuss the significance of sacrifice and offerings to the faith of Israel
- Relate holiness in Leviticus to the Christian emphasis on holy living
- Discuss the positive and negative aspect of the story of Israel in the wilderness, based on the narrative in Numbers
- Describe the theological principles promoted by the Shema
- Discuss the significance of the covenant renewal and the theology of blessings and curses

ey Words to Understand

Burnt offering
Grain offering
Peace offering
Sin offering
Guilt offering
Day of Atonement
Holiness code
Kadesh
Moab
King's Highway
Plains of Moab
The Shema
Deuteronomic theology

Questions to consider as you read:

1. Why is it necessary to have rules and regulations for worship?
2. Why is it difficult to trust God in the midst of difficult situations in life?
3. What does "you shall love the Lord your God with all your heart" mean to you?

The three remaining books of the Torah (Leviticus, Numbers, and Deuteronomy) continue the theme of the covenant relationship with God that was established at Mount Sinai. Mount Sinai is the starting point of Israel's journey with God as a holy people. However, the destination of this journey is the land that God had promised to give them through His covenant with their ancestors Abraham, Isaac, and Jacob. These three books not only anticipate the fulfillment of the ancestral promises but also set the agenda for Israel's life in the Promised Land. How does Israel demonstrate holiness as a way of her life and relationship with God and others in the world? What is Israel's distinctiveness as Yahweh's people? What sets them apart from the neighboring peoples? What does it mean to journey with God? What are some of the peculiar challenges ahead of this nation's journey with God? What kind of life should Israel live in the Promised Land? These are some of the critical questions answered in the remainder of the Torah.

The Book of Leviticus

Setting

The English title Leviticus comes from the Greek and Latin translations of the Old Testament. The title implies that this book was an instruction manual for Israel's priests. We cannot give a precise date for its writing. The laws promulgated at Sinai were most likely expanded during Israel's later history. It is likely that most of these complex laws existed in a written form around 700 B.C.[1] The consensus among most modern critical scholars is that the laws and regulations found in this book are the work of Israel's priestly writers (P), dated approximately to 400 B.C. In its canonical placement, the content of the book is located in the setting of the covenant making at Mount Sinai (see Leviticus 27:34).

Content

Though the content of the book is often addressed as God's speeches to Moses, and occasionally to Aaron, it is clear that the people were to be the ultimate recipients of these words (see the recurring formula, "The LORD said to Moses, 'Speak to the Israelites,'" throughout this book). The content of the book may be outlined as follows:

Sacrifices and Rituals	1:1—16:34
Holy Living	17:1—27:34

■ Holy God, Holy People

Holiness of God and holiness of Israel are central themes in Leviticus. We briefly look at the various sections in this book that teach and promote holiness and holy living.

Chapters 1—7 present offerings and sacrifices as a provision established by God for Israel to maintain holiness in her relationship with God. An offering (in Hebrew *qorban* from a verb stem meaning "to approach" or "to bring near") is a gift that brings a person to the holy presence of God.

In the **burnt offering** the whole animal was burned on the altar to symbolize the worshiper's total dedication to God. Through the acceptance of this gift, God accepted the worshiper. The **grain offering** was a gift to God in recognition of His authority. The **peace offering** symbolized the harmonious relationship between God and the worshiper. The **sin offering** and **guilt offering** indicated the need to remove sin and guilt from the worshiper. The guilt offering implied that any wrong done against God or others must be corrected through proper restitution.

The consecration and ordination of Aaron and his sons as priests to minister in the Tabernacle is the subject of Leviticus 8—10. The primary concern of these chapters is the sanctity of those who are called to serve as mediators between the worshiper and God. They must maintain the highest standard of holiness and model holiness before the people.

Chapters 11—15 deal with various types of uncleanness and prescriptions to remove them. Dietary laws and laws of clean and unclean show God's concern for the health and well-being of the covenant community. Removal of all forms of impurity from the community is a divine mandate in these chapters.

Leviticus 16 focuses on the complex procedure by which the nation as a whole was cleansed from sin and its consequences on a designated day known as the **Day of Atonement**. This was the only day in which the high priest entered the holy of holies. God instituted this day as an annual day for Israel to seek the divine cleansing of sin from the nation (vv. 29-31). This day was for Israel a day of Sabbath, rest not only from work but also from the power of sin.

Leviticus 17—26 contain miscellaneous laws, connected by the theme of holiness. This section is popularly known as the **holiness code.** The holiness code addresses areas such as proper worship, eating, sexual activities, social conduct, conduct of the priesthood, the religious calendar, blasphemy, fair and equitable justice, restoration of the land and prop-

Blood Sacrifice and Atonement

The shedding of the blood of an animal was God's gracious provision to sinners (see Leviticus 17:11). The blood made "atonement" for one's sins. The word *atonement* conveys the idea of "covering" something; in this case, the covering of sin by the blood. But, it also involved the cleansing from sin. In the Old Testament, the blood cleansed a sinner from all sins (16:30). The animal sacrifice was a substitute act with which a sinner received from God both His justice and mercy. Blood sacrifice was thus effective in gaining forgiveness, restoration, and cleansing from God.

New Testament writers describe the death of Jesus as God's provision of atonement for all humanity. The writer of Hebrews states that "the blood of Christ . . . cleanse[s] our consciences from acts that lead to death, so that we may serve the living God" (9:14).

erty ownership, and reward and punishment from God.

The instructions in the Book of Leviticus end with detailed regulations concerning making special vows to God (chap. 27).

The Book of Numbers

The Book of Numbers continues the theme of holiness set forth in the Book of Leviticus by its emphasis on the centrality of the Tabernacle and the guidance of God in the journey of Israel through the wilderness. The book contains narratives about Israel's murmuring and rebellion against God when they were faced with the difficult realities of life in the wilderness. The story of this book takes Israel from Sinai to the plains of Moab.

The English title derives from the Greek and Latin translations (*arithmoi* in Greek and *numeri* in Latin). This title reflects the cen-

Holiness in Leviticus

The call to holiness ("be holy") is an important theme in the holiness code (see 19:2; 20:7, 26; 21:6, 8). The holiness code describes the arena of daily life as the most appropriate context to practice holy living. Holiness in Leviticus is not a private affair for the enjoyment of the individual. It is the community's business to be holy so that it would be the mediating agency of God's holiness in the world. The Law insists on "love your neighbor as yourself" as the operative principle for achieving this goal (19:18). The New Testament emphasis on "love your neighbor as yourself" (Matthew 22:39; Romans 13:9; James 2:8) also reiterates the centrality of the law of love in Christian conduct.

sus accounts in chapters 1 and 26. The Hebrew title *bemidbar* ("in the wilderness") fits well with the geographical setting of the book. The book in its canonical form presents the wilderness context in the 13th century B.C. However, we also recognize the fact that the book in its present form and arrangement may have been the work of later generations. Critical scholars find in this book a mixture of J, E, and P materials.[2]

Setting

Various events described in Numbers 1:1—10:10 took place in the vicinity of Mount Sinai in the second year of Israel's departure from Egypt. Israel departed from Mount Sinai on the 14th month after they left Egypt. Their immediate destination was the wilderness of Paran, directly north of Mount Sinai. They arrived at **Kadesh,** probably an oasis located just south of the border of the Promised Land. From Kadesh, Moses sent out 12 spies to look over the land of Canaan and the strength of its inhabitants (12:16; 13:26). In the 40th year of their journey, Israel arrived at **Moab,** the region directly east of Jericho, beyond the river Jordan (20:22; 22:1).

We do not know for sure where Israel spent the time during the intervening years (approximately 38 years). It is possible that Israel, after the initial arrival at Kadesh, stayed there for a few months then left that region and wandered aimlessly in the wilderness for 38 years. They eventually returned to Kadesh to begin the final phase of the journey that took them to Moab. The narratives do not cover the entire history of Israel in the wilderness. The focus is on years 2 and 40 of Israel's journey. The book, as it stands in the Bible, covers Israel's history between 1280 and 1240 B.C.

Content

The narratives in Numbers can be assigned to the following three sections:

Preparations for Departure
from Sinai   1:1—10:10
Journey from Sinai to
Moab   10:11—21:35
Israel in the Plains of
Moab   22:1—36:13

■ Israel in the Wilderness

Preparation to leave Mount Sinai included a census taking to organize the nation as an army, in anticipation of opposition and war with enemies on the road to the Promised Land. The tribes of Israel were positioned around the Tabernacle. The Levites who were designated to assist the priests encamped around the Tabernacle to preserve the sanctity of the sacred space.

Numbers 10:11-28 describes Israel's journey from Sinai under the guidance of the cloud of God's presence. The Levites who carried the sacred objects were at the middle of the marching line. Those who carried the ark of the covenant were at the front line to give Israel a visible sign of God's leadership during their journey (see v. 33; see also Joshua 3:14).

The narratives in the next few chapters give us a glimpse of Israel's rebellion and complaint along the way. People were unhappy with Moses' leadership and the lack of food and water in the wilderness. Perhaps the most serious complaint came when they were camped out at Kadesh (chaps. 13—14). Ten of the 12 spies that Moses sent out to spy out Canaan came back with a negative report about the formidable task of conquering the Promised Land. This prompted the people to misconstrue God's good intentions and promises as

The possible route of Israel's journey from Mount Sinai to the plains of Moab.

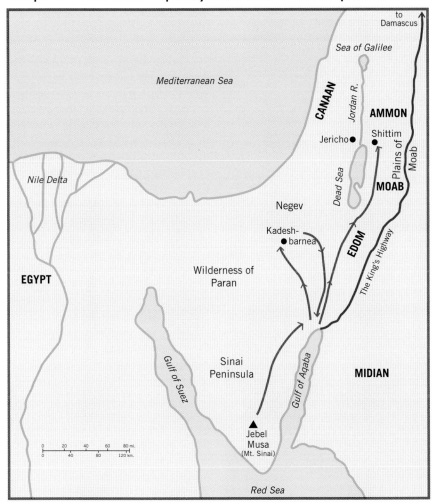

T A God-Centered Community

The positioning of the tents of Israel with the tent of God's dwelling at the center conveys the theme of the God-centered life of the people of God (2:1-2). On every side, the tents of Israel faced the Tabernacle. This theme of God-centered community and family existence speaks powerfully against our tendency to give God only a marginal place in our life. When God is no longer the center of our life, life becomes empty and void of holiness. The result is a life dominated by materialism, self-sufficiency, and pride.

His evil plans aimed at their destruction. As a result of this rebellion, God punished the people with the judgment of their wandering in the wilderness for 40 years and the eventual death of everyone who left Egypt, except Joshua and Caleb, the two spies who presented a favorable report.

Various miscellaneous laws interrupt the narrative of Israel's journey in the wilderness (chaps. 15, 18, 19). Numbers 20—21 describes the last segment of Israel's journey in the wilderness. At Meribah, the people rebelled again because there was no water. Though God commanded Moses to take his rod and speak to the rock, in a moment of rage he struck the rock twice with his rod. Though water came out of the rock, God pronounced the judgment upon His disobedient servant that he would not lead Israel into the Promised Land.

The narrative also includes the report about Israel's journey around Edom because the king of Edom refused to let Israel travel on the **King's Highway,** an ancient route from the Gulf of Aqaba region in the south to Damascus in the north. On the way to the plains of Moab, Israel encountered and gained military victory over the king of Arad; Sihon, king of the Amorites; and Og, king of Bashan.

Chapters 25—36 relate various incidents that took place in the **plains of Moab.** While camped out there, Israel worshiped Baal and engaged in the Canaanite fertility cult. Later records show that Balaam—a magician and seer recruited by Balak, king of Moab, to pronounce a curse upon Israel—was the one who led them to this corrupt and idolatrous behavior (see chaps. 21—24; 31:16; Revelation 2:4). God's judgment came upon the nation because of idolatry and immoral sexual practices (Numbers 25).

The book concludes with a number of miscellaneous matters, including the inheritance laws, appointment of Joshua as Moses' successor, laws of special offerings and religious vows, and boundaries of the Promised Land (chaps. 26—34). Moses designated 48 cities for the settlement of the Levites and 6 cities as cities of refuge for those who were guilty of unintentional murder (chap. 35).

We have traveled with Israel from Mount Sinai to the plains of Moab. Here Israel, a new generation, mostly children born in the wilderness, the second generation of those who have left Egypt, waited for instructions to enter

The plains of Moab where the Israelites camped at the end of their wilderness journey.

the Promised Land. We will now turn to the Book of Deuteronomy to examine Moses' final instructions to Israel on how life should be lived in the Promised Land.

The Book of Deuteronomy

According to tradition, the Book of Deuteronomy contains Moses' farewell speeches to the nation that was ready to occupy the Promised Land. Those who composed the historical books (Joshua, Judges, 1 and 2 Samuel, and 1 and 2 Kings) found this book to be the theological source for their interpretation and evaluation of Israel's history. Both Jews and Christians regard this book as one of the most important books in the Hebrew Bible. Frequent quotations from Deuteronomy in the New Testament indicate the significant role it played in the life of the early Christian church.

The English title comes from the Greek title *Deuteronomion* ("the second law"). Deuteronomy is "the second law" in the sense that it is the Law given or repeated a second time. Deuteronomy sums up

Gilead in modern Jordan. The tribe of Gad inherited this area.

the essence of the Law that God gave to Israel at Mount Sinai.

The book in its present canonical form contains Moses' exhortations to the Israelites who were preparing to enter the Promised Land. That would presuppose a 13th century B.C. context for the content of the book. Some modern critical scholars view this book as a document produced in the late 7th century B.C. in the context of King Josiah's religious reforms. It is very likely that the basic core of instructions in the Book of Deuteronomy belongs to the Mosaic period. It is also possible that later inspired writers would have expanded the Mosaic instructions to address specific theological

---

T Life in the Wilderness

We learn three theological lessons from Israel's wilderness journey. First, *in our daily walk with God, we must depend on the mysterious and gracious provisions of God.* God's provision of daily bread is His graciousness toward us. And for that, we must be grateful. The gospel also invites us to trust in the gracious provisions of God (Matthew 6:25-34).

Second, *we must trust in the unseen, yet powerful reality of God's presence with us.* The visible and life-threatening forces of life often have the capacity to distract us from the invisible reality of God's presence with us. The apostle Paul said: "If God is for us, who can be against us?" (Romans 8:31).

Third, *we must be submissive to God's faithful leadership.* Israel's rejection of both human and divine leadership cautions us about the peril of individualism and autonomy. Submission to the authority of responsible and God-directed leadership is a mark of holy living.

The Shema

Deuteronomy 6:4-9 is part of the morning and evening prayer of Judaism. In Jewish daily worship, this text is recited along with 11:13-21 and Numbers 15:37-41 as "Recitation of **the Shema.**" The name *Shema* comes from the opening word *hear* in 6:4 (in Hebrew *shema*).

The Shema begins with the confession that "the LORD our God, the LORD is one" (v. 4). This confession explicitly calls for a life of relationship with God in which there is no room for other gods. The covenant calls for absolute loyalty to God. This confession invites us to reflect on the words of Jesus, "No one can serve two masters" (Matthew 6:24).

Moses also invited the people of God to demonstrate their exclusive loyalty to God through their wholehearted, exclusive, and energetic expression of love for Him (Deuteronomy 6:5). The call to love God is without doubt the most central challenge of the Book of Deuteronomy. Jesus called this command to love as "the first and the greatest commandment" (Matthew 22:38). Here we find the summons to model love in the most intimate way, involving the heart, soul, and strength of the believer.

The Shema is God's gracious invitation to holy living. The call to love God is first and foremost a call to live in the experience of God's faithful and unfailing devotion to us. Only then can we truly love Him. John states, "God is love. Whoever lives in love lives in God, and God in him. . . . We love because he first loved us" (1 John 4:16, 19).

challenges of their particular religious contexts. However, it is difficult to determine a precise date for the final shaping and the arrangement of the content of this book. The book may very well have existed in the written form long before the Josianic reform in the 7th century B.C. (see 2 Kings 22:8-13).[3]

Setting

The opening verses (1:1-5) identify the plains of Moab as the setting of the content of Deuteronomy. The wilderness journey is over. The nation would soon witness a momentous event in their history. They would enter the land that God had promised to give Abraham as an inheritance for his descendants. God's promise to make Abraham a great nation was already fulfilled. Their entry into Canaan would set the stage for Israel to become a blessing to "all peoples on earth" (Genesis 12:3).

Content

The introduction to the book presents its content as Moses' explanation of the Law *(Torah)* that God gave to Israel at Horeb (Deuteronomy 1:5). Torah, usually translated as "law," receives in this book a new meaning. Here the Law is more than what God prohibits or permits, rather it is God's gracious will, His *instructions* for one's conduct and life. We may appropriately call this book God's guiding principles for Israel's faithful and obedient living in the Promised Land. The book has the following major sections:

Remembering the Past
1:6—4:43
There Is No Other God
5:1—28:68
Covenant Renewal
29:1—30:20
The Epilogue 31:1—34:12

■ There Is No Other God

Deuteronomy begins with a recital of some of the significant events in the wilderness journey of Israel. God's love and concern for Israel is a key theme in these narratives (1:6—4:43). This remembrance of the past sets the stage for Deuteronomy's central affirmation of Israel's faith that Yahweh alone is God (6:4). Therefore, Israel's fundamental duty is to love God with all their heart, soul, and strength (v. 5). Both of these theological issues are key to Israel's life and future as the covenant community in the Promised Land. Deuteronomy also challenges God's holy people to order their lives with constant attentiveness to the instructions of God (Torah). God's people must be preoccupied with the Torah and let it shape and influence their thinking, feeling, desires, and actions. Deuteronomy further establishes the Torah as the foundation and the guiding truth for the Israelites' existence at home or outside the home (vv. 6-9).

The centrality of God in the life of Israel is reiterated throughout Deuteronomy. The Torah instructs God's people to categorically reject the temptation to go after other gods (vv. 10-19). Loyalty to God is instilled in the hearts of children by parents who take seriously their responsibility to tell them the story of redemption and challenge them to remain faithful to the Lord (vv. 20-25).

Israel when it enters the Promised Land should remember the wilderness as a place where God tested and humbled His people so that they would learn the truth that He is their sole Provider (8:1-10). The book also portrays the land of promise as a gift God is giving to His people, and therefore they have no natural right to the land. Neither can they claim that they occupied the land by the power of their hands. Deuteronomy sternly warns Israel that they would face the tragedy of destruction if they forget Yahweh their God who brought them to the land (vv. 11-20).

■ God's Requirement

Deuteronomy places before Israel the sum of all the commands of God. God's great requirement to His people is that they fear Him, walk in all His ways, love Him, serve Him with their whole being (heart and soul), and keep the covenant commandments (10:12-22). In order for this to become a reality, the people must circumcise their hearts; that is, submit themselves to God's Torah. Meeting this requirement also meant an intense commitment to care for the widows, the father-

T Israel's Social Responsibility

Deuteronomy challenges the covenant community to be a compassionate people who love and care for the widow and the alien in the land—the oppressed and the marginal in the society. They represented a group that seldom received any protection from the powerful and oppressive social and political systems in the ancient world. The emphasis on Israel's social responsibility is found in Deuteronomy 14:29; 15:7-11; 24:19-22; 26:12-15. We are reminded here to be "imitators of God" by doing righteousness, by promoting justice, and by giving food and clothing to the poor among us. At the heart of the Christian gospel is the call to live the compassionate life of Jesus, the One who was moved with compassion when He saw the oppressed, harassed, and the marginal in His own day (Matthew 9:36; James 1:27).

H Israel's Pilgrim Festivals

Israel remembered and celebrated God's saving actions and His blessings through various annual festivals. The Passover celebrated Israel's redemption from Egypt. The Feast of Unleavened Bread commemorated the removal of leaven from the Israelite household and eating the unleavened bread for seven days. During the Feast of Weeks the Israelites presented the firstfruits of their wheat harvest to the Lord. Weeks refer to the seven-week period of harvest that began with the cutting of barley and concluded with the wheat harvest. The celebration happened on the 50th day following the Passover (so the name *Pentecost*). Later in Israel, the Pentecost festival became a commemoration of the giving of the Law at Mount Sinai. The Feast of Booths marked the completion of the agricultural year. This festival also reminded Israel of her wandering days in the wilderness. This feast is also known by the names the Feast of Tabernacles and the Feast of Ingathering. The people set up booths and dwelt in them for seven days to remind themselves of their tent dwelling days in the wilderness. These festivals were pilgrim festivals that required every Israelite male to appear before God in Jerusalem with an appropriate offering to express gratitude to God (Deuteronomy 16:16-17).

less, and the sojourner in the land.

Among the various and miscellaneous rules and regulations in Deuteronomy 12—26, we find repetitions and adaptations of laws from other legal collections in the Pentateuch, along with some new laws and regulations. These instructions serve as guidelines for the establishment of an orderly life in the Promised Land. Instructions in these chapters cover topics such as legitimate and authorized ways of worship, the destruction of idolatry, laws of clean and unclean animals, tithing, and religious festivals. The beneficiaries of tithing included the Levites, the sojourner, the widow, and the fatherless. The concern for the poor is also reflected in the laws that deal with the release of debt and the freeing of slaves in the seventh year.

Guidelines for Israel's life in the Promised Land also included steps for proper judicial process, rules for the conduct of kings who would govern God's people, the prohibition of divination, and the establishment of the prophetic office to continue the ministry of Moses (chaps. 17—18). Deuteronomy reminds God's people that gratitude to God is the most appropriate way to respond to His gracious gift of the land (chap. 26). At harvesttime, they must not only bring some of the firstfruits in a basket at the appointed place of worship but also recite the story of redemption from Egypt and the gift of the land as a thanksgiving response to God. Again, God's gracious actions on behalf of Israel in the past constituted the theological basis of these guidelines for her life in the Promised Land. What was at stake was the future of Israel as God's people. And that future rested on their commitment to live in obedience to God's instructions.

Deuteronomy instructs Israel that life in the land must begin with specific rituals, which included the pronouncement of blessings and curses, blessings for covenant faithfulness and curses for covenant breaking (chaps. 27—28). Scholars label this theology of blessings and curses as **Deuteronomic theology.**

■ Covenant Renewal

Instructions in chapters 29—30 aim to promote loyalty and single-minded allegiance to God through the renewal of the covenant with God. The covenant with God is crucial to Israel's future in the Promised Land. Breaking of the covenant would have serious consequences. However, God is a forgiving God who promises restoration to those who repent of their sin. The divine promise also includes the circumcision of the hearts of God's people so that they would love Him with all their heart, soul, and strength (30:1-10). This section ends with the challenge to choose life or death. Obedience means life and blessings; disobedience means death and destruction. Israel's life in the land depends on her decision to choose life (vv. 15-20).

■ The Epilogue

The final chapters of the Book of Deuteronomy (chaps. 31—34) make up the epilogue, the conclusion of the book as well as of the entire Pentateuch. This section contains the farewell song of Moses, which reminds the people of God's faithfulness in spite of their unfaithfulness. The book concludes with the narrative of Moses' seeing the Promised Land from Mount Nebo, his death, and his burial by God in the land of Moab. The book ends with a fitting eulogy that "since then, no prophet has risen in Israel like Moses, whom the LORD knew face to face" (v. 10).

The challenge underlying the concluding words of the Torah is clear. It is an invitation to Israel to rise up as a people who live in the experience of seeing God and knowing Him "face to face" as Moses did. Only Israel can fill the void left by the death of Moses. Moses was dead, but Israel lives on.

We have followed the story of Israel from Egypt to the plains of Moab. The dream of the Promised Land will soon be fulfilled in the history of God's people. We will now see what kind of destiny Israel chose for herself when she entered the Promised Land. This is the story we find in the Books of Joshua, Judges, and Ruth.

Mount Nebo. Moses saw the Promised Land from this site before his death.

Summary Statements

- Holiness is separation from the secular influences of the world and consecration to God.
- Maintaining holiness in all areas of life and relationship is a necessary component of holy living.
- God guided and provided for Israel in the wilderness.
- The wilderness became a place of judgment because of Israel's rebellion and complaint.
- Remembering God is an important theme in Deuteronomy.
- Moses challenged Israel to obey, love, and serve God with all their heart and all their soul.
- Social responsibility to the widows, orphans, and aliens in the land is an important part of Israel's covenant life.
- Israel's future in the Promised Land depended on her commitment to live by the requirements of God.
- Blessings for obedience and curses for disobedience is the underlying principle of Deuteronomic theology.

Questions for Reflection

1. Discuss ways to maintain holiness in our everyday Christian life.
2. What are some of the areas where we tend to erase the boundary between the sacred and the profane?
3. What are some practical ways to atone for our sins, other than repentance and prayer for forgiveness?
4. What are the things that tend to bring anxiety, doubt, and fear for existence today?
5. Using the Book of Deuteronomy as a guide, make a list of the guiding principles that would give us directions to live a faithful life in the secular world in which we live today.

Bible Study Assignment

Read Deuteronomy 30:15-20 and answer the following questions:

1. What is the significance of this text in the present literary arrangement of Deuteronomy? (Review the materials preceding this text and the narrative that follows this text.)
2. What choices does God place before His people? Why?
3. What is the intended purpose of the "if . . . then" statements in this text?
4. What are the conditions for Israel to enjoy life?
5. What are the actions that would bring death and destruction upon God's people?
6. What role does God assign to heaven and earth? Why?
7. What is involved in choosing life (how does one gain life)?
8. What lesson do you find in this text about God?
9. What particular teaching of Jesus reiterates this theme of choosing and gaining life? How does Jesus portray himself in the Gospels?
10. What does this text offer as hope to those who pursue the path of death and destruction in our world today?

Resources for Further Study

Craigie, Peter C. *The Book of Deuteronomy.* In *New International Commentary on the Old Testament.* Grand Rapids: Eerdmans. 1976.

Kaiser, Walter C., Jr. *The Book of Leviticus: Introduction, Commentary, and Reflections,* in vol. 1, *The New Interpreter's Bible.* Nashville: Abingdon Press, 1994. Pages 985-1191.

Miller, Patrick D. *Deuteronomy.* In *Interpretation: A Bible Commentary for Teaching and Preaching.* Louisville, Ky.: John Knox Press, 1990.

Thompson, J. A. *Deuteronomy: An Introduction and Commentary,* in *Tyndale Old Testament Commentaries.* Downers Grove, Ill.: InterVarsity Press, 1974.

Wenham, Gordon J. *Numbers: An Introduction and Commentary,* in *Tyndale Old Testament Commentaries.* Downers Grove, Ill.: InterVarsity Press, 1981.

UNIT III

THE COVENANT
COMMUNITY IN CRISIS

Your study of this unit will help you to:

- Describe the early days of Israel's life in the Promised Land
- Evaluate the circumstances that led to the establishment of Israel as a political nation
- Describe the events that resulted in the destruction of the kingdoms of Israel and the exile of the nation
- Summarize the story of Israel's restoration to the Promised Land

■ Israel in the Promised Land:

Joshua, Judges, and Ruth

■ Israel Becomes a Political Kingdom:

1 and 2 Samuel

■ Israel's Exile from the Promised Land:

1 and 2 Kings

■ Israel's Restoration to the Promised Land:

Chronicles, Ezra, Nehemiah, and Esther

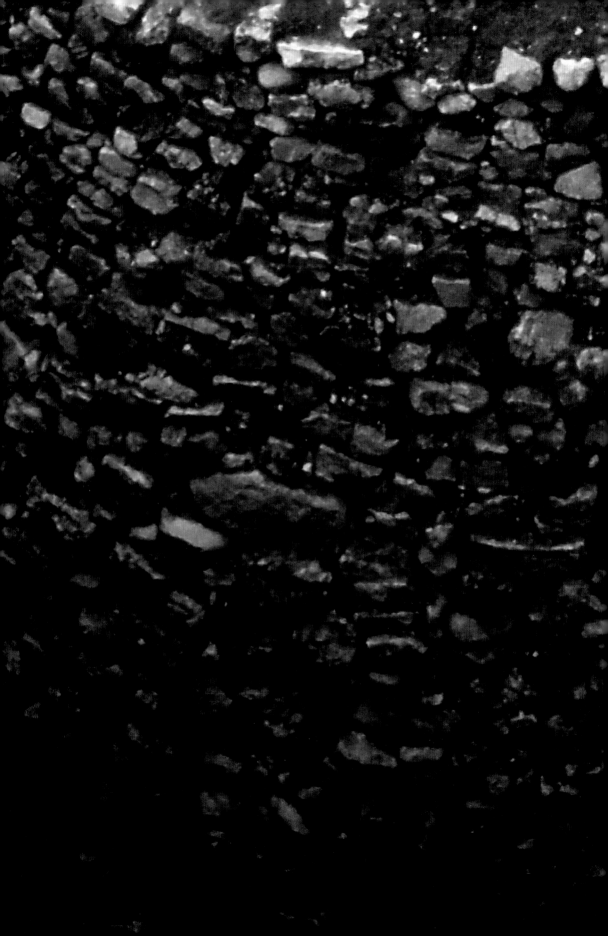

7 Israel in the Promised Land:
Joshua, Judges, and Ruth

 Objectives:

Your study of this chapter should help you to:

- Describe the relationship of Deuteronomistic history to the Book of Deuteronomy
- Discuss the manner in which the people entered, possessed, and distributed the land of promise
- Discuss the religious and cultural challenges the Israelites faced during the early years of their settlement in Canaan
- Describe the role of the judges
- Explain the cycle of retribution in the context of the Deuteronomistic history
- Describe the central messages of the Book of Ruth

 Key Words to Understand

Former Prophets
Deuteronomistic history
Holy war
Cherem
Cycle of retribution
Judges
Baal
Deborah
Gideon
Levirate marriage
Samson
Philistines
Megilloth

Questions to consider as you read:

1. What is a "holy war" today?
2. What are some of the distinctive features of Christian culture that stand in opposition to the culture in which you live?
3. What happens to a people when they lose memory of their traditions or disconnect themselves from the previous generations?

The second major portion of the Old Testament, known as the Prophets or the *Nebi'im* is concerned to tell "the rest of the story" of the people of God. As the people settled in the land of promise, would they be faithful to live in wholeness of heart, soul, and strength, as Moses instructed them? Would the people ultimately place their trust in other gods, in idols, or even in their own schemes? If so, what would happen to them? These questions reflect the primary concerns of the Prophets *(Nebi'im)*. The first part of the *Nebi'im* is commonly known as the **Former Prophets,** a collection of books that contain Israel's history from the nation's settlement in Canaan to its exile to Babylon.

The Deuteronomistic History

In biblical studies, the Former Prophets has often been referred to as the **Deuteronomistic history.** This designation recognizes that the story of Israel told in its final shape in Joshua, Judges, Samuel, and Kings is a single work written with the concerns and theological convictions of Deuteronomy in mind.

The writers of the Deuteronomistic history drew their information from various sources, such as "the book of the annals of the kings of Israel" and "the book of the annals of the kings of Judah" (see 1 Kings 14:19, 29; 15:7, 31). It is likely that various other lists, annals, and stories not specifically mentioned in the text were utilized by the writers as well. Nevertheless, when reading these and other history books (such as the chronicler's history, comprised of 1 and 2 Chronicles, Ezra, and Nehemiah), we should recognize that the primary concern of the writers is not to present a "colorless" list of disconnected events but rather a connected story that interprets the life of Israel from a prophetic perspective. For the Deuteronomistic history, that perspective is found in the sermons of Moses in Deuteronomy.

The Book of Joshua

Setting

The Book of Joshua, the first book in the Deuteronomistic history, deals primarily with the manner in which the Israelites entered and possessed the land of promise. The book in its present form presupposes a setting in the 13th century B.C. Joshua emerged as the leader of Israel following the death of Moses. The book deals with the entrance of Israel into Canaan from the plains of Moab, on the eastern side of the Jordan River. The stories of the book may be placed during the period between 1240 and 1225 B.C.

Content

The Book of Joshua depicts the stories of entering, possessing, and distributing the land as a solemn act of worship. Instructions in Deuteronomy introduced the land as a gift from God. The stories in Joshua show how Joshua and Is-

Jericho was one of the oldest cities built in Canaan (8000 B.C.); this was the first city taken by Israel when they entered the land.

Holy War and the Kingdom of God

The various stories of battles in the Book of Joshua reflect the ancient practice of **holy war.** In this practice, people fought the war in the name of God. God gave them victory. Because the battle belonged to God, all that was conquered also belonged to Him. Therefore, everything conquered was dedicated or sacrificed to God through total destruction or ***cherem.***

These stories present modern Christians with a challenge. However, the stories of such wars must be understood first in light of their theological perspective. The Deuteronomistic emphasis upon holy war points to the necessity for the people of God to reject the ways of the world. The Deuteronomistic history also reveals the painful truth that war, destruction, and death were part of the redemptive history of Israel in the Old Testament. The reality of war and destruction of enemies in no way characterize Israel as a morally superior people who were charged with the mandate of a holy war against the pagan world. Therefore, in the Christian reading of these stories, the Old Testament practice of holy war should never be taken as a model for the establishment of the kingdom of God. The cross of Jesus demonstrates that the conquering power of the people of God is not found in killing the enemy, but rather in giving up our own lives as a sacrifice for others.

rael claimed the land as their worshipful response to God's faithfulness. The stories of Joshua can be arranged under four sections:

Entrance into the Land
               1:1—5:15
Possession of the Land
               6:1—12:24
Distribution of the Land
               13:1—21:45
Joshua's Farewell Speeches
               22:1—24:33

■ Entrance into the Land

Although the entrance into the land began a new era for the people of God, the new era was directly related to what God has been doing in the previous generation. God gave Joshua the assurance of His presence with him and commissioned him to complete the task to which God called Moses.

Joshua began his task by instructing the Israelites to prepare for their entrance into Canaan. He sent two spies to Jericho to search out the land, where they were assisted by Rahab, a non-Israelite, who recognized the power of God at work among the Israelites. The journey into Canaan began with Israel crossing the River Jordan on dry ground, which connected this new generation with the preceding generation that crossed the Sea of Reeds (Exodus 14). The two stories of divided waters demonstrate the full picture of God's saving activity for His people. God both delivered the people *from* the captivity of the Egyptians and delivered them *to* life in the Promised Land.

Once the procession across the Jordan was complete, the people responded in three significant acts. They set up 12 stones at the Jordan as a memorial of God's deliverance for future generations, and at the encampment at Gilgal, Joshua circumcised all male Israelites as a sign of their membership in the covenant community. Finally, the nation celebrated the Passover for the first time in the Promised Land.

■ Possession of the Land

This section begins with the familiar story of the taking of Jericho. The narrative in chapter 6 shows great liturgical precision, with the repetition of the number seven throughout the story. The emphasis upon the *total* destruction of the city and all of its inhabitants points to the nature of the taking of Jericho as an act of worship. Everything was to be put under *cherem* or the sacrificial ban.

The military campaign against Canaan was carried out in three directions—the central, southern, and northern part of the land. Jericho and Ai were conquered during the central campaign. The southern campaign brought cities such as Lachish and Hebron in the south under Israel's control. The northern campaign crushed the coalition of city-states in the north led by the king of Hazor. The narratives show that these central, southern, and northern campaigns enabled the Israelites to take possession of the Promised Land. The stories of conquest end with the statement: "So Joshua took the whole land, just as the LORD had directed Moses, and he gave it as an inheritance to Israel according to their tribal divisions" (Joshua 11:23).

Lachish, one of the oldest cities in Canaan (dated to 8000 B.C.), located 30 miles southwest of Jerusalem. Joshua and Israel conquered and took this city.

■ Distribution of the Land

In chapters 12 through 21, we find specific detail concerning the allotments of land to each of the tribes. From the Deuteronomistic perspective, the land was God's property, and He had given to each tribe a plot of land as an inheritance to be kept within each family unit in perpetuity. For this reason, Israel's prophets such as Elijah, Amos, Micah, and Isaiah made harsh criticisms against the practice of stripping families of their inheritance of land (1 Kings 21; Amos 8:4-6; Micah 2:1-2, 9; Isaiah 5:8).

Once the land was distributed to the various tribes, Joshua established 6 cities of refuge (Joshua 20) and 48 Levitical towns (chap. 21), according to the instruction of Moses (Deuteronomy 18:1-8; 19:1-10). The cities of refuge allowed for persons accused of capital crimes to have a fair hearing. The Levitical towns provided a place for the Levites to reside, since no specific territory had been set aside for these traveling priests.

■ Joshua's Farewell and the Covenant Renewal

The story of the conquest and settlement of Israel in Canaan concludes with worship. After the settlement of the tribes, the people gathered for a farewell discourse from their leader (Joshua 23) and a renewal of their covenant with God and each other (chap. 24). The leadership of Joshua ended in the same way that Moses ended his leadership. The final act of both leaders was leading the nation in a covenant renewal service (see Deuteronomy 27—28). In the covenant renewal service at Shechem, Joshua called the people to make a commitment to live a life of "complete" and "whole" devotion to God (Joshua 24:14). He also challenged the people to cast aside any gods to whom they might turn.

Yahweh (the LORD) alone was the God who saved them; therefore, the Lord alone would be the object of their reverence and service.

The people enthusiastically responded that they would never forsake God to serve other gods. Joshua concluded the service of renewal by making a covenant with the people, writing down various statutes, and finally by setting up a stone as a witness to the people's decision to serve God wholeheartedly (vv. 25-27).

The book concludes with the report about Joshua's death (vv. 29-30) and the burial of Joseph's bones at Shechem. Prior to his death, Joseph anticipated that God would visit His people and bring them into the land that He promised to give to their ancestors (Genesis 50:24-25). Here we find not only the fulfillment of that hope but also a proper closure to the story of Joseph. The exiled son of Jacob found a final resting place in the Promised Land.

Now that the promise of God to Israel had been fulfilled, the question remains: Would the people of Israel remain faithful to their covenant with God? Would they wholeheartedly serve Him? Would they reject the gods of Canaan? Would they reject the culture of Canaan?

These questions receive attention in the next book, the Book of Judges.

The Book of Judges

After the death of Joshua, the people of God began the long process of making the Promised Land their permanent home. The new beginning of Israel in the Promised Land was met with difficult challenges. The nation was

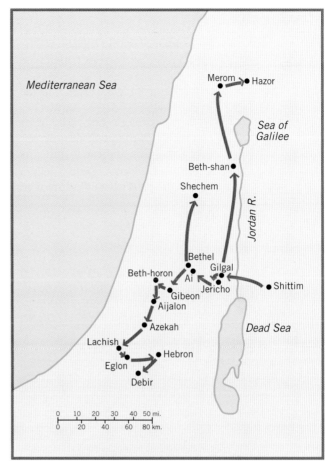

Israel's conquest of central, southern, and northern parts of Canaan.

somewhat settled in the land, though there were still many areas of the land still under the control of the Canaanites. It seems that the people of Israel became more and more concerned about adopting new strategies for survival in the land than continuing the conquest of the rest of the Promised Land. The Book of Judges shows that this stage in their history took the nation through great cultural, moral, and spiritual crises.

The title of the Book of Judges is appropriately named after the central characters in its stories. Though this book is part of the Deuteronomistic history composed at a later period, the stories in the book go far back to the time when the warrior heroes and heroines of Israel would have lived. It is very likely that various tribes would have told and retold for generations the great feats, faith, and failures of certain warrior judges. Each new generation would have learned both the positive and the negative traits of these leaders, as persons to follow in some cases or as examples to avoid in other cases.

Setting

For about 200 years (approximately from 1220 B.C. to 1050 B.C.), Israel struggled to establish themselves in the land that was dominated by the religious, cultural, and political ideologies of the Canaanites. After Joshua's death, there was no national leader to unite the various tribes of Israel. The tribes of Israel lacked unity and strong national leadership. Family, clan, and tribal leaders provided local leadership at various levels. This period presented the people of God with two significant challenges: first, the difficulty of making a transition from a seminomadic desert dwelling way of life in the past to the settled life of agriculturalists; second, ordering life in the society as a covenant people without the assistance of a strong national leader. The story in the Book of Judges relates that on both of these areas, Israel succumbed to the pressures of the dominant culture that surrounded them.

The settlement of the 12 tribes of Israel.

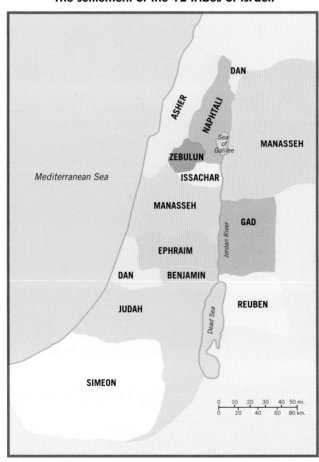

Content

The characteristic feature of the Book of Judges is the repeated fourfold cycle lived out by the Israelites. In the first place, the Israelites repeatedly turned from their worship of God to worship Baal, or did what was "evil in the eyes of the LORD" (2:11). In response to their apostasy, God handed them over into the hands of an invading nation (v. 14). As a result of the oppression by an enemy nation, the people cried out for help (vv. 15, 18). Finally God sent a deliverer or a "judge" to fight off the enemy (vv. 16, 18). For the remainder of the judge's life, the land remained at rest. However, when the judge died, the cycle was repeated once again. This **cycle of retribution** provides the general framework for the various stories of the judges.

This fourfold pattern of apostasy, deliverance into the hand of an enemy, outcry, and deliverance reflects very clearly the primary theological concerns of the Deuteronomistic history. With this paradigm as the backdrop, a large portion of the remainder of the book provides specific instances in which this cycle is played out.

The narratives in Judges can be outlined as follows:

Strangers in a Foreign Land
1:1—2:23

The Judges of Israel   3:1—16:31

Miscellaneous Narratives
17:1—21:25

■ Strangers in a Foreign Land

The opening two chapters set the stage for the story of the book. In spite of Joshua's final instructions, most of the tribes failed to continue the expulsion of the Canaanites from the land. The narrator then summarizes the cycle of retribution that Israel experienced in the next 200 years (2:11-23).

■ The Judges of Israel

In the early days of Israel's life in Canaan, the 12 tribes were only loosely organized as a larger unit, perhaps more as a confederation of relatively independent tribes. It seems that family leaders or elders made important decisions that affected the clans and families within each tribe. However, intertribal

The First Mention of Israel

The *Hymn of Victory of Mer-ne-Ptah* contains the earliest mention of Israel that has been discovered. Near the end of the 13th century B.C., the Egyptian king Mer-ne-Ptah led a successful campaign against rebels in Canaan. In a hymn celebrating the victory, the statement is made that Israel has been laid waste and has no survivor. However, the term *Israel* in the hymn refers to a group of people rather than to a geographical location. At this point the people appear to have still been in the process of settling into the land.[1]

disputes appear to have been left to the jurisdiction of **judges** (in Hebrew *shophetim*) whom we find in the Book of Judges. Although some of the earliest leaders of the Israelites are not specifically identified as judges, the Hebrew verb used of their primary activity (*shaphat,* which means "to judge") indicates this role. The one who does the activity of *shaphat* is one who renders justice or makes legal decisions.

The primary role of judges, however, was to lead the tribes in their fight against enemies who sought to take control of the land. Throughout the Book of Judges, the Spirit of God empowered various persons to lead in military campaigns. Once victorious, the

The Canaanite Religion

Baal worship was the characteristic of the Canaanite religion. As a fertility religion, baalism functioned to meet the needs of an agricultural people. The worship of **Baal** was grounded in a cyclic myth in which Baal was taken captive into the underworld by the god of death (Mot). The Canaanites connected drought and famine and the lack of productivity of the ground to the captivity of Baal. They also believed that, in due time, Baal's consort, Asherah (or in some accounts Ashtart or Anat), would descend into the underworld and release Baal. Baal and his consort subsequently engaged in sexual activity, which in turn made the ground to be fertile and productive. This cycle was repeated annually, which made it possible for the land to produce crops again and again.[2]

An ancient Canaanite altar at Megiddo.

a left-handed man, to deliver the people. After Ehud, Shamgar delivered Israel from the Philistines.

Chapters 4 and 5 contain the story of the prophetess/judge **Deborah** who appointed Barak to bring deliverance to Israel from Jabin, king of Hazor. As Israel fought back, Sisera, Jabin's commander, fled to an ally, Heber the Kenite. While he was resting in the tent, Heber's wife hammered a tent peg into the temple of his head. As gruesome as the details are in this story, once again the emphasis is upon God's victory through the weak and powerless in the world.

God raised up **Gideon** to deliver the Israelites from the Midianite oppression. He gave victory to Gideon with 300 most unlikely soldiers that he selected from the 32,000 member Israelite army. Jephthah, the son of a prostitute and an outlaw, delivered Israel from the Ammonite oppression. Before going to battle, he vowed that he would sacrifice whatever came first out of his house to meet him upon a victorious return. When he returned home after his victory, the first person to greet him was his daughter, his only child. To fulfill his vow, Jephthah carried out human sacrifice, an act that was an abomination to the people of God.

military leader continued his role as judge over Israel for the remainder of his or her life.

Chapter 3 presents the stories of three judges. The cycle of retribution began with Israel's turning away from God and the worship of Baal. God handed them over to the king of Aram. When they cried out to God for help, the spirit of the Lord empowered Othniel to overthrow the power of the king and to deliver the Israelites. For the remainder of his life, the Israelites were at peace. Following the death of Othniel, the Israelites once again turned away from God. King Eglon of Moab overran Israel and ruled for 18 years. In response to the outcry of the Israelites, God prepared Ehud,

T   Theology of Weakness

The various stories of the judges demonstrate two significant traits. The description of the enemies includes special mention of their strength, wealth, or power. The one whom God raises up as "judge" is often a person of weak or lowly status. In all of these cases, the Spirit of the Lord is the empowering agency. Judges gain victory not by their strength but by the strength of the Lord. The stories very clearly express the conviction that God demonstrates His strength through the weak and the powerless.

Centuries later the apostle Paul claimed that God's power is made perfect in human weakness. Reflecting on his own experience, he declared to the church at Corinth, "When I am weak, then I am strong" (2 Corinthians 12:10).

Levirate Marriage

In ancient Israel, the Law did not permit family properties to be sold because of the belief that God owned the land. If a family property had to be sold due to hardship, then the redeemer or *go'el*, the nearest relative, was responsible for buying it back or redeeming it (Leviticus 25:25-28). In the Deuteronomic law, the *go'el*'s role includes marrying the widow of a childless brother. This custom is known as **levirate marriage** (Deuteronomy 25:5-10). The man who became the husband of his deceased brother's wife thus became her *go'el*.

In **Samson** (chaps. 13—16), we see the ultimate degeneration of the office of the judge. The story of Samson begins with a reference to the apostasy of Israel. This time, the oppressors were the **Philistines,** who occupied the southwestern part of the coastal plain of Canaan. Though he was raised by his parents as a Nazirite, the stories of Samson show that the Nazirite vow of faithfulness to God meant little if anything to him. However, in spite of the unfaithfulness of Samson, God remained faithful and filled him with His Spirit, thereby enabling him to do great wonders.

In the closing five chapters of the Book of Judges, we sense just how loosely knit the tribes really were. Scattered throughout the book, we often catch a glimpse of the relative "independence" of each tribe. In this section, the narrator includes two specific examples of the growing tension that existed among the tribes. The tribe of Dan decided to migrate northward due to the increasing threat from the Philistines. However, on the way, the Danites not only stole objects of worship but also took a priest from the tribe of Ephraim. Once arriving in the north, this tribe established the city of Dan and set up the stolen object of worship as an idol. Eventually, the city of Dan became one of the two worship sites established by Jeroboam I as a rival to Jerusalem (see 1 Kings 12:26-30).

Judges 19—21 relate the tragic events that led to Israel's war with the tribe of Benjamin. The rest of the tribes of Israel decided to punish the Benjamites, because some wicked members of that tribe had abused the concubine of a Levite who was passing through their territory. In the war, the Benjamites were nearly annihilated to the point that special provisions had to be made to repopulate the tribe.

The closing statement of the Book of Judges provides both a postlude to the premonarchic period and a prelude to the next chapter in the life of Israel: "In those days there was no king in

Excavations at Hazor, located 10 miles north of the Sea of Galilee. During the period of the judges, King Jabin of Hazor oppressed the Israelites.

Israel; all the people did what was right in their own eyes" (21:25, NRSV). Certainly, to do what was "right in their own eyes" assumes that the people were not living according to the Torah as instructed by Moses and Joshua. In the absence of a king who promoted the Torah as the standard for the conduct of God's people, Israel lived the first 200 years in Canaan by their own law that they devised for themselves. The next chapter in Israel's history shows further steps that Israel took to declare their autonomy from God.

The Book of Ruth

The Book of Ruth is among one of the finest and best-loved short stories in the Old Testament. We do not know who wrote this book. Translators of the Septuagint placed the Book of Ruth between the books of Judges and 1 Samuel. This was done most likely due to the reference in the opening verse that places the story of Ruth in the period of judges (see 1:1). However, the book was not originally a part of the Deuteronomistic history. Neither does Ruth reflect the familiar thought and language of the books of the Deuteronomistic history.

Within the Hebrew Bible, the Book of Ruth is found in the third major section known as the *Kethubim* or the Writings. This book and four other books (Song of Songs, Ecclesiastes, Lamentations, and Esther) are frequently referred to as the **Megilloth** (scrolls) or the Festal Scrolls. The Book of Ruth was traditionally read at the Feast of Weeks, later called Pentecost, which celebrated the giving of the Law at Mount Sinai.

Lessons from the Book of Ruth

Ruth's historical setting in the period of judges provides a significant theological corrective to the cultural, religious, and social attitude of that period. We learn the following significant lessons from this book:

First, Ruth's story relates very clearly that God's providential care extends over all people regardless of their national origin. The stories of war and defeat of other nations in Judges might persuade one to conclude that Israel's God was simply a nationalistic God, siding with Israel against all others. However, the story of Ruth protests a narrow sense of nationalism that would limit the activity and the grace of God to any one particular national or ethnic group. The God who mysteriously intervenes in this story is the God of all peoples.

Second, Ruth depicts a sense of unity even in the midst of diversity. Family unity and the unity between an Israelite and a Moabite that we find in Ruth stand in great contrast to the warring factions and tribal competitions depicted in the Book of Judges. Ruth's famous words to Naomi, "Your people will be my people and your God my God," demolish the walls of division expressed in nationality, race, and socioeconomic status.

Third, the story of Ruth is one of fidelity and communal concern at various levels. Such fidelity and communal concern were qualities lacking in Israel during the period of judges. Ruth, a non-Israelite person, modeled for the covenant community how to show loyalty and covenant fidelity at the social level. Throughout this story, we find the expressed desire not for individual concerns but for the well-being of the community and particularly the well-being of weaker members within the community. Ruth in that sense is the ideal that God's people are to follow, whether they live with or without a human king.

Setting

Although the setting of the story is the premonarchic period, the writing of the story seems to have taken place at a later period. Some scholars think that the book was written during the early days of the monarchy, perhaps to trace the ancestry of King David (Ruth was David's great-grandmother). Others place the book during a period in the life of Israel when narrowness and overt nationalism was prominent. Such an atmosphere of exclusivity emerged during the postexilic period (particularly the fifth century B.C.) when the people of God were attempting to redefine their identity often through narrow and rigid means. During this period, foreigners were kept at a distance, and Jewish men were even encouraged to divorce their foreign wives (see Ezra 10:1-5 and Nehemiah 13:23-27). In the midst of this situation, the Book of Ruth would have sought to combat a narrow nationalism by demonstrating David's Moabite ancestry.

Content

The story of Ruth has the form of a play with four scenes. The story begins with famine, death, and tragedy; however, it ends on a happy note with marriage, homebuilding, and children to keep posterity. The story has the following parts:

Naomi and Ruth	1:1-22
Boaz and Ruth	2:1-23
Naomi's Plan	3:1-18
Boaz Marries Ruth	4:1-21

■ A Story of Great Fidelity

The story of Ruth begins with a famine at Bethlehem ("house of bread"), which prompted an Israelite couple and their two sons to relocate to Moab, where the two sons married women from the Moabite culture. Soon tragedy struck, and all the male members of the family died, leaving the three women to widowhood. Naomi the mother decided to return to Bethlehem and encouraged her daughters-in-law to go back to their own families. However, Ruth, wife of one of the sons, responded in great fidelity: "Where you go I will go, and where you stay I will stay. Your people will be my people and your God my God" (1:16).

Upon Ruth and Naomi's return to Bethlehem, Ruth encountered Boaz, a relative of her father-in-law, when she went to collect leftover stalks in the field of Boaz. The Law stipulated the practice of leaving the leftover stalks so that the poor may gather it for food (see Leviticus 19:9-10). Boaz was impressed by Ruth's devotion to Naomi. He invited her to eat with him, and he instructed his servants to deal kindly with her when she gleaned in the field. Naomi instructed Ruth in ways to win the favor of Boaz so that he might marry Ruth. Taking Naomi's advice, Ruth endeared herself to Boaz. Boaz promised Ruth that he would seek means to act as her redeemer *(go'el)*. Another man who was nearer in kinship to Ruth's deceased husband declined to marry Ruth, and this opened the door for Boaz to become Ruth's *go'el*, and he took her as his wife. The story concludes with the birth of a son to Boaz and Ruth, Obed. In the closing verse of the book, we discover that Obed is the father of Jesse, and Jesse is the father of David.

Summary Statements

- The Deuteronomistic history interprets the life of Israel through the lenses of Moses' sermon in Deuteronomy.
- The Book of Joshua seeks to connect directly the generation that entered the land to the generation of Moses.
- Israel entered Canaan and occupied that land as an act of worship, in gratitude to God who had given the land to His people.
- The call to serve God in totality is based entirely upon the gracious act of God and the present identity of Israel as the people of God.
- The Book of Judges portrays the repeated struggle and temptation of the Israelites to find religious systems that they could manipulate.
- In the midst of the weaknesses of the judges, God's power is made visible.
- The cycle of retribution shows clearly the Deuteronomistic themes of religious rebellion, divine judgment, call to repentance, and hope for divine aid.
- In the story of Ruth, the kingdom of God is broadened beyond nationality or race.
- The Book of Ruth traces David's ancestry to Ruth, a Moabite woman.

Questions for Reflection

1. In what ways can the people of God faithfully transmit the faith from one generation to the next?
2. How can the people of God remain distinct from the dominant society in which they live?
3. How does the Book of Joshua convey the possession of the land as an act of worship?
4. Where do we see the cycle of retribution repeated in our own lives?
5. How do the stories of the judges reflect the Bible's perspective on human strength and weakness?
6. How does God use persons "outside" the community of faith as seen in the Book of Ruth?

Bible Study Assignment

Read Joshua 24:14-15 and answer the following questions:

1. What is the historical, cultural, and religious setting of this passage?
2. What is the literary setting of this passage (the text that comes before and the text that follows the passage of your study)?
3. Identify the key action words in this passage and describe how they relate to Joshua's challenge to Israel?
4. What is the significance of the word *serve* in this text? How should one serve the Lord? What is the historical and theological basis for this call to "serve"? (see vv. 2-13).
5. What are the choices that Joshua has placed before Israel? What are the implications of these choices?

Bible Study Assignment, *cont.*

6. Why did Joshua set an example for the Israelites? What did it mean for Joshua's descendants?
7. What is the theological challenge of this text to modern readers?
8. Discuss practical ways to fulfill the call to serve God in our day. What are the hindrances to serving God today? How do we respond to Joshua's challenge today?

Resources for Further Study

Coote, Robert B. *The Book of Joshua: Introduction, Commentary, and Reflections,* vol. 2 in *The New Interpreter's Bible.* Nashville: Abingdon Press, 1998. Pages 553-719.

Grey, John. *Joshua, Judges, Ruth,* in *New Century Bible Commentary.* Grand Rapids: Eerdmans, 1986.

Olson, Dennis T. *The Book of Judges: Introduction, Commentary, and Reflections,* vol. 2 in *The New Interpreter's Bible.* Nashville: Abingdon Press, 1998. Pages 723-888.

Robertson Farmer, Kathleen A. *The Book of Ruth: Introduction, Commentary, and Reflections,* vol. 2 in *The New Interpreter's Bible.* Nashville: Abingdon Press, 1998. Pages 891-946.

Woudstra, Marten H. *The Book of Joshua,* in *New International Commentary on the Old Testament.* Grand Rapids: Ferdmans, 1981.

8 Israel Becomes a Political Kingdom:
1 and 2 Samuel

 bjectives:

Your study of this chapter should help you to:
- Articulate the transitional role of Samuel in the story of Israel
- Make assessment of Saul's kingship
- Describe the manner in which David consolidated his power
- Describe the significance and meaning of the Davidic covenant
- Articulate the manner in which David's household disintegrated

 ey Words to Understand

Philistines
Shiloh
Samuel
Messiah
Saul
David
Jonathan
Mount Gilboa
Hebron
City of David
Jerusalem
Davidic covenant
Zion theology
Solomon
Royal theology

Questions to consider as you read:

1. Why do some people seek "to be like" others who are more affluent and accepted in society?

2. What are some of the temptations of those who possess great power?

3. What strategies do political leaders adopt to bring stability and unity to their government today?

4. Why is it important for a leader to have impeccable moral conduct?

The Book of Judges closed with the observation that Israel had no kings during the early days of the nation's existence in Canaan. This closing statement sets the stage for the next segment in the Deuteronomistic history. The Book of 1 Samuel relates the story of how Israel made the transition from the Spirit-equipped, charismatic military leadership to the more permanent institution of kingship.

This book is named after Samuel, who was Israel's last judge and the first of the prophets. He occupied the place between the era of the judges (premonarchic period) and the era of statehood and kingship (monarchic period). He thus stood at the crossroads of divine rule and human rule. He, like Moses and Joshua, challenged Israel to trust in God alone.

Although 1 Samuel is part of the completed work of the Deuteronomistic history, it is likely that various narratives within the book were part of Israel's oral tradition. It is equally possible that some of these narratives existed in written form long before the completion of the Deuteronomistic history itself.

Setting

The stories of 1 Samuel belong to a period approximately between 1050 and 1000 B.C. In the previous 200 years, Israel went through a series of national, cultural, and religious crises and a total breakdown of law and order in the society. The crisis within the nation was compounded by the threat of external enemies, most notably the powerful **Philistines** who pushed their border in the southwest coastal region into the territories of Israel. The early chapters of the book also indicate that even the priestly family in charge of the Tabernacle at **Shiloh** was corrupt and abusive in their dealings with the worshipers. This is the context in which God called Samuel to give leadership to Israel.

Content

The story of 1 Samuel deals with the leadership of Samuel and Saul, Israel's two key national figures in its early history in the Promised Land. The content of this book can be divided into two major sections:

Samuel and the Transition to
Monarchy   1:1—12:25
Saul and David   13:1—31:13

The early part of the book (chaps. 1—12) summarizes the story of the rise of Samuel as the nation's last charismatic leader. This part also shows how Israel made the transition from charismatic leadership to monarchy.

T

The Song of Hannah

The Song of Hannah contains her praise of God for elevating her from her lowly position. Also, it looks forward to God's exaltation of the humble and the humiliation of the proud in the world. This theme is reflected throughout the Deuteronomistic history. Appropriately, the Song of Hannah is later reflected in Mary's Magnificat (Luke 1:46-55). Paul echoes this theme in his analysis of the cross of Jesus Christ: "God chose what is weak in the world to shame the strong . . . so that no one might boast in the presence of God" (1 Corinthians 1:27, 29, NRSV).

The second part of the book (chaps. 13—31) focuses on the rise and fall of Saul, Israel's first king.

■ Samuel and the Transition to Monarchy

The account of the rise of monarchy in Israel begins with the birth story of **Samuel.** The circumstances surrounding the birth of Samuel somewhat reflect the birth accounts of other key figures in the Bible, such as Isaac, Jacob, Samson, and John the Baptist. Hannah, a barren woman, during an annual visit to Shiloh, made a vow to God that if He would grant her a son, she would consecrate him as a Nazirite. She returned home with an assurance from Eli the priest that God would answer her petition. Later she conceived and gave birth to a son whom she called Samuel. She returned to Shiloh later and offered her son back to God for His service. What she asked from God, she lent back to Him. This was truly an act of worship in which there was no selfishness or attempt to hoard God's gracious gift. The birth narrative of Samuel concludes with Hannah's song of praise to God.

Samuel grew up at Shiloh as a young boy who found favor with both God and the people. As a result of the self-serving evil of Hophni and Phineas, Eli's sons, an anonymous prophet declared to Eli that his sons would die and that his descendants would be removed from their priestly office. At that critical time in Israel's history, God called Samuel at a young age to rise to the position of leadership in Israel.

Israel's defeat by the Philistines and the capture of the ark serve as the immediate context of the rise of Samuel as a charismatic

T Samuel's Call

The story of Samuel's call reflects two Deuteronomistic concerns. First, *God would not abandon His people without proper leadership.* He provides for them His chosen leaders to guide them through the dark days of their existence. Second, *each generation is responsible for the faithful transmission of the faith to the next generation.* Although God was calling Samuel, Eli of the outgoing generation directed Samuel to be attentive to God. The faithfulness of Eli thus opened the way for Samuel to respond to the call of God.

military leader. With the ark taken away from the land of Israel, all hope appeared to be gone. However, the ark narrative (4:1—7:1) does not end with defeat! Soon the Philistines learned the valuable lesson that their god Dagon was no equal or superior to the God of Israel. A plague that came upon the Philistines prompted them to return the ark to Israel with gifts and offerings. Upon the return of the ark to the Israelites, Samuel gathered the people at Mizpah. Like his predecessors Moses and Joshua, he called the people to return to God with all their heart, to put away the foreign gods that were among them, and to serve Him alone (7:3). Samuel faithfully served the nation as a charismatic military leader, priest, prophet, circuit judge, and wise counselor.

When Samuel reached the age of retirement, the people demanded that he set over them a king so that they would be like other nations in the world. Though at first Samuel was extremely reluctant, he fulfilled their request after God authorized him to do so. In His conversation with

Anointing as a Ritual

Though anointing was part of the installation ritual of the priests, the anointing of persons as kings receives a distinct meaning in the Old Testament. In this ritual, the officiating priest would pour olive oil upon the head of the person nominated to be the new king. This act symbolically conveyed the empowerment of this person by God's Spirit. Once the anointing with oil had occurred, the king would then be referred to as the *mashiach* (**messiah**), or literally the *anointed one.* The Greek equivalent of this term is *christos*, from which comes the title *Christ*.

Samuel, God indicated that the people's desire to have a king was in reality the sign of their rejection of God himself.

God himself selected Israel's first king. (chaps. 9—10). Through strange circumstances God brought **Saul**, a Benjamite, to Samuel's house (see the intriguing story in 9:3-14). Samuel announced to him that God had designated him as Israel's first king. Saul responded to Samuel with humility and acknowledged his unworthiness to be God's instrument (v. 21). The next morning, Samuel took a flask of oil and poured it upon Saul and thus anointed him as Israel's prince.

With Saul as king over Israel, Samuel retired from his office as Israel's judge. In a closing address to the people (chap. 12), Samuel proclaimed the core prophetic conviction that if the people and the king would live in obedience to God, all would be well. He challenged the people to fear God and serve Him faithfully with all their hearts.

In spite of Saul's early days of faithful leadership, the remainder of his reign was one of great tragedy. The downfall of Saul does not appear to be related to a despotic rule. In fact, unlike those kings who would come after him,

Saul levied no taxes, conducted no military draft, and carried out little if any international trade. In many ways, Saul appeared much more like the judges before him than like the kings after him. However, the downfall of Saul was directly related to his outright disobedience to Samuel's explicit instructions. On one occasion, he intruded into the priestly office and officiated a sacrifice (13:1-15). At another time, he disobeyed the *cherem* commandment (15:1-9). On both occasions, Samuel rebuked him and announced God's rejection of his kingship.

■ Saul and David

Samuel had already indicated to Saul that God was seeking a person after "his own heart" to take over the leadership of Israel (13:14). Chapter 16 introduces **David** from the tribe of Judah as that chosen person. The story very clearly relates the truth that God looks at the heart of people and not their appearance when He calls them to do His special work. Also we find here the Deuteronomistic affirmation that God uses the weak to confound the strong. Samuel anointed David as the next king over Israel. At the moment of David's anointing, the Spirit of the Lord came upon him, equipping and empowering him for leadership. At the same time, the spirit of the Lord departed from Saul (vv. 13-14). The narrator relates the familiar story of David's victory over Goliath to authenticate the Spirit's empowerment of David as God's anointed one (chap. 17).

From this point on, the story focuses on the rivalry between Saul and David and the tragic events that led to Saul's death. Increasingly, Saul became estranged from everyone around him, and he found himself isolated in his own private, tormented world. Meanwhile David shared an intimate friendship with Saul's son, **Jonathan.** The people-at-large viewed David to be a greater warrior than Saul. Saul's jealousy toward David turned to fear, and he schemed different ways to bring David to his demise. Saul's continued attempts to take David's life prompted David to escape to the land of the Philistines where he became their ally and a mercenary soldier for Achish, king of Gath (chaps. 25, 29—30).

Meanwhile the Philistines had made significant advance into the Israelite territory. Saul's army could not stop them from further invasion into the land. The final chapter of Saul's life took place on **Mount Gilboa.** Three of Saul's sons, including Jonathan, were killed in the battle against the Philistines. Surrounded by the invading Philistine army, and facing certain defeat, Saul took his own sword and fell upon it. The following day, the Philistines cut off Saul's head and publicly displayed his corpse on a city wall in Beth-shan. The people of Jabesh-gilead, whom Saul saved from the

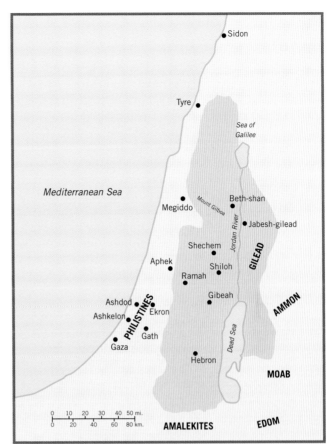

The boundary of Saul's kingdom.

Ammonites, showed their gratitude to him by giving their king a proper burial.

With Saul now dead, the stage was set for David to assume the role of king. However, as we shall see in the next chapter, the road to kingship was no easy path for David. The next book, 2 Samuel, begins with the trials of David before he finally established himself as Israel's second king. We shall now turn to this story.

2 Samuel

The Book of 2 Samuel traces David's consolidation of power over Israel and the subsequent disintegration of that power. In the story of David's rise and fall, we once again see the Deuteronomistic portrayal of God's promise of hope to His people as well as His judgment upon sin. As in 1 Samuel, here also we find the power of the blessings and curses in Deuteronomy at work in the history of Israel.

Again, this book belongs to the broader context of the Deuteronomistic history. However, it is very likely that some of the materials in this book may have existed as independent documents before they became part of the Deuteronomistic history.

Setting

The story of 2 Samuel covers the period approximately between 1000 and 960 B.C. The story shifts focus from Saul and the tribe of Benjamin to David, the tribe of Judah, and the whole nation Israel. This book narrates the story of the establishment of David as king first by the people of Judah and later by the rest of Israel. The threat of border invasions by the Philistines came to an end. During the reign of David, Israel became a kingdom-building nation by annexing neighboring countries and lands. Though David had to deal with

some internal troubles, from a political perspective, this period may be designated as the golden years in the history of Israel.

Content

The Book of 2 Samuel can be divided into four parts:

The Establishment
of a Dynasty 1:1—8:18
Covenant Faithfulness and
Covenant Breaking
9:1—12:31
David's Family Troubles
13:1—18:33
Restoration of David's
Reign 19:1—24:25

■ The Establishment of a Dynasty

When the news of Saul's death came, David was careful not to seize power immediately. He knew that Saul's surviving son Ishbosheth would be a legitimate contender for his father's throne. Also, he was well aware of the significant influence of Abner, Saul's military commander. We see in these narratives a reflection of both his respect for Saul's family and more importantly his political savvy, a trait that helped him later to secure his kingship.

David took the first step to establish his kingship by seeking the approval of his own tribe Judah, who crowned him as king at **Hebron.** He made Hebron his capital and ruled as king over Judah for the next seven years (1000 B.C. to 993 B.C.).

Meanwhile, Saul's son Ishbosheth began his rule as king over the remaining 11 tribes. He had on his side Abner, who was the real power behind the throne. With this faction among Israel's tribes, conflict, confrontation, and

Elah Valley, the site where David killed Goliath during Israel's battle with the Philistines.

struggle for power were inevitable. Second Samuel 2—4 relates the tragic stories of treachery and bloodshed carried out by Abner and David's commander Joab. This civil war period saw the violent deaths of Abner and Ishbosheth, which finally cleared the path for David to consolidate his power as king over all Israel.

Early in his reign as king over Israel, David carried out numerous successful military campaigns. Although Jebus had been taken earlier by the Israelites, it remained a stronghold of the Canaanites. With his personal army, David was finally able to overcome the Jebusite stronghold and claim it as his own city. He renamed it the **city of David.** He also established this neutral city located between the tribes in the north and Judah in the south as the capital of his kingdom. At a later period, the city of David came to be called **Jerusalem** (meaning "foundation of peace"), a reflection of the role it played in bringing peace in the land.

As a leader, David's next attempt was to establish a common

Samuel's tomb.

identity for his people. He did this by bringing the ark of the covenant from Kiriath-jearim to Jerusalem. This initiative provided for Israel a central place to gather together to worship the God who brought them out of Egypt. Jerusalem thus became both the political and religious capital of his kingdom. Israel's later traditions recognized Jerusalem as the symbol of God's presence among His people because the ark resided in that city.

Once Jerusalem became the place for the ark of the covenant,

Beth-shan. The Philistines fastened the body of Saul to the walls of Beth-shan. The old city of Beth-shan is the tell (mount) in the background; remains of the Roman city Scythopolis are in the foreground.

The City of David (Jerusalem) during David's time.

ple of his tragic failure to keep justice and righteousness in interpersonal relationships (chaps. 9—12). In a display of lavish generosity, he invited Jonathan's crippled son, Mephibosheth, to remain under his custody for the remainder of his life and to receive income from his grandfather's property. Similarly, David sought to provide covenant faithfulness to the son of the Ammonite king following his father's death (see 10:1).

David made plans to build a Temple, which would be a "house" (in Hebrew *bayit*) for the ark, and thus a "house" for God (see 2 Samuel 7:1-3). Although the prophet Nathan at first supported David's plans, he returned to David with the announcement that David's descendant who would sit on his throne would fulfill this desire. Through Nathan, God promised to make David's descendants a permanent, hereditary dynasty or royal "house" *(bayit)*. He also promised to enter into a father-son relationship with David's descendants. This oath of promise that God gave to David is known as the **Davidic covenant** (see vv. 12-17).

Chapter 11 shows how David, who exemplified covenant faithfulness to Saul's house, transgressed God's covenant and destroyed not only a marriage but also an innocent human life. In this familiar story of David's sin with Uriah's wife, Bathsheba, we see the portrait of an oriental despot who manipulated people to accomplish his plans. Through careful scheming, he arranged for Uriah's death in the battlefield so that the door would be open for him to marry Bathsheba with whom he committed adultery. When the news of Uriah's death came, David did what seemed to be the most honorable thing for a "just and righteous" king to do. He married his dead soldier's widow, a shrewd public relations ploy and a cover-up for his sin. The narrator concludes this tragic story with the report that this matter "displeased the LORD" (11:27).

■ Covenant Faithfulness and Covenant Breaking

The stories of David include two examples of David's "just and right" actions, as well as an exam-

T

David: A Repentant Sinner

Psalm 51 has been associated with David's prayer for forgiveness when Nathan confronted him. In this prayer, the psalmist conveys his intimate acquaintance with human sin and its powerful influence upon his life from birth. The psalm also recognizes God's forgiving grace, cleansing from sin, and the gift of a new heart as the solution to human depravity.

T Zion, the City of God

With the transfer of the ark, the "city of David" became "the city of God." In the next generation of the monarchy, the palace of the king and the Temple of the Lord sat side by side, often one providing legitimacy to the other. Religion and politics thus became inseparable twins, which later led to the rise of religious nationalism in Israel.

Jerusalem's establishment as the religious center led to the development of **Zion theology** in Israel's theological traditions. During the premonarchy days, Zion was a fortified hill within the Jebusite stronghold. Once the Temple was built on the hill at this location, the Temple Mount itself became known as Zion. This name later became the name for the entire city of Jerusalem. Zion in the Old Testament reflects the security found on the holy mountain of God. Reflecting the mighty kingship of God himself, the term evoked images of God's protection of His people and God's power in battle. It vividly embodied God's victory, sovereignty, and invincibility. Various psalms (see 46, 48, 76, 84, 87, 122, 125, 132) celebrate Zion's beauty and God's reign upon Mount Zion. Though this understanding evoked a deep sense of trust, it often led to a sense of false security and even invincibility for the people and the city itself. Later prophets, such as Micah and Jeremiah, preached against such false security.

The prophet Nathan, who had previously spoken about God's covenant with David, confronted David and revealed to him God's judgment because of his sin. The prophet announced that the evil that David had done to Uriah would come upon David and his household (12:11). Ironically, the first two acts of evil to take place within David's family were sexual misconduct (Amnon's rape of Tamar) and murder (Amnon's murder by Absalom).

At this point in the story, David shows himself as a genuinely repentant sinner. He acknowledged his act as sin against God. Though Nathan pronounced God's forgiveness, subsequent stories show

The city of Jerusalem today.

The Succession Narrative

Old Testament scholars describe 2 Samuel 9—20 and 1 Kings 1—2 as the succession narrative or court history. This lengthy narrative describes the struggle for power within David's family and the claims of various royal family members to David's throne. The stories graphically portray David's dysfunctional family and make no attempt to cover up for anyone. The presence of this material within Scripture demonstrates the manner in which the Bible is concerned with all of life. In these stories, there are no ideal heroes. However, we learn the lesson that the sinfulness of God's people brings only more brokenness to an already broken world.

the long-lasting results of David's sin, beginning with the death of Bathsheba's child. Later, she conceived once again and gave birth to a son. David named the child Jedidiah, who later received the throne name **Solomon.**

■ David's Family Troubles

Although David repented of his sin, subsequent stories in 2 Samuel show that Nathan's word of judgment against his household came to fulfillment. The royal palace became the setting for a

great power play that involved adultery, murder, and rebellion.

Amnon, the eldest son of David, developed an unhealthy love for his half-sister, Tamar, and devised a scheme to molest her. Tamar's brother, Absalom, killed Amnon to retaliate the rape of his sister. Fearing that David might take action, Absalom became a fugitive and fled from Jerusalem (chap. 13). Two years later, David welcomed Absalom to his palace and the two were reconciled to each other. However, soon Absalom began to make aggressive moves to overthrow his father from the throne. Within four years, Absalom succeeded in gaining enough support to declare himself as king at Hebron. David, fearing for his life, fled Jerusalem with his loyal supporters. The father-son struggle ended in the death of Absalom by Joab, David's commander.

■ Restoration of David's Reign

David restored his power after the death of Absalom. In the closing chapters of 2 Samuel (21—24), we find various materials that reflect the final years of David's reign. These materials are not arranged in chronological order. The final episode of 2 Samuel

Royal Theology

God's covenant stands in direct continuity with the Sinai covenant and God's covenant with Abraham. However, the focus here is on a household rather than the entire Israelite community. The Davidic king was God's "son" who ruled Israel, God's "people," with whom He made the Sinai covenant. The development of this **royal theology** engendered the belief that the reign of the Davidic king represented God's reign over the people. Various psalms reflect this understanding of kingship (see 2, 18, 20, 21, 72, 89, 110, 132). Over time, the term *anointed one* (Hebrew *mashiach*) came to represent the ideal Davidic king who would properly embody the just reign of God over Israel.

deals with David's census of Israel and the subsequent judgment that came upon him (chap. 24). When he realized that his action was not pleasing to God, he confessed his guilt. As punishment, God sent a pestilence throughout David's kingdom that killed 70,000 persons in the land. David saw God's messenger, who was the agent of destruction, standing by the threshing floor of Araunah. David went to Araunah and purchased the floor and set up an altar there for future generations as the place of worship in Israel (vv. 18-25). Later, this site became the place where Solomon built the Temple.

Second Samuel ends with the optimistic note about God answering David's prayer for the land. In the end, a sinner confessed his sins, made amends, and pleaded for God's mercy. A gracious and compassionate God responded to his prayer with forgiveness and healing for His people. In the midst of sin and judgment, He made His presence known to a sinner under judgment. God's acceptance of David's offerings gave the king and his people the assurance that indeed God dwelt among them.

Would the next generation and the generations to come live by this truth about God? The Deuteronomistic history we find in 1 and 2 Kings answers this question. We shall now turn to this continuing story of Israel and her God in these two books.

The area under the political and economic control of Israel during the reigns of David and Solomon.

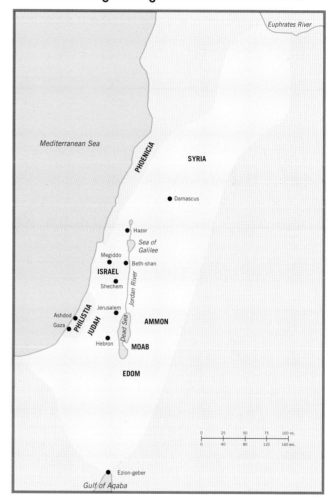

Summary Statements

- Samuel gave leadership to Israel as judge, priest, and prophet in the period of transition between judgeship and monarchy.
- Israel's decision to have a human king was a sign of their rejection of God's kingship over them.
- The role of Samuel in Saul's life reflects the nature of the prophetic ministry in that he was both a voice of promise and a voice of judgment.
- The story of Saul's downfall depicts the tragic results of the human attempt to take life into one's own hands.
- David ruled as king over Judah for seven years before he consolidated his kingship over all Israel.
- David established Jerusalem as his capital and brought the ark to the city and thus made it also the nation's religious center.
- David sinned against God, but he also sought God's mercy and forgiveness.
- David suffered family troubles as the consequence of his sin.

Questions for Reflection

1. How do the stories of 1 Samuel challenge you to love God wholeheartedly?
2. In what ways do we continue today to seek to have "kings" in place of God?
3. What lessons do you learn from the fall of Saul?
4. How does God demonstrate His continuing faithfulness in our lives even in the midst of our own disobedience?
5. In what ways do you see David as a "man after God's own heart"?

Bible Study Assignment

Read 1 Samuel 8:4-9 and answer the following questions:

1. What is the historical, religious, and cultural setting of this passage?
2. What was the request of Israel to Samuel? Why did they make this request? What cultural custom is reflected in the text? What was an underlying desire of Israel when they made this request?
3. Why did this request cause concern to Samuel?
4. What theological issue is at the center of this request? How did God respond to this request? Why do you think God responded the way He did? What does this text say about God's response to His people when they want to go against His plans for them?
5. In what ways does this text address contemporary issues in the life of God's people? In what ways do we seek to be like others in the world today?
6. What theological challenges do you find in this text? Discuss ways to keep a unique identity as God's people in a world that bids us follow its customs and patterns of life.

Resources for Further Study

Baldwin, Joyce G. *1 and 2 Samuel: An Introduction and Commentary,* in *Tyndale Old Testament Commentaries.* Downers Grove, Ill.: InterVarsity Press, 1988.

Birch, Bruce C. *The First and Second Books of Samuel: Introduction, Commentary, and Reflections,* vol. 2 in *The New Interpreter's Bible.* Nashville: Abingdon Press, 1998. Pages 1199-383.

Brueggemann, Walter. *First and Second Samuel.* Louisville, Ky.: John Knox Press, 1990.

...had obtained part of this mi...
...ery.

18 * Now this man purchased a f...
...ith the reward of iniquity, and fall...
...eadlong, he burst asunder in the mi...
...d all his bowels gushed out.

19 And it was knowen vnto all...
...wellers at Jerusalem, insomuch...
...hat field is called in their pro...
...ongue, Aceldama, that is to say, F...
...eld of blood.

20 * For it is written in the book...
...of Psalmes, Let his habitation be...
...late, and let no man dwell ther...
...And his ‖ Bishopricke let anot...
...ake.

21 Wherefore of these men wh...
...aue companied with vs all the t...
...hat the Lord Jesus went in and...
...mong vs,

22 Beginning from the Baptism...

9 Israel's Exile from the Promised Land: 1 and 2 Kings

Objectives:

Your study of this chapter should help you to:
- Evaluate the positive and negative impact of Solomon's kingship
- Describe the nature and purpose of the Temple in Jerusalem
- Describe the factors leading to the division of the Davidic kingdom and the eventual destruction of the divided kingdoms of Israel
- Discuss the role and message of the prophet Elijah
- Make assessment of the ways in which the stories of the people of God in 1 and 2 Kings reflect core Deuteronomistic convictions

Key Words to Understand

Jeroboam
Rehoboam
Dan
Bethel
Omri
Samaria
Ahab
Elijah
Elisha
Jeroboam II
Uzziah
Tiglath-pileser III
Ahaz
Syro-Ephraimite war
Hezekiah
Sennacherib
Josiah
Zedekiah

Questions to consider as you read:

1. What are some of the negative outcomes of mixing politics with religion?

2. What are some of the factors that contribute to political and religious instability?

3. What role does religion play in bringing about radical changes within a culture?

4. What are some of the modern-day examples of national tragedies because of corrupt and oppressive leadership?

Near the end of David's reign, rivalry and political intrigue developed within the house of David to settle the question of who would be the legitimate heir to the kingdom. First Kings narrates the developments that led to the rise of Solomon as David's successor. The rest of the narratives in this book show the continuing struggle for power in the land. This struggle led to the division of the kingdom into two kingdoms. The Book of 2 Kings resumes the story of covenant breaking that has become a characteristic way of life for the citizens of both kingdoms. Second Kings narrates the story of how both of these kingdoms lost their national and political existence due to God's judgment that came upon them as punishment for their sin.

1 Kings

The Books of First and Second Kings were originally one composition that continued the story of Israel's kingdom following the death of David. The title indicates that these books deal with the history of kingship in Israel. Again, these two books together make up the final part of the Deuteronomistic history. Deuteronomistic historians utilized various sources such as "the book of the annals of Solomon" (1 Kings 11:41), "the book of the annals of the kings of Israel" (14:19), and "the book of the annals of the kings of Judah" (v. 29) to compose their work. It is also likely that they would have drawn from other written or oral sources that had circulated long before these books received their final form.

Setting

First Kings covers the story of Israel from about 960 B.C. to 850 B.C. The book begins with the declining years of David. The stage is thus set for the transition of power to the next generation. Though the opening verses of the book attempt to paint a picture of relative calm and stability in the kingdom, the rest of chapter 1 suddenly shifts to shrewd political maneuverings and palace plots to establish a successor to the dying king.

Content

The first two chapters of 1 Kings serve as an appropriate introduction to the story of Solomon's reign. Scholars consider these chapters as the conclusion to the succession narrative begun in 2 Samuel 9.

The Book of 1 Kings can be divided into the following two major sections:

The Reign of Solomon
                1:1—11:43
Divided Kingdoms   12:1—22:53

The second part has extensive narratives about the ministry of Elijah the prophet, beginning with chapter 17.

■ The Reign of Solomon

The question of the legitimate successor to David nearly divided the royal family and David's political and religious advisers into two

International Treaties and Marriage

The narrator of 1 Kings reports that Solomon had 700 wives and 300 concubines. In the ancient world, a king's possession of a large harem was not as much an expression of sensuality as it was international diplomacy. "Family ties" represented "political allies." Solomon's marriage relationship with other nations was thus a political strategy through which he secured stability for his kingship. The price Israel paid for this unholy alliance with pagan nations was the introduction of foreign gods into Jerusalem.

camps, one favoring Adonijah and the other favoring Solomon. However, before his death, David declared Solomon as the legitimate heir to the throne (960 B.C.). The dying king reminded Solomon that God's promise of an eternal Davidic dynasty was conditional. Fulfillment of this promise depended upon the future generations' obedience to God and their walk before God with all their heart and with all their soul.

The early chapters of 1 Kings show how Solomon secured his kingship through an extensive political housecleaning that included the murder of his rival Adonijah and the banishment of Abiathar, David's high priest who supported Adonijah. He also ordered the death of Joab, who also supported Adonijah, as punishment for the murder of Saul's general Abner.

The narrator begins and ends the story of Solomon by making reference to his marriage relationships. The story begins with Solomon's marriage alliance with Egypt.[1] The concluding chapter of this narrative section observes Solomon's marriage alliances and love for foreign women whom he had taken from many of the neighboring countries (11:1-8). He thus violated the Law of Moses that sternly warned against Israel's intermarriage with pagan people (Deuteronomy 7:3-4). Solomon not only married pagan women but also worshiped their gods and became an influential patron of pagan religions in the land.

Early in his reign, Solomon traveled to Gibeon in order to make a sacrifice to the Lord. There he requested from God "a discerning heart" so that he would have the capacity to rule with wisdom and distinguish be-

Syncretism in the Temple

The construction of the Temple shows evidence of syncretism, or the blending of religious ideas, during the reign of Solomon. Architectural features of the Temple reveal the strong influence of religious ideas from neighboring areas, especially Phoenicia. The two bronze pillars at the entrance door of the Temple perhaps stood as the symbol of the ancient Near Eastern view that the earth rested upon its foundation pillars. The molten sea supported by 12 oxen likely reflected the primeval waters conquered at creation. Engravings in the doors included cherubim, flowers, and palm trees, all Near Eastern symbols of fertility.

tween right and wrong (1 Kings 3:9). God gave this gift of wisdom to Solomon, and his fame as a wise king spread throughout the ancient Near East.

Solomon's wisdom was evident in his skill as an effective administrator. He reorganized the 12 tribes of Israel into 12 administrative districts for the purpose of taxation and conscription. Solomon's administrative policy also included forced labor to complete his building projects, which took the nation back into the days of political bondage.

Solomon's greatest accomplishment was the construction of the Temple in Jerusalem. This project took seven years for its completion. Solomon depended heavily upon the architecture and artisanship of the Phoenicians to complete the Temple building project. Solomon's dedicatory prayer over the completed Temple (chap. 8) reflects Israel's conviction that God did not dwell in an earthly building. Throughout his prayer of dedication, Solomon declared that even the heavens

A horned altar found at Beersheba, the southern border of ancient Israel.

could not contain the Lord, much less the Temple (v. 27).

Solomon's other building projects were a royal complex, which included his own palace, a house for his Egyptian wife, and various other state buildings. In addition to numerous buildings in Jerusalem, he also constructed other royal buildings at Gezer, Hazor, and Megiddo.

In spite of the diverse accomplishments of Solomon, Deuteronomistic historians give a negative final evaluation of his kingship. At the end of Solomon's reign, vari-

ous rebellions against the Davidic house took place. Deuteronomistic historians relate these incidents as the beginning of God's judgment upon Solomon. Of particular significance was the rebellion of **Jeroboam,** Solomon's officer for slave labor. The prophet Ahijah announced to Jeroboam that God would give him 10 of the 12 tribes of Israel.

After Solomon's death (922 B.C.), the people gathered at Shechem to make Solomon's son **Rehoboam** his successor and king over Israel. However, he refused to grant the petition of the northern tribes to give them relief from their labor and heavy taxation. This prompted them to break away from the Davidic kingdom and to set up their own kingdom under the leadership of Jeroboam. The Davidic kingdom that Rehoboam inherited was thus reduced to the tribes of Judah and Benjamin in the south. The 10 northern tribes (the Northern Kingdom) subsequently became known as Israel or Ephraim. The Southern Kingdom

Solomon fortified Megiddo and made it one of the most influential centers of his kingdom.

under the Davidic house came to be known as Judah.

Early in his reign, Jeroboam reestablished Shechem as the political center of his kingdom. He also set up **Dan** and **Bethel** as centers of worship for his citizens, where he constructed a golden bull to serve as an alternative symbol to the ark of the covenant. The bull, which was the symbol of the Canaanite fertility god Baal, thus became for Israel the object of their worship. Deuteronomistic writers cast a negative judgment on Jeroboam's action by referring to it as "the sin of Jeroboam."

■ The Divided Kingdoms

Throughout the remainder of 1 and 2 Kings, the writers evaluate the various kings in light of their faithfulness or lack of faithfulness to God. For northern kings, the writers describe subsequent rulers as continuing in the sin of Jeroboam. All of the northern kings receive a negative appraisal from the writers. On the other hand, some of the southern kings receive positive and some receive negative evaluations. Those who lived according to the instructions of the Torah were those who did what was "right in the eyes of the LORD." Those who continued in their idolatry were those who did what was "evil in the eyes of the LORD."

The lack of a permanent dynasty resulted in volatile and violent political conditions in the Northern Kingdom. Assassinations and relatively brief reigns of kings were characteristic of the first half century. In contrast, the Southern Kingdom of Judah showed relative stability, since successors to the throne were already determined by means of the Davidic dynasty. Conflict and

The entrance to Dan, in the Northern Kingdom of Israel.

war characterized the relationship between these two kingdoms in the early years (915-873 B.C.). Later, these kingdoms enjoyed a brief period of peace and friendship (873-842 B.C.).

Up until the time of **Omri,** the Northern Kingdom had been unable to establish a permanent succession of kings. However, with Omri, relative political stability and economic prosperity was achieved for over three decades. Omri not only established a dynasty that would last through four kings but also built **Samaria** as his new political capital.

Although the Deuteronomistic writers give Omri's reign only minimal attention, they describe Ahab's reign in great detail. In order to seal the political relationship with Phoenicia, Omri married his son, **Ahab,** to the Phoenician king's daughter, Jezebel. As an ardent supporter of the Phoenician god, Baal, Jezebel imported hundreds of prophets of Baal into Israel and subsequently constructed numerous sanctuaries for these prophets. Soon, the masses of Israelites were worshiping Baal alongside Yahweh.

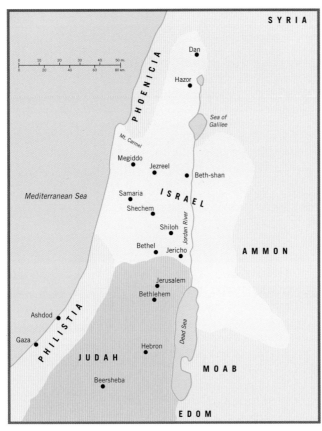

Boundaries of the kingdoms of Israel and Judah.

him" (18:21). At Mount Carmel, Yahweh demonstrated himself as Israel's God and the God over nature, and He exposed the futility of following Baal and Asherah.

The Book of 1 Kings begins and ends with narratives that deal with Israel's splendor and downfall. Both the Solomonic and the Omride kingdoms represent opulence, wealth, security, and national splendor. Ironically, both periods also show tremendous injustice, corruption, and utter disloyalty to God. In 2 Kings, the final book of Deuteronomistic history, we shall see the tragic outcome of Israel's breaking of the Mount Sinai covenant and their determination not to walk in the ways of Yahweh, their God.

2 Kings

Second Kings begins with a major turn of affairs that resulted in the overthrow of the Omri dynasty in the Northern Kingdom. Again, this is the final part of the Deuteronomistic history that covers Israel's history from the theological perspectives of the Book of Deuteronomy. The historians who compiled this book very vividly portray God's judgment that came upon Israel and Judah as the unleashing of the covenant curses stated in Deuteronomy. The narratives cover the period from around 850 B.C. to 587 B.C.

Content

The content of the Book of 2 Kings can be divided into the following two major sections:

When baalism was running rampant in Israel, God sent the prophet **Elijah** to the Northern Kingdom to champion the cause of Yahwistic faith in that nation. His mission was to challenge the dominant system of baalism and to declare Yahweh alone to be the God of Israel. Elijah declared a showdown between Baal and Yahweh at Mount Carmel. Challenging 450 prophets of Baal and 400 prophets of Asherah, Elijah called upon the people to make a decisive choice as to whom they would serve. For Elijah, the problem was not necessarily the people's refusal to serve God. Rather, their hearts were divided between the Lord and Baal. Elijah challenged the people: "If the LORD is God, follow him; but if Baal is God, follow

■ The Downfall of Israel

One of the final tasks of Elijah was to transfer the prophetic ministry to his disciple **Elisha** and to appoint him as his successor, before he disappeared into the heavens in a fiery chariot. Elisha picked up the mantle of his "prophetic father," which symbolized the transfer of prophetic activity and the power to perform miraculous things.

In contrast to Elijah who made his mark by religious and political confrontations, the stories of Elisha focus upon various miracles performed by the prophet. His miracles for the most part were directed to helping the people who needed water and food, healing the sick, and raising the dead. More specifically, his primary ministry was to instigate a revolution to overthrow the Omri dynasty. He played a vital part in the rise of Jehu, who massacred the entire house of Omri, as Israel's king.

The dynasty that Jehu established ruled Israel for the next four generations. Although the Deuteronomistic writers praised Jehu's attempt to wipe out Baal worship, in the final evaluation of his reign they observed that he "did not turn away from the sins of Jeroboam" (10:29, 31).

Jehu's revolution resulted in significant diplomatic and political changes in Israel's relation to their neighboring nations. Relationships with Phoenicia developed by Omri and Ahab were severely broken with the murder of Jezebel. Likewise, Jehu's murder of Judah's king Ahaziah, who was visiting the Northern Kingdom, severed Israel's relation with Judah. Without the support of

Northern and Southern Kings in 1 Kings

Northern Kings	*Southern Kings*
Jeroboam I (922-901)	Rehoboam I (922-915)
	Abijah (915-913)
Nadab (901-900)	Asa (913-873)
Baasha (900-877)	
Elah (877-876)	
Zimri (876)	
Omri (876-869)	Jehoshaphat (873-849)
Ahab (869-850)[2]	

Phoenicia and Judah, Israel became considerably more vulnerable to the attacks of Syria.

Israel regained its political and economic strength under the reign of **Jeroboam II**, the great-grandson of Jehu. Jeroboam's reign of economic prosperity and political advancement coincided with similar wealth and development in Judah. Under King **Uzziah** (also called Azariah in the biblical text), the Southern Kingdom expanded its borders eastward across the Jordan and westward into the Philistine territory, putting Judah in control of major commercial thoroughfares. Following nearly a half century of peace and prosperity under the reigns of Jer-

Wadi Qelt in the Judean desert; tradition holds that Elijah stopped here on his way to Horeb.

Northern and Southern Kings in 2 Kings[3]

Northern Kings	Southern Kings
Ahaziah (850-849)	Jehoram (849-843)
Jehoram (849-843/2)	Ahaziah (843/2)
Jehu (843/2-815)	Athaliah (842-837)
Jehoahaz (815-802)	Joash (837-800)
Jehoash (802-786)	Amaziah (800-783)
Jeroboam II (786-746)	Uzziah (783-742)
Zechariah (746-745)	Jotham (742-735)
Shallum (745)	
Menahem (745-737)	
Pekahiah (737-736)	Ahaz (735-715)
Pekah (736-732)	
Hoshea (732-724)	
	Hezekiah (715-687/6)
	Manasseh (687/6-642)
	Amon (642-640)
	Josiah (640-609)
	Jehoahaz (609)
	Jehoiakim (609-598)
	Jehoiachin (598/7)
	Zedekiah (597-587)

Steps of Megiddo from the early Israelite kingdom period.

oboam II in the north and Uzziah in the south, the situation changed dramatically. Soon after the death of Jeroboam II, the Northern Kingdom returned to its earlier practice of royal assassinations and coups. During Menahem's reign, the Assyrian king **Tiglath-pileser III** forced Israel to pay a large tribute in order to preserve its relative independence. Although Menahem's son, Pekahiah, followed his father to the throne, his two-year reign came to an end when Pekah assassinated him. In order to defend the kingdom against the Assyrian invasion, Pekah entered into an alliance with the Syrian King Rezin. Together, Pekah and Rezin attempted to force King **Ahaz** of Judah to join them against the Assyrians. The joint **Syro-**

Ephraimite (Syria and Israel in alliance) **war** against Jerusalem prompted the Judean King Ahaz to seek help from Assyria. He did this against the wise counsel of the prophet Isaiah, who called Ahaz to put his trust in the Lord. Though the Assyrians delivered Judah, they entered Damascus and brought an end to Syrian power. Judah thus became a vassal of Assyria and was forced to pay tribute as well as to adopt Assyrian practices of worship (16:5-16).

During the reign of Ahaz over Judah, the Northern Kingdom experienced its final violent coup d'etat that resulted in the murder of Pekah by Hoshea. Though Hoshea remained a vassal of Assyria during the early part of his nine-year reign over Israel, later he joined Egypt in a plot against Assyria and subsequently withheld tribute from Assyria. In retaliation against this breach of loyalty, the Assyrian King Shalmaneser V

High Places

High places, often mentioned in 1 and 2 Kings, were sanctuaries located on high hills surrounded by green trees. Israel established such places of worship patterned after the Canaanite high places where the Canaanites worshiped Baal and Asherah. The Law of Moses prohibited such places of worship in Israel. However, as a practice these places provided the people with local shrines, in addition to the established and legitimate place of worship in Jerusalem. These places were furnished with altars for sacrifice, pillars, and poles and other objects of idol worship. According to 1 Kings, Solomon was the first king of Israel to build such places of worship in Israel. This practice was continued by his son Rehoboam and many of the northern kings (see 1 Kings 11:7-8; 14:23; 2 Kings 17:9).

besieged Israel for three years. Following Shalmaneser's death, his successor, Sargon II, completed the task of bringing an end to the nation of Israel in 721 B.C.

A Story That Continues: Grace in the Midst of Judgment

The tragic destruction of Jerusalem is not the final story of 2 Kings. Though the covenant nation Israel lost its political existence and religious freedom, the future was not filled with gloom and despair. The final narrative in this book casts a glimmer of hope for the nation in exile. The Deuteronomistic historians who compiled this book and other parts of Israel's past history knew very well that the exile was not God's last word to His people. Time and time again, they have recalled for the nation God's gracious dealings with His people and His mighty deeds of salvation performed for them since He brought them into the land of promise. They were convinced that God would again return to His people with His grace and mercy during the darkest days of Judah's exile in Babylon. They saw the release of Jehoiachin from prison by the Babylonian king Evil-Merodach as the harbinger of the good days to come for the exiled community. The writers note that the Babylonian king "spoke kindly" to the exiled king of Judah and "gave him a seat of honor higher than those of the other kings who were with him in Babylon" (25:28). This note of optimism is, in the final analysis, the message of 1 and 2 Kings. Judah's future is with her God who is her covenant God. And that future depends solely on the gracious compassion of God, who had long ago promised to restore His scattered people from the lands of their exile (Deuteronomy 30:1-5).

■ The Downfall of Judah

While his father Ahaz had yielded to Assyria by not only paying regular tribute but even by building an Assyrian altar in the Jerusalem Temple, **Hezekiah** led the people of Judah into an era of religious renewal and political strength. He removed the places of Baal worship, including the Asherah poles and Baal altars. Furthermore, Hezekiah moved to centralize all worship at the Temple in Jerusalem. These religious reforms clearly signaled Hezekiah's intent to liberate Judah from its political bondage to Assyria.

In 701 B.C., Hezekiah joined a revolution against Assyria, supported by both Babylon and Egypt. Though Isaiah had counseled Hezekiah to remain neutral, he joined the revolt. The Assyrian King **Sennacherib** responded quickly (chaps. 18—20; also Isaiah 36—39) and surrounded Jerusalem with his army and laid a siege against the city. Through God's intervention, his army withdrew and the city was miraculously spared of destruction.

The Deuteronomistic writers have given Hezekiah an unqualified positive evaluation. They observed that no one before or after Hezekiah was like him in his faithfulness to God. However, this was not the case with Manasseh, who rebuilt the high places and practiced and promoted astral worship, human sacrifice, and sorcery. Manasseh's grandson **Josiah** carried out a massive religious reform intended to restore true worship in Judah and to shake the nation free from its bondage to Assyria. This reform included a covenant renewal prompted by the discovery of the "book of the law" by workers who were engaged in the repair of the Temple. Most scholars think that the "book of the law" contained the core of the present Book of Deuteronomy (chaps. 12—26).

Following the covenant renewal ceremony, Josiah purged the Temple of all objects dedicated to other deities and religions. Furthermore, he destroyed the shrine and the altar established by Jeroboam I at Bethel. The reform of Josiah was finally culminated in the national observance of the Passover, the first of its kind since the time of the judges. The historians observe that there was none like Josiah, either before him or after him, who served God wholeheartedly and with undivided loyalty.

Meanwhile, changes in international politics prompted Josiah to become involved in the affairs of the ancient Near East. Toward the last quarter of the seventh century B.C., the allied forces of the Medes and the Babylonians destroyed Nineveh, the capital city of the Assyrians, and moved westward and captured Haran, Assyria's last major stronghold. Pharaoh Neco II of Egypt set out to offer assistance to Assyria to recapture Haran from the Babylonian-Medes allied forces. King Josiah, who attempted to stop the Egyptian army, was mortally wounded in the battle at Megiddo in 609 B.C. Egypt gained control of Judah and deposed Jehoahaz, Josiah's son, and replaced him with his brother Jehoiakim. Later in 603 B.C., Jehoiakim transferred his allegiance to Babylon's King Nebuchadnezzar. Two years later, when the Babylonian army suffered a temporary setback in the war with Egypt, Jehoiakim decided to rebel against Babylon. Nebuchadnezzar sent his army against Judah to punish the rebellious vassal. However, Jehoiakim's death in 598 B.C. spared him from seeing the outcome of the Babylonian invasion of Judah. Jehoiachin, his son, who assumed the throne, could keep his kingship only for three months. The Babylonians carried Jehoiachin and many of Jerusalem's prestigious political and religious leaders into captivity in Babylon in 597 B.C.

The Babylonians installed **Zedekiah** as king over Judah with the understanding that he would encourage faithfulness to Babylon. However, when Zedekiah rebelled, Nebuchadnezzar returned to Jerusalem in 587 B.C. and carried out its final destruction. The Baby-

lonians looted the Temple treasury and set fire to the Temple, the royal palace, and other adjacent buildings. Zedekiah was forced to witness the murder of his sons, and he was blinded and taken captive to Babylon. The majority of the population was carried into exile, and the Babylonians left in the land only the poorest and weakest members of the nation. Even among this group there was treachery and violence. A rebel group murdered Gedaliah, who was appointed by Babylon as Judah's governor. This rebel group finally escaped to Egypt, fearing reprisal from Babylon.

Summary Statements

- Although the political and economic developments of Solomon's reign were far-reaching, they also provided the seed for destruction.
- God's judgment of Solomon resulted in the division of his kingdom.
- Dan and Bethel became the "measuring rod" for the Deuteronomistic writers' evaluation of the northern kings.
- The message and ministry of the ninth century B.C. prophet Elijah reflect the central Deuteronomistic conviction that the people of the Lord must serve their God with an undivided loyalty.
- In spite of the thoroughgoing reforms of Jehu, Jehoash, Hezekiah, and Josiah, the people of God were not capable of ultimately changing their ways.
- The ultimate consequence of Israel's covenant breaking with God was the loss of their political and religious freedom.
- The destruction of Samaria and the destruction of Jerusalem were evidence of the covenant curses at work.
- The Deuteronomistic history concludes on a note of optimism that God holds the future open.

Questions for Reflection

1. How do our subtle "alliances" with the world in which we live lead to "divided hearts"?
2. How might symbols of God's presence, such as the Temple in Jerusalem or Jeroboam's golden bulls, become worshiped as idols in our lives? What might some of these symbols be?
3. When is an appropriate time to take a stand for God, as the prophet Elijah did?
4. What can be accomplished through religious revivals or reforms? What are their limitations?
5. What brings on exile in the lives of the people of God?

Bible Study Assignment

Read 1 Kings 19:9-18 and answer the following questions:

1. What is the historical, cultural, and religious setting of this passage?
2. Where was Elijah when this encounter with God took place? Why did he go there?
3. What is the theological intent of God's question to Elijah (vv. 9, 13)?
4. What does Elijah's response to the above question convey about his spiritual and emotional condition and his attitude toward his ministry?
5. Describe the various manifestations of God in verses 11-12. What is the theological purpose of this theophany narrative? Contrast these appearances with the "still small voice."
6. How does the narrative conclude? What was God's commission to Elijah?
7. What are some of the theological lessons that you find in this narrative?
8. How would you relate the lessons of this narrative to modern-day situations?

Resources for Further Study

Bright, John. *A History of Israel,* 4th ed. Louisville, Ky.: John Knox Press, 2000.

DeVries, Simon J. *1 Kings,* vol. 12 of *Word Biblical Commentary.* Waco, Tex.: Word, 1985.

Hobbs, T. R. *2 Kings,* vol. 13 of *Word Biblical Commentary.* Waco, Tex.: Word, 1985.

Wiseman, Donald J. *1 and 2 Kings: An Introduction and Commentary,* in *Tyndale Old Testament Commentaries.* Downers Grove, Ill.: InterVarsity Press, 1993.

10 Israel's Restoration to the Promised Land:

Chronicles, Ezra, Nehemiah, and Esther

bjectives:

Your study of this chapter should help you to:

- Describe the theological issues that Israel faced during the period of exile and restoration
- Articulate the message of Chronicles to its first audience
- Describe the historical setting and content of the Books of Ezra, Nehemiah, and Esther
- Evaluate the significance of the message of Ezra, Nehemiah, and Esther to their first audience
- Assess the biblical prescription for reforming and maintaining a vital community of faith

K ey Words to Understand

Cyrus the Great
Postexilic history
Priestly history
Ezra
Nehemiah
Sheshbazzar
Zerubbabel
Haggai
Zechariah
Esther
Additions to Esther
Purim

Q uestions to consider as you read:

1. What lessons can you learn about your relationship to God by looking at your nation's history?

2. How significant are symbols for your faith?

3. Why is worship such an important part of a relationship to God?

4. What does it mean to follow God completely?

The Crisis of Exile and Its Outcome

The events of the Babylonian exile precipitated a major theological crisis for those who survived. The covenant people remained without the symbols of God's special blessings—their Temple, kingship, and nationhood. This crisis led them to reflect and raise questions about the nature of God and their destiny in the world as His covenant people.

Central to their concerns were questions about God's fairness and trustworthiness. Survivors of Jerusalem's destruction wanted to know why this evil had happened. Also important were questions about identity. How could the exiles or refugees be Israelites if there was no nation called Israel? Without the Temple and kingship, could the Israelites still be God's people? Such questions led to concerns about the future. Is there a future for the exiles? What is their destiny and mission in the world?

These questions led the exilic community to reflect on their past, present, and future. Their reflection on the past led them to the great historical and theological traditions of their ancestors. In these ancient traditions they found evidence of God's power and faithfulness. The Books of Moses most likely received their final canonical shape during the Exile. The Books of Joshua, Judges, Samuel, and Kings were also compiled at this time to provide an extended narrative explanation for the Exile (Deuteronomistic history). As they contemplated their present conditions, they composed highly emotional poems such as Lamentations and Psalm 137 to express the deep feelings of living the nightmare of exile. Also, they

gathered the writings of the prophets and recognized their credibility and authenticity as God's true prophets to Israel. They found in the words of these prophets God's plans and purposes for their future. The words of these previous prophets were reiterated and recast into new words of hope and comfort by their own prophets who were in exile (see Isaiah 40—55). It is also likely that a number of other books such as Psalms and Job also received their final form during the Exile.

The Exile was thus a turning point in Israel's history. It gave them a new vision for their future. We know from their later history that they took the identity as Yehudites (Jews) during this period. Also, they learned Aramaic, the language of their Babylonian captors, and made it their spoken and commercial language. We also think that the Exile introduced them to commercial and business enterprises, which became the primary vocation of their descendants. The absence of the Temple and rituals prompted the exilic community to meet together in private homes for prayer and praise and the reading of Scripture. This gathering eventually led to the establishment of the synagogue, the educational and teaching center of later Judaism.

Restoration Period

The Babylonian empire began to decline in power in the mid-sixth century B.C. As Babylon was weakening, a gifted prince among the Persians, who became known as **Cyrus the Great,** was beginning to gain prominence in the lands to the east. He took control of the vast empire of the Medes and Afghanistan in the east be-

The Cyrus Cylinder

The Cyrus Cylinder records the capture of Babylon in 539 B.C. and refers to new policies instituted by Persia's King Cyrus the Great. Part of the text of the cylinder reads: "As far as Ashur and Susa, Agade, Eshnunna, the towns of Zamban Me-Turnu, Der, as well as the region of the Gutians, I returned to these sacred cities on the other side of the Tigris, the sanctuaries of which have been ruins for a long time, the images which used to live therein and established for them permanent sanctuaries. I (also) gathered all their (former) inhabitants and returned (to them) their habitations."[1]

fore turning his attention to Babylon. In October of 539 B.C. the armies of Persia entered the city of Babylon. The Jewish exiles saw the rise of Cyrus as God's plan for their liberation from Babylon (see Isaiah 44:28—45:6).

Cyrus's decree (see sidebar) permitted the Jewish exiles to return to their homeland in 538 B.C. Though many in the exiled community remained behind in the secure and familiar environment of Babylon, a significant number made the perilous journey to reclaim their homeland. As we shall see later, their immediate goal was to rebuild the Temple and reestablish worship in their homeland.

Life in Judah throughout the Persian period did not turn out as bright and hopeful as Jeremiah, Ezekiel, and the exilic writer of Isaiah 40—55 envisioned it. Unrealized dreams of the glorious renewal projected by earlier prophets apparently led people to distrust the God of their fathers. Some scholars also think that this period witnessed the rise of party movements within Judaism and conflicts within the community on matters of worship, rituals, and other religious issues (see Isaiah 56—66; Haggai; Zechariah; Ezra; Nehemiah; and Malachi).

Despite such problems, the community of Israel discovered

new depths to their faith through this time of testing. The next set of historical books (Chronicles, Ezra-Nehemiah, and Esther) outline for us some of the theological perspectives that were developed during this critical period in Jewish history. These theological perspectives set the agenda for the nation's future for the next several centuries to come.

1 and 2 Chronicles

Chronicles begins the second section of the historical books of the Old Testament. This section is made up of Chronicles, Ezra, Nehemiah, and Esther. These books are often called the **postexilic history** because they were all written after the Exile and contain records of the events of that period. However, the narrative in Chronicles begins with David around 1000 B.C. and ends with the time of Nehemiah around 430 B.C.

The two Books of Chronicles offer one more overview of Israel's history before the Exile. While they repeat information from previous books of the Old Testament, they do not simply rehash the same thing. There is new material and a fresh look at Israel's experience with God. More than simply recording events, these books contain new theological perspectives aimed to give the present and future generations direction for their life as God's people.

The author of Chronicles is unknown and is often simply called the chronicler. Some scholars have suggested that the chronicler may have been either Ezra or Nehemiah. Though this could be possible, we simply do not have enough evidence. These books do not appear to have much in common with the Books of Ezra and Nehemiah. So, it is unlikely that Chronicles is the work of either Ezra or Nehemiah. Some scholars suggest that the chronicler may have been a Levite since he gives so much attention to the ministry of the Levites.[2]

The Books of Chronicles were some of the last books of the Old Testament to be written. Evidence in the text suggests that they were composed sometime around 400 B.C.

Setting

The Books of Chronicles were composed during the time of unrest in the western part of the Persian Empire (around 400 B.C.). A number of provinces were in revolt against the empire, and the people of Judah were caught in the middle. The future of the Persian Empire, and the Jews as well, was un-

Modern Jewish settlement in Israel.

certain. Further, the Jews still remained disillusioned with their lot in life. Restoration of their community had not come about as hoped. The economy still struggled, and foreign powers still dominated. The first audience to hear Chronicles was wrestling with questions of God's interest in His people and their future.

Content

The two Books of Chronicles are a unified composition. They were originally written as one unit and only later divided for convenience. The chronicler relied upon many sources to compose his history. Most obvious is the material from 2 Samuel, 1 Kings, and 2 Kings. About half of Chronicles is drawn directly from these books. The chronicler, however, was selective in using the material. He employed only those parts that fit his purposes and re-arranged them as needed.

Chronicles focuses upon the lives of David and Solomon. They are the primary examples of faithful worshipers of God. Introductory and concluding sections frame the stories of the reigns of these two kings. The books divide into the following four sections:

Genealogies
　　1 Chronicles 1:1—9:44
David Narratives
　　1 Chronicles 10:1—29:30
Solomon Narratives
　　2 Chronicles 1:1—9:31
Kings of Judah Narratives
　　2 Chronicles 10:1—36:23

■ Genealogies

The first nine chapters of Chronicles give a list of Israel's ancestors from Adam to Saul. This seems unusual to the modern reader. To the ancient Jew, howev-

Chronicles as Priestly History

Chronicles, along with Ezra-Nehemiah, could be called the **priestly history** because it presents Israel's history from the perspective of the priests. By contrast, the Deuteronomistic history analyzes Israel's past from a prophetic viewpoint.

It is this difference in perspective that accounts for the kind of material that is either included or omitted in Chronicles. A large amount of material in Chronicles focuses upon the Temple, its ritual, and its personnel. The Deuteronomistic history shares some of this material, but Chronicles adds much more. The lists of Levites in 1 Chronicles 24—26 and the worship service of Jehoshaphat in 2 Chronicles 20 are good examples.

er, genealogies were significant. They clarified relationships and emphasized connections to the past. Genealogies also affirmed that God's blessing rested upon His people. A list of generations meant that God had made them fruitful and increased their number (see Genesis 1:28).

Genealogies are a kind of history writing.[3] They can cover a vast amount of time quickly. Chapter 1 moves from Adam to Israel and so connects the Israelites to the entire human race. God's salvation is not reserved for a few; it is universal. All members of humanity, as well as "all Israel," may participate in God's redemption.

Chapters 2—8 delineate the descendants of the various tribes of Israel. Two groups, the Levites and the Judahites, are highlighted by the amount of space given to them and by the arrangement of the text. Both groups are significant in the book—the Levites because of their relationship to the Temple and the Judahites because they were the tribe of David.

Chapter 9 brings the history down to the time of the first readers. It mentions those who returned to Judah after the Exile and lists descendants into the fifth century B.C. This section closes with the genealogy of Saul, which prepares the reader for the narrative in chapter 10.

■ Reign of David

The second section of Chronicles focuses upon the life of David. It deals first with the establishment of David's kingdom and then turns to how David prepared to build the Temple. David served as the chronicler's best example of a godly king. The reason God prospered David, according to the chronicler, was because of his godly character. Chapters 13—16 describe the salient points that make David the ideal leader of God's people. He inquired regularly of the Lord and placed a priority on worship. His efforts to bring the ark of the covenant to Jerusalem symbolized his deep desire to place God at the center of his kingdom. David's hymn in chapter 16 stands as a model for true worship. It lifts up God and confesses total reliance upon Him.

Chapter 17 forms a climax for this section of Chronicles. David desired to build a house for God (the Temple). But God determined to build a house for David (a dynasty of kings). David's faithfulness brought divine blessing, a promise of an everlasting kingdom. For the first readers of Chronicles, this was an important word of hope.

Most of the material in chapters 22—29 is unique to Chronicles. It records how David organized the Levites for worship service and charged Solomon to carry out the plans for the Temple. Worship of God was no afterthought. Extensive plans were made because worship at the Temple was a primary means of demonstrating faithfulness to God.

■ Reign of Solomon

The chronicler presents in 2 Chronicles chapters 1—9 an ideal picture of Solomon by careful selection of material. As with David, his intention was not to gloss over imperfections or realities. Rather, he simply sought to highlight the ways in which Solomon did things right. He saw patterns in David's

and Solomon's lives that served as models for believers.

The chronicler presents Solomon as a true seeker of God. He, like his father David, went before God to receive direction for life. His Temple dedicatory prayer illustrates his piety and trust in God. He presented the Temple as a place of healing, forgiveness, and genuine encounter between God and His people. God's response to the prayer laid out the conditions to continue that relationship.

The key verse for this section, and the entire book, is the well-known verse in 7:14. It reads, "If my people, who are called by my name, will humble themselves and pray and seek my face and turn from their wicked ways, then will I hear from heaven and will forgive their sin and will heal their land." It concisely expresses the central

View of the Temple Mount from the Mount of Olives. The second Temple was located where the Dome of the Rock is today.

The Western Wall, known as the Wailing Wall, is the only part of the second Temple complex that exists today.

theme of the book. A forgiving, healing relationship with God depends on a humbling, seeking, repenting posture before God. This text invites us to examine our hearts when we come before God through prayer and worship.

■ Reigns of the Other Kings of Judah

The final section of Chronicles illustrates the main points of the book by means of a survey of the rest of Judah's kings. The fortunes of *each* king are told in reference to how well he followed David's model. Those who imitated David were blessed, but those who pursued other patterns were cursed.

Positive examples are given the most space. These include Asa (chaps. 14—16), Jehoshaphat (chaps. 17—20), Hezekiah (chaps. 29—32), and Josiah (chaps. 34—35). They did what was right in eyes of God, sought the Lord, prayed, humbled themselves before God, and paid attention to the Temple.

Negative examples of kingship are found in Jehoram (chap. 21), Ahaziah (chaps. 22—23), Ahaz (chap. 28), Amon (chap. 33), Jehoiakim (chap. 36), Jehoiachin (chap. 36), and Zedekiah (chap. 36). Their pattern was to do evil in God's eyes and walk in the ways of the kings of the Northern Kingdom. Other kings of Judah provided mixed examples. One of the most interesting kings in this category is Manasseh. According to 2 Kings 21, he was one of Judah's worst kings, leading the nation into its darkest period of apostasy. The chronicler, however, records his humbling before God when the Assyrians took him as a prisoner, and God's answer to his prayer. Manasseh was restored to his kingship and he became a true servant of God (2 Chronicles 33:1-20).

ah. Ezra came from a family of high priests and apparently held a position in the Persian court as an adviser on Jewish affairs. Jewish tradition holds Ezra almost on a par with Moses. Nehemiah was cupbearer to the king in the Persian court in Susa.

Ezra and Nehemiah are treated as a unified work in the Hebrew tradition. The division of the two books obscures the interrelation of ideas in these books. They are also similar in structure, themes, and literary techniques. Here, we will deal with these books as one unified work.

We do not know for sure who composed Ezra-Nehemiah. Tradition places Ezra as the author. It is also likely that Nehemiah or an unknown person may have compiled these books. The last dated event in these books is the beginning of Nehemiah's second term as governor of Judah (Nehemiah 13:6-7). This would have been around 430 B.C. It is likely that the materials were compiled into Ezra-Nehemiah around 420-400 B.C.

This confirms that God holds out hope even for the most treacherous sinner.

The Books of Ezra, Nehemiah, and Esther continue the theme of God preserving a community of faith in the midst of adverse conditions. These books maintain the hopeful expectation of Chronicles that God is shaping the future of His people.

Ezra-Nehemiah

The main characters in these books are a scribe named **Ezra** and a layperson named **Nehemi-**

Setting

The biblical text presents the ministry of Ezra and Nehemiah during the reign of the Persian King Artaxerxes I (464-424 B.C.). Some scholars think that Ezra served under Artaxerxes II (404-

The Broken Walls of Jerusalem

In the ancient world, city walls were a symbol of strength and stability. Jerusalem was scarcely populated because of its broken-down walls. A city without secure walls was vulnerable to attack. But the ruined walls meant more than lack of security to Israel. Nehemiah called the broken-down walls of Jerusalem a disgrace (Nehemiah 1:3 and 2:17). The ruined wall and the unprotected city portrayed Israel's God as powerless among the nations. They also signified that restoration had not fully taken place. The rebuilding, on the other hand, symbolized God's continued blessings upon Israel and His protection of His chosen city.

359 B.C.). It is likely that Ezra came to Jerusalem in 458 B.C. and Nehemiah in 444 B.C. We do not know much more about Ezra's dates except that he was present at the wall dedication in 444 B.C.[4] Nehemiah was governor for 12 years, and then he went back to Susa in 432 B.C. His next term as governor probably began a few years later and lasted shorter than the first.

The ministry of Ezra and Nehemiah took place at a crucial period in the postexilic history. The Jewish national and religious life was in crisis. Though the Temple was rebuilt and worship restored, the Jewish community fell victim to spiritual apathy and community tensions. The restored community needed religious instruction in the Law of Moses. Intermarriage with non-Jewish people and lack of covenant commitment seriously affected the spiritual condition of the nation. These spiritual lapses also affected the social life of the Jewish community.

Content

Ezra-Nehemiah is composed of various materials. Diary-like writings by Ezra and Nehemiah are

Nehemiah was concerned with the rebuilding of Jerusalem's walls. The walls around Jerusalem today were built by Suleiman the Magnificent in the 16th century A.D.

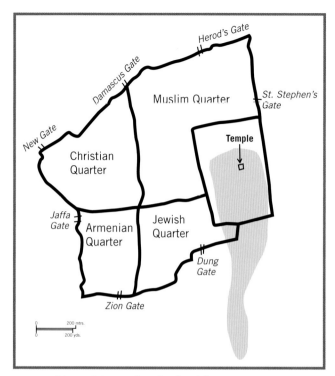

Map of Jerusalem in the 4th century B.C. (shaded areas). The outline shows the modern boundary of the Old City of Jerusalem.

among the sources of these books. The Ezra Memoirs may be found in Ezra 7—10 and possibly Nehemiah 8—9. The Nehemiah Memoirs consist of Nehemiah 1—7 and 11—13.

Ezra-Nehemiah material may be divided into the following four major sections:

Restoring the Temple
    Ezra 1:1—6:22
Restoring Purity
    Ezra 7:1—10:44
Restoring the Walls
    Nehemiah 1:1—7:73
Restoring Law
    Nehemiah 8:1—13:31

Each of these sections contains a pattern of the following four regularly occurring elements: (1) royal decrees, (2) return of the people, (3) opposition to rebuilding, and (4)

success over the opposition. The sections also parallel one another. Nehemiah 1—7 recalls Ezra 1—6 by its focus upon a physical building project. Both sections also include celebrations of feasts and dedication ceremonies. Nehemiah 8—13 echoes Ezra 7—10 by emphasizing the role of law in rebuilding God's community.

■ **Restoring the Temple**

The first section of Ezra-Nehemiah tells of the trials and triumphs of those who first returned to build the Temple in Jerusalem. An edict from the Persian King Cyrus allowed the return.

Sheshbazzar, a member of the royal family, led the first group of returnees in 538 B.C. Like the Exodus from Egypt hundreds of years earlier, Israel once again made their way to the Promised Land, but this time from the homeland of their ancestor Abraham. When **Zerubbabel** came with another group, he took over leadership of the community along with Jeshua the high priest. They built an altar and began laying the foundation of the Temple. Opposition from neighboring peoples brought an abrupt halt to the project, and work on the Temple ceased.

About 18 years after the first returnees arrived in the land, the prophets **Haggai** and **Zechariah** (520 B.C.) began to inspire the Jews to take up the task of rebuilding the Temple again. This evoked questions from Tattenai, the governor of the Trans-Euphrates satrapy. Darius the Great reissued the decree allowing the Jews to rebuild the Temple. The Jews completed the Temple around 515 B.C. Though it was not of the scale and grandeur of Solomon's Temple, it served as the center for worship of Israel's God for nearly 600 years. Construction of this second Temple was an important event in the history of God's people. It affirmed once again God's presence with His people. The rebuilding ended with a celebration of the Temple dedication and the Passover.

■ Restoring Purity

There is a gap of 50 years between Ezra 6 and 7. The focus shifts to the return of Ezra the scribe in 458 B.C. and the reforms he undertook upon his arrival.

The Persian King Artaxerxes I commissioned Ezra to return, along with others who wished to go, and teach the law of their God. Such a commission fits with what historians know of Persian policies and practices. The effect of Ezra's teaching of the Law was a new awareness of the problem of mixed marriages. Ezra was heartbroken by this sin and repented. Others followed his lead, and the community confessed its sin. Then specific steps were taken to deal fairly with each improper marriage.

■ Restoring the Walls

The story of the rebuilding of the walls of Jerusalem is the subject of Nehemiah 1—7. About 10 years after the events in Ezra 10, Nehemiah received news of the condition of Jerusalem's walls and set out to rebuild them.

Through divine providence, the Persian king granted permission to Nehemiah to accomplish his goal. When he arrived in Jerusalem, he laid out a plan for the project but immediately encountered opposition. Neighboring peoples evidently feared that the Jews might gain

The Persian Empire.

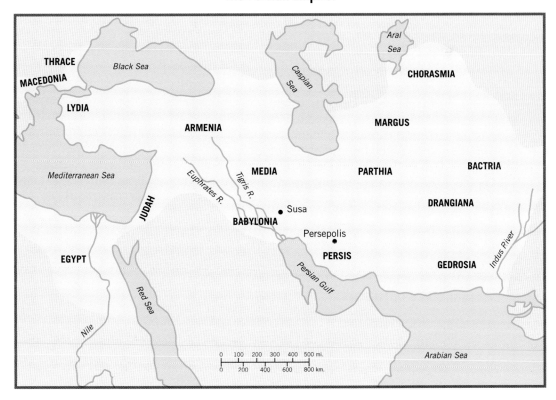

too much strength and influence in the region.

Showing exceptional tenacity and leadership skills, Nehemiah eventually overcame the opposition and completed the restoration of the walls in 444 B.C. As with the Temple, this success came about not because of Nehemiah's skills but because of God (6:16). The message of Nehemiah 1—7 echoes Ezra 1—7. We can trust in God's control over His world.

■ Restoring the Law

The final section of Nehemiah focuses on the reading of the Law of Moses (Torah) and the renewal of the covenant with God. This is what the rebuilding of the community was all about. The ultimate aim was recommitment to the God who continued to work in the history of His people. In his prayer, Ezra reflected on God's graciousness toward His people from the time of creation to the Exile, to remind the nation that apart from God's grace, there is no hope for the community.

In a dramatic moment, the community recommitted themselves to follow the Law. They determined to avoid mixed marriages, to take care of the Temple, and to repopulate the city of Jerusalem. Once the commitments have been made, the community celebrated the dedication of the wall.

The main goal of Israel's restoration was not an ideal societal structure but a committed, trusting relationship with the living God. The material of Ezra-Nehemiah points us in that direction. Israel understood the character of God as "a forgiving God, gracious and compassionate, slow to anger and abounding in love" as the basis for covenant renewal (Nehemiah 9:17). References to God's compassion and goodness are abundant in the Old Testament. The possibilities of restored covenant hinged on God's faithfulness and compassion toward His people. Because God is who He is, we have hope in becoming who we should be—a forgiven and redemptive community in the world in which we live today.

Esther

The Book of Esther is a well-known story of the dramatic deliverance of the Jews that took place during the Persian period. This drama unfolds with considerable intensity, and affirms throughout that God is in control of this world and that He cares for His people.

One may assume that the author of this book wrote soon after the events and that this person would be one of its main characters, either **Esther** or Mordecai. This assumption may be right, but there is little evidence to confirm or deny it. Consequently, scholars have suggested various other possibilities for the author and time of writing. Most of the

L Additions to Esther

The lack of reference to God in Esther prompted an unknown author in the second century B.C. to add six major **additions to Esther** with explicit reference to God. The Septuagint translators added this version of the story to their work. These additions are part of the apocryphal books.

suggested dates fall within a time frame beginning just after the events in the book to the end of the Persian period in 330 B.C.[5]

Setting

By contrast with Ezra and Nehemiah, the events in this book take place solely in Susa, one of the three main administrative centers of the Persian Empire. Originally the ancient capital of the Elamites, Susa became the winter capital when Darius I built a large palace complex there. Esther and Nehemiah lived in Susa, along with numerous other Jews who had high positions in the royal court. The events of the book took place during the reign of Xerxes I (Ahaseurus in Hebrew) who ruled over the Persian Empire from 486 to 464 B.C. We do not know anything about the religious condition of the Jews of this period. Ironically, the book does not mention God or any of the traditions of Israel.

Content

Esther contains many elements that traditionally make for a good story. There are interesting characters, life-and-death suspense, comic relief, ironic twists, and a happy ending.

The story of Esther may be outlined as follows:

Background Events	1:1—2:23
The Conflict	3:1—5:14
The Climax	6:1—7:10
Final Resolution	8:1—10:3

■ Background Events

The first two chapters of the book establish the background for the events in the story. The Persian King Xerxes I gave a royal banquet and displayed his vast

Purim

Esther explains the origins of the Feast of Purim and its regular observance. This holy day became known as **Purim** because lots *(purim)* were cast to determine what day the Jews would be destroyed. Purim is celebrated on the 14th and 15th of Adar (February or March). The Feast of Purim celebrates God's sovereign hand in the history of His people. It affirms His special selection of Israel as His people and His constant protection of Israel throughout the generations. The Book of Esther is read during the feast.

wealth and power. His queen, Vashti, refused to attend his banquet, and so the king banished her from her position. This led to a search for a new queen and the opportunity for Esther, a poor young Jewish woman, to enter the king's court. Though she rose to high position, she remained as a woman of principle with a teachable spirit and loyalty to her heritage. Mordecai raised his orphaned cousin Esther and continued to give her guidance.

■ The Conflict

Dramatic tension in the story develops with the introduction of Haman, the arrogant villain. He held a powerful position in Persian politics, second only to the king. His hatred for Mordecai the Jew evolved into a sinister plot to exterminate not only Mordecai but his people as well. Xerxes was deceptively drawn into the evil plan, a date for the extermination was selected, and a decree sent throughout the kingdom.

In response, Mordecai challenged Esther to take advantage of her position in order to rescue the Jews. Esther rose to the occasion and designed a counterplan. She called her people to fast and took the risk of presenting her request to the king. Though God's name is not mentioned, there is no question that He is the key player. His people, the Jews, are endangered by the powers of this world. Esther's call for a fast (4:16) is an obvious acknowledgment of the need to trust God for His people's deliverance. In the context of the biblical story, from the Garden of Eden to the restoration, God is the only source of deliverance for those who trust Him.

■ The Climax

The tables turned quickly in the narrative with an ironic comical twist. Haman, whose hatred drove him to build a gallows on which to hang Mordecai, ended up showing honor to Mordecai. Haman's evil plot to exterminate the Jews was revealed at Esther's banquet. Haman suffered the fate he intended for Mordecai. He was entrapped by his own plans. The story confirms the proverbial saying that "the wicked are brought down by their own wickedness" (Proverbs 11:5).

■ Final Resolution

Though the villain was removed, the consequences of his actions continued. The plan to exterminate the Jews remained in effect since Persian law was inviolable. Esther and Mordecai received permission from the king to issue another decree allowing the Jews to defend themselves. The result was the elimination of thousands of enemies of the Jews throughout the kingdom.

The final verses of the book encourage those who experienced God's deliverance as well as future generations to commemorate this event regularly. The things God has done must not be forgotten.

The Book of Esther provides a fitting conclusion to the historical narrative of the Christian Bible (Genesis through Esther). It emphasizes once more that God will not abandon His people. The book affirms God's promise to Abraham: "I will bless those who bless you, and whoever curses you I will curse; and all peoples on earth will be blessed through you" (Genesis 12:3). The faithfulness of God to His people is one of the primary themes of biblical history.

Summary Statements

- The Babylonian exile pushed Israel into a theological crisis of major proportions.
- Persian policy allowed exiled Israelites to return and restore their nation.
- Genealogies are a kind of history writing that emphasizes connections to the past.
- Kings who did not follow the model of David brought disaster upon themselves and their nation.
- The first readers of Ezra-Nehemiah were the Jews who struggled to survive the hardships of the restoration period.
- Ezra-Nehemiah communicates the themes of trusting God, connecting with one's spiritual heritage, and shaping one's life by God's Word.
- The Book of Esther affirms God's sovereignty in this world and His faithful protection of His people.

Questions for Reflection

1. Why did the community of Judah experience spiritual disillusionment during the restoration?
2. What are some of the important symbols of faith and God's presence in our lives?
3. Compare and contrast the issues that confronted the Jews of the fifth century B.C. with the issues that God's people face today.
4. In what practical ways does Scripture give guidance for organizing and maintaining societies?

Bible Study Assignment

Read 2 Chronicles 7:11-18 and answer the following questions:

1. What is the historical and religious setting of this passage? Read 2 Chronicles 5:1—7:10 to study the background.
2. Read Solomon's prayer in chapter 6 and review the conditions he sets forth for God's response to the prayers of His people. Make a list of these conditions ("if" statements) in this chapter.
3. What is God's promise to Solomon in response to his prayer?
4. What are the conditions that the people of God should meet in order to receive God's forgiveness and healing?
5. What specific promises does God make to Solomon concerning the future of his kingship?
6. What lessons do you learn about prayer from your study of this passage?
7. What lessons do you learn about God from your study of this passage?
8. What are the contemporary applications of this text to our personal and community life?

Resources for Further Study

Baldwin, Joyce G. *Esther: An Introduction and Commentary,* in *Tyndale Old Testament Commentaries.* Downers Grove, Ill.: InterVarsity Press, 1984.

Kidner, Derek. *Ezra and Nehemiah: An Introduction and Commentary,* in *Tyndale Old Testament Commentaries.* Downers Grove, Ill.: InterVarsity Press, 1979.

Selman, Martin J. *1 Chronicles: An Introduction and Commentary,* in *Tyndale Old Testament Commentaries.* Downers Grove, Ill.: InterVarsity Press, 1994.

_____. *2 Chronicles: An Introduction and Commentary,* in *Tyndale Old Testament Commentaries.* Downers Grove, Ill.: InterVarsity Press, 1994.

UNIT IV

ISRAEL: A COMMUNITY WITH SAGES AND POETS

Your study of this unit will help you to:

- Discuss the role of wisdom in ancient Israel
- Describe the theology reflected in the wisdom books in the Old Testament
- Evaluate the significance of psalms to the community of Israel
- Discuss various features of the poetic books in the Old Testament

■ Wisdom of the Community: Job, Proverbs, and Ecclesiastes

■ Songs of the Community: Psalms, Song of Songs, and Lamentations

11 Wisdom of the Community:
Job, Proverbs, and Ecclesiastes

O bjectives:

Your study of this chapter should help you to:
- Explain the theological basis of wisdom thinking
- Outline the content of Job
- Compare the arguments of the main characters
- Explore ways to comfort those who are suffering
- Apply proverbial wisdom to life situations
- Analyze different approaches for gaining meaning for life

Q uestions to consider as you read:

1. What is wisdom in our cultural thinking?

2. What thoughts go through your mind when you hear about tragedy and loss of life?

3. What are some of the meaningful proverbial sayings in our contemporary world?

4. What is the common attitude toward life in secular society today?

K ey Words to Understand

Job
The Satan
Eliphaz
Bildad
Zophar
Sheol
Elihu
Righteous
Wicked
Proverb
Qoheleth

What Is Wisdom?

The Books of Job, Proverbs, and Ecclesiastes are the product of Israel's wisdom teachers. Who were the wise and from where did they receive their wisdom? Moses brought down from Mount Sinai the Ten Commandments, written by God himself. The prophets stood in the throne room of God to receive their messages. However, there is little appeal in the wisdom books to divine revelation as the source of wisdom. Rather wisdom looks to the created order. The arguments of the wise (see Job and Ecclesiastes) come from observing how God has structured the world. One studies the world to gain understanding and insight into how to live well.

Wisdom *(hokmah)* in the Old Testament can generally be grouped into four broad categories. One who is skilled as an artisan or craftsman is said to possess wisdom in making things.

Solomon asked for wisdom, and God granted his request.

The Old Testament also mentions those who possessed encyclopedic knowledge among the wise in ancient Israel. Solomon had vast knowledge of animal and plant life and was the author of a large number of proverbs. A third use of *wisdom* concerns those who are adept in social skills. Biblical wisdom, for the most part, focusses on the understanding of one's obligations to God and service to Him with awe and respect. "The fear of the LORD is the beginning of knowledge" sums up this biblical principle of wisdom (Proverbs 1:7). Israel identified wisdom with God's revelation of the Torah or Law. To know the Law was to know God's revealed wisdom. This wisdom included not only knowing what was written in the Law but also applying it to everyday life (Psalm 119). A person with such wisdom would be happy or blessed in life (Psalm 1).

Wisdom in the Ancient Near East

Wisdom was a shared phenomenon in the ancient Near East. In addition to Israel, other cultures and peoples of the ancient Near East also had their own proverbs, sayings, riddles, stories, and poems from their study of the universe. As these peoples were in constant contact through trade, diplomatic missions, and even wars, they shared with each other their insights. Since Israel was situated on the main trade routes between Egypt and Mesopotamia, the two main ancient cultural centers, she also shared in this cultural interchange. One example of this migration of knowledge may be seen by comparing the *Sayings of the Wise* in

Proverbs 22:17—24:34 to the Egyptian work titled *Instruction of Amen-em-Opet.*[1] The two literary works have so many parallel sayings that it appears that some type of borrowing took place between them. Works similar in theme to Job and Ecclesiastes, but shorter in content, are found in the Mesopotamian cultures.[2] The wise of many nations observed and recorded their insights and then were willing to share their wisdom with others.

Scope of Wisdom Literature

There are several types of wisdom literature in the Old Testament. The Book of Proverbs communicates wisdom through short, easy-to-remember statements that deal with the practical issues of life. We may label this book as an example of *practical wisdom* or *proverbial wisdom.* There is also a speculative side to wisdom. The Book of Job explores whether or not one may live a blameless life before God, and if so, why does one who is innocent suffer evil? Ecclesiastes examines the question of the purpose of life and finds that it is vanity; that is, empty of meaning. These books are examples of *speculative* or *philosophical wisdom* in the Old Testament.

Wisdom, however, is not confined to a select group of books. A number of psalms are classified as wisdom psalms because of the contrast between the godly and the wicked (Psalms 36, 37, 49, 73, 78, 112, 127, 128, 133). The Wisdom of Solomon and the Wisdom of Jesus Ben Sirach are two wisdom books included in the Apocrypha.

Wisdom was taught at the city gate in ancient Israel.

The Book of Job

Many have heard that Job patiently endured great suffering (James 5:11). How many, however, know him as a man of protest? Did you know that his patience was not cheerful and his suffering was not done in silence? Rather, he became quite angry over his situation and directed his anger toward God. Most people hold an image of Job based on the first two chapters of the book. When we turn to chapter 3, we encounter a different Job. The rest of the book is made up of long, wordy speeches of various individuals, which conclude with

Theology of Wisdom

Biblical wisdom has a theological foundation. Israel connected wisdom with God's creation of the universe. When God created all things, His first creation was wisdom (see Proverbs chapter 8). At the time of creation, He placed the principles of wisdom—a divinely established moral order—within the universe so that it functions or works according to those principles. The "fear of the Lord" includes one's recognition of this truth. What are those principles that tend to make life longer, safer, healthier, more successful and prosperous? One discovers them by studying the created order and seeing what works. The wise who structure their lives according to these principles enjoy a long and good life. Fools never learn the principles. Even when they are taught wisdom, they reject it to live a pleasure-seeking, self-willed life. The end of such a life is poverty, illness, disgrace, and death. Thus ultimately wisdom comes from God. To study His created order is to learn about God himself and His will for humanity and the created order.

speeches of God. What happened? Welcome to the world of the Book of Job.

Scholars have proposed various views on the date and authorship of the Book of Job, ranging from Moses in the 13th century to someone in the 2nd century B.C. The patriarchal setting in the first two chapters has led some to conclude that the book is quite old, possibly the first book of the Old Testament to have been written. The sophisticated theological arguments in the rest of the book compel us to place the book at a much later period in Israel's history. Many scholars tend to date the book in the 7th or the 6th century B.C.[3]

Content

The following is a general outline of the Book of Job:

Prologue	1:1—2:13
Job's Monologue	3:1-26
Three Cycles of Speeches	
	4:1—27:23
Poem on Wisdom	28:1-28
Job's Monologue	29:1—31:40
Elihu's Speeches	32:1—37:24
God's Speeches	38:1—42:6
Epilogue	42:7-17

Prologue

The first two chapters contain five scenes alternating between earth and heaven. The opening scene describes **Job,** a blameless and upright man and a man of great wealth. The scene quickly shifts (v. 6) to a day when the angels (literally "the sons of God")

Divine Justice

The Book of Job closes without answering the question of divine justice. The question "Why do the righteous suffer?" remains an enigma. Yet it does illustrate a proper response to evil. Job passionately questioned God's justice, yet God did not count it as sin. He learned from God's speeches the greatest truth about God. God is intimately involved with His creation. The relationship of God to the world included Job and his suffering. Job's world of suffering was within God's providential care. Job's response was repentance, a turning away from anger and back to trusting God. It is difficult to trust God when we are angry and hurt. Jesus later experienced the bitterness of human injustice and the agony of divine silence in the moment of suffering. There is a quiet comfort to be gained through trusting the One who knows the depth of human affliction.

gathered to present themselves to Yahweh. **The Satan** who was among the angels challenges God to take away Job's wealth to see if he would still keep his piety before God. God accepted the challenge and allowed the Satan to take away all that Job had.

The next scene (vv. 13-22) shows a succession of calamities that came upon Job. Job responded to this with a solemn confession of his faith in God (v. 21). Scene four is another meeting of the angels again in heaven. At this time, the Satan claimed that Job would curse God if he was inflicted with pain and suffering. In response, God allowed the Satan to make Job suffer. The final scene on earth portrays Job's intense suffering. Even though his wife encouraged him to curse

God, he did not sin. His three friends—Eliphaz the Temanite, Bildad the Shuhite, and Zophar the Naamathite—came to comfort him. They sat in silence with Job seven days, the normal time of mourning in the ancient time.

■ Three Cycles of Speeches

Job broke the silence at the end of seven days with a lament, in which he cursed the day of his birth and wished for death to bring an end to his miserable existence. This defiant speech of a blameless and upright Job sets the stage for the three cycles of dialogue in the book. At this point, the focus of the book shifts to the problem of suffering, particularly the suffering of Job. Job's friends tackle this problem from the perspective of the tradi-

The Ancient Near Eastern Background and Literary Parallels

The Book of Job was not the first work in the ancient Middle East to ask questions about the suffering of the righteous. Egypt produced a number of works that dealt with this problem during the 12th dynasty (1990—1785 B.C.). A good example is *The Admonitions of Ipuwer.* This work contains the lament of Ipuwer over the strife and social turmoil in the land. He complained that even the gods did not take notice of the situation. "There is no pilot in their hour. Where is he (God) today? Is he then sleeping? Behold, the glory thereof cannot be seen."[4]

Mesopotamia also produced several similar works. The poem *A Man and His God,* a Sumarian work of the second millennium, describes the complaint of a sufferer to the gods about his tormented situation. The Babylonian poem *I Will Praise the Lord of Wisdom* deals with a sufferer's struggle with the inscrutable will of deity. He had performed the rituals required by the gods but was uncertain that they would have any effect.[5] *The Babylonian Theodicy* (1100 B.C.) is similar to Job in that it is a dialogue between a sufferer and his friend. The friend maintained an orthodox position while the sufferer listed his grievances against the gods. In the end he offered up a prayer that the gods might take note and help him.[6]

The Book of Job shows no direct dependence on any of these works. Job, however, is similar to these works in that it represents Israel's attempt to grapple with the problem of the suffering of the righteous. What sets Job apart from other ancient wisdom works is its comprehensive treatment of the topic. Job also shows a variety of literary forms or genre, such as laments, disputations, lawsuits, hymns, wisdom instructions, petitions, avowals of innocence, and affirmations of trust in God. In summary, we believe that Job's intellectual roots lie in the wisdom tradition that spanned many cultures. Its theological concepts, however, belong to Israel's religious traditions contained in the Old Testament.[7]

tional doctrine of reward and punishment. **Eliphaz** related suffering to the inherent nature of humanity as mortals who cannot be pure before God. **Bildad** affirmed the idea that God punishes the wicked. **Zophar** thought that Job's punishment was much less than what he deserved. In all the three cycles of speeches, Job's friends forcefully defended the orthodox concept of divine justice and upheld the integrity of God as a God who blesses the righteous and punishes the wicked. As the debate progressed, they concluded that Job's suffering was the consequence of his wickedness. However, they also appealed to their friend to put away sin from his life and seek God, so that he could be restored to his former state of wealth and blessedness.

Job's speeches show that he, too, believed in the traditional doctrine of reward and punishment. However, he introduced into this doctrine the element of human experience, particularly his own experience as a righteous person, whom he saw as the victim of God's unbridled and violent actions. He believed that God established the moral order of the universe. However, he complained that God did not honor the rules He established, and that he was the victim of a perverted system of justice, which seemed to favor the wicked. His speeches, on the one hand, show his utter hopelessness and his fear of death and the impending journey to **Sheol,** the dwelling place of the dead. On the other hand, Job's speeches also demonstrate his unwavering faith in his ultimate vindication. He called for an arbitrator (9:33) and believed that in the end a "witness," an "intercessor" would plead his case with God (16:19-21). Later in a strong statement of faith he called God his Redeemer (*go'el,* a kinsman who defends and delivers) and confessed with assurance that even after death he would see God (19:25-27). Although the Hebrew in these verses is difficult, it is clear that Job in his suffering had risen to a new level of faith and spiritual insight.

The debate over the issue of Job's suffering ended without resolution. Neither Job's friends nor Job succeeded in proving their argument. In the end, Job took an oath of innocence once again to establish his righteousness before God. At this point **Elihu,** a fourth speaker, appears on the scene with a new theological perspective. Elihu claimed that suffering has a disciplinary function. Punishment is remedial, to call the sinner back to God who is exalted in power and majesty. Elihu's de-

Satan

The term *satan* means adversary, opponent, one who brings accusations, and so forth. The New Testament identification of Satan with the devil is lacking in the Old Testament. In the Book of Job, the term is always used with the article, *the* Satan, in order to designate an office. From the conversation between God and the Satan it appears that his job was to investigate persons and bring offenders to God's notice. He functioned as the heavenly prosecuting attorney, hence the title "the Satan," meaning the adversary.

scription of God's majesty sets the stage for God's speeches out of the storm (38:1—41:34).

■ God's Speeches

The speeches of God conclude the poetic section of the book. The author introduces here the wisdom theological perspective on God. God's speeches began with a series of questions addressed to Job. These questions establish the power and majesty of the Creator and His providential care for everything in the universe. God's speeches show how the smallest animals as well as the most monstrous and terrifying creatures are under His control. The divine speeches do not resolve Job's dilemma. His questions are not answered; he is neither acquitted nor found guilty of the charges brought against him by his friends. However, the speeches make one thing very clear. There is a vast gulf that separates God and humanity. Humans cannot claim to know the mysterious ways in which God works in the universe. Though God remains mysterious, the speeches convey the truth that Job and his world of suffering are not removed from the providential care of the Creator who ordered and structured the whole universe.

It is the recognition of this mystery about God that led Job to repent of the words he spoke about God. He admitted that he spoke of things he did not understand (42:3). He recognized the truth that he was human and that he could not understand how God ordered the universe. Everything God does and the ways by which He relates to the universe remain a mystery. From now on, he would abandon his presumptive thinking about God. He would take the path of

Artist's depiction of Job and his friends.

trust rather than protest. Faith would replace anger.

The story ends with God restoring to Job double for all the possessions and wealth he had lost. He received all his children back. Is there a subtle hint here that even in death, Job and his wife had not ultimately lost their children?

The Book of Proverbs

How does one discover the way to the good life? Israel maintained the view that God had placed within creation itself the principles of wisdom (Proverbs 8). By studying the outcomes of the choices people had previously made, one could discern what tended to make life long or short, prosperous or poor, and peaceful

God asked Job: "Do you know when the mountain goats give birth?" (Job 39:1).

Solomon, and probably some even earlier. However, the book as we have it today went through a process of editing and compiling, perhaps taking final form sometime during or just after the Babylonian exile.

Content

The following is a broad outline of the materials in the Book of Proverbs:

Poems on the Way of Wisdom	1:1—9:18
Proverbs of Solomon and Other Sayings of the Wise	10:1—29:27
Closing Material	30:1—31:31

■ The Way of Wisdom

The prologue (1:1-7) states the purpose of the book: to give wisdom and discipline for both the simple and the young and to enable the wise to learn more. The foundation of wisdom is in one's respect and reverence for the Lord.

The first main section (1:8—9:18) is composed of 10 instructions, usually beginning with the formula "Listen, my son." These instructions instruct and challenge the youth to avoid the path of sin and choose the way of wisdom. These instructions also warn against sexual immorality and call for fidelity in marital relationship. The way of wisdom in this section also includes admonitions about sound business practice and diligence in work.

Wisdom is personified as a woman (Lady Wisdom) in chapters 8 and 9. She calls the people to enter her house and receive life, honor, and wealth. She was with God in creation, and through wisdom God brought everything into existence. Those

or troublesome. The wise could see the lessons before them and structure their lives for good. The foolish reject wisdom and live an undisciplined life that leads to destruction. In Israel's wisdom tradition, those who fulfilled God's pattern were righteous and wise; those who did not were the wicked and foolish.

While many Old Testament books are anonymous, Proverbs begins by stating: "The proverbs of Solomon son of David, king of Israel." In addition 10:1 has the title, "The proverbs of Solomon." These statements might lead one to think that Solomon wrote the book as we have it. However, 25:1 notes: "These are more proverbs of Solomon, copied by the men of Hezekiah king of Judah." This note tells us that the book was not completed until at least the time of Hezekiah (715 to 687 B.C.). The book also contains other collections of sayings such as "Sayings of the Wise" (22:17—24:22), "Further Sayings of the Wise" (24:23-34), "Sayings of Agur" (chap. 30), "Sayings of King Lemuel" (31:1-9), and a poem on "The Wife of Noble Character" (31:10-31). There is no reason to doubt that some of the material goes back to

"Righteous" and "Wicked"

The terms **righteous** and **wicked** are often used in the Old Testament to designate relationships rather than moral conditions. The individual lived as a member of the family, clan, tribe, community, and so forth, and each area imposed certain expectations. When one discharged the obligations demanded in each situation, then the person was righteous. A person is righteous only when obligations are met in all levels of relationships. In Proverbs the term *wicked* is used for those who are immoral (12:12), as well as those who violate social obligations (v. 26).[8]

who enter her house will feast on the finest of foods. With her, life will be good. In contrast Dame Folly invites the simple to her house where stolen food is delicious. Hers, however, is the house of the dead.

■ Proverbs of Solomon and the Wise

Chapters 10—29 are composed of short, two- to four-line sayings. These are the types of sayings usually associated with the term *proverbs*. A **proverb** (Hebrew *mashal*) is a short, pithy saying that contains an idea or truth. There seems to be no connecting or unifying theme to this section.

This section covers a wide range of topics. We find in this section warning against illegal business practices, laziness, idle chatter, dishonest scales, pride, sexual indiscretion, gossiping, slandering, foolish talk, false witnesses in courts, fraud, gluttony, envy, lying, and rulers who oppress the poor. Also there are proverbs here that call for trust in God; disciplining oneself, one's children, and one's servants; generosity; care for the poor; maintaining right relations within the family; diligence in working; thrift; patience; and above all attaining wisdom. Basic to wisdom is the

fear (respecting and obeying) of God.

■ Closing Materials

The final material of the book comes from several sources. The sayings of Agur make up chapter 30. The sayings of King Lemuel begin the final chapter (31:1-9). The final collection in this book is an acrostic poem on the qualities of a worthy wife (vv. 10-31). The woman's qualities are described in typical wisdom pattern. While her piety is noted, it is her industry that receives emphasis and praise in this poem. Choose a wife (and the advice relates to choosing a husband as well) not according to physical beauty but according to her ability to work diligently, to conduct business shrewdly, and to run the household efficiently. Such a choice is wise.

The Book of Ecclesiastes

Israel's wisdom sages, though they were proponents of the orthodox doctrine of reward and punishment, also knew that human existence was far more complex than this neatly packaged religious belief. They questioned, argued, and proposed new perspectives that would shed light into the complexities of human existence. The disparities and disillusionment of life made some pessimistic even about their view of the world and human existence. Can any human really know the purpose of life? Does life have any meaning? These questions seem to occupy the thoughts of the writer of Ecclesiastes.

The writer called himself **Qoheleth,** sometimes translated "Teacher." The term has something to do with one who collects or gathers. Does Qoheleth gather a group to hear his words, students to teach, or sayings to publish? It is not certain, but it may have been that he did all three. The superscription (1:1) states that he was a son of David and, according to 1:12, a king over Israel in Jerusalem. Because of these statements, tradition has assigned this book to Solomon, suggesting that Qoheleth was a type of pen name. Most scholars today

place the book in the postexilic period and suggest that the author assumed the role of a king to test intellectually the various opportunities that life presents.[9]

Content

There has been much discussion over the plot of Ecclesiastes, but scholars have come to no consensus. The book moves from one topic to another with little internal structural development. The book also contains diverse literary forms, such as poetry, prose, rhetorical questions, proverbs, curses and blessings, and autobiographical narrative. This variety adds to the richness of the thought but detracts from its purposeful development. The reader is thus confronted with an anthology of assorted materials compiled for the purpose of demonstrating the emptiness of life.

Ecclesiastes can generally be divided into three parts:

Prologue	1:1-11
Various Discourses	1:12—11:6
Epilogue	11:7—12:14

The second section and bulk of the book contains loosely connected literary units that cannot be outlined without making numerous exceptions. The final part begins with an epilogue on youth and aging (11:7—12:14). The book concludes with an appendix that reflects traditional wisdom and an orthodox perspective (12:9-14).

■ Futility of Life

"Meaningless! Meaningless!" says the Teacher.
"Utterly meaningless!
Everything is meaningless" (1:2).

So the author begins. Life is meaningless, vain, and empty of purpose. The prologue (vv. 3-11)

T

Contemporary Relevance of Israel's Proverbs

How trustworthy are these ancient proverbs for guiding a person's actions today? Are they absolute truth? How are they to be understood when some proverbs seem to contradict each other, such as those contained in 26:4-5?

Do not answer a fool according to his folly,
    or you will be like him yourself.
Answer a fool according to his folly,
    or he will be wise in his own eyes.

Should one answer or not answer a fool? Wisdom knows the answer. These proverbs illustrate that while all proverbs are true in that they capture an aspect of life, not all are universal and applicable in all circumstances. The wise know not only what to say or do but also the appropriate time. The fool does not. Wisdom is not purely an intellectual endeavor, memorizing lists of proverbs, but a pragmatic application of insight into how to live well.

Proverbs vs. Ecclesiastes

Both Proverbs and Ecclesiastes deal with God, humanity, and critical concerns of human life. Proverbs is more positive about these matters. God's will is knowable. One may succeed in life by working diligently according to the divine will. The Teacher is not as confident as Proverbs. God seems more remote, unknowable, and wrapped in mystery. Whatever proposals are made, one is never sure how God will respond. In the end, both the righteous and the wicked suffer the same fate; they die and are forgotten. Proverbs approaches life with optimism. However, the Teacher is pessimistic. Death hangs over every aspect of life. What separates him from the philosophy of living only for the moment is his recognition that there is a God and that it would be foolish to live so as to anger Him.

Both books are scripture and require the believer to come to grips with their teachings. Neither presents God's final revelation, so they must be held as incomplete and partial. These books recognize our human finitude and invite us to worship our God who has revealed himself only partially, trusting that He is good.

develops this thought by describing the endless cycle of life. People are born, die, and are forgotten. Nature continues on its ceaseless cycle of seasons and nothing new arises. What is accomplished?

The Teacher explored the various facets of life in order to discover its purpose. He indulged himself with things that brought pleasure, which proved to be meaningless. The Teacher also found work as meaningless (2:17-26). He concluded that nothing is better than enjoying life by eating, drinking, and finding satisfaction with work. Enjoyment of life is God's gift to humanity.

The discussion about work is interrupted by what may be the most famous poem of the book (3:1-8):

"There is a time for everything,
and a season for every activity
under heaven" *(v. 1)*.

Matched antithetical pairs fill out the poem: a time to be born and to die, to plant and to harvest, to kill and to heal. There is a time for each. The problem is, of course, knowing when is the proper time to engage in each activity. Is now

the time for war or for peace? How do we know? Perhaps the intent of the author is that humans cannot alter the divinely established order of time for everything that happens. If this is the case, what, then, is the purpose of human existence? The writer thus paints before us the language of despair and pessimism.

The Teacher saw oppression, envy, and discontentment all around him (chap. 4), and everything was meaningless, a grasping after the wind. The Teacher thought that one should not be too zealous even in serving God (5:1-7). If one is so rash as to make a vow to God, then that person should certainly pay it. The Teacher next explored the folly of wealth, because it does not endure (5:8—6:12). The wealthy are not content and are driven by an insatiable appetite.

The Teacher found seven things that are good, or better—a good name, death, sorrow, mourning, rebuke of the wise, wisdom, and inheritance are among the good things in life (7:1-14). He called for contentment in all circumstances, for both good and evil times come from God. Traditional wisdom taught that there is only one God and that He is good. Yet the Teacher claimed that all things, whether good or evil, come from Him. How can this be? This is the problem Job struggled with and what still puzzles modern thinkers.

Even in his pessimistic mood, the Teacher recognized the importance of proper behavior (chap. 8). Though an immediate punishment did not come to the wicked, he concluded that a God-fearing life was better than a life filled with wicked schemes.

The Teacher returns to the theme of death as the end of life for both the wicked and the righteous (9:1-10). So, what is the advantage of one over the other? With the living there may be hope, but it is tarnished with the thought that all will die and their memory be forgotten. The best one has is this life, so one should enjoy it as fully as possible.

The Teacher concludes the book with a collection of miscellaneous proverbial sayings. He contrasts wisdom and folly and gives advice to the young on how to succeed in life. He invites the young to enjoy life, a continuing refrain of the book. Yet all restraint is not to be cast off. One must still be aware that God brings one into judgment. Also, old age comes and one must live with the end as well as the beginning in mind. A beautiful poem describes pictorially the aging process (12:2-7). Finally, the opening words of the book are echoed again:

"Meaningless! Meaningless!" says the Teacher. "Everything is meaningless" (v. 8).

The last two verses bring the book to a close. The purpose of humanity is known: keep God's commandments. Why? For God will bring everything into judgment. These words reflect a more traditional approach to the religion of Israel, more in keeping with the pragmatic wisdom of Proverbs and the theology of Deuteronomy.

Summary Statements

- Wisdom in the Old Testament includes four broad categories, one of which is the fear of the Lord.
- Job, Proverbs, and Ecclesiastes are the primary examples of wisdom in the Old Testament.
- The Book of Job is mostly poetry, and it is for the most part in the form of a dialogue.
- Job's friends defended the traditional doctrine that suffering is the evidence of sin in one's life.
- Job maintained his innocence and hoped to be vindicated by God.
- Elihu's speeches relate suffering to the idea of divine discipline and instruction.
- God's speeches emphasize His relationship to the world and His governance of everything He has created.
- Proverbs focuses on the theme of living a good life and living up to one's potential as a responsible member of society.
- Ecclesiastes presents a pessimistic view of human life.

Questions for Reflection

1. What wisdom have you learned from others around you (parents, teachers, or others with life experience)?
2. What lesson do we learn from the example of Job's friends about how not to comfort one who is suffering? What might be more helpful approaches?
3. How can proverbs created by a culture promote responsible life in society?
4. Is life as meaningless as the Teacher thought? How does one discover life's purpose?

Bible Study Assignment

Read Job 4:1—5:27 and answer the following:

1. Who is the speaker in this passage? How does he begin his speech? What does he say about Job?
2. What does the speaker say about the innocent? What does he say about the wicked?
3. What is the speaker's perception of humanity in general? What is the source of his knowledge of humanity?
4. What seems to be the point the speaker is attempting to make in 5:1-4? Do you think he is referring to Job in these verses?
5. What ideas about sin and suffering does the speaker introduce in this speech?
6. What counsel does the speaker give Job? Why does he counsel Job (what underlying conviction about Job is the basis for this counsel)?
7. What is the speaker's understanding of God? Is it consistent with the biblical perspective of God?
8. What is your evaluation of this speech in light of the introduction of Job in Job 1:1? Do you think the speaker affirms what is said about Job in 1:1? Explain your answer.

Resources for Further Study

Garrett, Duane A. *Proverbs, Ecclesiastes, Song of Songs,* in *New American Bible Commentary.* Nashville: Broadman, 1993.

Hartley, John. *The Book of Job,* in *New International Commentary on the Old Testament.* Grand Rapids: Eerdmans, 1988.

Newsome, Carol A. *Job: Introduction, Commentary, and Reflections,* in vol. 4, *The New Interpreter's Bible.* Nashville: Abingdon Press, 1996. Pages 319-637.

12 Songs of the Community:
Psalms, Song of Songs, and Lamentations

bjectives:

Your study of this chapter should help you to:
- Identify the main characteristics of Hebrew poetry
- Identify the various types of psalms
- Analyze the message of individual psalms
- Develop a biblical view of human sexuality and its proper function
- Evaluate the theology of the Book of Lamentations

ey Words to Understand

Parallelism
Acrostics
Tehillim
Psalmoi
Hermann Gunkel
Form criticism
Hymns
Laments
Mashiach
Song of thanksgiving
Royal psalms
Wisdom psalms
Psalms of trust
Canticles

Questions to consider as you read:

1. What are the various themes of songs and hymns we sing during our corporate worship on Sundays?

2. Should complaints to God be a regular part of our corporate worship? Explain why or why not.

3. What are the various reasons why you praise God?

4. How do people view sex and sexuality in our contemporary society today?

Hebrew Poetry

Nearly one-third of the Hebrew Scriptures is in poetry. Most of the works of the Prophets, wisdom books, all of the Psalms, Song of Songs, and Lamentations are composed of poetry. To understand these books, a basic knowledge of how the Israelites composed their songs and sayings is needed.

The basic building block of Hebrew poetry is parallelism of thought. **Parallelism** refers to the relationship between two or more lines of verse. The three basic forms of parallelism are: synonymous, antithetical, and formal. In *synonymous parallelism,* the first line makes a statement and the second line repeats the thought, as illustrated in the following example:

Show me your ways, O LORD,
teach me your paths.
—*Psalm 25:4*

In *antithetical parallelism* the first line makes a statement and the second stands in contrast to it, as illustrated in the following example:

The sluggard craves and gets
nothing,
but the desires of the diligent
are fully satisfied.
—*Proverbs 13:4*

In *formal parallelism,* sometimes called *synthetic parallelism,* the first line makes a statement and the second carries the thought on, or expands it without repetition or contrast, as illustrated in the following example:

Do not be quickly provoked in
your spirit,
for anger resides in the lap of
fools.   —*Ecclesiastes 7:9*

In addition to parallelism, there are a number of literary devices in Hebrew poetry that cannot be reproduced in a translation. *Alliteration,* the repetition of the same consonantal sounds, and *assonance,* the repetition of the same vowel sounds, are two such devices. Some poems were written as **acrostics.** The first word of a verse or stanza began with the first letter of the Hebrew alphabet, the first word of the second verse with the second letter, and so on, through the 22 letters of the alphabet.

The Book of Psalms

The Book of Psalms is one of the most widely read and appreciated books in the Bible. Both the synagogue and the Church continue to read, sing, and pray the Psalms. Whereas other books of the Old

Steps that lead to a ceremonial bath *(mikveh).* Ceremonial bathing was a required ritual to maintain holiness in ancient times in Israel.

Testament represent God's word to humanity, the Psalms bring humanity's voice to God. They articulate our cry to God for help or express our gratitude for His care and deliverance. The Psalms explore our depth of need and the height of our praise. Worshipers are able to locate their various phases of life in the words of the psalmists and find comfort in praying them anew. These ancient words also provide us with the language to express our hope and confidence that God's grace will sustain us in the midst of difficult experiences of life.

The Hebrew title for the Psalms is **tehillim,** meaning "songs of praise." **Psalmoi,** which also means "songs of praise," is the title of the book in the Septuagint. The Latin version called it *Liber Psalmorum.* The Greek and Latin versions are thus the source of the title "Book of Psalms." The ancient titles convey that the book contains Israel's songs of praise to God.

The development of the book covered a long span of time, perhaps over a thousand years. While most of the psalms come from the time of the monarchy, it was not until after the Exile that the book as a whole took final shape. There are presently five sections or books of Psalms, each ending with a doxology. These sections are Psalms 1—41, 42—72, 73—89, 90—106, and 107—150.

Most of the psalms have titles or captions. These titles often identify the person or group with whom the psalm is associated. They also contain some instructions for musical accompaniment. Of the 73 Davidic psalms, 18 have notes associating them with events of David's life as recorded in 1 and 2 Samuel. This would indicate that

the titles were not added until after those books were written and thus sometime after the psalms themselves were first created. Fifty psalms have no authorship and are sometimes called *orphan psalms.*

It is likely that psalm writing and singing of songs were activities associated with worship in Israel that goes back to the pre-monarchy period. Later, many psalms were most likely written specifically for the shrine erected by David and the Temple built by Solomon. An organized choir, musicians, and psalm singing were part of the Temple worship in the postexilic period. Most scholars refer to the Book of Psalms as the Hymnbook of the Second Temple, thus giving it a prominent place in Israel's worship in the postexilic period.

Jews praying at the Western (Wailing) Wall; psalms are prayers of the faithful who trust in the mercy of God.

Types of Psalms

The modern study of Psalms took a major step forward with the work of a German scholar named **Hermann Gunkel.** He noted that many of the psalms were structured according to identifiable patterns or forms. This analysis of literary works according to structure is known as **form criticism.** By identifying the form of a psalm, a reader is able to identify how its thought and message are developed. Gunkel's work also helped us place the psalms in the context of Israel's worship. They belonged to the congregation of the faithful who used them to express both their praise and needs to God.

Hymns

Gunkel realized that while not all psalms could be classified by their forms, a sizable number of them could be placed into the categories of hymns, laments, and songs of thanksgiving. Scholars have accepted his classification with minor adjustments. The simplest category is that of hymn. **Hymns** usually begin with a call to the community to praise God. Some hymns celebrate Yahweh's rule of creation and history (33; 145; 146; 147). Hymns that proclaim the kingship of Yahweh *(enthronement psalms)* may have been part of a ritual where the recognition of the kingship of Yah-

weh over the created order was reenacted (93 and 95—99). Hymns of Zion celebrate God's choice of Zion as His dwelling place (48).

Laments

Over a third of the psalms may be classified as **laments,** cries to God for help. This category is comprised of both personal and communal laments. In the *personal laments,* the psalmists call upon God in times of their personal misfortunes and trials. These laments reflect the contexts of sin, illness, economic distress, betrayal by a friend, false accusations, infertility, death, abandonment by God himself, and oppression by enemies. Often the precise situation cannot be identified. A number of psalms refer to the enemies of the worshiper. Psalms 6, 10, 13, 17, 22, 35, and 51 are examples of personal laments. *Communal laments* express the need of God's deliverance when the community faced military defeat, famine, pestilence, drought, or some other difficulty. The crises forced the community to raise agonizing questions. Was God with them? Was He angry over sin? Was He just in His treatment of His people? Psalms 12, 44,

---

T   **Attitude Toward Enemies**

O Daughter of Babylon, doomed to destruction,
     happy is he who repays you
     for what you have done to us—
he who seizes your infants
     and dashes them against the rocks *(Psalm 137:8-9).*

When we encounter hateful language like that of Psalm 137, we must keep in mind that calling God to carry out judgment was an important part of Israel's religious beliefs. The helpless people of God saw God as the only source of justice and help. They did not take matters into their own hands, but rather trusted God with His righteous judgment. As Christians reading the psalms, we should apply the love commandment as the basis of our relation with those who hate and persecute us (Matthew 5:43-45).

Jewish and Early Christian Interpretation of Psalms

In the later history of Israel, after the monarchy was swept away with the fall of Jerusalem in 587 B.C., the royal psalms became the voice of hope and expectation. The people longed for God to bring forth a royal leader who would once again, like David, restore the kingdom to Israel. The king was the *anointed one* (in Hebrew, the **mashiach** or messiah). In the postexilic community, these psalms were read as prophetic descriptions of the Messiah whom God would send to redeem His people. Instead of looking backward to a historic kingdom, they were viewed as looking forward to God's new act of redemption, which He would inaugurate with a messianic king. The early Christians applied many of the royal psalms to the life and ministry of Jesus the Messiah.

58, 60, 80, 90, 94, and 137 are examples of communal laments.

The lament has many variations, which are not difficult to recognize. The cry to God for help and the description of some type of difficult situation are distinctive markers. Some laments display the psalmist's claim of innocence or confession of sin. Trust and confidence in God's faithfulness and loyalty to His covenant with Israel are also found in some of the laments. Laments may also contain a brief section of praise and thanksgiving. The laments usually did not end in despair, but in hope and worship.

Songs of Thanksgiving

While the lament looks forward to the help of God, the **song of thanksgiving** arises as a response of gratitude for God having responded to prayer. God's forgiveness of sin, healing from sickness, and deliverance from enemies are usually the occasions of thanksgiving psalms (see 9, 18, 62, 118).

Not only the individual but also the community as a whole expressed its joy for God's blessing, particularly for bountiful harvests (Psalms 65 and 67), victory over enemies (75 and 124), and for bringing pilgrims safely to

Jerusalem for one of its times of annual festivals (107).

The song of thanksgiving may be confused with the hymn, as both open with a statement of intent to give praise to God. While the hymn begins with a call to the

> "On his law he meditates day and night" (Psalm 1:2).

community as a whole, similar to a community song of thanksgiving, it is the next movement that distinguishes between the two forms. In the hymn the call to praise is followed by a series of motive clauses. Both individual and community thanksgiving songs rehearse the problems that gave rise to a need for divine intervention and how God responded. Both make positive statements about the graciousness of God who does marvelous things for His people.

Other Types of Psalms

Many of the psalms cannot be classified by their form but by their rhetoric or content. They have some common theme that binds them together. The **royal psalms** represent one such group. These psalms were written by or for the king and often have the superscription "By David." Psalms 2, 72, and 110 were sung at the coronation of the king;

Psalm 45 at a royal wedding. In Psalm 118 the king led the congregation in worship. In Psalm 20 the king prepared to go to war; in Psalm 21 he returned in victory. Psalm 18 is a royal psalm of thanksgiving.

The **wisdom psalms** reflect the concerns of wisdom. These psalms draw a sharp contrast between the wise and the fool, the godly and the ungodly, and the righteous and the wicked (Psalms 37, 112). Psalm 1, which serves as an introduction to the entire book, focuses on the two ways of life—the way of godliness and the way of wickedness. In Psalms 49 and 73 the psalmists struggle with the complexities of the world. The common thought of the day was that God would insure justice; the righteous would be rewarded and the wicked punished. Yet the wicked prospered and suffered no punishment. This inequity pushed the psalmists to

T　Theology of Psalms

The Psalms may be humanity's prayer to God, but at their center is God, not humanity. There is one God, Yahweh who delivered Israel from Egypt, established His covenant with His special people, gave them the land, chose David as king and Jerusalem as His place of habitation. Yahweh jealously guards His people from their enemies but will not allow their sin to go unpunished. A primary task of Yahweh is the moral governance of this world. The righteous can rest secure in His justice that the wicked will be punished and the righteous rewarded. Israel's covenant relationship will be sustained by Yahweh's steadfast love (in Hebrew *hesed*, which also means covenant loyalty, unfailing love, faithfulness, etc.).

The Psalms view humanity as dependent creatures in need of God's help. The world has become a hostile place with powerful forces opposed to Israel. Even in the covenant community, the wicked seek to destroy the righteous. Only Yahweh can provide an adequate shelter. He sustains the warrior, brings justice to the oppressed, and defends the holy city. There is little hope beyond this life, so worshipers cry for immediate relief from oppression, the powers of death, the infertility of the earth. The Psalms show only faint hopes that the justice of God might reach beyond the grave. Sin will bring the wrath of God, yet restoration is possible through repentance. While the laments seem to color the emotional tone of the Psalms in dark hues, the joy of the presence of God stands in contrast. Even the laments ring with a confidence that God will hear and answer prayer. Life will be good again.

look beyond the present and into a confession of the hope for life beyond the grave (Psalms 49:15; 73:26). While this thought seems obvious from the standpoint of the New Testament, in Old Testament Israel it was innovative.

The **psalms of trust** are some of the best-loved psalms of the Bible. Psalm 23 is probably the best known of all the psalms. Other songs of trust include Psalms 11, 16, 62, 63, 91, 121, 125, and 131. The song of trust celebrates God's goodness and dependability in the midst of the troubles of life. At points the exuberance overflows into excessive claims of divine protection, particularly for the king, from all of life's calamities (Psalm 91).

Song of Songs

The Song of Songs celebrates human sexuality as a normal part of the love and affection shared by a married couple. The book captures in beautiful poetry the sexual passion and intimate conversations between lovers. Its view of love is consistent with other parts of the Bible in that love and sexuality are seen as normal expressions of human life, and thus gifts of God.

The phrase "song of songs" is a Hebrew expression meaning the greatest song. From the Vulgate or Latin translation the book took the name **Canticles.** The first verse of the book associates the work with Solomon, the patron of wisdom literature, and is thus often called the Song of Solomon.

Who authored the book is an open question. The traditional view ascribes the authorship to Solomon (1:1). Sometimes scholars can date a book by its style of poet-

> ### T Theology of the Song of Songs
>
> The book is unusual in that it lacks any divine voice, prophetic voice, or reference to Israel's laws, covenant, or sacred history. We hear only human voices that extol the pleasure and passion of sexuality. What theological message does it contain? Israel viewed Yahweh as the Creator of the physical universe. Whatever He created was a gift and a blessing to His creation. This includes our physical bodies and the physical enjoyment we receive in sexual love. Sexuality used as an expression of love and affection within the bounds of marriage becomes both a creative act, issuing in the birth of children, and an expression of companionship between a man and woman. Exploitation of sexuality outside of marriage or in unnatural or perverse ways is a perversion of God's gift. The song celebrates the goodness of God's gift of love.

ry or by historical references contained in the book. Neither of these methods offers a secure means for dating this book. Suggestions as to date of writing vary from the 10th century, written by Solomon himself, to the 4th century B.C. The dominant voice in the book is that of a woman, not a man.

Interpretation of this book has a long history.[1] Early Jewish scholars followed the allegorical method and interpreted it as an expression of God's love for Israel. Early Christian scholars followed the same pattern, only recasting it as Christ's love for the Church. Modern approaches have varied, some seeing it as a type of Greek drama complete with a chorus, or as originally coming from a pagan cultic ritual that celebrated the union of a god and goddess. Pope relates the song to the funeral festivals in which life and love were celebrated as the most powerful force that can cope with the fear of

Song of Songs is a celebration of love.

images drawn primarily from nature: gardens, animals, perfumes, spices, and trees. With expansive and redundant expressions, the poetry builds vivid word pictures of passionate love.

The speakers in the first two chapters alternate between the woman and the man. In these songs, the woman sings of her love and the man responds by praising her beauty and enticing her to depart with him. The song in chapter 3 describes the woman seeking her lover and enticing him into the wedding chamber. The physical beauty of the woman is the focus of the song in chapter 4. The language of this poem includes comparisons drawn from nature.

Songs in chapters 5 and 6 include the song of the woman searching for her beloved and the choral response of the young women of Jerusalem asking why she loves him so. The woman then describes his physical charms. Again the groom's voice is heard extolling the physical beauty of his bride who is more beautiful than all the women in the harem of a king.

Chapter 7 begins with a poem celebrating the beauty of the maiden. The groom speaks of the pleasure of her physical love. The woman responds by inviting him into the vineyards where she will give him her love. Her song continues into 8:1-4 where she expresses the desire to be with her lover openly as with a brother. The rest of chapter 8 consists of a number of short songs by the groom, the woman, and brothers or friends of the woman.

death.[2] A better way to view the book is to see it as a collection of love songs. While some poems may have been composed as songs for wedding festivals, others may simply be love poems composed by various individuals. When and by whom the diverse materials were brought together as a collection of love poems is unknown.

Content

The content of the book consists of a number of seemingly disconnected poems, and therefore, it is difficult to give a thematic outline to the book. The poems utilize a large number of

Lamentations

We live in a culture that has lost the capacity to cry out and express deep emotional distress over sudden death and destruction. So it is difficult for us to understand the depth of agony, suffering, and the fragmented world portrayed in the Book of Lamentations. Such lament poems were a part of the religious and literary tradition of the ancient world.[3] The Book of Lamentations introduces us to a world that knew how to express grief and how to cope with the reality of pain and suffering when horrifying tragedy occurred.

Lamentations is part of the Writings *(Kethubim),* the third division of the Hebrew canon. This book—together with Song of Songs, Ruth, Ecclesiastes, and Esther—make up the five Festal Scrolls *(Megilloth).* Readings from Lamentations are part of the liturgy of the Ninth of Ab, the Jewish remembrance of the Jerusalem Temple destroyed by the Romans in A.D. 70.

Ancient versions such as the Septuagint and the Vulgate attributed the authorship of Lamentations to Jeremiah and placed this book after the Book of Jeremiah. The introductory statements of both the Septuagint and the Vulgate cite the fall of Jerusalem and the captivity of Judah as the occasion of the writing of Lamentations. This tradition is followed in the English Bible. Most scholars today regard this book as the work of an anonymous writer who was an eyewitness of the tragedy of 587 B.C.

Content

The book is made up of five carefully crafted and structured poems that utilize a rich and elegant variety of metaphors. Each poem, except the last one, is constructed as an acrostic, using the 22 letters of the Hebrew alphabet. As typical of dirge poems, the thoughts of the author are often mixed, and move from one theme to another, showing discontinuity and fragmentation. However, the acrostic structure of these poems also shows the author's intention to deal with the details of the tragedy carefully and systematically without glossing over pain and suffering.

The book begins with a lament about the desolation of Jerusalem and God's withdrawal from His people (chap. 1). The author saw the destruction of the Temple as the evidence of God's anger against His people who were no longer holy to the Lord (chap. 2). Chapter 3 contains a personal lament of the author. Like Job, the author complained to God about his suffering. But unlike Job, the writer was convinced that he and his nation were suffering because of their sins. Nonetheless, he maintained hope in God's great

---

T **Theology of Grief**

Grief is not a private matter. The author challenges us to openly speak about our agony and pain and the chaos that surrounds our human existence. This is the courageous way to encounter suffering. We must also take time to examine, reflect, and come to grips with our pain. We must take time to pray, confess, and seek God's forgiveness. In the end, what sustains us in our suffering is the faithfulness and the love of God that surrounds us in the midst of trials and tribulations in life (3:23, 32; Romans 8:28, 38-39).

love, compassion, and faithfulness. In the midst of suffering, he proclaimed that God is good and called His people to wait quietly for their salvation. The true character of God's people is best revealed through their patient waiting upon the Lord (see Romans 5:3-5). The poet challenged the people to confess their sin and to acknowledge guilt before God so that they would once again experience His unfailing love.

The poet reminded the people that they were paying a terrible price for their sins (Lamentations 4). During the famine caused by the Babylonian siege, even the mothers lost compassion for their children. The responsibility for this tragedy was on the prophets and priests who failed to give the nation proper direction and leadership.

The poet once again acknowledges sin as the cause of the present misfortune of God's people (chap. 5). The community was under judgment because of the sins of both the present generation and the previous generations. The lament ends with an earnest appeal for the restoration of God's people. The poet was certain that the Eternal King and the Sovereign Lord would not reject or be angry forever with a repentant sinner.

Summary Statements

- Parallelism is a common feature of Hebrew poetry.
- Praise of God is the overall objective of the psalms.
- Psalms originated in the context of Israel's worship.
- Psalms provide us with the language to pray and praise God.
- Hymns, laments, psalms of thanksgiving, royal psalms, wisdom psalms, and psalms of trust are some of the major types of psalms.
- Song of Songs celebrates human sexuality and the love shared by a man and a woman.
- The author of Lamentations acknowledged sin as the cause of the destruction of Jerusalem and pleaded for God's mercy.

Questions for Reflection

1. Read through the Psalms and describe the psalmists' portrait of humanity.
2. Read through the Book of Psalms and describe the psalmists' portrait of God.
3. What is significant about the way most laments end?
4. Write a personal prayer of trust and confidence using the language of the psalmists.
5. How is sexuality viewed differently in the Bible than in the student's culture?

Bible Study Assignment

Read Psalm 2 and answer the following questions:

1. Identify the literary type of this psalm. Cite the verses that help us determine its literary type.
2. Outline the psalm following the subthemes. Give a label to each subsection.
3. Analyze each subsection. Discuss the meaning of key words in each section. What is the key idea of each subsection?
4. Make a list of the theological lessons of this psalm.
5. Consult a commentary or concordance to see how this psalm is interpreted by various New Testament writers. What conclusions do you draw from your study of the New Testament use of this psalm?
6. What is the contemporary application of this psalm? Relate the theological lessons to our personal and community life.

Resources for Further Study

Kinlaw, Dennis F. *Song of Songs*, in vol. 5 of *The Expositor's Bible Commentary*. Grand Rapids: Zondervan, 1991.

Mays, James L. *Psalms. Interpretation: A Bible Commentary for Teaching and Preaching*. Louisville, Ky.: John Knox Press, 1994.

McCann, Clinton J., Jr., *The Book of Psalms: Introduction, Commentary, and Reflections*, vol. 4 of *The New Interpreter's Bible*. Nashville: Abingdon Press, 1966. Pages 641-1280.

Whybray, Roger N. *The Book of Proverbs*, in *Cambridge Bible Commentary*. Cambridge: University Press, 1972.

UNIT V

ISRAEL: A COMMUNITY WITH PROPHETS AND VISIONARIES

Your study of this unit will help you to:
- Describe the nature of prophecy in Israel
- Evaluate the ministry and message of Israel's canonical prophets
- Describe the apocalyptic character of the Book of Daniel and evaluate the message of Daniel

■ God's Spokespersons to the Community: Isaiah

■ God's Spokespersons to the Community: Jeremiah and Ezekiel

■ God's Spokespersons to the Community: Hosea, Joel, Amos, Obadiah, Jonah, and Micah

■ God's Spokespersons to the Community: Nahum, Habakkuk, Zephaniah, Haggai, Zechariah, and Malachi

■ Apocalyptic Visions of the Community: Daniel

13 God's Spokespersons to the Community: Isaiah

Objectives:

Your study of this chapter should help you to:

- Summarize the history of the development of prophecy in ancient Israel
- Identify the key literary types (genre) found in the books of the prophets
- Describe the historical setting of the various parts of the Book of Isaiah
- Discuss the major themes of the Book of Isaiah
- Identify specific themes in Isaiah that have particular importance to the teachings of the New Testament

Questions to consider as you read:

1. When you hear the words *prophet* and *prophecy,* what thoughts come through your mind?
2. What is your perception of God?
3. What concerns you the most about the social and spiritual conditions of your time?

Key Words to Understand

Noncanonical prophets
Canonical prophets
Forthtelling
Foretelling
Messenger style speech
Uzziah
Ahaz
Hezekiah
Second Isaiah
Third Isaiah
The remnant
Immanuel
Servant of the Lord

Prophets and Prophecy

Prophets occupy a unique place in Israel's faith traditions. They have contributed to one-third of the content of the Old Testament. Who were the prophets? What prompted the appearance of prophets as religious leaders in Israel? What characteristics set them apart from other religious leaders? We will begin with some of these questions.

Israel's prophets were God's spokespersons to their nation during national crisis. When Israel was in bondage in Egypt, God called Moses as His spokesperson. Scholars think that the ministry of Moses laid the foundation for the prophetic office in Israel (see Deuteronomy 18:15-22; Hosea 12:13).

We do not have any record of prophetic activity in the early days of Israel's settlement in Canaan (see 1 Samuel 3:1). Samuel seems to be the first person to hold the prophetic office since Moses (vv. 20-21). He was known throughout Israel as a prophet. The last mentioned prophet in the Old Testament is Malachi, who is dated to the mid-fifth century B.C.

The Old Testament mentions individuals such as Gad, Nathan, Ahijah, Jehu the son of Hanani, Micaiah, Elijah, and Elisha among Israel's prophets during the next 200 years after Samuel. The Old Testament does not contain any writings that come from these prophets. Amos's book, dated to the mid-eighth century B.C., is considered to be the first literary product of Israel's prophetic tradition. Therefore, scholars assign the label **noncanonical prophets** (nonwriting prophets) to the prophets before the ministry of Amos.

During the eighth century B.C., prophecy became an ongoing religious phenomenon in Israel. Prophetic leadership and literary development of prophetic books continued through the mid-fifth century B.C. Scholars label this period as the classical period of prophecy in Israel (800-450 B.C.). Israel's **canonical prophets** (writing prophets) belong to this period.

The Old Testament contains several terms that describe the role of the prophet. *Seer, visionary,* and *man of God* are frequently found designations for non-writing prophets. *Nabi* (a spokesperson for God; *prophetes* in Greek) is the title usually given to the canonical prophets. Speaking on behalf of God was the primary task of Israel's prophets.

Israel's prophets were recipients of a special call from God to be His spokespersons. Amos, Isaiah, Jeremiah, and Ezekiel give us the record of their call and com-

Elijah challenged the prophets of Baal on Mount Carmel.

mission (Amos 7:10-15; Isaiah 6:1-13; Jeremiah 1:4-10; Ezekiel 1:1—3:15). As God-called individuals, one of their tasks was to bring to their nation's memory the great and mighty acts of God in events such as the Exodus and Sinai covenant, the wilderness journey, the conquest of Canaan, and God's covenant with David. Prophetic preaching also aimed to promote devotion to God through obedience, repentance, and life-transforming worship. Covenant loyalty and faithfulness, practice of justice by the covenant community, and care and concern for the poor were other key concerns of the prophets.

Prophetic preaching often included the prophet's evaluation of contemporary political, moral, social, or religious conditions. This function of the prophetic ministry is usually called **forthtelling.** The goal of forthtelling was to challenge the nation to repent and restore their relationship with God. Though preaching of an immediate message was a main feature, predictions **(foretelling)** were also an important component of the prophetic message. Prediction in the Old Testament is an announcement about the future. The prophets reiterated the Deuteronomic theology that God would send His blessing as the reward for faithfulness and curses for breaking the covenant (see Deuteronomy 28). Salvation and judgment are thus integral parts of prophetic predictions.

Israel's prophets often used various literary forms (genre) to convey the content of revelation they received from God.[1] The most common genre of prophetic speech is the **messenger style speech.** In the messenger style

speech, the prophet speaks God's word with an introductory formula, "Thus says the LORD." Messenger style speeches contain messages of judgment and warning or messages of salvation. A primary purpose of judgment speeches was to draw the audience to repentance and reconciliation with God. Messages of salvation brought hope and comfort to those under judgment.

Old Testament prophets more often spoke about present conditions than about future events.

The Book of Isaiah

The Book of Isaiah is undoubtedly the greatest prophetic book in the Old Testament. Both Judaism and Christianity regard this book as a highly significant theological work. The New Testament quotes this book more than any other Old Testament book.

The opening statement of the book labels its content as visions

In the parable of the vineyard, Isaiah reminded the Israelites that God planted them as His vineyard to produce good fruit.

of Isaiah ben Amoz, of whom the book gives no great details. The name *Isaiah* means "the LORD is salvation." Some scholars think that his family belonged to Jerusalem's aristocracy. The book tells us that he was married and had two sons (7:3; 8:3). He gave his sons symbolic names that conveyed God's message to Judah.

According to chapter 6, Isaiah received the call to be a prophet in the year of King **Uzziah**'s death (742 B.C.). The opening statement of the book (1:1) indicates that he was a prophet during the reign of Jotham, Ahaz, and Hezekiah. Scholars think that his ministry lasted until 690 B.C.

Setting

God called Isaiah to be a prophet during a critical time in the history of the kingdoms of Israel and Judah. Both of these kingdoms were under the threat of the Assyrian power that was expanding into the Syria-Palestine region. During the early part of Isaiah's ministry, he counseled King **Ahaz** (735-715 B.C.) to trust

in God when the Syrian-Israelite coalition led by the kings of Israel and Syria invaded Judah. Ahaz rejected this counsel and appealed to Assyria for help. Chapters 7—8 belong to this period. The Assyrian army invaded Syria and Israel, which eventually led to the destruction of Israel in 721 B.C.

Isaiah also counseled Judah's next king, **Hezekiah** (715-690 B.C.), and warned him of the consequences of making political alliances with neighboring nations (chaps. 20, 30). The Assyrian invasion of Judah in 701 B.C. is the setting of chapters 36—37. The first part of the book ends with the announcement of the Babylonian exile as punishment for Judah's continued attempt to make alliances with other nations. The events of 587 B.C. show the fulfillment of this judgment word pronounced by this eighth-century B.C. prophet.

Oracles in chapters 40—66 focus on God's redemption and the return of the exiled Judah from Babylon. Judgment, which is a dominant theme in chapters 1—39, is completely lacking in chapters 40—66. This section depicts the land of Judah and Jerusalem as destroyed and uninhabited. Oracles in chapters 40—66 also anticipate the rebuilding and repopulation of Jerusalem/Zion. These oracles, therefore, reflect a later historical situation.

Scholarly opinion on the setting of chapters 40—66 is not unanimous. Scholars who prefer to see chapters 40—66 as the work of a prophet during the Babylonian exile label this section as **Second Isaiah**. There are still others who limit the Second Isaiah section to chapters 40—55 and view chapters 56—66 as the work of a postexilic prophet **(Third Isaiah)**. They place chapters 56—66 in the religious and social context of the last quarter of the sixth century B.C. There is no unanimous opinion on this issue among conservative evangelical scholars. Some prefer the multiple authorship view. Others view the entire book as the work of Isaiah of the eighth century B.C.

Content

Although the materials in the Book of Isaiah may belong to two or perhaps three different historical settings, the book in its present canonical shape is the focus of our study and for that reason we shall treat the book in its entirety in this chapter. As we have mentioned earlier, a judgment theme dominates chapters 1—39.[2] The assurance of salvation and the restoration of Zion unify the various oracles in chapters 40—66.[3]

We group the various oracles of Isaiah under the following themes:

Rebellion and Judgment
1:1—39:8
Redemption from Babylon
40:1—55:13
Universal Salvation
56:1—66:24

■ Rebellion and Judgment

Isaiah's book begins with a series of oracles that deal with the theme of God's judgment upon His covenant people who have rebelled against Him (chaps. 1—5). Though the people are sinful, the prophet announced God's willingness to remove the deep stains of their sins if they would repent and make a commitment to live a transformed life (1:10-20).

The eschatological hymn in 2:1-5 highlights the Gentiles' desire

to follow God's law. Nations will come to Zion to learn the law of the Lord (Torah), and this will lead them to unilateral disarmament and peaceful coexistence in the world. Zion, which will be judged for her sin, will be redeemed and purified, and she will once again become a refuge and shelter for the redeemed people of God (4:2-6). Through a parable, the prophet portrayed Judah and Israel as not worthy to be kept as God's vineyard. God's people who were to promote justice and righteousness were guilty of bloodshed, violence, greed, self-indulgence, materialism, perverted moral thinking, pride, and bribery (5:1-31).

Chapter 6 narrates the call of Isaiah to become a spokesperson for God. This call came during the critical year of King Uzziah's death (742 B.C.). Isaiah responded to the vision of God's holiness with a confession of his own sinfulness and unworthiness to stand before the holy and awesome God. This confession brought forgiveness from God, and Isaiah responded without hesitation to God's call for a messenger to speak His words. God warned Isaiah that though Judah would not respond to the mes-

Remnant

Isaiah often spoke about God preserving a remnant. In some texts, **the remnant** refers to those who are left in Jerusalem, whose names are recorded for life (4:2-6). Other passages describe the remnant as a penitent group that God would bring back to Jerusalem from their exile. The prophet gave his son the name Shear-Jashub ("a remnant shall return") to convey this message (7:3; 10:20-23; 11:11 ff.; 27:12-13).

Holiness of God

God's holiness is a dominant theme in Isaiah. God is the "holy One of Israel," a description found in the book about 26 times. Holiness is the very essence of God. Holiness means separation from sin. Holiness also involves the idea of God's judgment of sin. Holiness of God is also the hope of humanity. Isaiah's experience of forgiveness and cleansing from his sinfulness can be our experience also. The holy God calls us to "wash" and make ourselves "clean" from sin (1:16).

sage, he must continue to preach until the judgment comes. After the judgment, God would raise up a holy seed—a faithful community of people.

Chapters 7—12 probably belong to the early part of King Ahaz's reign. Ahaz was panic-stricken because of the Syrian-Israelite army in Jerusalem (7:1-2). The king refused to trust the prophetic word that God would not allow the enemy to overtake Judah. Nonetheless the prophet spoke to the king that a "young woman" will give birth to a son as a sign of the trustworthiness of God. This child's name, **Immanuel** ("God with us"), conveyed the promise of God's presence with His people even in the midst of their lack of trust in Him. The prophet also announced that Assyria will devastate the lands of Syria and Israel, and that Judah will go through painful and tragic days (vv. 10-17; v. 18—8:8).

The prophet maintained firm trust and hope in the God whom the people rejected. Though the nation dwelt in spiritual darkness and political bondage, he anticipated the arrival of light, joy, and the end of warfare through "a child" who would be God's gift to His people (8:9—9:7). The child will be called "Wonderful Counselor," "Mighty God," "Everlasting Father," and "Prince of Peace." The prophet also anticipated that a Davidic king ("a shoot . . . from the stump of Jesse"), a Spirit-filled ruler, will rule God's people with righteousness (11:1-9). The symbolic description of the wolf living with the lamb conveys the idea of a peaceful order of life in the messianic kingdom.

Isaiah's *oracles against the nations* focus on judgment upon Babylon, Assyria, Philistia, Moab, Syria, Egypt, and Edom (13:1—

Immanuel Oracle

The Immanuel oracle has significance to both the Old and the New Testaments. The identity of the "young woman" (*almah* in Hebrew; *parthenos* [meaning "virgin"] in the Septuagint) in Isaiah 7:14 is not known. Some scholars think that she was Ahaz's wife. Others think that Isaiah was speaking about his own wife. The Gospel writer Matthew related this oracle to the manner in which Jesus was born of a virgin (Matthew 1:23).

23:18). This theme of God's judgment of the world is continued in chapters 24—27. The prophet anticipated the defeat of all evil and God's gathering of His remnant from the four corners of the world as His new vineyard.

There are six woe oracles—pronouncements of doom and destruction—addressed to Ephraim/Israel in chapters 28—33. Mixed with these woe oracles are also words about God's intent to lay in Zion a cornerstone aligned with justice and righteousness. Zion will be established as a peaceful and quiet dwelling place for God's people (33:17-22).

Chapters 36—39 narrate the sequence of events that culminated in the prophetic word about the exile of Judah to Babylon. Assyria laid siege around Jerusalem during the reign of Hezekiah (around 701 B.C.), and Sennacherib, the Assyrian emperor, demanded Hezekiah to surrender to his army. During this crisis, Isaiah spoke about the deliverance of Jerusalem. The city escaped destruction in a miraculous way (37:1-38). God's intervention in the life of Hezekiah during his near-death illness is the story of chapter 38. In chapter 39, the prophet repudiates Hezekiah's unwise alliance with Babylon and warns about the coming exile of Judah to Babylon.

■ Redemption from Babylon

Now we turn to the second part of the book, which deals with the impending deliverance of Judah from Babylon and her return to Zion.

With a profound sense of urgency and deep conviction in the redemptive power of God, the prophet spoke to the exiled Jews

> **I   Messianic Kingdom**
>
> The coming Messiah and His messianic kingdom is the theme of 9:2-7 and 11:1-9. The prophet anticipated that the ideal Davidic ruler would truly represent God for His people. As Israel's history shows, human rulers from David's family failed to realize this hope. From our Christian perspective, we think that the full scope of this text is to be found in the kingship of Jesus the Son of David and the Son of God.

that God, like a gentle shepherd, would lead them on a highway back to their homeland (40:1-31). This redeemer God is none other than the Creator who is incomparable in power and majesty. The prophet saw in the historical events of the day (the rise of the Persian Empire and the impending doom of Babylon in the second half of the sixth century B.C.), the unfolding of God's salvation plan for His people. The Persian king Cyrus is God's "shepherd" and "anointed"; his commission from God is to free Judah from Babylon (44:28; 45:1, 13). The prophet described Israel's salvation from Babylon as one of the "new things" that God would create for His people (43:18-19; 48:6-8). Coming out of Babylon will be a new exodus experience, far more glorious than the old exodus from Egypt.

In Isaiah 40—55, we find the portrait of a **Servant of the Lord** in four different passages. The first passage presents the servant as an individual whom God has called and endowed with His Spirit to bring forth justice to all the earth (42:1-4). The mission of the servant is to be "a light to the nations" (v. 6, NRSV), to give sight to the blind and freedom to those in bondage (v. 7). The second Servant poem (49:1-6) describes the call of the Servant even before His birth. The mission of the Servant is twofold: to bring Israel back to God and to be a light to the nations. In the third Servant poem (50:4-9), the Servant is the model of trust and obedience to those who remain in darkness (see v. 10). His ministry is to speak words that would comfort the weary and afflicted. He is obedient to God's teaching though He is the object of opposition and attack by His enemies. In the fourth Servant poem (52:13—53:12), the focus is on the redemption that would come through the suffering of the Servant. The prophet portrayed the Servant as despised and rejected and wounded for the sins of humanity. Though He was innocent, He voluntarily submitted to suffering. However, His suffering fulfilled God's plan to bring healing and wholeness to

sinners. The Servant, through His obedience to God, opened the way for sinners to be counted as righteous by God. The Servant's ministry included intercession for the transgressions of humanity.

The prophet compared Israel in exile to a barren woman, a woman forsaken by her husband. Though God was angry with His people, He promised to love them with His everlasting love and maintain His "covenant of peace" with them (54:10). Moreover, His salvation is free to all who seek it (55:1). The good news in Isaiah 55:1 is that God does not attach a price tag to our salvation. Those who seek the Lord with repentance will find Him. God will fulfill His word and lead His exiled people in joy and peace to their homeland.

■ Universal Salvation

There is no unifying theme to the oracles in Isaiah 56—66. These chapters focus on worship and rituals, issues of justice and righteousness, restoration and rebuilding of Zion, God's kingdom, and the universality of salvation. Some scholars see here the work of several prophetic voices. However, salvation to all who are righteous—both the Jews and the Gentiles—seems to be a connecting link in these chapters.

The postexilic community most likely included people who were sinful, oppressive, and sectarian in their thinking (56:9-12; 57:1-21). They were, however, very religious and performed rituals to please God (58:1-5). The prophet announced that rituals do not please God. He blesses those who promote justice and righteousness and who are contrite and humble in their hearts. God's

I The Identity of the Servant

There are various views about the identity of the Servant in Isaiah's Servant poems. The eunuch's question to Philip the evangelist reflects the Jewish uncertainty over this matter in the first century A.D. (see Acts 8:26-40). Some scholars see the nation Israel as the Servant. In their thinking, Isaiah was speaking of the sufferings of the Jews in their long history as part of God's redemptive plan for the whole of humanity. Some even think of the holocaust in terms of its redemptive purpose. Others think that the prophet was speaking about himself. A third view, popular among evangelical Christians, is that the prophet was speaking about the suffering of the future Messiah—events that were fulfilled in the life of Jesus of Nazareth. Philip found in the story of the Servant "the good news about Jesus" (v. 35). The Church proclaims Jesus the crucified as God's Suffering Servant through whom He demonstrates His suffering love for humanity.

house is a "house of prayer for all nations" (54:7), even those who were once barred by the Law (vv. 4-8). The mark of true religion is not false piety or one's racial purity but commitment to bring wholeness to the society. However, along with social concerns, the community of faith must also honor God by their careful observance of the Sabbath (58:13-14).

The return of God's glory to Zion is a key theme in chapter 60. Darkness will be lifted and light will shine on God's people. Israel shall become the light to the nations. Zion "the City of the LORD" (v. 14) will be ruled by peace and righteousness. The walls of the city will be called "Salvation" and her gates "Praise" (v. 18). God will accomplish His plan in the time appointed for it to become a reality.

The poem in chapter 61 announces the mission of a Spirit-filled individual. Some regard this individual as the Servant in chapters 40—55. The mission of the Servant individual is to proclaim the good news of freedom and God's favor to all who are afflicted, brokenhearted, bound, and oppressed. His ministry is to restore justice and thereby usher in God's sovereign rule on earth. The ruined land will be rebuilt. Those who spent their days in mourning and weeping would rejoice with "everlasting joy" (v. 7). God would clothe them with garments of salvation and righteousness. All nations in the world will see the work of the Lord through His Servant.

The exiles who returned to their homeland were disillusioned because of their continued struggle for existence and ongoing strife and struggle within their community. They became cynical and skeptical about God's power to restore Zion and their community life. In chapter 62, the prophet speaks about the end to all the past and present conditions. God will come like a warrior with victory and salvation to His people (63:1-6). God's relationship with Israel will be like a marriage relationship in which God will rejoice over His bride. His bride will take up a new identity—new names that characterize God's passion and love for His people.

Isaiah 63:7—64:12 is a community lament. The prophet mediates for the people and appeals to God for mercy by recalling His past deeds of compassion. This section also includes the prophet's confession on behalf of the people who were unrighteous through and through. The lament ends with a passionate plea to God the Father and the Potter to restore His city and His people to wholeness.

The prophet announces in 65:17-23 that God's plan is to restore wholeness and well-being, characterized by joy, long life, prosperity, and peaceful coexistence for His creation. The true servants of God will inherit the land. God will create a new heaven and a new earth.

A Jewish worshiper prays at the Western or Wailing Wall in Jerusalem.

The Gospel in Isaiah

The ministry of Jesus focused on giving freedom to the oppressed and harassed, sight to the blind, hearing to the deaf, healing to the sick and the demon possessed—bringing wholeness (shalom) to humanity. He saw himself as the fulfillment of Isaiah 61:1-3 (see Luke 4:16-21). Through Christ, God pronounces total forgiveness and freedom—the jubilee year—to our broken world that is in turmoil, bondage, and despair. That's good news to us today.

This world will be not only a restored world but also a transformed world. Prophetic hope expressed here is not just idealism but rather a vision of a reality that only God can bring about.

The prophet reminds the postexilic community that God required from His people humility and contriteness and not their meaningless sacrifices (chap. 66). He will restore joy, comfort, and prosperity to Zion and bring the scattered Jews to their homeland. God's restoration includes the nations (the Gentiles). Isaiah's oracles end with the eternal destiny of the wicked in unquenchable fire.

Jesus' words about the eternal destiny of sinners echo Isaiah's final words (see Mark 9:42-50). Isaiah's book ends with an implicit challenge and invitation to choose life and not death and hell, where "worms" do not die and "fire" burns forever.

Summary Statements

- The canonical period of prophecy began with Amos in the mid-eighth century B.C.
- The prophets were both forthtellers and foretellers.
- Various parts of the Book of Isaiah address communities of faith that belonged to different historical settings.
- Judgment is the dominant theme in chapters 1—39.
- Chapters 40—66 focus on the theme of salvation.
- God is a holy God, and He is the Creator and the Redeemer of His people.
- The remnant, Zion, the Davidic Messiah, and the Servant of the Lord are important themes in Isaiah.
- Isaiah taught that there is an essential link between spirituality and social concerns.

Questions for Reflection

1. What lessons do we learn from Isaiah's encounter with God's holiness (chap. 6)?
2. Describe Isaiah's portrait of God. Give illustrations.
3. Describe the Servant in Isaiah and develop a philosophy of Christian life based on the Servant's model.
4. Discuss the significance of Isaiah's vision of universal salvation to the Church and its mission to the world.

Bible Study Assignment

Read Isaiah 40:1-11 and answer the following questions:

1. Discuss the scholarly perspectives on the historical, political, religious, and cultural setting of this passage (consult commentaries on this issue).
2. What is the literary and theological relationship of this text to chapter 39 and 40:12-31?
3. Outline the text based on the subthemes of this text.
4. Study the meaning of key words and phrases.
5. What is God's opening message to His people? How does comfort come to God's people?
6. What is the message conveyed by the imagery of a "highway" in the wilderness?
7. How does the prophet contrast humanity with God's word in verses 6-8? What is the goal of this contrast?
8. How does the prophet describe God and His salvation in verses 9-11? What imagery is used here to describe God's relationship with His people?
9. How did the New Testament writers interpret verses 3-4? What particular theological perspective did they introduce into this text?
10. Summarize the key theological lessons of this text.
11. How do you relate the theological lessons of this text to contemporary situations?

Resources for Further Study

Hanson, Paul D. *Isaiah 40—66: Interpretation.* Louisville, Ky.: John Knox Press, 1995.

Motyer, Alec J. *The Prophecy of Isaiah: An Introduction and Commentary.* Downers Grove, Ill.: InterVarsity Press, 1993.

Seitz, Christopher R. *Isaiah 1—39: Interpretation.* Louisville, Ky.: John Knox Press, 1993.

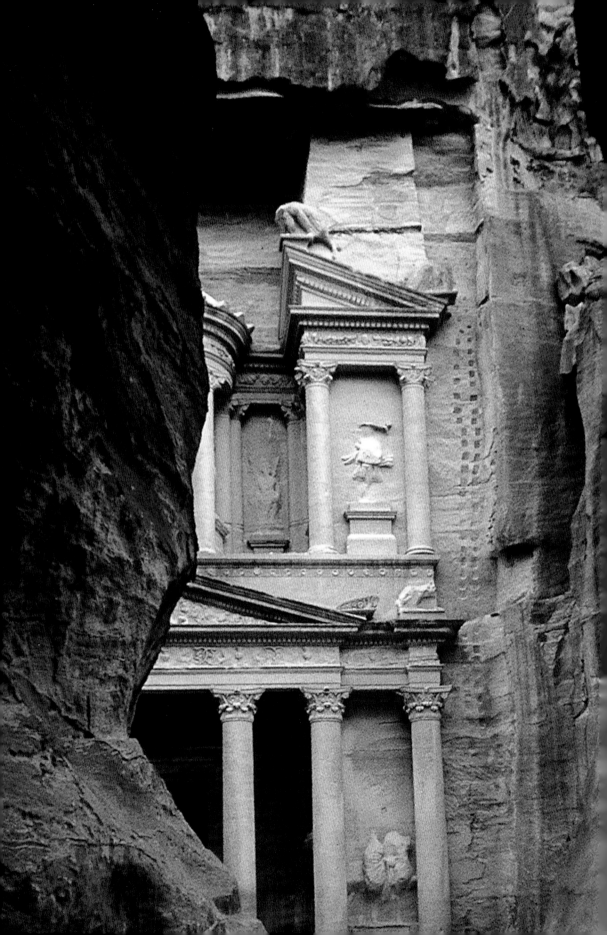

14 God's Spokespersons to the Community:
Jeremiah and Ezekiel

 **bjectives:**

Your study of this chapter should help you to:

- Summarize the historical setting of Jeremiah's ministry
- Discuss the major theological teaching of Jeremiah
- Identify the new covenant passage and discuss its significance to the message of the New Testament
- Summarize the historical setting of the ministry of Ezekiel
- Describe the key theological teachings of Ezekiel
- Relate the significance of Ezekiel's message to the New Testament

 ey Words to Understand

Josiah
Jehoiakim
Zedekiah
Babylon
Deuteronomic editors
Temple sermon
"Confessions"
Book of Consolation/Hope
New covenant
Son of man
Gog
Magog

uestions to consider as you read:

1. Often Jeremiah is referred to as a "weeping prophet." What does this label mean?

2. Why should a faithful preacher today agonize over the message of judgment?

3. Describe the feeling of displacement from home, church, and religious traditions that are important to you.

4. What would you say to a person who lives without any hope for the future?

The Book of Jeremiah

Jeremiah is one of the most passionate, outspoken, and courageous prophets in the Old Testament. It is likely that he belonged to a priestly family that descended from Abiathar, who was a high priest during the reign of David. He began his ministry in the 13th year of King **Josiah** (627 B.C.), and he prophesied during the days of Josiah, Jehoahaz, **Jehoiakim,** Jehoiachin, and **Zedekiah.**

Setting

Jeremiah's call came at a crucial time in Judah's history and world politics. Judah was under the rule of Josiah, a young king who was making plans to free the nation from Assyrian bondage. Five years after Jeremiah's call, Josiah (640-609 B.C.) began a religious reformation prompted by the discovery of the Book of the Law (2 Kings 22—23; 2 Chronicles 34—35). However, this reform did not produce any lasting change, except a resurgence of nationalism and spiritual pride. The political instability that followed Josiah's death (609 B.C.) serves as the background of much of Jeremiah's ministry. Judah's religious and political conditions deteriorated during the days of Jehoiakim and Zedekiah, and eventually the nation was destroyed by **Babylon.**

God showed Jeremiah a branch of almond blossoms to confirm the fulfillment of His word (Jeremiah 1:11).

Content

The Book of Jeremiah is not arranged in chronological order. In addition to numerous poetic oracles and prose sermons, the book also contains a number of historical and biographical accounts. Historical accounts parallel the accounts in 2 Kings. Jeremiah's prose sermons reflect the teachings of the Book of Deuteronomy. Some scholars attribute these sermons to the **Deuteronomic editors** of the book.

We give the following outline to the Book of Jeremiah:

Oracles of Judgment 1:1—29:32
Oracles of Hope   30:1—33:26
Historical and Biographical
    Accounts   34:1—45:5
Oracles Against the
    Nations   46:1—51:63
Historical Appendix   52:1-34

■ Oracles of Judgment

The book begins with an account of Jeremiah's call to be a prophet (1:4-10), followed by two vision accounts (vv. 11-12, 13-19) that authenticate the call. The call narrative shows that God called Jeremiah to be a prophet to the nations and consecrated him for that task while he was still in his mother's womb. Jeremiah's commission was to "to pluck up and to pull down, to destroy and to overthrow" the existing corrupt conditions and "to build and to plant" (v. 10) a new moral order in the world. The vision of the almond branch conveyed the assurance that God is watching over to fulfill His plan. The vision of the boiling pot conveyed God's plan to bring political disaster upon Judah because of the nation's wickedness.

Chapters 2—6 contain a collection of Jeremiah's oracles, all connected together with the theme of Israel's apostasy and God's response. Most commentators place these oracles in the early part of the prophet's ministry. Jeremiah describes Israel as a nation that has forsaken God, "the fountain of living water" (2:13, NRSV), and followed idols that have no worth. Israel is an adulterous nation; yet God is willing to take His unfaithful wife back to himself. The condition for the experience of God's mercy is repentance. Jeremiah returns to the theme of judgment in chapters 4—6. God's judgment will come through an enemy, a political nation from the "north." These chapters reflect the agony of the prophet who is heartbroken at the thought of the terrible destruction that is coming upon his nation. This judgment will affect the whole universe; chaos, darkness, and death will come upon the whole world because of the sins of God's people.

Jeremiah's **Temple sermon** (7:1—8:3, most likely preached in 609 B.C.; see 26:1) is a strong critique of Judah's false confidence in the indestructibility of the Temple. The people thought of the Temple as the sure guarantee of God's presence with them, even though murder, stealing, idolatry, and oppression of the poor characterized their lives. God's worshipers have made the Temple a "den of robbers" (7:11). The sermon ends with a warning of its destruction and the exile of the nation.

Chapters 8 and 9 contain Jeremiah's emotional appeal to the dying people of Judah to seek God, their "physician" and "balm

> **T**
> ## Repentance
>
> The only prerequisite to salvation is repentance. Repentance involves a complete turning away from sinful ways of life and a complete turning to God (3:12, 14, 19, 22; 4:1). Repentance unleashes God's healing power and brings wholeness to sinners who are incurably sick. Repentance cancels the death sentence upon us and prepares us to fully embrace God's grace that comes through Jesus Christ.

in Gilead" (8:12; see v. 4—9:3). God's refining judgment is coming upon His deceitful people, the outcome of which will be total devastation of the land. This is the destiny of all who are "uncircumcised in heart" (9:26), those who refuse to live on God's terms.

Judah's covenant breaking is a central theme in chapters 11—15. The curses of the covenant are already at work. Israel has broken the covenant with God; therefore, punishment is certain. This section also reveals the role of the prophet as an intercessor who confesses the nation's sin and seeks mercy and forgiveness from God. However, God reveals the finality of His decision; no one, not even Moses and Samuel, would be able to persuade God to change His mind.

God commanded Jeremiah not to marry and have the joy of normal family life, to symbolize the end of all joyous occasions in the land. God's judgment would send the people into captivity, but He would bring them back to their homeland (16:1-15). Idolatry is the clear evidence of the power of sin on the lives of God's people (17:1-4). The prophet compared the righteous in the land to a tree

God the Divine Potter

Jeremiah portrayed God as the divine Potter who comes to us with His sovereign free-dom of grace. The message at the potter's house shows that our ultimate destiny depends on the way we respond to God. Saying yes to God will lead to the fulfillment of His plans for our lives. Saying no, like Judah did (see Jeremiah 18:12), will only lead to death and destruction. Though God is our Potter, we also play a part in sealing our destiny by our pos-itive or negative response to God's will that is at work in our lives. The good news here is that sinners under God's judgment can hope in God's grace and mercy and receive a new lease on life through their repentance.

planted by water (vv. 5-8; see Psalm 1). He warned the wicked that God who sees their corrupt and wicked heart would bring them to judgment (Jeremiah 17:9-13). Using the illustration of the potter who reworked the spoiled clay into another vessel, Jeremiah proclaimed God's freedom to change His plans concerning Ju-dah and the nations (18:1-12). Sin-ful nations who are under the judgment of God would receive God's favor if they repent of their sin. Though Judah is God's chosen people, they stood under the threat of destruction because of their re-jection of God's plans for them.

Jeremiah performed a symbolic act of breaking a flask into pieces to show God's determination to destroy Jerusalem (19:1-13). The religious leaders who thought the Temple was an indestructible place arrested Jeremiah and put him in the stocks (v. 14—20:6).

We find a series of several com-plaints ("confessions") of Jeremi-ah in chapters 11—20. The first complaint is about the prosperity of the wicked (11:18—12:6). In the second complaint, he describes himself as a failure and asks if he could really trust God who seems to be deceptive in His dealings with him (15:10-21). In the third

complaint, the prophet appeals for protection from those who persecute him (17:14-18). In his fourth complaint, he seeks divine judgment against those who schemed to silence him (18:19-23; see v. 18). There are two com-plaints in chapter 20 (vv. 7-12, 14-18), the second of which is very much like Job's cry of despair (Job 3). Life has become unbear-able; so Jeremiah cursed the day of his birth.

Judah's ungodly kings, false prophets, and wicked priests are the subject of the oracles in Jere-miah 21—23. Oracles against the royal family hold the wicked kings of Judah accountable for the com-ing disaster of the nation. Jeremi-ah anticipated that God would es-tablish over the nation "a righteous Branch" (23:5) from the house of David who would initiate a new relationship between God and His people (see vv. 1-8).

The vision of the two baskets of figs describes the exile of 597 B.C. as God's way of preparing a fu-ture for Judah (24:1-10). God would restore, build, and plant the exiled community in their home-land. They would also receive from God the gift of an obedient heart and would enter into a new covenant relationship with Him.

Chapter 26 describes the consequence of Jeremiah's Temple sermon (see 7:1-15). The people were outraged that the prophet spoke about the destruction of the Temple. They demanded his death. During the trial that followed, some of the royal officials and certain elders spoke in favor of Jeremiah, citing Micah's speech about Zion's destruction nearly a century earlier. In the end, Jeremiah's life was spared.

Narratives in chapters 27—29 describe events that took place during the early part of Zedekiah's kingship (597-587 B.C.). The prophet appealed to Zedekiah to remain submissive to Babylon and not join in a rebellion led by the neighboring countries. He put yoke bars on his neck to symbolically convey the message that Judah's submission to the king of Babylon is God's will for the nation. However, Hananiah the false prophet discredited Jeremiah's words and broke the yoke bars with the announcement that God has broken the yoke of Babylon (chap. 28). Jeremiah later sent a letter (chap. 29) to the Judeans who were exiled to Babylon and instructed that community to live a normal life in the land of their captivity. God's plan is to bring them back to their homeland and to give them a future; but for that to become a reality, the exiled people must seek God with all their heart.

■ Oracles of Hope

Scholars label chapters 30—33 as the **Book of Consolation/Hope.** Various oracles in this section are connected together by the theme of Israel's restoration. God's offer of comfort will be realized in the future. Jeremiah thus spoke of Israel's restoration as an eschato-

logical (end time) event. God will restore Israel and the Davidic kingship. The covenant with God will be reestablished. God's love for Israel is everlasting, and He will build up the nation.

Jeremiah anticipated that God would establish a **new covenant** with Israel (31:31-34). The old covenant was broken. However, God would initiate a new covenant with Israel. The covenant is new in that God's law (Torah) will be written on human hearts. An added dimension of this new covenant is the promise that God would forgive and forget the sins of His people.

■ Historical and Biographical Accounts

Chapters 34—45 contain a number of historical and biographical events. Chapter 34 describes King Zedekiah and Judah as examples of covenant unfaithfulness and hypocritical religiosity. Chapter 35 contrasts the hypocrisy of Judah with the faithfulness of the Rechabites. King Jehoiakim's total disregard for God's word is the subject of chapter 36. This chapter identifies Baruch as the scribe who recorded the words that Jeremiah dictated to him. The king destroyed the first scroll, but Jeremiah dictated his words again to

---

T

The New Covenant

God fulfilled His promise of the new covenant through Jesus, His Son. The Lord's Supper reminds the Church of the "blood of the covenant, which is poured out for many" (Mark 14:24; see 1 Corinthians 11:25). The new covenant is a covenant of God's love, grace, and forgiveness. This covenant gives hope to our sinful world.

Baruch wrote the words of Jeremiah the prophet.

Baruch who prepared another scroll, to which many other oracles were added later.

Shortly before the fall of Jerusalem in 587 B.C., Jeremiah was arrested on charges of desertion to the enemy. While Jeremiah was in prison, Zedekiah secretly questioned him about God's plan for the nation. Jeremiah replied that the king himself would be a prisoner of Babylon. Jeremiah was later thrown into a cistern; but Ebed-Melech, an Ethiopian servant of the king, saved the prophet from death. He remained in the royal guardhouse until the Babylonian invasion (chaps. 37—38).

The account of the fall of Jerusalem to the army of Nebuchadnezzar (chap. 39) includes the tragic fate of Zedekiah. The Babylonians offered Jeremiah freedom and safe passage to Babylon; however, he opted to stay in Judah with the poor who were left in the land. Later a group of Judeans forced Jeremiah to go with them to Egypt. Jeremiah's last known oracles come from Egypt where he presumably lived until his death (43:8—44:30).

■ Oracles Against the Nations

Chapters 46—51 contain the prophetic word of judgment against Egypt, Philistia, Moab, Ammon, Edom, Damascus, Kedar and Hazor, Elam, and Babylon. The primary sin of these nations was their idolatry and refusal to acknowledge the God of Israel (50:17-18). God would bring His judgment upon these nations; however, they will also be restored when God fulfills His plan for the restoration of Israel.

Jeremiah's book ends with a summary of the destruction of Jerusalem and the exile of Judah (see the parallel account in 2 Kings 24:18—25:30), and a note about Jehoiachin's release from prison. This final note thus anticipates the freedom of the exiled nation. The ultimate goal of prophetic preaching is to announce God's grace and the hope of salvation to sinners. In that regard, this last chapter is a fitting conclusion to Jeremiah's book.

The Book of Ezekiel

Ezekiel was among the 10,000 Judeans who were taken to exile in Babylon in 597 B.C. by Nebuchadnezzar's army (2 Kings 24:14). He may have been a member of the influential Jerusalem priesthood. God called him to be a prophet in the fifth year of his captivity (593 B.C.). From 593 to 587 B.C., he prophesied God's judg-

T

God's Chariot Throne

Ezekiel's vision of God reflects a new theological perspective developed during the Babylonian exile. The traditional notion of God was that He dwelt in Jerusalem, confined to the boundaries of His Holy City. No wonder that this vision of God in a foreign land, in an unclean place, shocked and paralyzed Ezekiel, who was a member of the Jerusalem priesthood. God is dynamic, and His presence may be experienced regardless of who we are or where we live in the world today. Even though sin separates humanity from God's holy presence, the holy and gracious God visits sinners with the offer of salvation. This is the mystery of God's grace.

ment upon Judah and the coming exile of the nation. After the destruction of Jerusalem in 587 B.C., he began to speak about God's plan to restore His people back to their homeland. His last prophecy is dated to 571 B.C. (29:17).

Setting

Ezekiel's ministry took place during the darkest days of Judah's history. The events of 597 B.C. did not produce much change in the political, social, and religious life of the nation. Zedekiah proved to be an ineffective leader, and he succumbed to the political pressure to rebel against Babylon. The leaders gave false hopes to the people of Jerusalem about rebuilding the city. Idolatrous worship and pagan rituals continued even in the Temple precinct. Ezekiel's initial task was to address the stubborn and rebellious nation and warn them about the impending destruction of the city and the deportation of the people to Babylon (chaps. 1—24). The fall of Jerusalem in 587 B.C. is the setting of Ezekiel's oracles of restoration in chapters 33—48. During the latter part of his ministry, Ezekiel spiritually prepared the nation to anticipate their restoration and rebuilding of the city of Jerusalem.

Content

Some modern critical scholars have raised questions about the unity of the Book of Ezekiel. They think that there are many additions to the book by later editors. The book in its present form has a balanced structure, uniformity of style and language, and a clear chronological sequence. Except for the opening verses, the book is written in autobiographical style.

The following is a general outline of the major parts of Ezekiel's book:

Ezekiel's Call and
    Commission   1:1—3:27
Oracles of Judgment
    Against Judah   4:1—24:27
Oracles Against the Nations
        25:1—32:32
Oracles of Restoration
        33:1—48:35

I

Son of Man

God addressed Ezekiel over 90 times as **"son of man."** This term simply refers to Ezekiel as a mortal being, a part of humanity. In Daniel 7:13 and 8:17, this term designates a heavenly figure. In the intertestamental period, this designation became a messianic title. Jesus frequently used this title, perhaps to suggest both His human nature and His messianic role.

■ Ezekiel's Call and Commission

God's call came to Ezekiel through a supernatural vision. In the vision, Ezekiel saw God seated on His throne on a platform supported by four half human and half animal creatures. God's chariot moved in all directions without being confined to an earthbound route. Ezekiel could not adequately describe the majestic glory of God who was seated on His throne. He caught only a glimpse of the radiance and splendor of God. In shock, and in fear and awe, he fell on his face before God's holy presence.

God commissioned Ezekiel to speak to Judah, a rebellious and stubborn nation. He also demanded the prophet to demonstrate his obedience by eating a scroll that contained God's message to Judah. Ezekiel must first consume the message, digest it, and make it a part of his being. When he ate the scroll, God's word tasted like honey. Though God's demand was strange, obedience brought satisfaction and fulfillment to the prophet's life. Ezekiel's task was to be a watchman over Israel. He must warn the wicked to change their life, and challenge the righteous not to sin. Whether or not the people responded to God's word, Ezekiel must faithfully deliver the message.

■ Oracles of Judgment

Through various symbolic actions Ezekiel conveyed the fate of those who lived in Jerusalem (chaps. 4—5). The portrayal of the siege of the city with a diagram, paralysis that lasted for 430 days, eating unclean food, and shaving his head and beard all show the severity of God's judgment upon Judah.[1]

The mountains of Israel are judged in chapter 6 because they represent Judah's idolatry and unholy alliance with the Canaanite religion. Idolatry is seen at all levels of society, including the Temple. Judgment would bring an end to all evil and abominable practices of worship in Israel (chap. 7).

The visions in chapters 8—11 occurred in 591 B.C. The main message of the visions is the departure of God's glory from Jerusalem because of the abominations and idolatry in the city. The Spirit took Ezekiel from Babylon to Jerusalem in a supernatural vision, and there he found idols of Canaanite and Mesopotamian deities in the Temple. In the visions Ezekiel heard God commanding executioners to slay those who were idolaters. The slaughter of the guilty began in the sanctuary. Afterward, the city was purified by fire. Ezekiel was alarmed at the finality of God's word of judgment, and he ap-

God described Israel as sheep without a shepherd (Ezekiel 34:1-6).

pealed for God's mercy. God promised that He would restore the exiled people to their land and give them the gift of a new heart and a new spirit. The visions ended with the departure of the glory of God from the city. The glory of God stood on the mountain east of the city (Mount of Olives). God's departure made the city vulnerable and defenseless before the invading army of Babylon.

As instructed by God, Ezekiel prepared a baggage for his exile and dug a hole through the wall of his house and escaped at night (chap. 12). This action conveyed the message that in the same way, Judah would go into exile. Ezekiel announced that King Zedekiah himself would try to escape through the wall of Jerusalem, but he would be brought to Babylon and face his death there (see also Jeremiah 39:4-7).

Both Jeremiah and Ezekiel had to deal with false prophets who preached smooth words of peace and prosperity. The people believed such words and rejected God's true prophets. Ezekiel announced God's judgment upon all the false prophets, magicians, and diviners for their part in encouraging the wicked and disheartening the righteous in the land (chaps. 13—14).

Chapters 15—17 contain three parables that illustrate God's judgment and the future of Judah. Jerusalem has become like a vine in the forest, a worthless wood of the forest that will be destroyed (chap. 15). The second parable (chap. 16) summarizes the spiritual history of Jerusalem. The city, which God has chosen as His bride, has become unfaithful. The parable ends with the promise that God would again restore the city and enter into an everlasting covenant with her. The third parable (chap. 17) deals with King Zedekiah's rebellion against Babylon and its consequence. The narrative ends with the promise that God would place on the throne of David an ideal messianic ruler.

Chapter 18 affirms the truth that each individual is accountable to God. In a discourse in this chapter, the prophet responds to the criticism of the people that God is unjust in transferring the guilt of the parents to their chil-

Theology of Cleansing

The idea of divine cleansing is an important part of Ezekiel's understanding of restoration. According to the Mosaic Law, ritual cleansing from defilement was necessary to restore an individual's membership in the holy community of Israel (see Leviticus 14:52; Numbers 19:11-22). Ezekiel anticipated that God himself would cleanse His people by sprinkling clean water upon them. Holiness of God's people would no longer be determined by the cultic and ceremonial act done by the priests, but by God's own activity of cleansing. Moreover, he connected this cleansing with the gift of a new heart and a new spirit. The object of the divine cleansing is the human heart defiled with sinfulness and impurity. A clean heart has pure motives, a right attitude, and love for God and neighbor. Peter described the Pentecost experience as having "purified their hearts by faith" (Acts 15:9; see vv. 6-9; 2:1-4). God's gracious work in our lives includes not only our redemption from sin but also the cleansing of our hearts through the blood of Jesus Christ (Hebrews 9:13-14; 1 John 1:7-9). The Bible invites us to live a holy life by appropriating this gift through our faith in Jesus Christ.

"The bones came together . . . tendons and flesh appeared . . . and skin covered them" (Ezekiel 37:7-8).

Jehoahaz and Jehoiachin met their fate because of their wickedness. Zedekiah would soon be taken out of power and be exiled. None of these kings provided good leadership to Judah.

The theme of judgment continues in chapters 20—24. God's counsel is hidden from His people who have become sinners. God's sharpened sword of judgment is upon His people who have defiled themselves with idolatry throughout their history. Chapter 23 narrates the story of the idolatry of both Samaria and Jerusalem. These two sisters, Oholah in the north and Oholibah in the south, pursued the life of idolatry. God punished Samaria for her sins. Ezekiel warned the younger sister Judah, who did worse than the older sister, that she would suffer judgment by the hand of the Babylonians.

dren. He reminds his audience that the righteous would live and the wicked would die. God has no delight in the death of a sinner. This is the greatest truth in Ezekiel 18. An intentional commitment to break away from the world of sin is the key to the gift of life that God offers to sinners. God's will for His creation is life, not death (Ezekiel 18:32; see John 3:16).

Ezekiel's lament over the disastrous fate of the Judean kings Jehoahaz, Jehoiachin, and Zedekiah is the theme of chapter 19. Both

The allegory of a boiling pot and two woe oracles in chapter 24 convey the message of God's wrath upon the city. The content of this chapter is dated to January 15, 588 B.C., when Jerusalem came under the siege of the Babylonians. God is left with no other option but to burn and destroy the city that had so long rejected His offer of cleansing. As God had warned, Ezekiel's wife died to convey the message that God was about to hand His own pride and glory—the Temple—over to be destroyed by the Babylonians.

T A New Heart and a New Spirit

The promise of a new heart and a new spirit (see also Ezekiel 18:31; 36:26) is God's remedy for the sickness of sin that plagues humanity today. Our rebellion against God has its root in the sinful condition of our heart. A new heart means the end to our rebellious condition and the beginning of a life in conformity to God's Word. A new spirit means an attitude of loving obedience to God (Matthew 22:37; cf. Deuteronomy 6:5). God fulfills this promise now through His Holy Spirit who makes all things new in Christ (2 Corinthians 5:17).

■ Oracles Against the Foreign Nations

Ezekiel's judgment oracles against Israel's neighboring nations (chaps. 25—32) continue the pattern we have already noticed in Isaiah and Jeremiah. Tyre (26:1—28:19) and Egypt (29:1—32:32) receive more attention in Ezekiel's judgment speeches. Both nations were the symbols of wealth and glory in the ancient world. They boasted in their wealth and power. Ezekiel predicted that God would send Nebuchadnezzar, king of Babylon, to destroy Tyre and Egypt because of their pride and arrogance.

■ Oracles of Restoration

Jerusalem fell into the hands of the Babylonians in 587 B.C. In spite of Ezekiel's last-minute pleas and warnings, the citizens of Judah remained unrepentant and therefore the judgment came (chap. 33). The fall of Jerusalem directed Ezekiel to turn his attention to the future of Judah and God's plan for the restoration of His people and the rebuilding of the holy city. The restoration oracles begin with the portrait of God as the Good Shepherd who would come to seek and search for His flock (chap. 34).

God's people are scattered because of the corrupt and unfaithful shepherds of Israel (political and religious leaders). The prophet announced that God himself would come to gather His scattered sheep. He would rescue them and bring them to His good pasture. The people of God would dwell in peace and security in God's ideal kingdom filled with blessings and prosperity.

God's judgment came upon the people of Judah because they profaned His holy name through their idolatry. But God would gather them from the lands of their exile. He would act to restore the sanctity and credibility of His holy name. Ezekiel announced that God would make Israel clean from their uncleanness and give them a new heart and a new spirit (36:22-32). The covenant would be reestablished, and the people would live under blessed and prosperous conditions.

God assured Ezekiel of His power to fulfill the promise of restoration through a vision of a valley filled with dry bones (chap. 37). The bones that were dry and scattered meant no possibility of life again. However, God showed Ezekiel His power to bring life in the midst of death and destruction. This vision gave Israel the hope and confidence in their restoration from the Exile and the reemergence of their nationhood.

Chapters 38 and 39 are difficult to interpret primarily due to our lack of understanding of the iden-

A Jewish cemetery on the Mount of Olives. God promised Ezekiel that He would open up graves and give life to the dead (37:1-14).

I

Interpretation of Ezekiel 40—48

There is no consensus among Christians on the meaning and interpretation of Ezekiel 40—48. Did these visions already become a reality through the restoration of the exiled Jews back to their homeland and the Temple rebuilding? Some Christians think so. Some think that a literal fulfillment of these visions would take place with the second coming of Jesus Christ and the establishment of His kingdom. Some others think that these visions are being fulfilled in a spiritual sense in the life of the Church today. There are many other views on these chapters.

When we compare these chapters with Revelation 20—22, we find some parallels and also some key missing elements.[2] In Revelation, we do not find any of the earthly concerns of Ezekiel—the Temple, the priesthood, the sacrifices, and so forth. The visionary of Revelation saw the reality of the kingdom of God and God's ultimate rule from the perspective of his experience and religious traditions of the Early Church. Jesus' coming inaugurated a new era of God's activity in the history of humanity. The kingdom of God was established through the preaching of the gospel. The Church now waits in eager anticipation of the Second Coming and God's dwelling with His people forever.

tity of **Gog** and **Magog** and the many nations listed here as enemies of Israel. We do not know if these were nations that existed in the seventh and sixth centuries B.C. Revelation 20:8 also mentions these names. Perhaps these names symbolize all the evil powers in the world that are hostile to God's plans and purposes.

The setting of these chapters is the end time, and thus the oracles are eschatological in nature. The message is that in the end time, there would be a final battle between God and the evil forces in the world. God would defeat and destroy these forces that are antagonistic to His redeemed people.

The final chapters (chaps. 40—48) describe Ezekiel's visions of Israel beyond the days of her restoration and the defeat of her enemies. The first part of the visions contains elaborate details of the Temple, its courts, gates, chambers, and rules and regulations for various offerings and sacrifices. In the second part, Ezekiel deals with the boundaries of the land and the allotment of the land to various tribes of Israel. Significant to this section is the vision of a river that flows from the Temple that would bring productivity and life to the land. The visions end with the description of the city of Jerusalem and its 12 gates, each gate named after a tribe of Israel. The city would receive a new name, "THE LORD IS THERE" *(Yahweh Shamah)*.

Summary Statements

- Jeremiah prophesied during the final years of Judah's political existence.
- Jeremiah announced the Babylonian exile as God's judgment upon Judah.
- Jeremiah appealed to God's people to repent of their sins.
- Jeremiah anticipated God's new covenant with Israel.
- Ezekiel emphasized each individual's responsibility to live a righteous life.
- God promised to come as the Good Shepherd to restore Israel.
- God promised to give new life to the exiled nation, cleanse them, and give them a new heart and a new spirit.
- Ezekiel's end time teachings include the final defeat of God's enemies and the establishment of Jerusalem as the city of God.

Questions for Reflection

1. In what ways do we tend to forsake God today? What are the areas in our life where this is a crucial issue?
2. How do we maintain hope and courage in the midst of despair and hopelessness?
3. Ezekiel described Judah as a stubborn and rebellious nation. What are the areas in our personal lives where we show resistance to God's word?
4. Describe various ways in which we may experience God's life-giving power today.

Bible Study Assignmment

Read Jeremiah 2:4-13 and answer the following questions:
1. Consult a commentary to discover the possible historical, religious, and cultural setting of this text (approximate time when Jeremiah spoke this word).
2. What literary form does the prophet utilize to convey this word?
3. Outline this text based on its subthemes.
4. Discuss the meaning of key words and phrases in this text.
5. What are the charges that are brought against Israel in this text?
6. What are the past historical traditions of Israel that the prophet utilizes in this text to show God's faithfulness to His people?
7. What is the goal of the repeated question being asked in verses 6 and 8?
8. What is the theological function of verses 10-11?
9. What is the sin of Israel, according to verse 13?
10. Summarize the theological lessons of this text.
11. How do you relate the lessons of this text to contemporary situations?

Resources for Further Study

Fretheim, Terence E. *Jeremiah,* in *Smyth & Helwys Bible Commentary.* Macon, Ga.: Smyth & Helwys, 2002.

Taylor, John B. *Ezekiel: An Introduction and Commentary.* Downers Grove, Ill.: InterVarsity Press, 1969.

Thompson, J. A. *The Book of Jeremiah,* in *The New International Commentary on the Old Testament.* Grand Rapids: Eerdmans, 1980.

Weavers, John W. *Ezekiel,* in *The New Century Bible.* Grand Rapids: Eerdmans, 1969.

15 God's Spokespersons to the Community: Hosea, Joel, Amos, Obadiah, Jonah, and Micah

Objectives:

Your study of this chapter should help you to:

- Summarize the historical setting of the ministry of Hosea, Joel, Amos, Obadiah, Jonah, and Micah
- Describe the content of the Books of Hosea, Joel, Amos, Obadiah, Jonah, and Micah
- Describe the key theological teachings of Hosea, Joel, Amos, Obadiah, Jonah, and Micah

Key Words to Understand

Jeroboam II
Gomer
Jezreel
Lo-Ruhamah
Lo-Ammi
"The day of the LORD"
Bethel
Gilgal
Justice
Righteousness
Edomites
Sela
Nineveh
Bethlehem Ephrathah

Questions to consider as you read:

1. What is unconditional love?
2. Describe radical obedience.
3. What is the relationship of worship to common life?
4. What is the consequence of harboring hatred?

In addition to the Books of Isaiah, Jeremiah, and Ezekiel, the Prophets section of the Old Testament includes the books of 12 other prophets, commonly called the minor prophets. In the Hebrew tradition these books are collectively called the Book of the Twelve. In this chapter we will examine the message of the first 6 of these 12 prophets who have brought God's word to Israel at various times in the nation's history.

Hosea

Hosea's book is well known for its intense and passionate expressions of God's love, anger, agony, and despair. It is profound in theology and daring in approach to Israel's understanding of her covenant God.

Hosea's name (in Hebrew *hoshea*) means "salvation." Scholars think that he was a member of the Northern Kingdom of Israel. His oracles address the citizens of the Northern Kingdom, which he often refers to as Ephraim, the most prominent tribe in the north. The story of Hosea indicates that he was married and had three children, to whom he gave symbolic names to convey God's judgment upon Israel.

Setting

Hosea began his ministry perhaps around 750 B.C., during the reign of **Jeroboam II**, and continued until 722 B.C. This was a time of extreme political instability, the assassination of rulers, and unpredictable foreign policy in Israel. The nation also witnessed the breakdown of the social and economic structure. Baal worship was the popular form of religion in the land. The people regarded Baal as the provider of their agricultural productivity, flocks, and children. They offered sacrifices and took part in drunken and sexual orgies in order to benefit from Baal's procreative power. Even Israel's priests were guilty of promoting idolatry in the land.

Content

The Book of Hosea can be divided into the following parts:

Hosea, Gomer, and the Children	1:1—3:5
Sin and Judgment	4:1—11:11
Call to Repentance	12:1—14:9

The Book of Hosea begins with God's command to Hosea to marry a woman from a family of harlots. Hosea's marriage to **Gomer** may have been a way for God to speak to Israel through the prophet.[1] Gomer and her children are symbols of Israel's unfaithfulness to God and God's judgment upon His people who have broken the covenant with Him. **Jezreel** (God sows) conveys the message of the end of the political state of Israel. **Lo-Ruhamah** (not pitied) means God would not show pity to Israel. **Lo-Ammi** (not my people) symbolizes the end of God's covenant relationship with Israel.

Restoration and renewal of God's relationship with Israel is a key theme in chapters 2 and 3. God will punish Israel for claiming Baal as their provider; however, He will also restore them and enter into a new marriage relationship with them. Hosea's purchase of his estranged wife reiterates this theme. Though she had left him to go after other lovers, he purchased her and brought her to his home.

Chapters 4—11 contain numerous oracles, all connected with the theme of Israel's sin and God's judgment upon the nation.

This section begins with a lawsuit that charges the people with their failure to demonstrate faithfulness, covenant loyalty, and personal knowledge of God (4:1-3). The coming Assyrian invasion is evidence of God's withdrawal from His people who have forsaken Him. However, God would return to His people with compassion and grace if the people would seek Him and confess their guilt. What God desires from His people is not their rituals but permanence in their devotion to Him, covenant loyalty, and their commitment to know Him in a personal way (5:8—6:6).

Hosea portrays Israel as God's prodigal child in chapter 11. Though God raised His child with love and compassion, the child rebelled against the parent's love. The rebellious child deserves death; yet, God's compassion would not allow Him to hand His child over to destruction (see Deuteronomy 21:18-21). He is "God—the Holy One" among His people. Here we find the clearest expression of God's amazing grace to sinners who deserve nothing but death.

Hosea returns to the theme of repentance in chapters 12 and 14. Israel's hope for salvation rests on the nation's decision to seek God's favor just as their ancestor Jacob sought God at Bethel and later at Peniel. God's people must not only return to God (repent of their sins) but also make a commitment to love, do justice, and wait continually for God.

The oracles of Hosea end with one more appeal to Israel to return to God from their sinful ways of life (14:1-7). In a model prayer, Hosea acknowledges the guilt of the nation, recognizes the futility of seeking help from other nations and idols, and trusts in the mercy of God for the nation's salvation. The book concludes with the prophet's confidence that God's healing love and blessing would come upon His people. The final verse of the Book of Hosea is a wisdom statement. It is an exhortation to discern and walk according to God's ways. The righteous will find God's way as the source of life, whereas it will be a stumbling block to sinners.

Joel

The first Christian disciples saw in the events that took place on the Day of Pentecost the fulfillment of Joel's prophecy (Joel 2:28-32; Acts 2:17-21). The apostle Paul found in Joel's prophecy the promise of salvation to all who call on the name of the Lord (Joel 2:32; Romans 10:13).

Joel's identity is not clearly known. The name means "Yahweh is God." Since his oracles are

T
Hosea's God

Hosea described God as the loving and forgiving Husband, the compassionate and gracious Father, and the Healer of His people. These metaphors help us to discover the enormity of God's grace and His love for sinful humanity. The Gospel writer John captures the mystery of God's love in the statement, "For God so loved the world that he gave his one and only Son" (John 3:16). Here, then, lies the hope of a world that is estranged from God.

addressed to the people of Judah, it is generally assumed that he was a citizen of that nation.

Setting

The book also lacks any specific reference to the time of Joel's ministry. Scholars have proposed various dates for his ministry, ranging from the ninth century to mid-fourth century B.C. Though there are still advocates for a pre-exilic date for Joel, most scholars prefer to place this book in the postexilic period, somewhere between 500 and 350 B.C.

Content

The following is an outline of Joel's book:

The Day of the Lord   1:2—2:11
God's Response   2:12—3:21

Joel's book opens with an admonition to elders and all the people to preserve for the future generations the memory of the locust attack and a severe drought that devastated the land. Joel summoned the people to weep and wail over the ruin and destruction of crops, fruit, and pasture that the people and their livestock needed to sustain their life.

The locust plague gave the prophet the language and war imagery to describe the intensity of **"the day of the LORD,"** the day when God will bring His judgment upon those who oppose Him. No one can endure that dreadful day because God himself will be the commander of His army.

The second section of the book begins with God's summons to Judah to return to Him with their whole heart, with fasting, weeping, and mourning (2:12). God would respond to the repentance of His people by restoring the blessings of the land. He would also pour out His Spirit upon all people. Though the day of the Lord is a day of judgment, all who call upon His name will be saved from the wrath and judgment of God.

The final chapter in the Book of Joel contains several oracles of judgment against the nations in "the valley of Jehoshaphat," also called "the valley of decision" (vv. 2, 14). These are symbolic names that refer to the reality of God's final judgment of the wicked. God would sit in judgment against the nations. He would reclaim Jerusalem as His holy dwelling place. God's people would experience His blessings and forgiveness.

Amos

Scholars think that Amos was the first canonical prophet of Israel. In the 20th century, this book became a primary biblical resource for the advocates of justice and righteousness in our

T   The Promise of the Spirit

Our repentance with broken and contrite heart is necessary for the experience of spiritual blessings from God. The promise of the Spirit's outpouring is a reality today. The Spirit came upon the early Christians on the Day of Pentecost. The Spirit continues to come to our lives, not only to transform us but also to equip us to become His spokespersons in our day. Joel reminds us to live in newness of life through Christ and in the power of the Holy Spirit as we wait for the Second Coming.

world. Today, we hear even secular leaders citing Amos's passionate call for social justice: "But let justice roll down like waters, and righteousness like an ever-flowing stream" (5:24, NRSV).

The book contains only two brief references about Amos's personal background (1:1; 7:14-15). He was a shepherd and farmer from Tekoa, a village about 12 miles southeast of Jerusalem. Though he was a citizen of the Southern Kingdom, God called him to be a prophet to Israel, the Northern Kingdom.

Setting

Amos's ministry took place during the reign of Uzziah, king of Judah (783-742 B.C.), and Jeroboam II, king of Israel (786-742 B.C.). The book also refers to a more precise date for Amos—"two years before the earthquake" (1:1; see also Zechariah 14:5). Scholars connect this with a massive earthquake that destroyed Hazor around 760 B.C. Amos's ministry is thus dated to 763/762 B.C. We do not know the length of his ministry. It is possible that his ministry lasted only for a year.[2]

Amos came to the Northern Kingdom when the nation was at the height of its military and economic prosperity under Jeroboam II (2 Kings 14:23-29). Amos's oracles reflect the fact that the economic prosperity did not benefit the poor in the land. The rich who maintained winter and summer houses and houses of ivory lived a hedonistic life without any concern for the plight of the poor. The poor were traded as commodities and were the victims of economic exploitation, sexual abuse, legal and judicial corruption, and miscarriage of justice. Though oppres-

Amos was a shepherd before he became a prophet.

sion and violence were rampant in the land, there was also a revival of interest in religious festivals and rituals. **Bethel** and **Gilgal** were centers of idolatry that promoted false worship and false confidence in the presence of God with them. Amos's words were thus addressed to a people who failed to see any relationship between worship and the common life.

Content

Amos's book can be divided into the following parts:

Oracles of Judgment   1:3—9:10
Rebuilding and
    Restoration   9:11-15

The opening oracle announces the judgment theme, which dominates the entire book (1:2). This is followed by a series of oracles against Israel's neighbors—Syria, Philistia, Phoenicia, Edom, Ammon, Moab, and Judah (v. 3—2:5). The sin of the nations except Judah is their war crimes and ruthless and inhumane treatment of Israel. In these oracles, Amos portrays God as sovereign Judge of all humanity. Mistreatment and violent actions directed toward others are subject to God's judgment. Judah has rejected the instructions (Torah) of the Lord and therefore God's judgment is upon that nation.

Justice and Righteousness

The concern for **justice** (mishpat) and **righteousness** (sedaqah) is a key theme in the Book of Amos. We do "justice" when we fulfill our covenantal obligations to others. "Justice" is the fruit of our right relationship with others. Amos reminds us that our life should show evidence of our "hunger and thirst" for justice and righteousness. Jesus was a true friend of the marginal and the outcast people of His day. When justice and righteousness flow like an ever-flowing stream in our community life, then we would have met the preconditions for acceptable worship (5:24; see Matthew 5:6).

Beginning with 2:6, Amos focuses on the sins of Israel, which included slavery, oppression, sexual immorality, injustice, total disregard for the poor, and corrupt and idolatrous worship. The oppression of the poor by the rich is a recurring theme in Amos. The prophet gave ominous words of destruction to a people who trusted in their sacred sanctuaries for their salvation. Their future depended on their commitment to "seek the LORD" and "seek good, not evil" (5:6, 14).

The day of the Lord will come, not to bring salvation but judgment upon Israel. This will be a day of darkness and not light for Israel (vv. 18-20). The prophet instructed the religious community of Israel that was preoccupied with rituals and religious performances to "let justice roll on like a river, righteousness like a never-failing stream" (v. 24). Justice and righteousness are the necessary requirements for worship that is acceptable and pleasing to God.

The visions of the plague of locust, fire, the plumb line, basket of summer fruit, and the sanctuary continue the theme of the coming judgment (7:1-9; 8:1-2; 9:1-4). Neither in heaven nor in the depths of the earth will sinners find a place of escape from God's judgment.

Though Amos's oracles for the most part focus on judgment, the book ends with hope for the future. The promise of the book is that beyond judgment, there would be Israel's rebuilding, restoration, and return to the days of prosperity and blessing from God.

Obadiah

The Book of Obadiah is the shortest book in the Old Testament. The name Obadiah (meaning "the servant of the Lord") and its related forms are found a number of times in the Old Testament. The book gives us no reference to Obadiah's family or vocational background.

Setting

Lack of clear reference to any historical event makes it difficult to place Obadiah's book in a specific setting. Some scholars have proposed an early date in the ninth century B.C. based on the account of Edom's rebellion against Judah (see 2 Kings 8:20-22). There are others who place the book in the mid-fifth century B.C., during the Edomite occupation of the Negev.[3] Most scholars think that verses 11-14 refer to the Babylonian invasion of Judah and Jerusalem. That would place the book around 587 B.C. or immediately thereafter.

The pride and arrogance of the **Edomites**, descendants of Esau, is a key theme in this book. They lived in the area south of the Dead Sea, a region surrounded by deserts and mountains. The Old Testament frequently refers to the hostility between the Edomites and the Israelites, which continued throughout the history of both nations.

Content

Obadiah's oracle against Edom is preserved in one chapter. The author introduces the content of the book as "the vision of Obadiah."

The mountainous surrounding of **Sela** (means "rock" in Hebrew), the capital of Edom, provided the city the safety and shelter of a fortress. This led to the Edomites' prideful thinking that they were unassailable and inaccessible to invading armies. This little book announces God's plan to bring them down and humiliate them with utter destruction.

Obadiah describes Edom's ongoing hatred for Israel as its primary sin. When the enemy invaded Jerusalem, the Edomites joined with the enemies to plunder and destroy the city. Therefore, God will punish the Edomites with the same destruction they inflicted upon Judah. But "the day of the LORD" against Edom will be a day of salvation for Judah and Israel. The book ends with the confident hope that the kingdom of the Lord will ultimately be established in the world.

Jonah

Did Jonah spend three days and three nights in the belly of the fish? Readers of this unique book often get entangled in the debate over the literalness of Jonah's story. We invite you to hear the message of the book, rather than be concerned with the historicity of certain details in the book that we cannot prove or disprove with certainty.

Setting

The book lacks reference to any event that would help us to place Jonah in a particular time in history. The opening statement (1:1) identifies Jonah as the son of Amittai. Second Kings 14:25 refers to Jonah son of Amittai, a prophet from Gath Hepher, who prophesied about the restoration of the border of Israel during the reign of Jeroboam II. This would place Jonah somewhere between 786 and 746 B.C. Scholars have assigned various dates for the writing of the book, ranging from the eighth century to the third century B.C.[4] The book assumes the existence of **Nineveh** as a great and wicked city. The Babylonians destroyed Nineveh, the capital of Assyria, in 612 B.C. Jonah's ministry seems to have taken place before the rise of

The Nabatean rock city Petra, which most scholars identify as the location of Sela, one of the centers of the Edomites (Obadiah 3).

Assyria as a powerful empire under Tiglath-pileser III in the latter part of the eighth century B.C.

Content

The story of Jonah is like a drama with the following scenes:

Scene 1: Jonah Disobeys
God   1:1-16
Scene 2: Jonah in the
Belly of the Fish   1:17—2:10
Scene 3: Jonah's Goes
to Nineveh   3:1-10
Scene 4: Jonah's Anger and
God's Response   4:1-11

In scene 1, Jonah takes a ship to Tarshish in an attempt to escape from the presence of God who commanded him to preach to the Ninevites. A storm at sea prompts the sailors to look for the culprit responsible for this calamity. Jonah acknowledges his guilt and the sailors throw him overboard at his request to save their lives.

In scene 2, a great fish swallows up Jonah. We cannot speculate on the zoological identification of the fish; neither can we discard the narrative as fiction. Jesus described this event as a "sign" to His unbelieving audience (Matthew 12:38-40). In the belly of the fish, Jonah offers a thanksgiving prayer for God's deliverance of his life. He pledges to fulfill the vow he had taken in response to God's salvation. The fish vomits him after three days and three nights.

In scene 3 God commands Jonah a second time to go to Nineveh with His word of judgment against that wicked city. Jonah obeys the command; though it would have taken him three days to travel through the entire city, he travels only a day's journey to deliver his message. The whole city, however, responds to the message and shows signs of repentance. God cancels His judgment and saves the city.

In scene 4, we find an angry prophet who is upset about the salvation of the Ninevites. He goes outside the city and waits for God's judgment to come upon the city. God provides for Jonah a vine that gives shade to Jonah from the intense heat of the day. However, a worm eats the plant and Jonah is angry again because of the destruction of the vine. The scene closes with God's speech to Jonah in which He asks if He should not show concern for the

Joppa, the port city from which Jonah sailed to Tarshish (1:3).

Jonah's Silence

The story of Jonah ends with God's question to Jonah for which Jonah does not give an answer. Jonah received God's compassionate grace, but he failed to recognize others in the world as deserving the same grace. He was not moved by the marvelous work of God's grace. He was angry and then preoccupied himself with the things that brought comfort to him. When God asked the great question, there was silence—no angry words, no attempt to run away, but a cold silence.

The Book of Jonah invites us to free ourselves from our narrow worldview and prejudicial thinking and embrace the gospel of Jesus Christ as a gospel for all humanity. "When he [Jesus] saw the crowds, he had compassion on them" (Matthew 9:36). Ministering God's compassionate grace to our sinful world is the only way to break Jonah's silence.

people of Nineveh. The book ends without an answer from Jonah to God's question.

Micah

Except for the name Micah of Moresheth (1:1), we know very little about the person of the prophet. His name means "Who is like Yahweh?" He came from a town called Moresheth, about 25 miles southwest of Jerusalem. Micah identifies himself as a prophet "filled with power, with the Spirit of the LORD" (3:8), whom God called to declare to Israel her sin and transgression.

There is no consensus on the authorship of the oracles found in the book. The book in its final form is attributed to Micah of Moresheth. However, some scholars think most of chapters 4—7 belong to a later period, perhaps late exilic and postexilic period.

Setting

The title statement (1:1) indicates that Micah prophesied during the days of Jotham, Ahaz, and Hezekiah, kings of Judah. This would place his ministry sometime between 742 and 687 B.C. Jeremiah 26:17-19 places his ministry in the days of Hezekiah. Various oracles in the book indicate that Micah prophesied at a time when there was corruption, oppression of the poor, abuse of power, false piety, and false confidence in the indestructibility of Jerusalem. Micah shares in this book the same social and religious concerns of other eighth-century prophets (Amos, Hosea, and Isaiah).

Contents

Micah's book has the following parts:

Judgment and Restoration	1:2—5:15
God's Requirement	6:1-16
Micah's Faith	7:1-20

Micah's oracles begin with an announcement about God's coming to judge all humanity, which would produce a terrible and devastating effect upon the earth. The whole earth will suffer the consequence of the idolatry of Samaria and Jerusalem. When disaster comes, the powerful in the land who oppressed and defrauded their powerless victims would be deprived of their wealth. They will be exiled from the land. Shame and disgrace will

God's Great Requirement

Our daily walk with God is more important to God than our attempt to make things right with Him through certain religious rituals. Micah invites us to live a life appropriate for God's people. Justice, fairness, equity, covenant loyalty, and faithfulness are important qualities of the Christian life. Life lived in this world should also become a daily walk with God with humility and gratitude. When we live out these qualities, we will find freedom from the nagging questions of our self-worth, the merits of our deeds, and our capacity to save ourselves through our work. The outcome would be trust and reliance on God's forgiving and saving grace.

be the fate of the prophets who gave false hope to the nation.

The mark of a true prophet is his courage to preach God's word that his listeners do not want to hear. Micah demonstrates himself as a Spirit-filled preacher of God's word (3:8). We see him as a courageous prophet, unafraid of opposition, and bold in proclaiming the sinfulness of the leaders of the nation. His word about the desolation of Zion would have shocked those who maintained false confidence in God's commitment to protect His holy city (vv. 9-12).

Micah's oracles also reflect the prophet's hope in the restoration of Zion. Micah 4:1-3 is also found in Isaiah 2:2-4. God will restore Zion, and the nations will come to Zion seeking God's instruction (Torah). A ruler from a little, in-

significant town called **Bethlehem Ephrathah** will bring peace to God's people (5:2-4).

In chapter 6, we find a lawsuit (legal dispute) that God brings against Israel. Micah presents the mountains as the witness of this controversy between God and Israel. God the plaintiff wants to know how and why He has become a burden to His people. Defendant Israel responds with a sarcastic question, asking what it would take to please God. At this point in the lawsuit, the prophet announces God's requirement. What God requires from His people is justice, kindness, and a humble walk with God (v. 8). The lawsuit ends with the announcement of the utter ruin of Israel.

The last chapter of the book contains the prophet's expression of grief and sorrow over the sinful condition he witnessed among his people. This chapter also contains the hope of the prophet. Jerusalem, though fallen, will rise again. God will bring her out of her dark days into light to show His justice before the nations. Micah concludes his oracles with an affirmation of his faith in God as an incomparable God, forgiving and compassionate, the God who casts the sins of His people "into the depths of the sea" (7:19).

These ruins of an ancient city in Israel remind us of Micah's words of judgment, "Zion will be plowed like a field" (3:12).

Summary Statements

- Hosea described God as a forgiving Husband and a loving Father.
- Joel anticipated the spiritual restoration of Israel and the outpouring of God's Spirit on all people.
- Amos called for social justice as the prerequisite for God's acceptance of Israel's worship.
- Obadiah believed that God would ultimately establish His kingdom and bring an end to hatred and pride in the world.
- God's compassion for the sinful world is a key theme in Jonah.
- Micah proclaimed Zion's judgment and restoration and the coming of a ruler from Bethlehem.
- Micah summed up worship as doing justice, loving kindness, and walking humbly with God.

Questions for Reflection

1. Describe God's love, based on Hosea's book.
2. What does "calling upon God's name" mean, and what blessings does God bestow on those who call upon His name?
3. Give a list of the major human atrocities in our world in the last 50 years and discuss what Amos may be saying to us about judgment, justice, and righteousness.
4. What does Obadiah say to us about our unforgiving attitude to others?
5. Compare and contrast worship during Micah's time and our present-day worship. What will Micah say about the contemporary forms of Christian worship?

Bible Study Assignment

Read Amos 5:21-24 and answer the following questions:
1. What is the historical, political, social, and religious setting of this text?
2. Outline this text based on its subthemes.
3. Identify the key words and phrases that help us discover the meaning of this text.
4. Why do you think Amos describes rituals as displeasing to God? What parallels do you find between worship in this text and worship today?
5. What is the theological meaning of justice and righteousness in the Old Testament?
6. What does Amos convey through the use of imagery in verse 24?
7. What is the key theological truth of this text?
8. Based on this text, define worship.
9. How do you relate the theology of this text to our contemporary context?

Resources for Further Study

Limburg, James. *Hosea-Micah,* in *Interpretation: A Bible Commentary for Teaching and Preaching.* Louisville, Ky.: John Knox Press, 1988.

Mays, James L. *Hosea,* in *The Old Testament Library.* Philadelphia: Westminster Press, 1969.

_____. *Amos,* in *The Old Testament Library.* Philadelphia: Westminster Press, 1969.

_____. *Micah: A Commentary,* in *The Old Testament Library.* Philadelphia: Westminster Press, 1976.

16 God's Spokespersons to the Community:
Nahum, Habakkuk, Zephaniah, Haggai, Zechariah, and Malachi

Objectives:

Your study of this chapter should help you to:

- Summarize the historical setting of the ministry of Nahum, Habakkuk, Zephaniah, Haggai, Zechariah, and Malachi
- Describe the content of the books of Nahum, Habakkuk, Zephaniah, Haggai, Zechariah, and Malachi
- Discuss the major theological teachings of Nahum, Habakkuk, Zephaniah, Haggai, Zechariah, and Malachi

Key Words to Understand

Ashurbanipal
Nabopolassar
Babylonians
Theophany
Darius the Great
Zerubbabel
Joshua
Apocalyptic
"The LORD of hosts"
The Messiah
"Burden"
Imagined disputation

Questions to consider as you read:

1. What is your attitude toward those who belong to other races or religious and denominational backgrounds?
2. How do you worship God?
3. Why do people show a great deal of interest in building churches?
4. How does one regain a sense of passion for God when religious activities become boring?

Nahum

Jonah's book presents God's compassion and mercy to the people of Nineveh, who repented when they heard the message about their judgment. In Nahum's book, we see another portrait of Nineveh and God's response to cruelty and violence in the world.

The identity of Nahum is not clearly known. The name means "consolation" or "comforter." The prophet is called the Elkoshite. The exact location of Elkosh is not known.[1] Some scholars identify Elkosh with the original site of Capernaum (which means "the village of Nahum"), located on the northwest corner of the Sea of Galilee. The message of the book offers comfort to Judah. This has led many scholars to think that Nahum was from Judah.

Setting

The message of the book, which is a prediction about the impending doom of Nineveh, leads us to think that Nahum gave his oracle during the Assyrian domination of Judah (3:18). Assyria's power declined after **Ashurbanipal**'s death (627 B.C.). The Neo-Babylonian Empire emerged as a major player in international politics under **Nabopolassar** (626-605 B.C.). Nineveh, the object of Nahum's judgment speeches, was destroyed by the combined forces of Babylonians, Medes, and Scythians in 612 B.C. Nahum's oracle against Nineveh belongs to this period of sharp turns of events in history. We may date his ministry to sometime between 663 B.C. and 612 B.C.

Content

The Book of Nahum can be divided into the following sections:

God's Wrath	1:2-15
Get Ready for Battle	2:1-13
Woe to the City of Blood	3:1-19

The book begins with an announcement about God's power as the Creator to carry out His wrath against those who plot evil against Him. He will destroy Nineveh without leaving anyone to carry on its name. However, the faithful can depend on the faithfulness of God. Judah will be delivered from the oppressor. Chapter 1 ends with a summons to the citizens of Judah to look and see "the feet of one who brings good news, who proclaims peace" to them (1:15).

God will send an invading army to destroy Nineveh. Though the Ninevites will put forth their best effort, the invaders will plunder the city and exile the people. The strength of Assyria will be broken because God is against that nation (2:11-13).

Chapter 3 continues the theme of Nineveh's destruction. The city known for its bloodshed and plunder will be filled with dead bodies. God will reveal its shame and filth. The city will be in ruins, and no one will mourn for it. The troops of

The ruins of a 4th century A.D. synagogue in Capernaum. Capernaum (known as Kaphar Nahum, meaning the "village of Nahum") may have been the place of Nahum's birth or ministry.

> ## T God and Nineveh
>
> We find in Nahum a sharp change in God's dealing with Nineveh. The compassionate God of the Book of Jonah is portrayed here as a God of wrath and vengeance. His plan is to wipe out Nineveh from the face of the earth. Nineveh stands for the violent people in the world. God will deal with them according to His ways of judgment. But He will be a refuge to those who suffer violence and evil at the hands of God's enemies. This is the comfort Nahum proclaims to us today.

Nineveh will be helpless and powerless to protect the city from the impending siege. The book ends with a message to Assyria's king that he will suffer a fatal injury.

Habakkuk

This little book has been a source of inspiration for millions of believers. Many have found in the courageous faith of Habakkuk a challenge to go on trusting God in the midst of severe adversities and trials of life (see 3:17-19). The prophet's words, "the righteous will live by his faith," became the cornerstone for the apostle Paul's teaching on justification by faith (Habakkuk 2:4; Romans 1:17; Galatians 3:11).

The book contains no information on the personal background of Habakkuk. His name appears in 1:1 and 3:1. In both texts he is identified by the title "prophet." His name is also found in the Akkadian language for a garden plant. This prompted some scholars to think that he was a non-Israelite who had adopted the Jewish faith.[2] It is likely that he was a citizen of Judah.

Setting

The book lacks specific references to events or persons. The opening verses indicate a widespread growth of wickedness and violence and a total breakdown of law and justice in the land (1:1-4). The phrase "I am raising up the Babylonians" (v. 6) helps us place the book at the end of the seventh century or in the early part of the sixth century B.C. Most scholars think that the **Babylonians** refer to the powerful Neo-Babylonian Empire, which gained control of the Syria-Palestine region around 604 B.C. Like his contemporary Jeremiah, the prophet Habakkuk saw the Babylonian invasion as God's judgment against Judah.

Content

The Book of Habakkuk can be divided into the following parts:

Habakkuk's Complaint	1:1—2:4
Woe to the Oppressor	2:5-20
Habakkuk's Prayer	3:1-19

> ## T Habakkuk's Triumphant Faith
>
> Habakkuk was determined to live a triumphant life though evil continued to increase in his world. His resolve was not just to hang in there somehow but rather to live an active, meaningful, and productive life. He knew that God would faithfully carry out His plans. Living a faithful life through uncertain and difficult times is a mark of righteousness in relationship with God. Centuries later Paul quoted Habakkuk: "The righteous will live by faith" (Romans 1:17).

Habakkuk's book begins with the prophet's passionate complaint against the growth of violence and wickedness in the world in which he lived. There is no law and justice in the land. God answers the prophet that He is "raising up the Babylonians," a ruthless and violent people, as the instrument of His judgment. This answer only adds more frustration to the prophet. Why would a holy and morally pure God use a wicked nation to punish His people, who are more righteous than their enemy? The prophet takes his stand like a watchman and waits for God's answer to come. God responds with the assurance that justice will come at its appointed time. In the meantime, Habakkuk must model

righteousness by waiting for the fulfillment of God's word and by being faithful to God.

Chapter 2 contains a series of woe oracles that contain words of judgment against the wicked Babylonians (vv. 6-20). The last chapter is for the most part an elaborate description of God's appearance **(theophany)**. Some scholars view this chapter as an apocalyptic hymn added by the later editors of the book.[3] We regard this chapter as Habakkuk's own composition to give the book a fitting conclusion.[4] The book ends with a powerful expression of the prophet's triumphant faith and joy in the midst of uncertain times. The enemy is about to viciously rampage Habakkuk's country and destroy everything he would need for his survival; but he will rejoice and praise the God of his salvation (3:17-19).

Zephaniah

The identity of Zephaniah is not clearly known. Some scholars identify him as a member of the royal family by tracing his ancestry to King Hezekiah (see 1:1). His father's name, Cushi, means "Ethiopian," which also suggests an African heritage to the prophet. The Book of Jeremiah mentions a priest by the name Zephaniah on several occasions (Jeremiah 21:1; 29:25, 29; 37:3; 52:24) as an important person and a messenger of King Zedekiah to Jeremiah. This has led some scholars to identify this priest as Zephaniah the prophet.[5]

Setting

The opening verse (1:1) indicates that Zephaniah prophesied

A watchtower. Habakkuk said he would stand and watch for God's word to come (2:1).

during the reign of Josiah king of Judah (640-609 B.C.). The precise date of Zephaniah's prophetic ministry is not known. Zephaniah's oracle against Assyria's capital Nineveh indicates that he prophesied before the fall of Nineveh in 612 B.C.[6] Zephaniah may have been a contemporary of Jeremiah, who began his ministry in 627 B.C.

Content

The following is an outline of the Book of Zephaniah:

The Day of the Lord	1:1—2:3
Oracles Against the Nations	2:4-15
Against Jerusalem	3:1-8
Salvation to All	3:9-20

The opening oracle (1:2-3) focuses on the theme of God's judgment of everything on the entire earth. Everything on earth will be swept away by God's judgment. The language here indicates the reversal of the creative acts of Genesis 1. This is followed by a number of oracles of judgment against the wicked and idolatrous people of Judah and Jerusalem, all connected together with the theme of the "day of the LORD" (1:7; see v. 4—2:3). This day will be "the day of the LORD's sacrifice" (1:8). The idolatrous people will be the Lord's sacrificial victims. He concludes this section with a summons to the "humble of the land" (2:3) to seek God.

Verses 4-15 contain Zephaniah's oracles against the foreign nations. Philistia, Moab, Ammon, Cush, and Assyria will be judged because of their hostility toward God and His people of Judah.

In chapter 3, Zephaniah labels Jerusalem a city of oppression, rebellion, and defilement, a city

> ## Universality of Salvation
>
> God's plan of salvation is for all of humanity. Long ago, He promised to Abraham that through his family, all the families of the earth would receive a blessing (Genesis 12:3). This universality of salvation is an important theme in all the prophets. The promise of salvation includes the promise of His cleansing us from all defilement that would keep us from worshiping God with all our heart, soul, and strength.

where there is no evidence of covenant relationship with God (vv. 1-8). The inhabitants of the city and the leadership have failed to recognize God's justice at work among them. Therefore, God will destroy not only Judah but also the nations, because the people of God have become like the people of the world. Zephaniah concludes his oracles with the promise that God will "purify the lips of the peoples" (v. 9) and enable them to call upon His name (vv. 9-20). Here we find the hope that the nations that were once the object of God's wrath will receive God's favor and salvation. This eschatological day will also be the day of Israel's salvation. God will defeat Israel's enemies and bring His exiled people to their homeland.

Haggai

The book does not give any details on Haggai except his identity as a prophet. Jewish tradition holds that he had lived in exile in Babylon and was an old man when he spoke the words of this book. The name Haggai means "my feast." He may have been born during one of Israel's annual festivals. His interest in the Temple rebuilding suggests that he may have belonged to a priestly family.

Haggai dates his messages specifically to the second year of the reign of **Darius the Great,** king of Persia. According to the modern calendar, he gave the oracles between August 29 and December 18, 520 B.C. Though Haggai's recorded ministry lasted less than four months, we assume that he may have spoken other oracles, in addition to those recorded in the book.

Setting

The Jewish exiles who returned home from Babylon laid the foundation of the Temple amid great celebration and optimism (538 B.C.). Soon, however, political opposition and poor economic conditions prompted the Jews to discontinue the Temple rebuilding. The people also became busy with

building their own homes. The foundation of the Temple remained untouched for about 18 years.

The second year of Darius the Great (520 B.C.) was the beginning of a new era of prosperity and stability in the Persian Empire. Haggai perhaps saw the prospect of this period as a great opportunity for his fellow Jews to complete the Temple rebuilding.

Content

Haggai's oracles are addressed to **Zerubbabel** the governor and **Joshua** the high priest. They are predominantly motivational and encouragement speeches. His message can be outlined as follows:

First Message and Response	1:1-15
Second Message	2:1-9
Third and Fourth Messages	2:10-23

The first message challenges people to ponder their present situation and reevaluate their priorities. The prophet reminds the people that their current economic condition is the result of not putting God first. The ruined Temple is a reminder of the people's lack of priority for God. The message ends with a summons to honor God by returning to the Temple rebuilding program. The following narrative deals with the positive response of the leaders and people and the resumption of the Temple rebuilding.

The second message contains more encouraging words to those who were overwhelmed with the task of rebuilding the Temple. The Jewish exiles lacked sufficient resources to rebuild the Temple to its former glorious condition. Haggai concludes this message

Rebuilding the Temple was a primary concern of Haggai and Zechariah.

with the promise that the glory of the Temple they were building would someday outstrip the glory of Solomon's Temple.

The Temple in ruins had defiled the land, and it remained unproductive. The third message contains the promise of God's blessing of the land and crops as reward for resuming the Temple rebuilding. In the final message addressed to Zerubbabel (vv. 20-23), Haggai affirms the messianic hope of Israel. He announces Zerubbabel, a descendant of David, as God's chosen one to usher in a new era of His sovereign rule. This concluding message thus anticipates the restoration of the Davidic throne to its rightful heir. Christians see the fulfillment of this hope in the coming of Jesus the Messiah.

Zechariah

Zechariah was a contemporary of Haggai. While Haggai provided the initial motivation for building the Temple, Zechariah was responsible for follow-up. His messages supplied the encouragement needed to continue the project. Zechariah's name ("the LORD remembers") is a common name in the Bible. Over 20 different people bore this name, including kings of Israel. The book identifies him as "son of Berekiah, the son of Iddo" (1:1, 7). According to Nehemiah 12:4, a priest named Iddo returned to Jerusalem with Zerubbabel. This person may have been Zechariah's grandfather. Zechariah's priestly perspectives are obvious throughout the book. Also, his message shows his indebtedness to the prophetic tradition, especially to the interests and images of the Book of Ezekiel.

Setting

Based on the dates mentioned in the book (1:1, 7; 7:1) we believe that Zechariah was active during 520-518 B.C., when the Temple rebuilding was resumed by the Jews. The messages of Zechariah 1—8 belong to the Temple reconstruction period. We do not know how long he carried out his ministry. It is very likely that he continued his ministry for several years after the Temple's completion in 515 B.C.

The historical setting for Zechariah 9—14 cannot be easily determined. These chapters do not contain specific dates for the messages. Their content and vocabulary are markedly different from chapters 1—8. Chapters 9—14 (known as Second Zechariah) also show some resemblance to **apocalyptic** writings. These issues have led scholars to question the unity of the book and to propose various authors and dates for Zechariah 9—14. In spite of the lack of dates, vocabulary differences, and apocalyptic lan-

Yahweh Zebaoth

Haggai, Zechariah, and Malachi show a marked preference for the divine name Yahweh Zebaoth **("the LORD of hosts").** Of the 237 occurrences in the Prophets, these prophets punctuate their prophecies 91 times with the term.

The name emphasizes God's power and sovereignty in the world and His heavenly and earthly resources to accomplish His purpose. The prophets used the appellative to remind their audience that God was able to handle any and all situations. Though the sovereignty of God might be questioned because Israel had been humbled by foreign powers, the prophets declared that God was still in control of His world.

guage, chapters 9—14 show strong thematic and structural continuity with chapters 1—8. The book comes to us as a cohesive literary unit. For lack of compelling evidence otherwise, it seems reasonable to treat chapters 9—14 as part of Zechariah's work.

Content

Zechariah's message can be outlined as follows:

Call to Repentance	1:1-6
Eight Visions	1:7—6:8
A Symbolic Act	6:9-15
Joy of the Messianic Age	7:1—8:23
Triumph of the Messianic Age	9:1—14:21

The book begins with a reminder of the sins of the past generations to motivate the present generation to repent and return to God. The opening speech is followed by a series of eight visions. These visions describe the main features of the messianic age. The first vision (1:7-17) depicts horses that patrolled the earth, which affirms God's sovereignty over His world. The second and third visions (vv. 18-21 and 2:1-13) focus on judgment upon enemies of God's people and God's plan to dwell in Zion. Visions four and five (3:1-10 and 4:1-14) emphasize God's provision and empower-

ment of leadership. These visions present Joshua and Zerubbabel as representatives of the ideal agent of salvation, the messiah. These visions also affirm that God would raise up His servant, "the Branch." God would accomplish His purpose not through the power and might of human beings but by His Spirit. The sixth and seventh visions (5:1-4 and vv. 5-11) focus on God's war on sin. The final vision of horses roaming the earth (6:1-8) again affirms God's sovereign rule over His world.

The visions are followed by a symbolic act in which Zechariah makes a crown and places it on the head of the high priest Joshua (vv. 9-15). The crowning of Joshua symbolically represents the merging of the political and spiritual roles in the coming messiah.

Chapters 7—8 are a collection of messages that signal the joy that accompanies the new age. Zechariah affirms God's care for His people and His presence with them in Jerusalem. In the coming age, nations would express their desire to be joined with the Jews to worship God in Jerusalem.

Zechariah 9—14 takes us beyond the Temple building project. These chapters expand upon the picture of God's kingdom designs introduced in the first eight chapters. Through apocalyptic lan-

The Messiah

Zechariah's portrait of **the Messiah** blends concepts found in other prophets. The Messiah will be a conquering Branch from the Davidic line who also will perform priestly roles as a servant. He will come humbly and in peace and lead His people as a good shepherd. He also will suffer rejection before His ultimate triumph. Such a portrait accords well with the life of Jesus. It is not hard to see why early Christians turned to the Book of Zechariah in order to understand their Savior.

guage and imageries, the prophet describes here the painful struggles and ultimate triumph of the messianic kingdom. These chapters contain two evenly balanced sections of material: chapters 9—11 and chapters 12—14. Each section is introduced as a **"burden"** or "oracle" (Hebrew *massa'*). This term indicates the sense of obligation the prophet felt when a message from God must be delivered.

The first "burden" begins by asserting God's ultimate conquest of Israel's enemies and the preservation of the Temple. Then God's messiah would arrive to establish his kingdom and consolidate the victory. God, the good shepherd who will bring unity and other blessing to His people, will care for the new kingdom. The people would reject the compassion of the shepherd. As a result, judgment will come upon them.

The focus of the second "burden" (chapters 13—14) is on the final messianic kingdom of God. In the final days, God would conquer the nations and protect Jerusalem. God promised an outpouring of His Spirit of grace for His people as they mourn and receive forgiveness for rejecting Him. This section ends with a vision of God's ultimate rule over all the earth. In the messianic age, everyone and everything will be sacred unto God and all nations will worship the Lord as King.

Malachi

Malachi is the final book of the writing prophets. It serves as an appropriate conclusion to prophetic literature. It recalls once more, in its own unique way, many of the main themes found in other prophetic books.

I Difficulty of Interpreting Zechariah's Images

Many of Zechariah's images leave the interpreter uncertain about specific historical setting and meaning. Some of the difficulties include identification of the horsemen, the horns and the craftsmen (chap. 1), and the seven eyes on a stone (3:9). Also, particularly illusive is the interpretation of the three shepherds and the worthless shepherd in chapter 11.

In chapter 4, in one of the most significant visions of the book, the reader is hard-pressed to determine the relationship of the various images. How the two olive trees relate to the seven-channel lampstand is unclear in light of the message of the passage. God is the source of power for His projects (v. 6), yet the olive trees that supply oil to the lamp are Joshua and Zerubbabel (v. 14).

This is the nature of eschatological (end time) material. Often the authors are not so much interested in locating each image in time and space. They are painting pictures of realities to come without reference to historical setting. They move freely between present and future without clearly signaling transitions. Present experiences pale in significance to future hopes in such literature. This is clearly the case in Zechariah.

We know very little about Malachi. No family lineage is given and no historical events or political leaders are identified in the book. He is not mentioned elsewhere in the Old Testament.

The name Malachi means "my messenger." It is not a typical Hebrew name. Some have suggested that it is simply a general appellative and not a proper name. They feel it should be understood the same as when the word occurs in 3:1. There, "my messenger" identifies the person who will prepare the way for the coming of the Lord. Yet, the form of 1:1 is typical of introductions to prophetic books. We consider Malachi as the prophet's proper name.

The Golden Gate, also known as the East Gate of Jerusalem.

Setting

The setting for the ministry of Malachi appears to be very similar to that of Ezra and Nehemiah, around the middle of the 5th century B.C. Whether Malachi preceded Ezra and Nehemiah, followed them, or worked alongside of them is difficult to determine. We think his ministry took place around 460 B.C., just prior to the arrival of Ezra.

Members of the Jewish restoration community had grown lax in their worship and practice. The book suggests that the community was faced with issues such as poor spiritual leadership, marriage and divorce practices, injustice, tithing, serving God, among other things. Malachi's audience possessed a feeling of hopelessness. Their efforts at religious practice seemed futile to them.

Content

Malachi employs a rhetorical device that may be called **imagined disputation**. This feature, which was employed at times by other prophets, projects an argumentative dialogue between God and the people. The typical pattern is as follows: (1) God states His issue with the people, (2) the people respond with a question, and (3) God responds with a message of challenge.

The book consists of a series of six imagined disputes dealing with different, yet related, issues in the life of the community. They are:

Dispute over the Lord's Love	1:1-5
Dispute over Poor Spiritual Leadership	1:6—2:9
Dispute over Breaking Faith	2:10-16
Dispute over Justice in the Land	2:17—3:5
Dispute over Tithes and Offerings	3:6-12
Dispute over Futile Worship	3:13—4:6

The first dispute is over God's love for Israel. Malachi responds to the people's question about God's love with an illustration from the past, showing how His election of Jacob is an act of His love. Israel is still the object of God's love and care. The future that God promises to Jacob's descendants is a display of His love.

In the second dispute, Malachi charges Judah's spiritual leaders with the responsibility for corrupt and substandard worship practices. He challenges the priests and the Levites to honor God so He may be honored among the nations in the world.

In the dispute over breaking faith, Malachi deals with the problem of marriage and divorce in the land. He deplores the practice of men marrying women who worshiped pagan gods and divorcing their Jewish wives with whom they had made a marriage covenant. He emphatically states that God hates such unfaithfulness. God's people must be people of integrity and fidelity in their most important relationships of life.

In the dispute over justice, Malachi declares that God would establish justice in the land. The Messiah would come and bring justice. He would judge everyone like a "refiner's fire" that separates pollutants from pure silver. The New Testament writers describe John the Baptist as "the messenger" who would prepare the way for the coming of the Lord (3:1; see Matthew 11:10; Mark 1:2; Luke 7:27).

In the dispute over tithes and offerings, Malachi describes the act of withholding tithe as robbing God. The giving of tithes and offerings is a tangible evidence of one's repentance and return to God. Malachi sees a close relationship between giving to God and blessing in life. Blessing would follow our attentiveness to God.

The final dispute is about the people's sense of hopelessness in serving God. Malachi responds with a challenge to lift their eyes beyond the present circumstances to a future day when justice would be served. Evildoers will be consumed in God's fire of judgment, while those who fear and honor God will know the protecting power of "the sun of righteousness" rising "with healing in its wings" (4:2). This day would not come unannounced. God promised to send Elijah to prepare for its coming. The New Testament writers identified this forerunner as John the Baptist (Matthew 11:14; 17:12; Mark 9:11-13; Luke 1:17).

Malachi as the Final Book in the Old Testament

Malachi serves as a fitting conclusion to the Prophets with its emphasis on the role of the prophet as a messenger of God. He sums up the key emphases of the other prophets.

Malachi and other prophets of the Old Testament still speak to us and remind us of our responsibility to God who has made a covenant with us through Jesus Christ. God's love for us is an indisputable fact. He is intensely interested in the way we maintain our fidelity to Him, the way we worship Him, the way we honor Him through our devotion to Him. He desires from us integrity in our relationship with others. The restoration of relationship with God, which is a key theme in Malachi and other prophets, is now a possibility for us through our faith in Jesus Christ. This is the "good news" that awaits us in the New Testament.

Summary Statements

- Nahum proclaimed God's judgment upon Nineveh and salvation to Judah.
- Habakkuk, though he complained to God about the growth of wickedness, maintained faith and joy even in the midst of the difficult realities of life.
- Zephaniah announced God's judgment on all who are wicked, but salvation and cleansing to those who seek Him.
- Haggai emphasized that building the Temple would be a sign of putting God first.
- Zechariah told the people that they were participating in the messianic age by building the Temple and that God would supply all the resources they needed to do it.
- Zechariah anticipated the ultimate triumph of God over evil in the messianic age.
- Malachi challenged people to honor God and be faithful in their relationship with Him.
- Malachi announced the coming of a messenger to prepare the way for the Lord.

Questions for Reflection

1. Do we have the right to bring judgment upon those who are God's enemies? Explain your answer.
2. What should a Christian do in a world that seems to be overtaken by the power of violence and wickedness? Illustrate your answer using Habakkuk's life.
3. Why does building a temple for God show we are putting Him first in our lives?
4. How does a vision of the messianic age help us deal with the everyday tasks of life?
5. Why is honoring God so important to our spiritual well-being?

Bible Study Assignment

Read Habakkuk 3:17-19 and answer the following questions:

1. What is the historical, cultural, and religious setting of this text? (Read chapters 1 and 2.)
2. Based on your reading of chapters 1 and 2, what do you think is the key issue that Habakkuk wrestled with in his life? What question remained unanswered for him?
3. What are the key words in the passage that help us discover the meaning of this text?
4. What are the conditions that Habakkuk describes in verse 17 that would make life unbearable and difficult?
5. What is his resolution that he declares in verse 18?
6. What is Habakkuk's understanding of God, reflected in verse 19?
7. What is the key theological lesson of this text?
8. Based on this text, attempt to define faith.
9. How do you relate the truth of this lesson to your personal life?

Resources for Further Study

Baldwin, Joyce G. *Haggai, Zechariah, Malachi: An Introduction and Commentary,* in *Tyndale Old Testament Commentaries.* Downers Grove, Ill.: InterVarsity Press, 1972.

Bennett, Robert A. *The Book of Zephaniah: Introduction, Commentary, and Reflections,* in vol. 7 of *The New Interpreter's Bible.* Nashville: Abingdon Press, 1996.

March, Eugene W. *The Book of Haggai: Introduction, Commentary, and Reflections,* in vol. 7 of *The New Interpreter's Bible.* Nashville: Abingdon Press, 1996.

Ollenburger, Ben C. *The Book of Zechariah: Introduction, Commentary, and Reflections,* in vol. 7 of *The New Interpreter's Bible.* Nashville: Abingdon Press, 1996.

17 Apocalyptic Visions of the Community:
Daniel

Objectives:

Your study of this chapter should help you to:
- Describe the nature of apocalyptic literature and how to approach it
- Understand the main messages of the Book of Daniel
- Become familiar with the major events of the Greek period in Judah

Key Words to Understand

Apocalyptic
Darius
Cyrus
Nebuchadnezzar
Nabonidus
Belshazzar
Maccabean revolt
Antiochus Epiphanes IV
Daniel
Hasmonean Kingdom
Maccabees
Alexander the Great

Questions to consider as you read:

1. What fears and concerns do believers have about a hostile culture?
2. Where is human history headed?
3. Who really controls the affairs of nations?

Daniel is unique among the books of the Old Testament. Though the book is found among the Prophets in the English Old Testament, scholars usually classify it as an apocalyptic writing. The Hebrew Bible placed this book in the Writings section, thus separating it from the prophetic literature.

What is apocalyptic writing all about? The term **apocalyptic** comes from the Greek word *apokalypsis,* which means "revelation" or "unveiling." Apocalyptic writings focused upon revealing the future, especially the end of human history. Typical features of this literature include: (1) symbolic language and surreal images, (2) visions of the future that are guided by angels, (3) strong contrast between the present evil age and the future good age, (4) prediction of a climactic intervention of God in human history, (5) authorship falsely ascribed to a famous person, and (6) history written as if it were prophecy.

In the Old Testament, apocalyptic language is found in Isaiah 24—27, Ezekiel 38—40, and Zechariah 9—14. Scholars label Daniel and Revelation as apocalyptic books in the Bible. Both Jews and Christians produced a number of other apocalyptic writings between the third century B.C. and second century A.D. These books did not become part of canonical Scripture.

Scholars think that apocalyptic writings emerged in the context of intense religious persecution, which produced hopelessness and despair among the believers. The evil in the world seemed to overtake the faithful. These writings aim to give hope and courage to the oppressed, and convey to them the reality of God's ultimate victory over evil. The emphasis of such literature is clear. Salvation is coming. God remains in charge and will bring an end to evil in this world. He will rescue His saints and create a new kingdom on earth. Apocalyptic writings not only offer hope but also challenge the believers to remain faithful to God during crisis.

Historical Difficulties in Daniel

Some scholars have questioned the historical accuracy of Daniel, especially in regards to the Babylonian and Persian Empire. Each of these alleged inaccuracies, however, has a viable answer.

Daniel 5:31 mentions **Darius** the Mede as the one who conquered Babylon. Other sources name **Cyrus** the Persian as Babylon's conqueror. Some scholars suggest that the name Darius the Mede is a special throne name for Cyrus. In fact 6:28 could be accurately translated "Daniel prospered during the reign of Darius, that is the reign of Cyrus the Persian."

Another historical difficulty is **Nebuchadnezzar**'s madness in 4:32-33. This seems to fit better with what we know of one of his successors, **Nabonidus.** However, a period of 30 years is missing from the chronicles of Nebuchadnezzar's reign; so we do not know all the details of his life. It is believed that he suffered a severe illness just before his death.

In the past, many scholars assumed that the mention of **Belshazzar** as ruler of Babylon in chapter 5 was inaccurate. Babylonian records showed that Nabonidus was the last ruler of the empire. But now scholars recognize that Belshazzar was indeed coregent with his father Nabonidus. Further, Nabonidus absented himself from Babylon for over 10 years and left the kingdom in his son's hands. Belshazzar was the ruler of Babylon at the time of its fall.

Setting

Scholars continue to debate the date of the writing of Daniel. Some view it as a product of the sixth century B.C.; others think that the book belongs to the second century B.C.

Those who see it as a second-century document believe it was written around 165 B.C. to encourage the Jews during the **Maccabean revolt.** They note the increasing focus of the book upon this era and the appropriateness of many of its key themes for people living during that time. Chapter 11 provides great detail on the reign of **Antiochus Epiphanes IV.** By contrast, some details in the Babylonian and Persian periods appear fuzzy or perhaps even inaccurate.

The assumption of this above view is that the Book of Daniel is named after a great hero of the Jewish faith. Those who follow this view describe its content more as historical accounts than predictions. Scholars also think that the writer of this genre of literature stood in the ancient prophetic tradition that viewed God's establishment of His sovereign rule in the world. In the final analysis, the writer preserves and supports the theological convictions of his predecessors, the great prophets of Israel.

Those who support a sixth century B.C. date affirm that Daniel's prophecies are genuine predictions of the Persian and Greek Empires and beyond. The themes and messages of the book speak not only to the sixth-century period but also to the Jewish community of the Persian and the Greek period.

Dreams in the Ancient World

People of the ancient world took dreams very seriously. They understood them to be one way the gods communicated with people. Egyptians, Assyrians, Babylonians, and Greeks had specially trained experts in the art of dream interpretation. These experts served, much like Daniel, as professional advisers for kings. Some of their writings included instructions for interpreting dreams, dietary regulations for dreaming, and records of "fulfilled" dreams.[1]

Dreams are mentioned numerous times throughout the Bible. Those who heard God's message while dreaming included Jacob (Genesis 28:12-15), Solomon (1 Kings 3:5-15), prophets (Jeremiah 23:25-28), Joseph (Matthew 1:20; 2:13, 19, 22), the magi at Jesus' birth (2:12), Pilate's wife (27:19), and Paul (Acts 16:9; 18:9; 23:11; 27:23-24).

The two great interpreters of dreams in the Bible were Joseph and Daniel. Joseph interpreted dreams for his friends in prison and for Pharaoh (Genesis 40:5-22; 41:1-38). Daniel was called upon to interpret two dreams of Nebuchadnezzar (Daniel 2:1-47; 4:1-19). In both cases the interpretations served to bring honor for God.

Daniel the Hero

Daniel (meaning "God is my judge") was the younger contemporary of Jeremiah and Ezekiel. He was a young man when the Babylonians took control of the region of Judah in 605 B.C. The Babylonians took him along with other promising youth to serve the kingdom of Babylon. They gave him the Babylonian name Belteshazzar (meaning "protect his life").

Daniel possessed the gift of interpreting dreams and carried a reputation for exceptional wisdom. He held high-level positions in Babylon, including head of the wise men of Babylon (2:48) and the third highest ruler in the Babylonian Empire (5:29). Later he became one of the top three adminis-

Daniel deciphers God's handwriting on the wall.

7:28. We do not know why the author dropped Hebrew and picked up Aramaic as the language to continue the narrative in this section. The stories of this section reflect a Babylonian historical context. So it is likely that the author used Aramaic, the language of Babylon, to give authenticity to these stories.

■ Stories of Daniel

The first six chapters consist of selected stories from the life of Daniel and his friends. These are hero stories, but their purpose is not to lift up Daniel. Their aim, rather, is to emphasize God's control over the affairs of humanity. The primary message is clear: God is sovereign over the world; therefore His people can risk remaining faithful to Him.

These stories have a common pattern. Each moves from some sort of test to a divine deliverance. Three stories (see chapters 1, 3, and 6) focus on a test of faith. Biblical values and beliefs are confronted by a hostile culture. The other three stories (see chapters 2, 4, and 5) deal with a test of interpretation. Daniel is challenged to explain what God revealed to him through dreams and signs.

Chapters 1, 3, and 6 give three examples of those who had courage to maintain convictions in the midst of major tests to faith. In these stories, Daniel and his friends were confronted with a threat of severe consequences for holding on to their beliefs. If they did not compromise, the consequence was rejection from the royal court (chap. 1), death in a fiery furnace (chap. 3), or death in a den of lions (chap. 6). In each case they chose to remain faithful and trust God. They refused to

trators in the Persian Empire (6:2). That means he witnessed some of the major shifts in the political history of the ancient Near East—the rise and fall of Babylon and the emergence of Persia. The last date given in the book is "the third year of Cyrus king of Persia" or about 535 B.C. (10:1). He would have been well over 70 years old when he served the Persians.

Content

The Book of Daniel consists of the following two parts:

Stories of Daniel   1:1—6:28
Visions of Daniel   7:1—12:13

Both sections progress historically, from the earliest date to the latest. A uniqueness of the books is the Aramaic section in 2:4—

defile themselves by eating meat from the king's table, by bowing to an idol, or by ceasing to pray to their God.

Their conviction was rewarded. God rescued His faithful servants and revealed His unique power. The end result was that the most powerful kings on earth acknowledged the sovereignty of Israel's God. The Persian king confessed: "He is the living God, enduring forever. His kingdom shall never be destroyed, and his dominion has no end" (6:26, NRSV).

The truth of this statement is the key theme of chapter 2. Nebuchadnezzar dreamed of a large statue made of four metals. Daniel interpreted the dream by the power of God (2:27-28). Four kingdoms would arise on earth but none of them would survive. By contrast, God's kingdom "will never be destroyed, nor will it be left to another people" (v. 44). The precise identification of these four kingdoms is not the main issue. The point is that human kingdoms will not last, but God's kingdom will. Chapter 7 picks up this imagery and theme again.

Chapters 4 and 5 make the same point as chapter 2. They contain two stories about two prideful kings who are humbled before Israel's God. Both kings received divine messages that needed interpretation. Nebuchadnezzar had a dream (chap. 4), and Belshazzar saw handwriting on a wall (chap. 5). Daniel deciphered both messages, which foretold the humbling of these kings. The final outcome was the fulfillment of the prediction and an affirmation of God's sovereignty. The power of earthly kings ceased when God ordained it.

■ Daniel's Visions

The final six chapters of Daniel report four visions of the prophet. They are arranged in chronological order with an increasing focus on the details of the Greek Empire. They tend to stress the same themes as the earlier stories.

Chapter 7 gives a vision that Daniel saw in a dream during the first year of Belshazzar (550 B.C.), the year in which Cyrus the Persian began his revolt against the Median Empire. Daniel saw four beasts rise up out of the sea and the throne of God set up for judgment.

Nebuchadnezzar

Nebuchadnezzar was Babylon's most prominent and powerful monarch, reigning from 605 to 562 B.C. He was the son of the founder of the Babylonian Empire, Nabopolassar. He married Amytis, the daughter of the king of the Medes. His successes as a general in the Babylonian army prepared him to ascend the throne at his father's death. He continued to expand the Babylonian Empire over his long reign, pushing its boundaries to modern-day Turkey and Egypt. Such conquests brought great wealth to the city of Babylon and provided for major building projects such as the famed Hanging Gardens. He was a worshiper of Marduk, the patron god of Babylon, as well as other gods and goddesses.

The Bible mentions Nebuchadnezzar by name over 90 times. Daniel's characterization of him as proud and arrogant accord well with what we know of him otherwise.

Identity of the Four Kingdoms

One of the challenges of interpreting Daniel is identifying the four kingdoms mentioned in chapters 2 and 7. The first is clearly identified in 2:38 as Babylon. The other three are open to interpretation. There are two main schools of thought on this matter. One group identifies the four kingdoms as Babylonia, Media, Persia, and Greece. Another sees them as Babylonia, Persia, Greece, and Rome.

Many scholars believe that the kingdom of God will emerge following these kingdoms. If the Roman Empire represents the fourth kingdom, this would accord well with the coming of Jesus during Roman rule. If, however, the fourth kingdom stands for the Greek Empire, then the kingdom of God would be the **Hasmonean kingdom,** established by the descendants of the **Maccabees.**

The text does not necessarily suggest that the kingdom of God would come after the human kingdoms are destroyed. It may in fact emerge within them. The curious phrase "in the days of those kings" in 2:44 (NRSV) indicates that God's kingdom can arise in the midst of these kingdoms. The point of the text, then, would be that as human kingdoms rise and fall, God's kingdom continues on. This is truth for all time.

The meaning of the vision was interpreted by a heavenly being. The four beasts represent four earthly kingdoms (v. 17) and the throne of God represents God's dominion over the earth (v. 27). In this context Daniel saw the coming Messiah establishing His rule. He described Him as "one like a human being coming with the clouds of heaven" (v. 13, NRSV). All peoples would eventually acknowledge His dominion.

The passage does not identify the kingdoms of earth by name. Modern scholars have suggested several possibilities, but there is no consensus. Whatever the exact identification of these kingdoms,

the main point remains undisputed. Though human kingdoms rise and fall, God will have the final victory.

The vision in chapter 8 focuses upon two of the four kingdoms mentioned in chapter 7. This vision came about 547 B.C., during Cyrus's conquest and expansion of his empire. In this vision Daniel saw two animals, a ram and a goat. According to the interpretation given to Daniel, the ram represented the Persian Empire and the goat represented the Greek Empire (vv. 20-21). The vision predicted that the Greeks would conquer the Persians. Then the Greek Empire would split into four and one of these rulers would oppress the people of Israel and desecrate their sanctuary.

All of this did take place. The Greek general **Alexander the Great** conquered Persia in 331 B.C., and his kingdom divided into four at his death. One of these four kingdoms, the Seleucid Empire, eventually came to control Judah and oppressed its people. One of its kings, Antiochus Epiphanes IV, took over the Jerusalem Temple for pagan worship in 168 B.C. Chapter 11 gives more detail of his rule.

Daniel's third vision (see chap. 9) happened about 539 B.C. That year Cyrus conquered Babylon and the Exile was ended. The Jews were free to return home to Jerusalem. Daniel recognized that Jeremiah's prediction of 70 years of Babylonian dominance (609-539 B.C.) had been fulfilled. So he prayed a prayer of praise and confession.

In response to his prayer, Daniel received a vision about the coming of "an anointed prince" (9:25, NRSV). The timing of his coming is marked by "seventy 'sevens'" (v. 24). The precise meaning of this phrase is difficult to determine. Scholars give various interpretations since no arithmetic calculation renders a completely satisfactory solution. What seems clear is that a long period of time would elapse between the decree to restore Jerusalem and the coming of the Messiah. Once the Messiah comes, He would be "cut off" and suffering would follow (v. 26). These predictions found fulfillment in Jesus' death, but may await further fulfillment prior to the second coming of Christ.

The final vision of Daniel is recorded in chapters 10—12. It occurred during the third year of Cyrus (536 B.C.). At this time the first group of Jews returned to Jerusalem to begin restoring their land (Ezra 1).

Daniel's vision projects some of the intense struggles that the new community would face. It focuses with increasing detail upon oppression of the Jews under the Seleucids in the second century B.C. In 11:21-45 the tyrannical rule of Antiochus Epiphanes IV (175-164 B.C.) is clearly envisioned. His rule would be cruel and distressing. But Daniel also saw the end of this oppression and deliverance coming from heaven. Once again, God's rule wins out.

Some scholars believe that the visions in chapters 7—12 also deal with events at the end of human history. They think that though these visions were once fulfilled in the second century B.C., there would be a final fulfillment yet to come. The text refers to "the time of the end" (8:17, 19; 11:35 and 40). The Book of Revelation in the New Testament picks up on several images in Daniel and relates them to the end of human history when Jesus Christ will return. (See, for example, Revelation 12:3-4; 13:1; 14:14; 16:18.) This is the telescoping quality of biblical prophecy that focuses upon the immediate future and the distant future at the same time.

From this perspective, the cruel ruler of chapter 11 not only reflects Antiochus Epiphanes IV but also the Antichrist at the end of time. The suffering and wars are descriptive of the last days as well as the days of the Maccabees. The book thus anticipates the final judgment and victory of God over evil and the establishment of God's ultimate rule in the world.

Daniel's visions included a ram with two horns (8:3).

Summary Statements

- Daniel was a statesman and an interpreter of dreams.
- The Book of Daniel belongs to the literary type known as apocalyptic writings.
- There are two views on the date of the writing of Daniel, the sixth century B.C. and the second century B.C.
- Daniel is a carefully structured book made up of stories and visions.
- The visions of Daniel have an increasing focus upon the Maccabean period.
- The main message of Daniel is that God will win in the end, so His people can risk remaining faithful.

Questions for Reflection

1. What are some of the modern examples of severe tests of faithfulness in the history of the Christian Church?
2. While we wait for God's sovereign rule to become a reality through the Second Coming, what kind of life should believers live (use illustrations from Daniel)?
3. What does the Book of Daniel say about oppressive powers in the world today?

Bible Study Assignment

Read Daniel 12:5-13 and answer the following questions:

1. What does verse 5 indicate as the source (medium of revelation) of the message contained in this text?
2. Make a list of all the imageries, symbols, and numbers in this text. What can be easily explained? What is difficult to explain?
3. What is the primary issue/question raised by this text? What verse helps you to discover this question?
4. What answer is given to this question? What is being conveyed by the writer's words in verse 8?
5. What seems to be the main idea expressed in verses 9-11?
6. Consult various commentators to discover their opinions on the meaning and message of this text.
7. What does this text suggest to you about the nature of apocalyptic texts?
8. What does this text say to us about the end time events?

Resources for Further Study

Baldwin, Joyce G. *Daniel: An Introduction and Commentary,* in *Tyndale Old Testament Commentaries.* Downers Grove, Ill.: InterVarsity Press, 1978.

Murphy, Frederick J. *Introduction to Apocalyptic Literature,* in vol. 7 of *The New Interpreter's Bible.* Nashville: Abingdon Press, 1995.

Smith-Christopher, Daniel L. *Daniel: Introduction, Commentary, and Reflections,* in vol. 7 of *The New Interpreter's Bible.* Nashville: Abingdon Press, 1995.

Towner, Shelby W. *Daniel. Interpretation: A Bible Commentary for Teaching and Preaching.* Louisville, Ky.: John Knox Press, 1984.

UNIT VI

THE BEGINNING OF THE NEW COVENANT COMMUNITY

Your study of this unit will help you to:

- Describe the historical, political, cultural, and religious setting of the New Testament story
- Describe the Gospels as a particular literary type in the New Testament
- Outline the life and ministry of Jesus
- Describe the content and message of the Gospels of Matthew, Mark, Luke, and John
- Outline the story of the Church from its beginning in Jerusalem to Paul's journey to Rome

18 The World of the New Testament

bjectives:

Your study of this chapter should help you to:

- Describe the political events that culminated in the takeover of Judea by the Roman Empire, and the destruction of the Temple in Jerusalem
- Describe the significance of the Torah, the Temple, the Synagogue, and the Sanhedrin
- Discuss the theological perspectives of the Sadducees, the Pharisees, and the Essenes

ey Words to Understand

Hellenization
The Maccabean war
Hasmonean dynasty
Herod the Great
Zealots
Hadrian
Domitian
Synagogue
The Temple
Sanhedrin
Sadducees
Pharisees
Essenes
Herodians
"The people of the land"
Samaritans
Intertestamental period
Apocalyptic thinking

Questions to consider as you read:

1. What significant political events prepared the way for the advent of Jesus Christ into the world?

2. What are the cultural elements that shaped Jewish life in the first century A.D.?

3. What are the various theological perspectives that emerged within Judaism during the intertestamental period?

Historical Setting of the New Testament

The New Testament is the story of the fulfillment of God's redemptive plan through His Son Jesus Christ and the establishment of a new community of faith that responded to the mission and ministry of Jesus. Paul sums up this perspective most clearly in Galatians 4:4-5: "But when the fullness of time had come, God sent his Son, born of a woman, born under the law, in order to redeem those who were under the law, so that we might receive adoption as children" (NRSV). According to Paul, the coming of Jesus into the world took place at the "fullness of time." Paul seems to think that the time was ripe for the advent of Jesus Christ; God's redemptive plan intersected with world events at the most critical time in the history of humanity. It is also in this critical moment that we find the Christian community emerging with the message of Jesus the Messiah as good news for all humanity. Our goal for this chapter is to briefly survey some of the key events and religious ideas and movements that serve as the setting of the birth, life, and ministry of Jesus Christ, and the story and faith of the Christian community that we encounter in the New Testament. We will continue here the story of the Jewish nation that we left off in chapter 10.

■ Jews Under the Greek Rule

In the second half of the fourth century, the Persian Empire came under the control of Alexander the Great, who incorporated Judah into the Greek Empire in 333 B.C. When Alexander died in 323 B.C., the empire was inherited by his successors, of which two are important to the history of the Jews in Palestine. General Ptolemy who took control of Egypt annexed Palestine as part of his kingdom. General Seleucus established his kingdom in Syria, the boundary of which extended to India. Palestine remained as a disputed territory for over 100 years, until the Seleucid king Antiochus III defeated the Egyptians in 198 B.C. and made it a part of the Seleucid kingdom.

The Greek rule over Palestine brought significant changes to Jewish life. During the Ptolemaic rule, large numbers of Jews made Egypt their home and adopted the Greek culture and language. This eventually led to the translation of the Hebrew Scriptures into Greek (the Septuagint). As Greek language and culture rapidly spread throughout the Greek kingdoms, Jews who lived in Palestine as well as those who lived outside their homeland (Diaspora Jews) came under the Hellenistic (Greek) influence. The Diaspora Jews were quick to absorb the Greek culture and language. Obviously there were some Jews in Palestine who more readily supported the Hellenistic culture than those who were more traditional and conservative in their thinking; the traditionalists would have wanted to protect their faith and culture from any foreign influence.[1]

Hellenization

The Seleucid rule of Palestine at the beginning proved to be a period of good fortune for the Jews. Antiochus III granted special privileges to them, including a 3-year tax rebate, the right to worship, and assistance to repair damages to the Temple. However, within 23 years, steps were taken by his son Antiochus IV Epiphanes (175-163 B.C.) to foster Hellenistic culture and religion (**hellenization**) throughout the kingdom, which brought hardship and persecution to the Jewish population in Palestine. This program included the worship of Zeus, other Greek gods, and of the emperor himself as the visible manifestation of Zeus. Struggle for power among rival contenders to the office of the high priest only worsened the already deteriorating condition of the Jews. With the support of Menelaus, a high priest who supported hellenization, Antiochus IV looted the Temple treasury and built a citadel called Acra, a Greek city with total control over Jerusalem and the Jewish Temple. As an added measure to counter the Jewish resistance, Antiochus banned the practice of the Jewish religion, including festivals, Sabbath, and circumcision, and set up an altar to Zeus in the Temple in December 167 B.C.

The Maccabean War

Only a small group of loyal and faithful Jews (Hasidim) resisted the program of hellenization. The first act of open rebellion against Antiochus's decree took place at Modein, a village located 20 miles northwest of Jerusalem. When a Greek soldier demanded Mattathias, a local priest, officiate at a pagan sacrifice, he not only refused but also cut down the soldier and another apostate Jew who offered to carry out the sacrifice. He and his sons (John, Simon, Judas, Eleazer, and Jonathan) then fled to the nearby hills where other loyal Jews joined the freedom fighters. The group carried out guerrilla war against the Greek army and took actions to preserve the Jewish law and customs as they marched against the enemy. A year later, Mattathias died and Judas, also known by the nickname Maccabeus (meaning "the hammer"), assumed the leadership of the movement. This struggle for freedom came to be known as **the**

Maccabean war, after its prominent leader. Judas and his soldiers successfully defeated various Greek army contingents that tried to stop them as they marched toward Jerusalem. He and his supporters finally arrived at the citadel town of Acra and removed all the pagan objects from the Temple area, cleansed the Temple, erected a new altar, and rededicated the Temple in December 164 B.C. The Jewish festival Hanukkah commemorates the Maccabean victory over the Greek army and the Temple dedication.

Hasmonean Dynasty

The Maccabean war continued even after the recapture of Jerusalem in 164 B.C. to drive out the Greek army from the surrounding areas of Jerusalem and to destroy the pro-Hellenistic Jews. This ongoing war took the lives of all the Maccabean brothers except Simon, who finally succeeded in unifying the nation and securing complete freedom for the Jews from the Greek power (142-134 B.C.). This marks the beginning of the **Hasmonean dynasty,** the independent Jewish kingdom that ruled Judah from 142 to 63 B.C. Simon became the high priest, commander in chief, and the governor of the Jews. He entered into a treaty with Rome, which brought the Jewish state under the protection of Rome.

The subsequent story of the Hasmonean dynasty is filled with internal rivalry and struggles for power among its members. John Hyrcanus (134-104 B.C.), Simon's son, brought relative stability to the kingdom and expanded its boundaries. After his death, the kingdom struggled to maintain power and stability in the next four decades. Rome intervened and appointed John Hyrcanus II as high priest and ethnarch of Judea, subject to the authority of the Roman governor of Syria (63-40 B.C.). The independent Jewish state thus came to an end, with Judah being made part of the expanding Roman Empire in 63 B.C.

The political ambitions and power struggle in the ruling family brought discontentment among the loyal and pious Jews, who separated themselves into the Pharisaic movement as guardians and promoters of the Mosaic Law. Other devout Jews left the Jerusalem area to establish for themselves a strict religious community in the wilderness (Essenes). The priestly group who supported the Hasmoneans became the Sadducees. We will discuss more in detail the significance of these and other religious groups within Judaism later in this chapter.

■ Jews Under the Roman/Herodian Rule

Herod the Great

Though Hyrcanus II was the appointed ruler of the Jews, the real power behind the throne was Antipater, the governor of Idumea. Later in 37 B.C. the Ro-

man senate confirmed the appointment of Herod, one of the sons of Antipater, as king of Judea. Herod was a skillful and cunning diplomat, a military strategist, and a ruthless and murderous ruler. Though he was an Idumean (Edomite) by birth, he adopted the Jewish religion. He was Greek in culture but thoroughly loyal to Rome in politics. His actions were calculated to win the support of loyalty from his subjects, but he did not hesitate to kill anyone who stood in his way of securing power. His victims included his mother-in-law, wife, two sons, and brother-in-law, and some of his closest friends whom he suspected of disloyalty.

Herod's legacy as a master builder can be seen even today in Israel. Early in his reign, he rebuilt the Hasmonean fortress northwest of the Jerusalem Temple and renamed it Antonia in honor of Antony, his friend and patron. Other well-known Herodian fortresses include Herodium in Bethlehem and Masada in the far south of the land. He rebuilt Samaria and renamed it Sebaste in honor of Augustus. He undertook the building of numerous cities, the most important of which is the city of Caesarea on the Mediterranean coast, the later Roman capital of the Roman Palestine. His most calculated attempt to win the favor of the Jews was the restoration of the Temple, which he began in 19 B.C. It took 10 years to complete the initial work of reconstruction. The restoration work continued until A.D. 64, long after the death of Herod. Six years later, in A.D. 70, the Romans destroyed this magnificent structure.

Before his death in March 4 B.C. Herod named as his successors

Remains of Herod's palace at Caesarea.

Masada. Herod
built this fortress
and his palace as
a place of
escape.

Antipas and Archelaus, sons by his Samaritan wife, and Philip, son by another woman from Jerusalem. Antipas (4 B.C.—A.D. 39) received the region of Galilee and Perea; Archelaus (4 B.C.—A.D. 6) received the region of Judea and Samaria; and Philip (4 B.C.—A.D. 34) received the territory east and northeast of the Sea of Galilee. Philip rebuilt Banias and renamed it Caesarea Philippi, in honor of himself and Caesar. He also rebuilt Bethsaida on the northeast part of the Sea of Galilee and named it Julias in honor of Augustus's daughter. A few years after his death, Caligula gave his territory to Herod Agrippa I, grandson of **Herod the Great** (A.D. 37).

Rome removed Archelaus after 10 years because of his ruthless activities and placed Idumea, Judea, and Samaria under the administration of governors/procurators who were responsible for keeping peace and order and collecting taxes. Three such officials are important to the New Testament story: Pilate (A.D. 26-36), Felix (A.D. 52-60), and Festus (A.D. 60-62). Rome banished Antipas

Herodian Kingdom.

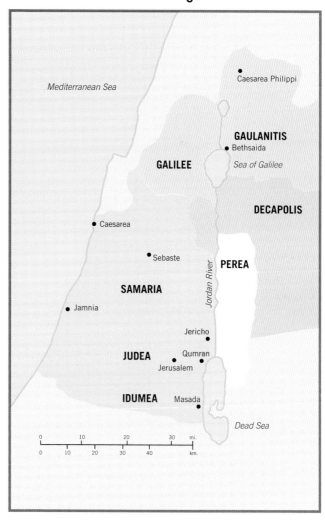

Roman Emperors Connected to New Testament History

Augustus (27 B.C.—A.D. 14)—the birth of Jesus

Tiberius (A.D. 14-37)—the ministry of Jesus

Caligula (A.D. 37-41)—demanded emperor worship

Claudius (A.D. 41-54)—expelled Jews from Rome

Nero (A.D. 54-68)—persecution of Christians; martyrdom of Peter and Paul

Vespasian (A.D. 69-79)—Jewish revolt and the destruction of Jerusalem, which was carried out by his son Titus

Domitian (A.D. 81-96)—persecution of Christians; John the apostle exiled to Patmos

because of his insubordination and placed the region of Galilee under the rule of Herod Agrippa I in A.D. 39. Later, in A.D. 41, the region of Judea and Samaria was added to his territory, which he governed until A.D. 44. He thus had control over the whole region, which was once ruled by Herod the Great. Agrippa I ordered the death of James the son of Zebedee, one of the 12 apostles. He also put Peter in prison to show his positive attitude toward the Jews (see Acts 12:1-4). After his death in A.D. 44 (see 12:21-23), his young son Herod Agrippa II was named the ruler of his father's territory. Paul appeared before this king while he was in Roman custody in Caesarea (25:13—26:32).

The Jewish Revolt

Judea was under the rule of 14 governors between A.D. 6 and 66. By and large, these governors were inept administrators who ruled Judea with a heavy hand and were cruel to anyone who opposed their rule. The Jewish population became more and more resentful of the corruption of the governors. Meanwhile, a nationalistic spirit flared up in the land under the leadership of a revolutionary leader named Judas the Galilean. The group he led, known as the **Zealots,** aimed to establish peace in the land by overthrowing Roman domination. Felix, before whom Paul stood trial, responded to the Zealots with harsh measures, which added more fuel to the anti-Roman sentiment in the land. A riot broke out in Jerusalem when governor Florus robbed the Temple and imprisoned a Jewish delegation that went to plead with him. The riot intensified in Jerusalem, and rebellion spread throughout the land. Nero sent Vespasian to restore order in Judea. Vespasian sent his son Titus to bring reinforcement from Egypt. The attack against the Zealots in Galilee resulted in the mass suicide of Galileans in the fortress city of Gamla. Vespasian moved to Jerusalem and besieged the city. Within the city itself, there was fierce fighting between the extremely fanatical and violent groups of Sicarii and Zealots and the moderate groups who wanted to make peace with Rome. Meanwhile, Vespasian became emperor and he assigned the military campaign against Jerusalem to Titus. The army entered the city in A.D. 70, and in the battle that followed mass destruction and death occurred, including the destruction of the Temple. Several thousand Jews were killed during this battle with Rome. Romans continued their campaign against the Zealots and followed them down to Masada, the fortress built by Herod the Great, where the Zealots took refuge from the enemy. After a three-year siege, the Roman army finally broke the walls of the fortress (A.D. 73), only to find the dead bodies of the freedom fighters, who took their own lives rather than surrender or be killed by the enemy.[2] Jewish leadership relocated to the Mediterranean coastal town of Jamnia, which became an important center of Jewish learning and literary activity. Another major outbreak of violence took place when Emperor **Hadrian** built a temple to Jupiter at the site where the Jewish Temple once stood (A.D. 132-135). Bar Kochba, a self-proclaimed messianic leader, led this rebellion. The Roman army crushed this rebellion by killing thousands of Jews and rebuilding Jerusalem as a Roman colony with the name Aelia Capitolina (A.D. 135). Rome prohibited Jews from entering this newly established city, which became mostly a camp for the Roman army.

Religious Context

■ Pagan Religious World

Christianity was born in the Greco-Roman religious world, and more specifically in the context of first-century Judaism. The influence of Greek culture and religion contributed to an assimilation of the Roman gods and goddesses into the Greek pantheon.[3]

Subsequently, for every Roman god/goddess, there was a Greek counterpart. Throughout the Roman Empire, there were temples built to the worship of the Greco-Roman deities. In addition, the imperial cult also became popular in the empire. **Domitian** was the first to enforce emperor worship, an act that was unacceptable to the monotheistic faith of both Jews and Christians.

The Greco-Roman culture also had its share of popular Greek, Egyptian, and Oriental mystery religions or cults. These cults offered purification and immortality of the soul to its adherents. Each cult centered on the myth of a god/goddess who died and was later resuscitated. Magic and other forms of superstitious practices were also common in the Greco-Roman culture. People consulted horoscopes and used other omens to predict the future. Exorcism by the use of magical formulas was a trade practiced by

Roman Governors of Judea (A.D. 6-66)

A.D. 6-9   Coponius
A.D. 9-12   Marcus Ambibulus
A.D. 12-15 Annius Rufus
A.D. 15-26 Valerius Gratus
A.D. 26-36 Pontius Pilate
A.D. 36-37 Marcellus
A.D. 37-41 Marullus
(Judea and Samaria under the kingship of Herod Agrippa I from A.D. 41 to 44)
A.D. 44-46 Cuspius Fadus
A.D. 46-48 Tiberius Alexander
A.D. 48-52 Ventidius Cumanus
A.D. 52-60 Felix
A.D. 60-62 Festus
A.D. 62-64 Albinus
A.D. 64-66 Florus

professionals who were skilled in casting demons out. Both Jews and non-Jews were attracted to these practices. Astrology was also popular in the first-century Roman Empire. Astrologers kept a careful record of the movement of the planets, which they consulted to ascertain the time of birth and destiny of people.

Jewish Religious Context

Judaism was a popular religion in the Greco-Roman world. Though it had always been associated with Palestine, the place of its origin, Jewish religion had infiltrated throughout the Greco-Roman world through Jews who had, for some reason or other, settled down outside of their homeland. These Diaspora Jews were primarily responsible for the growth of Judaism beyond the borders of Palestine.

By the middle of the second century, various theological perspectives emerged in Judaism, though the Law of Moses guided the everyday life of the Jews. The Law (the Torah) here is much more than the five books of Moses; rather, it is the whole will of God, the content of God's revelation that required Jews to live in submission to the commandments of God. The Torah provided the necessary guidelines for Jewish life and conduct. This significant place of the Law in the life of the Jews accounts for the origin of the scribes *(sopherim),* Jewish scholars who were the authoritative interpreters of the Law. In the early part of the intertestamental period, the priests carried out this task. Later, however, laypeople also became trained as scholars, who not only interpreted the Law but also took upon the task of copying and preserving the sacred Scriptures.

The center of the study and teaching of the Torah was the **synagogue.** It is likely that the custom of people meeting together to read and study the Torah originated in Babylon during the exilic period. During the intertestamental period, the synagogue became an established religious institution in Palestine. The syna-

Ruins of a fourth-century A.D. synagogue at Capernaum.

Jewish Religious Festivals

In addition to daily and weekly services, various religious feasts and festivals also played a significant role in the religious life of the Jews. The following is a summary of the key religious festivals, some prescribed by the Law of Moses and some established by later Judaism. These festivals also followed the religious calendar of Judaism. Pilgrims from throughout Palestine and from the Diaspora lands came to Jerusalem to participate in the three major festivals: Passover, Pentecost, and Tabernacles.

Passover and Unleavened Bread (observed during the month of Nissan/March-April) commemorated Israel's deliverance from Egypt. This festival also marked the beginning of wheat harvest. Seven weeks after the Passover came Pentecost or the Feast of Weeks, celebrated in commemoration of the giving of the Law at Sinai. This "50th day" event also marked the end of the wheat harvest (month of Sivan/May-June). The Jewish New Year or the Feast of Trumpets (Rosh Hashanah) was on Tishri 1 and 2 (September-October), which marked the beginning of the civil year and the end of the fruit harvest season. Eight days after the New Year came the Day of Atonement or Yom Kippur, the national day of repentance and fasting. The Feast of Tabernacles or Booths also was celebrated during the month of Tishri, in commemoration of Israel's tent dwelling days during their wilderness journey. To these religious days prescribed by the Law, Jews also added Hanukkah, or the Festival of Lights, to commemorate the cleansing and rededication of the Temple at the end of the Maccabean war (25th of Kislev/December), and Purim to celebrate the deliverance of Jews from the plot of Haman during the Persian period (14th and 15th of Adar/February-March).

gogue (meaning "assembly") was the center of Jewish life throughout the Greco-Roman world. A typical synagogue service included the recital of the Shema (Deuteronomy 6:4-9; 11:13-21; Numbers 15:37-41), prayer, singing of psalms, reading from the Law and the Prophets, a sermon, and a benediction. In addition to its religious function, the synagogue was also the center of the Jewish social, educational, and political life.

The Temple remained as the center for sacrificial worship in first-century Palestine until the Romans destroyed it in A.D. 70. The first-century Jewish Temple was a magnificent structure, surrounded by courts and colonnades. The Court of the Gentiles was a clearly marked area with specific instructions not to cross over into the Inner Court. The Inner Court included separate areas for the Israelites proper (men) and women. Within the Inner Court was the Court of the Priests, at the center of which stood the Temple. The altar of burnt offering was located just outside of the Temple. The Temple included the outer room (the holy place with its furnishings) and the holy of holies, the innermost and the most sacred sanctuary. A veil separated the holy place from the holy of holies. Private and public offerings and sacrifices were made at the Temple daily, weekly, and on special days such as the Day of Atonement. Songs by the Levitical choir accompanied by musical instruments, priestly prayers and benedictions, and blowing of trumpets were regular parts of the ceremonies at the Temple.

Multitudes of priests from several priestly families took turns officiating in the Temple rituals. By law, they all had to be descendants of Aaron. At the head of the priests was the high priest, who exercised very high authority over the Jewish people. He was the representative of the nation with whom political powers negotiated and made their treaties. It is likely that in the first century, the high priest also presided over the Sanhedrin, the highest judicial court of the Jews. High priests came from wealthy and aristocratic families. In the Greek period and during the Hasmonean period, this office was the most coveted office in the land due to the power that was vested in the high priest. The influence of the high priest continued until the destruction of the Temple in A.D. 70.

The **Sanhedrin,** the Jewish supreme court, handled all religious violations and breaking of the rules of the Torah. Since the Torah was the rule for both religious and civil life, there was no distinction made between civil and religious crimes. The Sanhedrin thus controlled every aspect of Jewish life. The Roman government recognized the authority of the Sanhedrin over the affairs of the Jewish people, and it intervened to exercise the Roman law only on matters of capital offenses, such as violation of the Roman law and treason against the empire.

▣ Jewish Religious Groups

We have noted earlier that in the Greek period, Judaism ceased to exist as a homogenous religious group. Within Judaism, there were those who were pro-Hellenists who were not only politically subservient to foreign rule but also willing to accommodate their religious faith to show their loyalty to those who dominated them. The Hebraic Jews, on the other hand, strived to remain religiously conservative and loyal to the traditions of their faith. Hellenistic culture perhaps changed the religious perspectives of the Diaspora Jews more significantly than those of the pro-Hellenistic group within Palestine. However, we find divergent theological developments and the rise of various sectarian movements within Palestine itself, which serve as the theological context in which Christianity was born in the first century. We shall now briefly survey the key religious groups that dominated the religious scene of first-century Palestine.

Sadducees

The **Sadducees** were considered to be the priestly aristocracy in Jerusalem, made up of families that controlled much wealth and power in the land of Palestine. Though no one clearly knows the origin of this name, one view is that the name originated from the Zadokites, the priestly group that claimed to be the legitimate successor of Zadok, the high priest of Solomon, and the Aaronic priesthood in Israel. Not much is known about this group because we have no literature available to us from them. Some trace the origin of this group to the second century B.C. during the period of John Hyrcanus, the Hasmonean ruler (135-104 B.C.). According to Josephus, Hyrcanus favored the Sadducees, who taught that the people should observe only those rules that are in the written word and reject those traditions that derived from the traditions of the ancestors.[4] Since the Torah and the rules and regulations that governed the Temple shaped their theological perspective, the Sadducees considered only the Books of Moses (the Pentateuch) as their central authority. They interpreted the Law literally and considered the Temple and the sacrificial system to be the fulfillment of God's faithful promises to Israel. They maintained the view that Israel's destiny in the world as God's chosen people is fulfilled through the Temple and its rituals. Though they did not reject the Prophets and the Writings (the rest of the Hebrew Scriptures), they did not regard them as authoritative. They rejected religious ideas not found in the Law, which include concepts such as resurrection, angels, demons, future reward, and apocalyptic thought that emerged in the pre-Christian period. Since their power and prestige was centered on the Temple, with the destruction of the Temple in A.D. 70 by the Romans, they disappeared from the scene without leaving any trace of their influence in the shaping of later Judaism.

Pharisees

Our knowledge of the **Pharisees** is also limited, since we do not know of any literature that comes directly from this group. It is commonly believed that this group descended from the Hasidim, the loyal and pious Jews who were staunch allies and supporters of the Maccabean family. The name Pharisee is associated with the idea of separation; thus the common meaning "separated ones" may be either a self-designation or a derogatory label given to them by their opponents.[5] Josephus remarks that the Pharisees taught the people a great many observances that are not in the Law and that there were disputes and differences between the Sadducees and the Pharisees. He also points out that though the Sadducees had only the rich on their side, the Pharisees had the general population ("multitude") on theirs.[6] This group was a "well organized political movement" during the Hasmonean period and continued to exert political power during the days of Herod the Great. Herod, though he had some friendly relationship with them during the early part of his reign, later considered them his enemies and executed several leaders of this movement.[7]

The Pharisees originated within the laity in Judaism and established themselves as teachers and scholars whose teachings laid the foundation of the vast collection of Jewish religious literature known as the Mishna and the Palestinian and Babylonian Talmuds. The synagogue was the center of their activity. The Pharisees, though they considered the Torah as central to the Jewish religious life, also respected the authority of the rest of the Hebrew Scriptures. It was at a Pharisaic council that met at Jamnia around A.D. 95 that the canon of the Old Testament was established.

As promoters of the Law, the Pharisees emphasized both the written Law and the oral Law, the latter of which is the interpretation of the Law handed down by previous generations of great rabbis. Since the Law was central to the life of the Jews in their thinking, Pharisees observed and taught strict obedience to both the written Law and the oral Law. They also promoted concepts such as the kingdom of God, the coming of the Messiah, the resurrection of the dead, and the future that God would usher in by destroying sin and evil in the world. Though they did not involve themselves in local politics or anti-Roman movements, they supported the national interests during the Roman invasion of Jerusalem in A.D. 70. They receive the credit for the recovery and survival of Judaism after that tragic date.

Essenes

The Dead Sea Scrolls, the discovery of which began in 1947, and Josephus provide us with our knowledge of this third religious movement in Judaism. Scholars think that this movement came out of the Hasidim during the Maccabean period. Koester thinks that they belonged to the priestly circles of the Hasidim who joined the Maccabean war in opposition to the appointment of Menelaus, a non-Zadokite person, as high priest by Antiochus IV.[8] When the Hasmonean ruler Simon appointed himself as high priest, they made the break with the ruling family, since this was an outright defiance of the Zadokite right to hold the high priestly office. Some think that the "wicked priest" in the Qumran texts may be an indirect reference to Simon, who ruled the nation with violence and cruelty.[9]

The **Essenes** established themselves as a self-exiled religious community at Qumran, on the northwest part of the Dead Sea. They made a complete break from the social, political, and religious life of Jerusalem and made Qumran their home perhaps around the middle of the second century B.C., during the early part of the Hasmonean rule. The remains of Qumran show a central complex with several rooms, including a scriptorium, an assembly hall, a meeting hall, common rooms, and many other surrounding buildings that were used for storage and as workshops. Cisterns and reservoirs of water and a bath for ritual cleansing (mikveh) were also found at Qumran. The nearby caves yielded a large number of manuscripts, which included copies of the Hebrew Scriptures, and the literature produced by this community. The literature from this community includes writings such as the *Damascus Document, Commentary on Habakkuk, Manual of Discipline* (or *Rule of the Community*), and *War of the Children of Light Against the Children of Darkness.*

The Qumran society saw themselves as members of the new covenant and as the true remnant of Israel. They also saw themselves as the poor who will one day inherit the earth. They regarded themselves as the children of light who were oppressed by the children of darkness. Those who were the children of darkness included the Roman Empire and the Jews who were apostate and unfaithful to the Law. They also believed that in the end, with the help of the heavenly hosts of God, the children of light would prevail against the children of darkness in the final battle, which would bring an end to all evil forces. The community lived with strong messianic expectations, in which their leader, the teacher of righteousness, seems to have played a key role. The community ceased to exist beyond A.D. 70. Some scholars believe that the

Roman army destroyed the sect during the siege of Jerusalem in A.D. 68. Anticipating the Roman invasion, the community took the measure of protecting and preserving their writings by hiding them in jars in nearby caves. The remarkable discovery of the Dead Sea Scrolls preserves for us their legacy, and more than that, a glimpse of the cultural, social, political, and religious conditions of the pre-Christian times.

Herod built this fortress about seven miles south of Jerusalem as a desert retreat for him and his family.

Zealots

Zealots were not a religious movement but a fanatical and political movement that opposed the foreign rule of Judea by the Romans. This revolutionary movement was intent on overthrowing the Roman power. They showed their resistance to Rome by refusing to pay taxes and causing uprising against the Roman army. This group is responsible for the Jewish revolt that led to the destruction of Jerusalem in A.D. 70 and the later revolt that led to the establishment of Jerusalem as a Roman colony in A.D. 135. Sicarii, who carried concealed daggers, were perhaps a more violent branch within this movement.

Other Groups

Herodians were likely a political party rather than a religious movement. They seemed to have exercised their influence in the Galilean area, where Antipas ruled. They were supporters of the Herodian dynasty. The Gospels mention them, along with the Pharisees, as opponents of Jesus (Mark 3:6; 12:13; Matthew 22:16). The masses of Jewish people, who were ignorant of the Law and who were indifferent to the customs of the Pharisees, are called **"the people of the land."** They did not have any political or religious power, though they constituted the majority of people in the land. Pharisees despised them because of their lack of knowledge of the Law and their association with Jesus. The **Samaritans,** who lived in Samaria, the area between Judea and Galilee, were a people despised by the Jews. The history of the Samaritans goes back to the Assyrian occupation of the Northern Kingdom (Israel) in 721 B.C. They were descendants of the Assyrian colonists and the Israelite population that was left in the land. The Jews viewed them as a mixed and defiled people who did not belong to the Jewish nation. The Samaritans considered themselves to be the true keepers of the Law and worshipers of Yahweh, the God of Israel. They had their own version of the Pentateuch *(The Samaritan Pentateuch),* and their temple, located at Mount Gerizim. The Jews avoided any contact with this group, and both groups were hostile toward each other, which often resulted in violence and murder. The Jews traveled around the Samaritan region because they considered even the land unclean. The Samaritans were not hospitable to the Jews who wanted to travel through their region (Luke 9:51-56). Jesus' travel to Samaria (John 4:1-42) and His conversation with a Samaritan woman display the revolutionary and life-transforming power of His gospel.

Another particular religious perspective that emerged during the **intertestamental period** also deserves our attention. During the period of intense religious persecution, despair, and disillusionment, Jewish visionaries began to promote the view that God would come suddenly to destroy all evil and set up His ideal kingdom. This perspective, known as **apocalyptic thinking,** may have its origin in the Old Testament visionary thinking found in Ezekiel 38—48 and Isaiah 56—66. Some scholars maintain the view that the Book of Daniel, the only apocalyptic book in the Old Testament, originated in the context of hellenization in the early part of the second century. Some of the popular Jewish apocalyptic writings include Enoch; the Assumption of Moses; 2 Esdras, also called 4 Ezra; the Apocalypse of

Baruch; the Sybylline Oracles; the Testament of the Twelve Patriarchs; and the Apocalypse of Moses. The apocalyptic writings portray their content as revelations about the future. Dualistic thinking, symbolic language, the use of numbers, and the final triumph of God over evil are some of the characteristic features of this type of religious thinking.

We conclude this chapter with this note. Jesus came into a world that was fractured by religious, social, political, and cultural tensions. Religious and political corruption, social oppression, and misguided theological perspectives were all characteristics of this period. Judaism itself was plagued by divergent political ideologies and religious perspectives. We had to limit our survey to some key events and people that identify for us what Paul perhaps meant by the phrase, "When the fullness of time had come" (Galatians 4:4, NRSV). Indeed the world was ripe for the coming of God's Son and the establishment of the new covenant community.

Summary Statements

- In the early part of the second century, Palestine became a part of the Seleucid kingdom.
- The Seleucid ruler Antiochus IV Epiphanes instituted the program of hellenization, which threatened to destroy the Jewish religion and culture.
- Under the leadership of the Maccabeans, the Jews were able to drive out the Greek rulers and establish an independent Jewish state.
- Struggle within the Hasmonean family led to the takeover of Judea by the Roman Empire.
- The Torah was central to Jewish life in the first century.
- Various religious groups within Judaism attempted to guide the destiny of the Jews with their particular theological perspectives.
- The Sadducees promoted the Temple and the sacrifices as necessary for the existence of Judaism.
- The Pharisees required strict adherence to both the written Law and the oral Law.
- The Essenes established a sectarian community at Qumran and identified themselves as members of the new covenant.
- Zealots were a nationalistic and revolutionary movement that attempted to overthrow the foreign domination of Judea.

Questions for Reflection

1. What parallels do you find between the theological and cultural conditions of Judaism in the first century A.D. and that of the Christian Church in the 21st century?
2. In spite of division and fragmented theological perspectives within Judaism, what are the forces that contributed to the unity of this religion in the first century? What does that say to the Church today?

Bible Study Assignment

Read Matthew 5:27-32 and identify the religious issue that prompted the Pharisees to criticize Jesus' behavior.

Read John 4:1-42. Based on this story, what were the peculiar customs and beliefs of the Samaritans that set them apart from the Jewish people? What would have been the response of a traditional Jew to Jesus' actions in this story? Explain your answer.

Resources for Further Study

Bright, John. *A History of Israel,* 4th ed. Louisville, Ky.: Westminster/John Knox Press, 2000.

Bruce, F. F. *New Testament History.* New York: Doubleday, 1972.

Kee, Howard C., Franklin W. Young, Karlfried Froehlich. *Understanding the New Testament.* Englewood Cliffs, N.J.: Prentice-Hall, 1965.

Koester, Helmut. *Introduction to the New Testament: History, Culture, and Religion of the Hellenistic Age,* vol. 1. New York: Walter de Gruyter, 1982.

Tenney, Merrill C. *New Testament Survey.* Grand Rapids: Eerdmans, 1961.

19 Jesus: The Mediator of the New Covenant

O bjectives:

Your study of this chapter should help you to:

- Describe the Gospels as a particular type of literature (genre) in the New Testament
- Evaluate the relationships among the Synoptic Gospels and the uniqueness of the Gospel of John
- Identify the major events in the life of Jesus
- Recognize the significance of the kingdom of God in the teachings of Jesus

K ey Words to Understand

Euangelion
Oral tradition
Synoptic problem
"Q"
Two-source hypothesis
Virgin Birth
Herod the Great
Bethlehem
Nazareth
Herod Antipas
Sanhedrin
Pontius Pilate

Q uestions to consider as you read:

1. Why are there so many similarities, as well as differences, between one Gospel and another?
2. Why did Jesus perform miracles?
3. In what sense are the parables of Jesus subversive?

Gospels as a Literary Genre

The four Gospels in the New Testament (Matthew, Mark, Luke, John)[1] provide us with the story of Jesus of Nazareth, whom the Christian faith confesses as the Son of God and the Lord and Savior of the world. These books constitute a particular type of literature (genre) in the New Testament. How did the word "gospel" (in Greek *euangelion*) become part of the title of the first four books of the New Testament? Obviously, the writers themselves did not give this label to their books. Mark uses the word in the first line of his Gospel, "The beginning of the gospel *[euangelion]* about Jesus Christ," and again in summarizing the message of Jesus as *euangelion* (1:14). It is possible that the Early Church was familiar with this word from two possible sources. First, the Greek translation of the Old Testament (the Septuagint), the Bible of early Christians, uses a form of *euangelion* to signify the good news that God was about to end the Exile and restore Jerusalem (Isaiah 52:7; 61:1). In the same way, the early Christian church saw the story of Jesus as the announcement of the good news of salvation. A second possibility is that the early Christians were familiar with Roman inscriptions that heralded the good news of peace brought by Roman emperors.[2] Though the word *euangelion* was already a part of the Christian vocabulary (4 times in Matthew, 8 times in Mark, and 60 times in Pauline writings), in the second century it developed into a literary type in Christian literature. Christians began to label the books that contained the message of Jesus as *"euangelion* according to Matthew," and so forth.

Even a casual reader of the Bible will note that the contents of the four Gospels are similar and even identical in many places. Yet a closer examination will reveal that these books are in fact significantly different from one another. We will now examine some of these general features of the Gospels and attempt to see how and why these books are similar, yet different from each other, before turning our attention to the life and ministry of Jesus portrayed in these writings.

The authors of the four Gospels would most likely have been familiar with popular biographies produced by Greek, Roman, and Jewish authors to entertain and instruct readers and hearers. While there may be some resemblance between the Gospels and Greco-Roman and Jewish biographies, New Testament scholars today agree that the Gospels were the unique product of early Christianity.[3] A significant feature of the Gospels is that they lack many of the details of a hero's life that would be part of an ancient biography. The birth of Jesus is told only in Matthew and Luke, but not in Mark or John. The Gospels tell us virtually nothing about Jesus' childhood, adolescence, and early adulthood, except for the single story of Him at age 12 at the Temple (Luke 2:41-51). Instead, the focus of the Gospels is on His teaching and healing ministry and His death and resurrection. They proclaim the good news of the kingdom of God inaugurated through Jesus' words, deeds, death, and resurrection. They simply tell in narrative form what God has done in Jesus to save the world.

The Gospels are thus primarily a theological narrative, the purpose of which is to tell the story of God's action in the world through the life, death, and resurrection of Jesus. This explains the lack of a precise, chronological account of the life of Jesus in the Gospels. Though we find in the Gospels many historical facts from the life of Jesus, they are not presented in a sequential, orderly, chronological manner. The Gospels often place the same event or saying of Jesus in two or three different settings. The theological character of the Gospel genre cautions us against making the incorrect judgment that the Gospels contradict each other.

A noteworthy characteristic of the Gospels is the extent to which they echo and indeed quote the Old Testament. The Gospel writers place the story of Jesus within the vast panorama of salvation history. Even though the Gospels portray the Christ event as a new thing that God has done in history, they nevertheless see continuity between what God had done in the past and what God did through the life, death, and resurrection of Jesus. The story of Jesus does not displace the Old Testament; it moves the story of God forward; it fulfills God's promises given in past ages (Matthew 5:17; Luke 24:44; John 5:39).[4]

How did the Gospel writers get their information about Jesus? Though the answer to this question is not certain, we think that **oral tradition** played a significant part in transmitting the story of Jesus. Those who heard Jesus teach or preach and saw the events in His life passed on these stories to others by word of mouth. It may be that some of the Gospel writers themselves were eyewitnesses of Jesus' life and ministry. Only Luke informs us that the details of his account of the life of Jesus have come to him through others who were eyewitnesses of Jesus (Luke 1:1-4). Oral tradition alone, however, does not explain the extensive similarities between the Gospels, particu- larly the first three Gospels (Matthew, Mark, and Luke), often called the Synoptic Gospels.

The Synoptic Problem

The word *synoptic* means "to see together or alongside one another." When scholars placed Matthew, Mark, and Luke side by side in order to compare them, they observed the following: (1) a substantial part of Mark's Gospel is identical to materials found in Matthew and Luke; (2) Matthew and Luke have many sayings of Jesus in similar and even identical Greek wording that are absent from Mark; (3) Matthew and Luke have materials unique to each of these two Gospels that are lacking in the other Gospels. These similarities and differences have led scholars to conclude that there must be some sort of connection between one Gospel and another. But what exactly is this connection? This question is what has come to be known as the **Synoptic problem.**

Modern studies in these three Gospels have led a majority of scholars to conclude that Mark was the first Gospel to be written and that Matthew and Luke depended on Mark but wrote independently of each other.[5] After studying the materials common to both Matthew and Luke, scholars formulated the hypothesis that Matthew and Luke were not dependent on one another but on another source that they both had access to independently of each other. Since no such document has ever been found, this remains only a hypothesis. The German scholars who first formulated this hypothesis named this source "**Q**," which stands for the German word *Quelle,* which simply means "source." By definition, then, a "Q" saying is one that is found only in Matthew and Luke but not in Mark. Most of the material identified in Matthew and Luke as "Q" consists of the sayings of Jesus and therefore "Q" is often referred to as the sayings source.

To conclude, the dominant scholarly hypothesis today is that Mark was the first Gospel to be written and that Matthew and Luke were dependent on the texts of Mark and "Q" as sources. This explanation has come to be known as the **two-source hypothesis** of the Synoptic Gospels, meaning that Mark and "Q" were the two sources for Matthew and Luke.

The two-source hypothesis does not answer the question of materials unique to Matthew and Luke. It is generally understood today that Matthew and Luke each had access to other sources not available to the other Gospel writers. The label "M" has been given to passages that are only in Matthew and "L" to passages that are only in Luke. "M" and "L" are considered traditions rather than well-defined documents. They are shorthand for passages that are only in Matthew or Luke respectively. An example of "M" would be the story of the wise men found only in Matthew 2:1-12. An example of "L" would be the parable of the Good Samaritan found only in Luke 10:29-37.

Whereas the texts of the Synoptic Gospels are clearly related to one another, as shown above, the Gospel of John stands alone in its wording, structure, and general characteristics. Its vocabulary is unique. The words of Jesus in John are considerably different from His words in the Synoptics. Although John seems familiar with the Synoptic tradition, there is no evidence that this Gospel was dependent on the written text of Matthew, Mark, or Luke.[6]

Major Events in the Life of Jesus

Today more than ever, there is intense interest in Jesus as a historical figure. Virtually everyone agrees that Jesus was a historical figure who lived in the first century A.D. and was crucified. Although many details are still debated among scholars, we can be certain of the major outline of His life and message.

■ Birth

The birth of Jesus is told in Matthew 1—2 and Luke 1—2. Though not the same, the two narratives agree that Jesus was conceived by the Holy Spirit and born of the Virgin Mary. In Galatians 4:4 Paul declares that Jesus was "of a woman." This unusual phrase may imply that Paul was familiar with the **Virgin Birth** tradition. The Gospels and Paul agree that Jesus had a human birth but was also the Son of God (Romans 1:3-4; Luke 1:31-32; John 1:1, 14).

Jesus was born during the reign of **Herod the Great** (Matthew 2:1), who was king over Palestine in 37-4 B.C. Because of his paranoia, Herod decreed the death of the children of Bethlehem who were two years old or under, in an attempt to get rid of Jesus whom the magi identified as king of the Jews (v. 16). Shortly thereafter, Herod died. Jesus must have been under two years old at the time of Herod's death. This puts the birth date of Jesus around 6 to 4 B.C.

Matthew and Luke concur that Jesus was born in **Bethlehem.**

Matthew finds this to be theologically significant in that Jesus fulfills the prophecy of Micah 5:2 that the Messiah will come from Bethlehem.

The details of the story in Matthew and Luke are not the same. Matthew 2:11 mentions a house where Joseph and Mary and the infant Jesus lived, implying that they were residents of Bethlehem but later moved to **Nazareth** of Galilee because of the political threat in Judea from Archelaus, a son of Herod the Great. Conversely, Luke indicates that Joseph and Mary lived in Nazareth and were temporarily in Bethlehem for taxation when Jesus was born (Luke 2:4-7). All four Gospels agree that Nazareth was Jesus' hometown (Matthew 2:23; Mark 1:9; Luke 2:51; 4:16; John 1:45).

The Gospels say virtually nothing about the childhood and adolescent years of Jesus, with the single exception of Luke's story of Jesus at the Temple at the age of 12 (Luke 2:42-52). Jesus had brothers and sisters (Matthew 13:55-56; Mark 6:3) who were not particularly sympathetic to His message during His lifetime (John 7:3-7; Mark 3:21, 31-35).

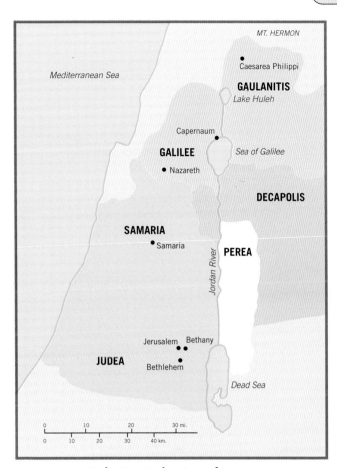

Palestine in the time of Jesus.

▪ Baptism and Temptation

The Gospels narrate the ministry of John the Baptist before getting into the public ministry of Jesus. It is certain that John baptized Jesus. The Gospel of John omits Jesus' baptism altogether, even though it tells about the ministry of John the Baptist (1:19-34; 3:22-30). Jesus' baptism poses a theological question. Why would Jesus, the sinless Son of God, come to John for a baptism of repentance (Matthew 3:14)? Jesus believed that John was a true prophet sent by God to prepare Israel for the final coming of the kingdom of God. Jesus intended to be part of that movement that announced the coming of God's kingdom. Later in His ministry, Jesus had high praise for John (11:7-11; Luke 7:24-28).

Immediately after His baptism, Jesus withdrew to the desert for a period of solitude. Satan tempted Him with self-serving strategies to accomplish His mission (Matthew 3:1-11; Mark 1:12-13; Luke 3:1-13). Jesus, however, refused to compromise His faithfulness to God even if it meant a hard road ahead. The supreme test came

Ritual of Baptism in Judaism

The readers of the Gospels often wonder how it was that John's ministry included the ritual of baptism. John was not the only one who practiced a water ritual. The Essenes at Qumran also practiced a ritual immersion in water to symbolize purification.[7] Other groups practiced ceremonial washing of the hands as a symbolic act of cleansing (Mark 7:3-4). Some of these ritual washings and immersions may go back to Old Testament regulations for priests (Leviticus 16:4, 24). John the Baptist insisted, however, that a mere ceremonial cleansing was far from sufficient. Repentance and a genuine change of lifestyle were necessary in preparation for the imminent coming of the final judgment (Mark 1:4; Matthew 3:7-12).

■ Ministry of Healing and Miracles

In spite of the philosophical bias of modern science against miracles, the historical-critical study of the Gospels strongly suggests that Jesus devoted a significant part of His ministry to healing and performing miracles. Even His opponents acknowledged that Jesus performed miracles, even though they attributed them to Satan's power (Mark 3:22). Jesus' own statement helps us to understand the function of miracles in His ministry. He states: "But if I drive out demons by the finger of God, then the kingdom of God has come to you" (Luke 11:20). Perhaps the intent of the miracles was to show those who followed Him that the kingdom of God had come.

Many in the first century viewed illness as God's judgment on sin, as illustrated in the question of the disciples to Jesus about a man born blind. "Rabbi," they asked, "who sinned, this man or his parents, that he was born blind?"

when Jesus was on the Cross. The spectators and religious leaders taunted Him and said, "Let this Christ, this King of Israel, come down now from the cross, that we may see and believe" (Mark 15:32). Jesus refused to compromise the integrity of His vision and His commitment to the divine purpose to the point of death.

The traditional site of Jesus' temptation.

Jesus, Temptation, and the Christian

Christian faith affirms that Jesus was truly human and was tempted as all of us. Jesus struggled in the desert in prayer and fasting over the issue of His ministry. To be tempted means that the possibility of yielding to it was available to Him, but He determined to remain faithful to God regardless of the cost. He is "one who was tempted in every way, just as we are—yet was without sin" (Hebrews 4:15).

Just as Christ was tempted, yet without sin, so also a Spirit-filled follower of Christ may still face temptations without yielding to them. Just as Christ faced temptations and resolutely rejected the lure of the tempter, so also a Christian is empowered by God to say no to the enticement of sin. Unlike the story of the Garden of Eden in Genesis 3, where the man and the woman yielded to temptation and sinned, Jesus remained faithful and obedient to the purposes of God. God offers all of us the possibility of a victorious life and empowers us to remain faithful under the most trying circumstances.

(John 9:2). Jesus replied that the blindness was not because of sin but that it provided the occasion for God to work in the man's life.

When Jesus was criticized for healing a crippled woman on the Sabbath, He said, "Should not this woman, a daughter of Abraham, whom Satan has kept bound for eighteen long years, be set free on the Sabbath day from what bound her?" (Luke 13:16). Quoting the words of Isaiah, Jesus described His ministry of healing as a demonstration of God's liberating power for the poor and oppressed (4:18-19). Sick people, the blind, and lepers were no longer social outcasts. To stress this point, He healed lepers by touching them, which the Law had forbidden (Leviticus 13). The kingdom of God had come, and it included them.

Scholars have been much more skeptical about the historicity of the so-called nature miracles, including the feeding of the 5,000 (Mark 6:32-44; John 6:1-15), the walking on the water (Mark 6:45-52; John 6:16-21), the stilling of the storm (Mark 4:35-41), the miraculous catch of fish (Luke 5:1-11; John 21:1-11), and the turning of water to wine (2:1-11). There is no reason to think that the Early Church invented these stories. The fact that at least three of these stories occur both in the Synoptic Gospels and in John attests to their historicity. Moreover, these stories take place in the Galilean setting of Jesus' ministry, such as crowds in the countryside without food, fishing and a storm on the Sea of Galilee, or a wedding in the Galilean village of Cana. There would be no reason for the Early Church to add such local coloring and significance if these stories were products of the church's imagination.

■ Disciples

Just as ancient Israel consisted of 12 tribes, Jesus chose 12 disciples to be the nucleus of a new Israel. After Israel had experienced the judgment of God in the Exile, Judaism hoped that someday God would restore Israel and establish His kingdom in a decisive way. Jesus believed that that time had come. His own ministry inaugurated the kingdom of God, and the 12 disciples were to be part of

The Gospels record the area around the Sea of Galilee as a place of Jesus' ministry.

fering them healing, but He also told subversive parables to issue a radical message to the hearers. Although the details of His parables came from everyday, familiar occurrences, Jesus invariably introduced a twist that puzzled the hearers. The parables of Jesus were not harmless illustrations of the status quo. They presented an alternate reality that stood at odds with the familiar.

There is not a single method of classifying the parables of Jesus. Some scholars classify them by making a distinction between parables that have a lengthy narrative plot, such as the prodigal son (Luke 15:11-32), and parables that are one-liners, without much of a plot, such as the mustard seed (Mark 4:31-32). Some scholars classify them by using the part of the social world from which Jesus drew the elements of His parables. On this basis, one scholar has classified the parables under three categories: (1) family, village, city, and beyond, (2) masters and servants, and (3) home and farm.[8] Regardless of the method, scholars agree that the parables of Jesus must be studied in the historical context of the life of Jesus without reading into them elaborate allegorical meanings derived from the later theology of the Christian Church.[9]

The kingdom of God is like a mustard seed, very small, but when it has grown it becomes a great shrub (see Matthew 13:32, NRSV). Mustard is a nasty weed that spreads rapidly and takes over a garden. The Kingdom is also like yeast that leavens a large quantity of flour (v. 33). Yeast was not always a positive symbol. The kingdom of God is revolutionary. It can be unobtrusive and subtle and yet

that inauguration. Jesus said to the Twelve, "I confer on you a kingdom, just as my Father has conferred one on me, so that you may eat and drink at my table in my kingdom and sit on thrones, judging the twelve tribes of Israel" (Luke 22:29-30; cf. Matthew 19:28).

The disciples often misunderstood the nature of the reign of God or the meaning of discipleship. They expected a triumphant, royal Messiah and a glorious kingdom, which was not what Jesus had in mind. Halfway through Mark, when Jesus told them that suffering and death awaited Him in Jerusalem, Peter rebuked Jesus (Mark 8:31-32). Jesus said that if they wanted to be His disciples, they must deny themselves, take up their cross and follow Him (v. 34). "If anyone comes to me and does not hate his father and mother, his wife and children, his brothers and sisters—yes, even his own life—he cannot be my disciple" (Luke 14:26). Some of His most radical statements about discipleship are in the parables that He told.

■ Parables of the Kingdom of God

Not only did Jesus act out the presence of the reign of God by associating with outcasts and of-so powerful and captivating that a laborer might sell all of his possessions to buy a field because he happened to find a treasure in it. It is like a merchant who sold everything he had to buy a single pearl of exquisite quality (vv. 44-45).

The parables of Jesus often made people uncomfortable and even angry, as in the case of the parable of the vineyard and tenants (Mark 12:12). The parable of the Good Samaritan (Luke 10:25-37) is particularly poignant. To test Jesus, a Jewish theologian asked Him what he must do to inherit eternal life. Jesus asked him what the Scriptures said. The theologian pointed out the two great commandments of loving God and loving one's neighbor. Jesus told him to do this and he would have eternal life. Embarrassed that the test was too easy, the theologian asked, "And who is my neighbor?" Jesus told him the story of the Good Samaritan and ended it by asking the theologian which of the three—the priest, the Levite, the Samaritan—proved to be a neighbor to the one victimized by robbers. The theologian could not even use the word *Samaritan*. Instead, he said, "The one who had mercy on him." Jesus said to him, "Go and do likewise."

Modern readers do not often grasp the offensiveness of that last statement. Jews despised Samaritans and did not associate with them. For Jesus to hold up a Samaritan as a model of virtue would be an ultimate insult to a Jewish theologian. To grasp the finer points of the parables one needs to understand the social world of Jesus.

Journey to Jerusalem

Halfway through the Gospels Jesus turns His face toward Jerusalem to carry His message to the very center of the religious and political establishment. Jewish pilgrims came to Jerusalem for Passover to celebrate ancient Israel's liberation from Egypt. Roman authorities knew that pilgrims, resentful of Roman occupation, could explode in their nationalistic feelings and start an uprising. Roman soldiers had standing orders to strike hard at the least sign of disturbance. Jewish leaders felt responsible to keep pilgrims calm.

The Gospels say that Jesus predicted three times that He would suffer and die in Jerusalem (Mark 8:31; 9:31; 10:33-34). Roman crucifixions of Jews were common during His lifetime. He was cer-

---

T

Messianic Expectation in First-Century Judaism

There is no doubt that the Jewish people in the first century fervently expected the Messiah, the Anointed One. Several messianic movements besides the Jesus movement got underway, but they were all crushed violently by the Romans. But what type of messiah did people expect? Passages in the Gospels and Acts, the writings of the Essenes at Qumran, as well as the writings of the first-century Jewish historian Josephus, attest to the fact that Judaism longed for deliverance from bondage to Roman domination and the dawning of a golden age. The Dead Sea Scrolls, the library of the Essenes at Qumran, indicate that this Jewish sect seems to have expected a royal messiah as well as a priestly messiah.[10] Even the followers of Jesus hoped for a messiah who would bring political victory to Israel. After the feeding of the 5,000, the crowd wanted to take Jesus by force and make Him king (John 6:15). James and John asked Jesus that they sit on His right and left in His kingdom (Mark 10:37). After the resurrection of Jesus, the disciples asked Him, "Lord, are you at this the time going to restore the kingdom to Israel?" (Acts 1:6).

tainly aware that **Herod Antipas,** the son of Herod the Great, executed John the Baptist (chap. 6) and was threatening to kill Him also (Luke 13:31). The Herodian family and the Romans were suspicious of anyone who spoke of another kingdom.

Jesus entered Jerusalem riding on a donkey as a deliberate act of messianic demonstration. The religious leaders and the crowd of Jewish pilgrims perfectly understood the symbolism of this act from the messianic prophecy of Zechariah 9:9. The crowd shouted a psalm (118:25-26) that celebrated victory over Israel's enemies: "Hosanna! Blessed is he who comes in the name of the Lord! Blessed is the coming kingdom of our father David! Hosanna in the highest!" (Mark 11:9-10).

Why did Jesus deliberately stage such a messianic demonstration, given the fact that in His Galilean ministry He avoided it? He intended to proclaim the arrival of the kingdom of God into the tightly controlled precincts of Jerusalem and the Temple. This staged drama did get the attention of the religious authorities (Matthew 21:10). They said to Jesus, "Teacher, order your disciples to stop" (Luke 19:39, NRSV). They feared that this much public demonstration might lead to a major crackdown by nervous Roman authorities (John 11:47-48). The kingdom of God threatened their vested interests and political power structures.

Jesus went to the Temple and drove out the buyers and sellers and overturned the tables of the moneychangers (Mark 11:15-17), quoting to them Isaiah 56:7 and Jeremiah 7:11, "Is it not written: 'My house will be called a house of prayer for all nations'? But you have made it 'a den of robbers'" (Mark 11:17). Jesus became angry at the chaotic merchandising going on in the outer court of the Temple, the only part where Gentiles could enter. The Temple had become a noisy bazaar, far from a house of prayer for all nations. The Temple leaders confronted Jesus and asked Him by what authority He was doing this. They began to look for a way to take Him into custody (vv. 18, 28).

While Jesus engaged in public activity and debate, He also met with His disciples privately. The Last Supper and the subsequent prayer in Gethsemane are particularly intriguing because they give us a glimpse into Jesus' understanding of His own death. The different accounts of the Last Supper (Mark 14:22-25; Matthew 26:26-29; Luke 22:17-20; 1 Corinthians 11:24-25) agree on several points. First, the death of Jesus, symbolized by the bread and wine, would be a renewal of the Old Testament covenant celebrated at Passover. Second, His death was to be for others. Third, His death would not be the end but part of the kingdom of God with a future dimension.

The Gethsemane episode shows the utter horror with which Jesus faced the prospect of His own death. He was distressed, horrified, and agitated (Mark 14:33-34). He prayed that this hour pass from Him, that God remove this cup from Him. The final line of His prayer, however, was, "Not what I will, but what you will" (v. 36). He would be faithful to God regardless of the consequences.

■ Crucifixion and Resurrection

The **Sanhedrin,** the highest Jewish council in Jerusalem,

charged Jesus with blasphemy because He claimed divine prerogatives by identifying himself as the Son of Man of Daniel 7:13 seated at the right hand of God and coming on the clouds of heaven (Mark 14:61-64). The Sanhedrin invoked the law in Leviticus 24:16 that imposed the death sentence on anyone who "blasphemes the name of the LORD" (NRSV). However, only the Roman governor, not the Sanhedrin, could impose the death penalty (John 18:31). The Gospels portray **Pontius Pilate,** the Roman governor, as reluctant to condemn Jesus but forced to do so under pressure from the Jewish elite (Matthew 27:24-25; Mark 15:9-11; Luke 23:4-5; John 19:12). Since Jewish scruples against blasphemy would not carry much weight with the Romans, the religious leaders brought the more political charge that Jesus was aspiring to be king (Luke 23:2; John 18:33-35). Jesus was condemned to death by Pilate in collaboration with the Sanhedrin.

The crucifixion of Jesus could not put a stop to the kingdom of God. After His death, the followers of Jesus testified that He appeared to them. In spite of diversity in details, the Synoptic Gospels, John, and Paul attest to the resurrection of Jesus. The differences in details actually strengthen the evidence. If all the witnesses said the same thing, we would suspect that they harmonized their stories.

Paul mentions the appearances of the resurrected Jesus to Cephas (Peter), the Twelve, 500 people, James (Jesus' brother), all the apostles, and last of all to Paul himself (1 Corinthians 15:3-8). The Gospels and Acts provide parallels to some of these appearances, but not all. According to the Gospels, Jesus appeared to Peter (Luke 24:34) and the other disciples (Matthew 28:16-17; Luke 24:33, 36). Acts 9:4-5 recounts Jesus' appearance to Paul. The Gospels and Acts do not mention the appearances to the 500 or to James.

Paul wrote First Corinthians around A.D. 55-60. He says that he had passed on to them the story of Jesus' death and resurrection (15:3), which he had heard from eyewitnesses. Here we have a very early tradition to attest to the resurrection of Jesus. Paul does not mention the appearance of Jesus to Mary Magdalene, as Matthew and John do (Matthew 28:1, 9; John 20:14-18). Given the

Some Christians identify Golgotha with this stone with skull-like features, outside of the wall of the Old City of Jerusalem.

Crucifixion in the Roman World

Since the Romans used crucifixion as a deterrence, it was always carried out in a public place. It was generally reserved for non-Romans, revolutionaries, the lowest classes, and the most dangerous criminals. Prior to crucifixion, the convict was stripped and brutally flogged with the Roman flagellum, which was a whip with sharp bones or metal pieces attached to it, calculated to tear the flesh. The convict was then led to the place of crucifixion and was attached to the horizontal and vertical beams of the cross with ropes or nails. Death often came slowly, only after several days of sheer agony. The victim died of asphyxiation when the legs and arms could no longer provide the needed support to fill the lungs with air.[11]

Some Christians regard this tomb located in the setting of a garden, outside the wall of the Old City of Jerusalem, as a possible site of Jesus' burial.

low status of women in the first century, it is unlikely that these Gospels invented a resurrection appearance to a woman. If they wanted to create stories, noteworthy apostles such as Peter, James, and John would have been better candidates for Resurrection appearances.

A more theological question has to do with the nature of the Resurrection itself. The Gospels affirm that the body of Jesus was resurrected, thus leaving the tomb empty. Other writings, such as 1 Corinthians 15:3-8, speak of Resurrection appearances without the mention of an empty tomb. Christ's bodily resurrection means that God intends to redeem all of creation, including the material part. In the resurrection of Jesus, God did something utterly new. He ushered in a new reality in history. Just as Jesus was raised, so also will be those who are in Christ. Believers in Christ have already been raised spiritually to a new way of life, but they will also be raised bodily in the final resurrection (Romans 6:8-9; 1 Corinthians 15:20-23).

Summary Statements

- The Synoptic Gospels are Matthew, Mark, and Luke and are literarily related to one another, whereas the Gospel of John stands alone.
- According to the two-source hypothesis, Matthew and Luke were dependent on Mark and "Q."
- The Gospels affirm that Jesus was born as a human being but also that He was the Son of God.
- The baptism and temptation of Jesus are signs of His identification with humanity.
- The miracles of Jesus were a demonstration that the kingdom of God had come.
- The disciples often misunderstood the nature of the reign of God or the meaning of discipleship.
- The parables of Jesus illustrate the kingdom of God inaugurated through His life and ministry.
- The resurrection of Jesus is the basis of the hope of the resurrection of all who are in Christ.

Questions for Reflection

1. In what way can a Gospel become for you good news from God?
2. If Jesus were alive today, in what circles would we most likely find Him?
3. What does it mean to make the kingdom of God the central focus of your life?

Bible Study Assignment

Read Matthew 20:17-19; Mark 10:32-34; Luke 18:31-34. Put these three passages in parallel columns. Using different color schemes, identify the words and phrases that are exactly alike in all the three Gospels (green). Identify words and phrases found only in Matthew (red). Identify words and phrases found only in Mark (yellow). Identify words and phrases found only in Luke (blue). Give a summary list of similarities and differences among these three Gospel accounts, and explain how these similarities and differences introduced by each writer contribute to our understanding of this narrative about Jesus.

Resources for Further Study

Cosby, Michael R. *Portraits of Jesus: An Inductive Approach to the Gospels.* Louisville, Ky.: Westminster/John Knox, 1999.
Senior, Donald. *Invitation to the Gospels.* New York: Paulist, 2002.
Strobel, Lee. *The Case for Christ.* Grand Rapids: Zondervan, 1998.

20 Jesus in the Gospels: The Gospels of Matthew and Mark

Objectives:

Your study of this chapter should help you to:

- Describe the authorship and purpose of the Gospel of Matthew
- Summarize the prominent themes in Matthew
- Discuss Matthew's portrait of Jesus
- Describe the authorship and purpose of the Gospel of Mark
- Discuss Mark's portrait of Jesus
- Make conclusions about the meaning of discipleship in Mark

Key Words to Understand

Royal Messiah
Sermon on the Mount
Ekklesia
Great Commission
Narrative
Discourse
Beatitudes
Antitheses
Eschatology
Olivet Discourse
Passion narrative
Caesarea Philippi
Passion predictions
Disciples

Questions to consider as you read:

1. Why is Jesus as a kingly messiah and teacher important for Matthew?

2. How does Matthew relate the story of Jesus to the Old Testament?

3. Why does Mark describe Jesus as the powerful miracle worker only to shift gears at midpoint to focus on the suffering and death of Jesus?

4. How does Mark portray the disciples?

The Gospel of Matthew

Authorship and Date

There is no scholarly consensus on the authorship and date of the first Gospel. Early Christian tradition ascribes this book to Matthew the disciple, also called Levi, a former tax collector. A statement from Papias (A.D. 100) quoted by Eusebius (A.D. 325) mentions Matthew composing in Aramaic the sayings of Jesus that others translated into Greek. Modern scholars tend to reject the view that Matthew the disciple wrote this book. Some scholars ascribe the book to a Jewish Christian who was highly educated in the Hebrew Scriptures, while others view the book as the product of the disciples of Matthew the apostle. Several internal elements in the Gospel support the traditional view. The structure and organization of the Gospel reveals the skill of a tax collector. This is the only Gospel that preserves the story of Jesus paying the Temple tax (17:24-27). The writer uses the apostolic name Matthew in his account of the call of the disciple (9:9; 10:2-4), rather than the name Levi, used by Mark and Luke. Scholarly views of the date range from A.D. 45 to 150. The book assumes the existence of the Temple (24:1-2), and it is therefore likely that the book belongs to a period shortly before the Temple was destroyed in A.D. 70.

The Purpose of Matthew

By comparing and contrasting the different Gospels, scholars have discovered that Matthew used at least 80 percent of the material in Mark.[1] However, the contents of Matthew are at least 50 percent more than Mark. This additional material in Matthew, which is not in Mark, happens to be in Luke also and consists mostly of the sayings of Jesus ("Q"). In addition to Mark and "Q," Matthew may have had access to other traditions that are part of his Gospel but not in Mark or Luke. Matthew sensed the need to add these materials to Mark's story of Jesus.

A good clue for understanding Matthew's purpose is the opening statement of the Gospel: "An account of the genealogy of Jesus the Messiah, the son of David, the son of Abraham" (1:1, NRSV). Following this opening statement, Matthew lists the ancestors of Jesus in a more detailed genealogy. The fact that Matthew shows Jesus to be a descendant of David, Israel's most venerated king, and of Abraham, Israel's primal ancestor, alerts the reader to the fact that Jesus is a **royal Messiah** whose ancestry is firmly rooted in Jewish history. As the royal Messiah, Jesus fulfills all the hopes and messianic expectations of the Old Testament.[2] This connection of Jesus to the Old Testament is one reason why the Gospel of Matthew ended up as the first book of the New Testament canon.

A second purpose, which is related to the above, is that Matthew as a Jewish-Christian writer wrote his Gospel to show that the Christian movement arising from Jesus was not a departure from Judaism but its ultimate fulfillment. More than any other New Testament writer, Matthew shows how the life and teachings of Jesus fulfill prophecies of the Hebrew Bible.

Third, by adding the sayings of Jesus to Mark's Gospel, Matthew intended to highlight the teachings of Jesus. Matthew's focus on Jesus as Teacher is evident from other features of the Gospel, such as large blocks of teaching material and explicit references to the teaching ministry of Jesus. In the **Sermon on the Mount** (chaps. 5—7), Jesus is presented as One who has authority to give a definitive interpretation of the Torah, the Hebrew Scriptures. Yet Matthew is careful to say that Jesus has come not to abolish but to fulfill the Law and the Prophets (5:17).

Matthew's purpose, however, goes even beyond that. Not only does the authority of Jesus surpass that of Moses and the prophets from the past, but it also extends to the future life of the church. Of the four Gospels, Matthew is the only one where we find the term *ekklēsia,* the Greek word for *church.* After Peter's confession of Jesus as the Christ, Jesus says to Peter, "Blessed are you, Simon son of Jonah . . . And I tell you that you are Peter, and on this rock I will build my church" (16:17-18). Chapter 18, which is one of the major discourses of Jesus in Matthew, is devoted to issues related to life in the church. People in the church must make every effort to forgive and be reconciled to one another, and to seek and save the lost. Jesus gives the church extraordinary authority and responsibility when He says, "Whatever you bind on earth will be bound in heaven, and whatever you loose on earth will be loosed in heaven" (v. 18).

However, the Church does not have a privileged position independent of Christ. Matthew's understanding of the nature of the Church is that the Church must live its life under the authority of Jesus and receive its identity in relation to Christ.[3] It must maintain its faithfulness to Jesus by living a righteous life, serving others, and bearing witness to the gospel. Otherwise, it might find itself under judgment on the final day (7:21-25; 25:12). Matthew concludes his Gospel with what has come to be known as the **Great Commission.** In this final word, the resurrected Christ meets with His disciples and commissions them to go and make disciples of all nations (28:18-20).

This word of Jesus underscores several concerns that Matthew has for the Church. The Church must live under the authority of Jesus, which is not of human origin but part of a trinity of Father, Son, and Holy Spirit. The Church must bear witness to Jesus by making disciples of all nations. Whereas earlier Jesus sent His disciples to the house of Israel (10:5-6), now He sends them out to all the nations of the world. The gospel is not exclusively for Israel. Finally, as the Church engages in mission, Jesus promises that His presence in the Church will continue to the end of time.

Content

Matthew organizes his materials into **narrative** and **discourse** sections and presents them in an alternating manner. The six narrative sections (chaps. 1—4, 8—9, 11—12, 14—17, 19—23, and 26—28) include stories about Jesus. The discourse sections (chaps. 5—7, 10, 13, 18, 24—25) contain the teachings of Jesus. The alternation between narrative and discourse is a key feature of the structure of this Gospel.

Scholars have proposed another simple threefold structure to the Gospel based on an identical statement at two significant junctures in the Gospel: "From that time on Jesus began to . . ." (4:17; 16:21).

Literary Structure of Matthew

The alternation between narrative and discourse material is one of the ways that scholars have understood Matthew's literary scheme.

Narrative (chaps. 1—4)	Birth, baptism, and temptation
Discourse (chaps. 5—7)	Sermon on the Mount
Narrative (chaps. 8—9)	Miracles of Jesus
Discourse (chap. 10)	Instructions to the Twelve
Narrative (chaps. 11—12)	Opposition to Jesus
Discourse (chap. 13)	Parables of the kingdom of God
Narrative (chaps. 14—17)	Miracles, Peter's confession, passion predictions, and transfiguration of Jesus
Discourse (chap. 18)	Instructions on Christian community
Narrative (chaps. 19—23)	Controversies with scribes and Pharisees
Discourse (chaps. 24—25)	The eschatological discourse
Narrative (chaps. 26—28)	Passion and Resurrection narratives

The Journey of Jesus to Jerusalem and His Suffering, Death, and Resurrection   16:21—28:20

Matthew tends to place similar materials in groups of three, as in the following examples: threefold division of the genealogy of Jesus (1:17); three illustrations of righteousness (6:1-5); and three eschatological parables (chap. 25). Matthew may have been influenced by the Law of Moses that requires two or three witnesses as evidence of authenticity, another instance of Matthew's Jewish tendencies (Deuteronomy 19:15; cf. Matthew 18:16).[4]

Matthew's Gospel shows frequent use of the Old Testament.[5] There are over 60 quotations from the Old Testament in Matthew, not counting a great many allusions. Understanding Matthew's use of these quotations is a challenge. Although Matthew frequently uses the word *fulfill* to indicate the relationship between Jesus and an Old Testament text, our popular notions of prediction and fulfillment are inadequate to explain what Matthew has done. Some of the quoted texts are simply descriptions of past events and not predictions of future events (see, for example, 2:17-18, where he quotes Jeremiah 31:15). In Matthew's use of the Old Testament, he begins with Jesus and then looks back to the Old Testament to show the continuity. In his mind, *fulfill* means that the life, message, death, and resurrection of Jesus bring fuller meaning to the Old Testament Scriptures.

Prominent Themes in Matthew

■ The Law and the Prophets

No other Gospel uses the phrase "the law and the prophets," or a variant of it, as extensively as Matthew does. This is an indication of Matthew's Jewish roots and his intention to show that Jesus and the Old Testament Scriptures are a single, continuous story of revelatory events. Jesus has not come to abolish the Law or the Prophets but to fulfill them (5:17). He encapsulates all the commandments of the Old Testament in the two great commandments of loving God with all the heart, soul, and mind and loving one's neighbor as oneself. "All the Law and the Prophets hang on these two commandments" (22:40).

■ Righteousness

Correlated with Matthew's emphasis on the Law and the Prophets is the theme of righteousness, particularly in the Sermon on the Mount (chaps. 5—7). The **Beatitudes,** the nine statements that begin with "Blessed," are the opening words of the Sermon on the Mount. In one beatitude Jesus says, "Blessed are those who hunger and thirst for righteousness, for they will be filled" (5:6). In another beatitude He says, "Blessed are those who are persecuted because of righteousness" (v. 10). In verse 20, another key passage in the Sermon on the Mount, Jesus states, "Unless your righteousness surpasses that of the Pharisees and the teachers of

the law, you will certainly not enter the kingdom of heaven." The rest of the Sermon on the Mount is in effect an elaboration of the theme of righteousness.

The next major section of the Sermon on the Mount consists of six **antitheses** (5:21-48). All six are constructed the same way, contrasting what was said earlier in the Hebrew Scriptures and what Jesus was saying now: "You have heard that it was said . . . but I tell you . . ." Each antithesis is an illustration of the principle stated in 5:20 that the righteousness of the disciples must exceed that of the Pharisees. For example, it is not enough to refrain from murder; one must not even be angry.

The theme of righteousness continues in 6:1-18, where Jesus warns against practicing one's piety (literally, "righteousness") before others to be seen by them. Almsgiving, prayer, and fasting are to be done secretly and without fanfare, to be seen by God rather than by people.

Instead of worrying over food and clothing, one must "seek first

This hillside may have been the site of the Sermon on the Mount.

"Christian Perfection" in Matthew

Far from being less demanding, Jesus reminds His disciples of the true meaning of the Old Testament commandments. Obedience to God is a matter of one's heart rather than merely a matter of external conduct.

The antitheses in Matthew 5 conclude with the highest possible standard of life when Jesus says, "Be perfect, therefore, as your heavenly Father is perfect" (v. 48). The context makes it clear that this perfection of the Christian is perfect love that refuses to return evil for evil. Perfect love is forgiving and charitable to both friends and enemies. The pattern of Christian perfection is God, who "causes his sun to rise on the evil and the good, and sends rain on the righteous and the unrighteous" (v. 45).

his kingdom and his righteousness, and all these things will be given to you as well" (6:33). A true disciple acts on the words of Jesus and lives a fruitful life (7:15-29).

The theme of righteousness continues beyond the Sermon on the Mount. In a scathing denunciation of the Pharisees in chapter 23, Jesus likens them to "whitewashed tombs, which look beautiful on the outside but on the inside are full of dead men's bones and everything unclean. In the same way, on the outside you appear to people as righteous but on the inside you are full of hypocrisy and wickedness" (vv. 27-28).

Matthew directs the charge of hypocrisy not only toward outsiders but also to members of his own Christian community, to those who may have made a confession of faith in Jesus but whose lifestyle and ethic did not show it. In the eschatological discourse of chapters 24—25, where Jesus speaks of "the end times," several parables target those who were inside the Christian community rather than those who were outside.[6] In the parable in 25:1-13, all 10 bridesmaids were waiting for the return of Christ, the Bridegroom. But 5 of them did not have enough oil for their torches. While they were gone to purchase oil, the bridegroom came and shut the door. When they returned, they found themselves left out of the wedding party. These bridesmaids represent those who profess the name of Christ but do not live the life of righteousness demanded by Christ. In the end they will find themselves under judgment. Earlier, in the Sermon on the Mount, Jesus says, "Not everyone who says to me, 'Lord, Lord,' will enter the kingdom of heaven, but only he who does the will of my Father who is in heaven" (7:21).

The last parable in Matthew 25 is a scene of the final judgment when the Son of Man makes a distinction between the righteous and the unrighteous as a shepherd separates the sheep from the goats (vv. 31-46). In this parable, it is the Gentile nations that are being judged (v. 32). Those who welcome and care for "the least of these" will be invited to "take your inheritance, the kingdom prepared for you since the creation of the world" (v. 34). Christ the Judge identifies the least of these as "these brothers of mine" (v. 40), that is, the missionaries whom Christ will send out to all nations (28:19). Those Gentiles who have ministered to the needs of the hungry, thirsty, estranged, naked, sick, and imprisoned messengers of Christ have unwittingly rendered service to Christ. On the other hand, the unrighteous are those who have failed to serve Christ by neglecting the needs of "the least of these." They will hear this word of judgment: "Whatever you did not do for one of the least of these, you did not do to me" (25:45).

To summarize, Matthew's indictment of unrighteousness targets not only the Jewish community and his own Christian community but also the whole Gentile world. Matthew issues a serious call to everyone to heed the demands of righteousness proclaimed and lived out by Christ.

■ The End of the Age

A final theme in Matthew is **eschatology,** the theology of the end of the age, particularly the issue of Christ's return. All three Synoptic Gospels contain the **Olivet Discourse** (chaps. 24—25), so named after the Mount of Olives where Jesus spoke these words (24:3; Mark 13:3).[7]

The setting in which Jesus gives the discourse is found in Matthew 23:38—24:3. A sequence of events precedes this discourse. The events begin with Jesus' lament over Jerusalem (23:38). Later, when the disciples point out to Jesus the buildings of the Temple, Jesus predicts that the Temple will be destroyed (24:2). The disciples then ask Him for the sign of the end time (v. 3). The Olivet Discourse is Jesus' response to the disciples' questions about the time of (1) the destruction of the Temple, (2) the coming of Christ, and (3) the end of the age. The discourse of Jesus weaves together these three matters.

In the first part of the discourse, Jesus warns against anxious speculations about the end time. When Matthew wrote this Gospel, speculations about the end of the world would have been very much up in the air. In such a context Matthew reminds his readers Jesus' words that wars, famines, earthquakes, and other cataclysmic events are not the signs of the coming of Christ and the end of the age (v. 6).

Second, no one knows the time of Christ's coming except God (v. 36). Therefore, it would be futile to look for signs of its nearness. It will happen suddenly and without warning (vv. 36-44).

Third, there are indications in the Olivet Discourse that the coming of Christ may be delayed. In

Matthew and Anti-Semitism

Many Jewish as well as Christian interpreters view statements in Matthew's Gospel that are directed against the Pharisees (chap. 23) as evidence of anti-Semitism in the Gospel of Matthew. Does Matthew, the most Jewish Gospel, indeed show an anti-Semitic attitude?

Unfortunately, the future history of Christendom, which became overwhelmingly Gentile, was checkered with prejudice and persecution against all Jewish people, who were labeled as "Christ killers." That kind of polemic ultimately led to the most radical form of anti-Semitism, namely, the genocide of 6 million Jews in Nazi Germany during World War II. Such sinful acts against the Jewish people no doubt found biblical support, however illegitimately, in Matthew and other New Testament writings, in much the same manner as Christian slaveholders used the Bible to support slavery in America.

One must remember that in the first century A.D. there were several Jewish groups that debated passionately with one another about what it meant to be Jewish. Matthew's Jewish Christian community and a Jewish synagogue led by Pharisees saw themselves as two rival Jewish sects rather than two different religions. For Matthew, faith in Christ did not mean accepting a religion different from Judaism. Consequently, the charge of anti-Semitism, which is really racial rather than religious, does not fit the historical context of Matthew.

the parable in 24:45-51, the slave whose master has gone away acts wickedly because he thinks to himself, "My master is staying away a long time" (v. 48). In the parable of the 10 bridesmaids, the bridegroom arrives later than anticipated (25:5).

Matthew's Portrait of Jesus

■ Royal Messiah

As noted earlier, Matthew's opening statement, "Jesus the Messiah, the son of David, the son of Abraham" (1:1, NRSV), is a clear indication that Matthew intends to portray Jesus as the fulfillment of Jewish messianic expectations. As a descendant of David, He is a royal Messiah, an anointed King. Matthew's account of Jesus' birth is full of references to His royal status. When the wise men come to King Herod's palace looking for the infant Jesus, they ask, "Where is the one who has been born king of the Jews?" (2:2).

Alarmed to learn of the birth of a rival king, Herod assembles the religious leaders to inquire of them where the Messiah was to be born. They quote to him Micah 5:2 that speaks of Bethlehem, the city of David, as the town out of which "will come . . . one who will be ruler over Israel." Of the three Gospels, Matthew by far has the most occurrences of "Son of David" as a title used by people to address Jesus, another indication of Matthew's interest in portraying Jesus as a royal descendant of David and therefore Messiah, or Christ.

■ A Teacher Greater than Moses

In Matthew Jesus is much more than a Davidic Messiah. As noted earlier, He is also portrayed as the Teacher who has a greater authority than Moses. Just as Moses received and then delivered the Ten Commandments from Mount Sinai, so now Jesus also delivers the Sermon on the Mount with an authority that surpasses that of Moses. Jesus speaks as the supreme Teacher whose word has greater authority than the Law of Moses.

■ Son of God

In Matthew, Jesus is not only a Jewish Messiah and a Teacher greater than Moses, but, above all, the Son of God. Although all four Gospels make this affirmation, Matthew does it in a unique way. Matthew connects the divine Sonship of Jesus to the Hebrew Scriptures and to Israel.

The announcement of the angel to Joseph concerning the conception of Jesus clearly focuses on the theme of Jesus as the Son of God (1:20-23). Jesus is conceived by the Holy Spirit, His name means Savior, and His birth signifies that God is with us (see Isaiah 7:14). Old Testament echoes are unmistakable in affirming that Jesus issues from the very being of God and thus He is the Son of God.

When Jesus walks on the water to the disciples in the boat and calms the storm, they fall down and worship Jesus and say, "Truly you are the Son of God" (Matthew 14:33). The confession of Peter in 16:16 has the additional affirmation that Jesus is "the Son of the living God," which is lacking in Mark 8:29. When Jesus was on the Cross, even the Roman centurion and the soldiers who watched the Crucifixion exclaimed, "Surely he was the Son of God!" (27:54).

Finally, the two most significant statements in Matthew about the intimate relationship between Jesus and God as Son and Father happen to be on the mouth of Jesus himself. Jesus says, "All things have been committed to me by my Father. No one knows the Son except the Father, and no one knows the Father except the Son and those to whom the Son chooses to reveal him" (11:27).

The second statement about the relationship between the Father and the Son is in the Great Commission, which is found only in Matthew. The resurrected Jesus commands the disciples to baptize "in the name of the Father and of the Son and of the Holy Spirit" (28:19). Although the doctrine of the Trinity emerged later, the foundations of it are found here in Matthew as well as in several other places in the New Testament.

The Gospel According to Mark

Authorship and Date

Most scholars believe that Mark was the first Gospel to be written. However, we have no clear indication in the Gospel that supports this view. An early Christian tradition (Papias, A.D. 100) describes Mark as the interpreter of Peter; Mark interpreted what Peter preached and later wrote down what he remembered, but not in exact order.

Several New Testament passages mention a person by the name of Mark. According to Acts 12:12, a young man by the name John Mark was the son of a prominent woman in Jerusalem in whose house the church met. This Mark traveled with Paul and Barnabas on their first missionary journey but deserted them and returned to Jerusalem (13:13). Later, Paul refused to take him on a second journey and had a sharp disagreement with Barnabas so that the two parted company (15:36-40). Apparently, Barnabas wanted to give Mark another chance, partly because the two were cousins (Colossians 4:10). Eventually Mark turned out to be a faithful coworker both of Paul and of Peter (2 Timothy 4:11; Philemon 24; 1 Peter 5:13).

Although some scholars question whether Papias's Mark is the same as the New Testament Mark,[8] other scholars find the statement of Papias consistent with the New Testament picture about John Mark, his associations with Christians in Jerusalem, his Jewish descent, and his close relationship with Peter and Paul.

More important than the issue of authorship for our understanding of the purpose of Mark is the question of when and where it was written. There is considerable agreement that it was written in Rome in the late 60s of the first century during or shortly after Nero's persecution of Christians and a year or two before the destruction of Jerusalem by the Romans in A.D. 70.[9]

The Purpose of Mark

Since Mark does not state the purpose for his Gospel, we must deduce this through careful reading of the Gospel. The clearest indication of Mark's purpose is perhaps his opening words: "The beginning of the gospel about Jesus Christ, the Son of God" (1:1). Mark's primary purpose was to tell the good news of Jesus.

Mark's further designation of Jesus as Christ and Son of God is significant for our understanding of the nature of this good news. Jesus is the Christ, the Anointed One of God. He is the Son of God. The good news is that Jesus has come to inaugurate "God's sovereign rule, the Kingdom, through his words and deeds."[10]

Content

Although Mark designates his story of Jesus as good news, it is a story of conflict, opposition, and death. Exactly how it is good news will not be clear until we have read the Gospel and noted its main features.

Mark's story of Jesus is a "Drama in Three Acts"[11] as outlined below:

Jesus' Ministry in
Galilee   1:1—8:21
Journey to Jerusalem
                           8:22—10:52

Arrest, Trial, and
Crucifixion   11:1—16:8

In this last section of Mark, known as the **passion narrative** among scholars, Jesus dies in utter humiliation. All of His followers desert Him. How can this be good news when it seems nothing but a story of failure? Jesus is buried, but when three women come to the tomb after the Sabbath they find it empty. A young man in a white robe tells them that Jesus has been raised and that they ought to go and tell His disciples. The story ends abruptly in 16:8; verses 9-20 are a later addition. The Gospel ends with the women fleeing from the tomb in utter terror and saying nothing to anyone. The reader is left perplexed as to how it is that a story that was supposed to be good news comes to such an anticlimactic and terrifying end.

If Mark intended to end his Gospel at 16:8, what was his purpose? The opening words of the Gospel, "The beginning of the gospel," and the open-ended conclusion in 16:8 may give us a clue. Jesus in His lifetime was the embodiment of the reign of God in the world. But He was opposed, ridiculed, abandoned, and executed. His disciples ran away. Even the women were terrified and told no one that Jesus was resurrected.

Yet Mark has written his Gospel to address a community of Christians four decades after the events of the life and death of Jesus. The story of Jesus *had* been told after all. The Gospel of Mark was most likely written in Rome to encourage a community of Christians persecuted by Roman authorities (10:30). The persecuted believers whom Mark addressed with his Gospel were proof that

The Ending of Mark

Almost all English translations of the Bible place the ending of Mark (16:9-20) either in brackets or in a footnote. The reason is that these verses are later additions to Mark, possibly from the second century. Even though these verses are present in many manuscripts of the Gospel of Mark, they are absent from Codex Sinaiticus and Codex Vaticanus, two important fourth-century manuscripts, which happen to be among the oldest of New Testament manuscripts. Some manuscripts of Mark have a shorter ending, and others have the longer ending of verses 9-20, most of which consists of the Resurrection appearances of Jesus from the other Gospels. Early copyists apparently tried in various ways to provide a better closure to the story of Jesus.

Scholars have proposed various theories about the Gospel of Mark. Some have suggested that Mark's original ending was somehow lost. Others have suggested that for some reason Mark was not able to finish his Gospel. Still others have proposed that Mark intentionally ended his Gospel at 16:8.[12]

Remains of Peter's house in Capernaum, the center of Jesus' Galilean ministry.

the story of Jesus did not end at 16:8. What Mark wrote in his Gospel was just "the beginning."

Mark's Portrait of Jesus

Throughout the Gospel, Mark presents Jesus as the powerful Son of God whose mission leads to suffering and death. The Gospel begins with the Christian affirmation that Jesus is the Son of God (1:1). The voice of God confirms this at the baptism and transfiguration of Jesus (v. 11; 9:7). Even demons recognize Jesus as the Son of God, but Jesus silences them (1:24-25; 5:7). In spite of His mighty works of healing and exorcisms, people respond to Jesus with doubt, anger, and murderous plots (2:6-7; 3:6, 22; 6:2-6). Even the disciples are often perplexed and flounder. After Jesus walks on the sea and calms the storm, the disciples are "completely amazed, for they had not understood about the loaves; their hearts were hardened" (6:51-52; cf. 8:17-21).

The incident at **Caesarea Philippi,** where Peter confesses

Jesus to be the Messiah or Christ, is a turning point in the Gospel (vv. 27-30). In spite of his great confession, Peter and his fellow disciples are about to face a crisis. Peter rebukes Jesus when he learns that Jesus must undergo great suffering, be rejected and killed, and be raised after three days (vv. 29-33). Three times Jesus makes such **passion predictions,** and each time the disciples demonstrate an utter lack of comprehension (v. 32; 9:32; 10:32-45).

This sort of misunderstanding and opposition to Jesus reaches a crescendo when the Sanhedrin in Jerusalem asks Jesus if He is "the Christ, the Son of the Blessed One" (14:61). When Jesus answers, "I am" (v. 62), they determine that He has committed blasphemy and condemn Him as deserving death. The Roman governor Pilate imposes the death sentence and crucifies Him.

The closing scene in Mark is the discovery of the empty tomb by the three women and the declaration of the heavenly messenger that Jesus has been raised

A Crucified Son of God

The only human recognition in Mark that Jesus is the Son of God comes from a most unlikely source and in a most unlikely context. As Jesus dies in utter agony and humiliation, the Roman centurion who most likely had a role in the execution exclaims, "Surely this man was the Son of God!" (15:39). Mark's point is clear. Rather than refuting the divine Sonship of Jesus, His death evokes a Roman soldier's confession that He is the Son of God.

For 2,000 years, Christians have recited the creeds that affirm Jesus as the Son of God and have almost taken it for granted. Not so with Mark. What Mark did was nothing short of a subversive act. Only the Roman emperor, the symbol of ultimate power, could be called the son of a god. Yet Mark and other Christians dared to proclaim that the One who was crucified by Roman authorities was the true Son of God.

(16:6-7). This is the final divine confirmation that Jesus is indeed the Son of God.

◼ Discipleship in Mark

Next to Jesus, the most signifi-cant characters in the Gospel of Mark are the **disciples.** Mark weaves into the story of Jesus their attitudes, responses, and conduct.

Mark's portrayal of the 12 disciples seems ambivalent at best. The disciples have both positive and negative attributes. On the positive side, when Jesus calls the disciples, they immediately leave everything and follow Him (1:18, 20; 2:14). Jesus calls them to have a part in His own mission, "that they might be with him and that he might send them out to preach and to have authority to drive out demons" (3:14-15; cf. 6:12-13). The call comes from Jesus; they are not volunteers as such.

When Jesus' own family come to take custody of Him because they think He has gone mad (3:21), He says in exasperation, "Who are my mother and my brothers?" (v. 33). Looking at His disciples and others around Him, He says, "Here are my mother and my brothers! Whoever does God's will is my brother and sister and mother" (vv. 34-35).

Some of Jesus' early disciples were fishermen. This boat is a model of fishing boats in the first century A.D.

In spite of this positive portrait of the disciples, Mark repeatedly points out their shortcomings and failures. He says that their hearts were hardened (6:52; 8:17-18). In the end, one of His disciples, Judas, will betray Him. Peter, the leader of the Twelve, will deny Jesus three times. The other disciples will abandon Him and run away.

The picture is even more disheartening in the second major section of Mark (8:22—10:52), when Jesus begins to instruct His disciples concerning upcoming events in Jerusalem.

The section begins with the healing of a blind man (8:22-26). At first, his healing is partial. He can see people but "they look like trees walking around" (v. 24). When Jesus touches him again, his sight is fully restored. At the end of the section there is a second story of a blind man, that of Bartimaeus (10:46-52). Mark's concluding comment that Bartimaeus "received his sight and followed Jesus along the road" (v. 52) clearly implies that he became a disciple.

These two stories of blind men function as brackets that enclose the whole section of Mark 8:22—10:52 on the theme of discipleship. After the healing of the first blind man, Mark weaves various materials together on the subject of discipleship (8:27—9:29; 9:30—10:31; 10:32-45). The backbone of this section consists of three passion predictions (8:31; 9:31; 10:33-35). The section concludes with the healing of blind Bartimaeus.

In the instruction that follows the first passion prediction, Jesus instructs His blind and resistant disciples on the true meaning of discipleship (8:34—9:1). Discipleship means denying oneself, taking up the cross, and following Jesus. Those who lose their life for Jesus' sake will save it. Following His second passion prediction (v. 31), He instructs that whoever wants to be first must be a servant to all, even to a child (vv. 35-37).

When the disciples reprimanded parents for bringing their children to Jesus (10:13-16), He instructs them that the kingdom of God belongs precisely to children. One must receive the kingdom of God as a child. Discipleship to Jesus means a radical reevaluation of previous social hierarchies. Children, the weakest members of society, matter to God and they must matter to disciples.

Discipleship also means a radical reevaluation of wealth. A rich man asks Jesus what he must do to inherit eternal life (vv. 17-22), assuming that he can obtain eternal life by *doing* things. Jesus tells the man to keep the commandments, but interestingly Jesus cites the second half of the Ten Commandments, which have to do with social relationships. The rich man says that he has kept the commandments since his youth. The final word of Jesus and the man's response bring the story to a soul-searching climax. Jesus says, "One thing you lack. Go, sell everything you have and give to the poor, and you will have treasure in heaven. Then come, follow me" (v. 21). Jesus puts His finger on the central issue. The man leaves grieving because he had many possessions. Discipleship begins with one's commitment to the first and most important of the Ten Commandments: "You shall have no other gods before me" (Exodus 20:3).

The third passion prediction deals with what will happen in Jerusalem (Mark 10:33-35). Yet, ironically, and oblivious to what

Jesus has repeatedly said, James and John request that they sit on His right and left in His glory. When the other 10 disciples hear this, they are angry. For the last time, Jesus teaches them what discipleship means (vv. 42-45). They are not to be like the rulers of the Gentiles who lord it over them as tyrants. If they wish to become great, they must become a slave to all, for even Jesus himself "did not come to be served, but to serve, and to give his life as a ransom for many" (v. 45).

Mark's purpose in this section is to show how blind and uncomprehending the disciples were during the lifetime of Jesus. However, Mark also knows that in spite of their failures, Jesus never gives up on them.

After the crucifixion and burial of Jesus, the final word of the heavenly messenger to the women at the empty tomb is for them to go and tell the disciples and Peter that Jesus has been raised and is going ahead of them to Galilee; there they will see Him (16:7). The good news that Mark has told is that in the end Jesus will still meet with His faltering disciples and they will finally see clearly who Jesus is and what it means to be His disciples.

Garden of Gethsemane where Jesus prayed before He was arrested.

Summary Statements

- Matthew portrays Jesus not only as a royal Messiah and as an authoritative Teacher, but above all as Son of God.
- Jesus teaches that righteousness must come from within and be a quality of the heart.
- The Gospel of Matthew indicts hypocrisy not only among outsiders but also among those in the Church.
- In the Great Commission, the resurrected Jesus sends out His disciples to make disciples of all nations.
- Mark's purpose was to announce the good news of Jesus as the Son of God, even though it involved conflict, misunderstanding, opposition, suffering, and death for Jesus.
- The disciples could not fully comprehend Jesus' words about His suffering and death.
- Mark gives instructions on what it means to follow Jesus.

Questions for Reflection

1. Why is it important to trace the roots of the story of Jesus in the Hebrew Scriptures?
2. How can one be sure that one's righteousness is truly from the heart and not hypocritical?
3. What are the implications of our faith affirmation that Jesus is the Son of God?
4. Do you find Mark's portrait of the disciples encouraging or discouraging? Explain your answer.

Bible Study Assignment

Read Matthew 18:1-35 and identify the common theme that connects the various stories in this chapter. What do you think Matthew is saying to us about how discipline should be carried out in the church today?

Read Mark 1:9—3:12. How does Mark portray Jesus in the various narratives in this section? What do you think is the message Mark is conveying to us about Jesus through these stories?

Resources for Further Study

Best, Ernest. *Following Jesus: Discipleship in the Gospel of Mark*. Sheffield: JSOT, 1981.
Juel, Donald. *The Gospel of Mark*. Nashville: Abingdon, 1999.
Senior, Donald. *The Gospel of Matthew*. Nashville: Abingdon, 1997.

21 Jesus in the Gospels: The Gospels of Luke and John

Objectives:

Your study of this chapter should help you to:
- Describe the authorship of the Gospel of Luke
- Discuss the content and message of the Gospel of Luke
- Make assessment of Luke's distinctive concerns for women, the poor, and sinners
- Describe the unique features of the Gospel of John
- Explore the major themes in John
- Gain insight into John's portrait of Jesus

Questions to consider as you read:

1. What did Jesus experience in His relationship with fellow Jews at home in Nazareth, and as He traveled about Galilee and Judea?

2. In what ways does Luke's Gospel express Jesus' concern for the underprivileged and oppressed?

3. Why are the miracles of Jesus in John called signs?

4. How does John portray the person of Jesus?

Key Words to Understand

"We" sections
"L" material
John the Baptist
New Testament
    Apocrypha
Galilee
Sepphoris
Capernaum
Johannine literature
The beloved disciple
Logos
Incarnation
Farewell discourse
Prologue
Paraclete
"I am" sayings

The Gospel of Luke

Authorship and Date

Early Christian tradition ascribes the Gospel to Luke, an early companion of Paul and evidently a physician (Colossians 4:14). This author combines two significant strands of early Christian history in a way that makes him a unique biblical writer. As a historical researcher, Luke documents the life of Jesus in light of earlier sources (Luke 1:1-4). He then goes on to tell the story of the early Christian movement in the Book of Acts, something no other author's extant work does. This two-volume work comprises almost a quarter of the New Testament and makes Luke one of the most significant authors in the Bible.

> Though we do not know much about the identity of the author, we think he was a Gentile and a traveling companion of Paul. Scholars often cite the **"we" sections** in Acts (16:10-17; 20:5-15; 21:1-18; 27:1-29; 28:11-16) as evidence in support of Luke's authorship of the Gospel and Acts. The writer of Acts changes the third-person narrative to first-person plural in these sections. It is possible that Luke may have joined Paul's traveling team at Troas during his second missionary journey. The Book of Acts also begins with an address to Theophilus, and the author of Acts presents his work as a continuation of his "former book" (Acts 1:1). It is very likely that the first book is the Gospel of Luke.
>
> It is difficult to assign a precise date for the writing of Luke's Gospel. Some scholars assign this book to the early 60s. They also think that Luke would have completed his second volume (Acts) before Nero's persecution of Christians in A.D. 64. Some others place the Gospel in the second century.

We believe that Luke utilized materials found in Mark's Gospel, which was composed in the late 60s. This would put the writing of Luke in the late 70s or early 80s.

Purpose of Luke

Luke's purpose and method is described in the prologue to his Gospel. Writing to Theophilus, or "lover of God," Luke states his purpose: "to draw up an account of the things that have been fulfilled among us . . . so that you may know the certainty of the things you have been taught" (1:1, 4). He indicates that he has scoured existing sources for information on Jesus' life. Of the numerous sources that were already in circulation in his day, Luke depends heavily on Mark and "Q" and his own special material, or **"L" material**, that contains many of the themes and parables found only in his Gospel.

Content

The content of Luke's Gospel may be outlined as follows:

Jesus' Birth and Early
   Life   1:1—2:52
Beginning of the Ministry
   of John and Jesus   3:1—4:44
Jesus and His Ministry
                       5:1—19:48
The Final Days in
   Jerusalem   20:1—24:53

■ Birth and Early Life

The information on the birth and early life of Jesus is an interesting feature of Luke's Gospel. The story of Zechariah and Elizabeth (1:5-80), parents of John the Baptist, is a good example of the kind of personal detail that Luke preserves about the events surrounding Jesus' early life. It also demonstrates the importance of women to the Gospel history, a theme that will prove to be of particular concern to Luke.

Luke not only gives us more information about Jesus' birth than any other evangelist but also preserves the only information we have about His childhood. The account of the boy Jesus in the Temple at age 12 (2:39-52) describes how He amazed the elders and teachers with His wisdom. Jesus shows a sense of destiny with regard to the Temple that will be seen through the remainder of the narrative. After being left behind in Jerusalem on a family pilgrimage trip, He asks His parents, "Didn't you know that I had to be in my Father's house?" (v. 49). For Luke, from birth (vv. 28-32) to death (19:45-48), Jesus was filled with passion for Jerusalem and the Temple.

of additional information on the birth and early ministry of John reinforces this status. In Luke, the births of both men are miraculously announced by an angel (1:11, 26); the two mothers have a poignant meeting while pregnant (vv. 39-45), and hymns of praise are raised for each (vv. 46-55, 67-69). Luke presents John as a transitional figure who heralds the One who is to come (3:1-20).

The narrative shifts its emphasis from John to Jesus at the heavenly voice in 3:21-22. Jews of the first century A.D. came to believe that prophecy ended in the

Shepherd's Cave in Bethlehem.

■ Beginning of the Ministry of John the Baptist and Jesus

Among men, **John the Baptist** is second in importance only to Jesus in Luke (7:28). Luke's inclusion

The New Testament Apocrypha

If early biblical sources were reticent to describe the early life of Jesus, the so-called **New Testament Apocrypha,** or "revealed" documents, were not so reserved. Some have argued that a few of these sources, such as the Gospel of Thomas, are as old as the Gospels themselves. Apocryphal New Testament documents contain gospels, letters, apocalypses, acts of the apostles, and liturgy. One recent source listed 75 such extant works. It is easy to see why the church chose not to include such material in the Bible. For example, the Infancy Gospel of Thomas, written about A.D. 150, tells the story of Jesus being criticized as a five-year-old for making clay pigeons on the Sabbath. He clapped His hands and said, "Off with you," and the clay pigeons came to life and flew away! In another story, Jesus is playing in the second story of a home with another child. When the child accidentally falls to his death, his parents accuse the young Jesus of pushing him out the window. Jesus raises the child from the dead to prove His innocence! These exuberant stories were the pulp fiction of ancient Christian literature. Students of the New Testament can read these and other stories in collections of the New Testament Apocrypha.[1]

postexilic times, and they antici-pated God to speak to humankind with a voice from heaven. Thus, it is significant that Jesus is pro-claimed God's Son by such a voice: the new age of communica-tion has come!

The Gospel focuses more on the ministry of Jesus in chapter 4. Following His temptation (vv. 1-13), Jesus begins His public min-istry. Again, it is Luke who gives us greater detail of Jesus' first days of ministry. Jesus begins His ministry as a teacher in the syna-gogues, and a report about Jesus spreads around Galilee (v. 14).

A key theme of chapter 4 is the rejection of Jesus by His home-town people. Initially, the people responded positively to Jesus' reading from Isaiah 61 in the syn-agogue at Nazareth (Luke 4:22). When the people asked Him to perform healing in His own hometown, Jesus reminded them of the stories of Elijah and Elisha performing miracles and healing among the foreigners (vv. 25-27). Luke's interest in the inclusion of the Gentiles in the gospel of Jesus is clearly evident here. Intense parochial support for Jewish na-tionalism and ethnicity led them into a rage, and they drove Him out of town to throw Him off a cliff. As far as we know, Jesus never returned to His home, and He remained an outcast to the end of His ministry.

Following this incident, Jesus returned to **Capernaum** approxi-mately 10 miles away, to the house of Peter where he was of-ten a guest.

■ Jesus and His Ministry

Chapters 5—19 form the middle portion of Luke's Gospel. The compression of time in this cen-tral section is so great that these few chapters represent almost three years of events and teach-ing. As a result, Luke carefully se-lects his material to show his con-cerns in retelling the gospel story. As we have noted, he also brings a source to his writing that the other Gospel authors did not have. Much of what we will dis-cuss now comes from that distinc-tive "L" material. The following themes represent Luke's perspec-tive on Jesus and His story.

Jesus' Ministry in His Jewish Environment

Luke's narrative frequently places Jesus in the synagogue, es-pecially the many incidents of conflict with fellow Jews. On two occasions, Jesus heals in the syn-agogue on the Sabbath to demon-strate that compassion for the sick comes before considerations of law and religious propriety (6:6-11; 13:10-17). Jesus also re-mains loyal to the Temple in

The Galilee and Nazareth

The **Galilee** ("the District") was a largely ru-ral and agrarian area of northern Israel. It was di-vided into two regions, upper and lower, and was known for its olives, figs, grapes, grains, and fish-ing. The Galilee was also situated on an important trade route, which explains the presence of trou-blesome toll collectors. There were several sub-stantial towns there, Capernaum and Tiberius among them. Though not mentioned in the Bible, the most prominent city was the Roman adminis-trative center **Sepphoris,** a city of 30,000 just four miles north of Nazareth. Nazareth, however, was so small that it is never mentioned in the Old Testa-ment or any existing extrabiblical source, including Josephus, who catalogues 54 towns in the Galilee. The famous Sea of Galilee is actually only a lake, and known as Kinneret, or harp, in the Gospels be-cause of its shape.

Jerusalem. Luke tells us He encouraged those who were healed to make the appropriate offerings to local priests (5:14; 17:14). However, Jesus was also convinced of the need to reform the Temple practices. His disruption of Temple trade was perhaps the primary cause of the hostility He met in Jerusalem (19:45).

Luke also presents Jesus' debate with His fellow Jews on a wide range of issues, such as work on the Sabbath, ritual washing, tithing practices, the source of His authority, fasting and prayer, and the issue of fellowship with known sinners. Jesus' perspectives on these matters show His intense concern for a proper understanding and practice of the Torah. He affirms the Jewish way of life, but He believes the practice has been corrupted, especially by some of the Pharisees.

Before leaving the subject of the Jewish environment in the life of Jesus, a word must be said about the place of Jerusalem in Jesus' life. It is clear from the Gospel accounts that Jesus loved this city. However, we find in Luke's Gospel the portrait of Jerusalem as the city of destiny for Jesus. This is made clear in Luke 9:51: "As the time approached for him to be taken up to heaven, Jesus resolutely set out for Jerusalem." This consuming passion drove Jesus ever closer to the sacred city (13:22), and He declares: "I must keep going today and tomorrow and the next day—for surely no prophet can die outside Jerusalem!" (v. 33). Other references detail His focus on the city (17:11; 18:31 ff.; 19:28), and Jesus foresaw the destruction of Jerusalem, still 40 years away in A.D. 70 (19:41-44; 21:5-6, 20 ff.).

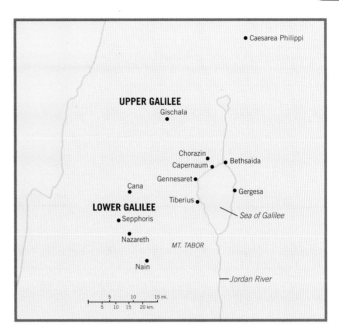

Upper and Lower Galilee.

Women in Luke

Women play a prominent role in Luke and are a significant part of Jesus' entourage (8:1-2). Two passages in Luke particularly highlight Jesus' concern for women. First, Luke gives us a personal glimpse into the lives of Martha and Mary from Bethany (10:38-42). Martha is "distracted by all the preparations" (v. 40) during Jesus' visit to her home while Mary sits at His feet and learns from His teaching. To welcome a female student was a radical departure for a rabbi; this story shows Jesus' egalitarian concern for women.

Second, in one of the most emotional scenes in the New Testament, Jesus extends kindness and forgiveness to a woman known to be a sinner, possibly a prostitute (7:36-50). While Jesus is eating in the home of a Pharisee, the woman enters and weeps at Jesus' feet, anoints Him with ointment and tears, and then dries His feet with her hair. It is a poignant scene of

Capernaum, Jesus' Home Base for Ministry

Capernaum is one of the most interesting archaeological sites in the Galilee. The Franciscans excavated the almost completely undisturbed site in the first years of the 20th century. The ruins of an impressive 4th-century A.D. synagogue made of limestone were uncovered. Beneath that was a basalt foundation wall and flooring believed to be from the 1st-century synagogue of Jesus' ministry. It is also the site of the events of John 6:25-59, where Jesus describes himself as the Bread of Life. His comments there stirred such controversy that He was eventually expelled from Capernaum (Luke 10:15-16). Thirty meters from the synagogue is Peter's House, a hexagonal church built in the 4th century. This site is believed to have been the place of Christian worship since the late 1st century. Tradition associates this site with Peter's house, also the location of Jesus' home during His Galilean ministry. A modern hexagonal-shaped Catholic church now stands over the site, preserving the original remains.

penance from a broken woman and characteristic of the way Luke highlights compassion for women. Jesus tells the woman, "Your sins are forgiven" (v. 48). Luke certainly shows us the side of Jesus that was tender and compassionate to the plight of women.

Sinners Find Repentance

The central message of the Gospel of Luke is repentance, and the central section (chaps. 5—19) tells the stories of five sinners. The first story is about Levi the toll collector who gives a banquet for all of his friends in Jesus' honor (5:29-32). When the Pharisees complain about this unseemly gathering of toll collectors and sinners, Jesus answers with a key phrase for Luke's Gospel: "It is not the healthy who need a doctor, but the sick. I have not come to call the righteous, but sinners to repentance" (vv. 31-32).

The second sinner is the woman who anoints Jesus' feet (7:36-50), whom we have already considered. The third passage is the whole of chapter 15, the so-called heart of the third Gospel. This moving chapter once again

places its message in the context of the Pharisees' complaint that Jesus eats with sinners (15:1-2; cf. 5:27). There are three parables in chapter 15. In the parable of the lost sheep (vv. 3-7), one lost animal is the main concern of the shepherd. The second is the parable of the lost coin, where a woman searches the whole house, having lost one of her 10 coins (vv. 8-10). The third is the famous parable of the prodigal son, who is welcomed back by his father (vv. 11-32). It is significant that all these stories appear only in Luke, which demonstrates his particular concern for forgiveness for sinners.

The poignant and almost comical story of the Pharisee and the tax collector presents the fourth sinner in the central section of Luke (18:9-14). The tax collector is typical of all Luke's sinners who always respond rightly to God, in contrast to the religious people who cannot see the truth. In this reversal of expectation, the sinners become the heroes of the Gospel story and the religious the antiheroes!

The theme of repentance finds its ultimate fulfillment in Luke's delightful story of Zacchaeus the tax collector (19:1-10). When Jesus invites himself to stay at Zacchaeus's house, the people who see it grumble that Jesus had "gone to be the guest of a 'sinner'" (v. 7). Zacchaeus repents, and Jesus proclaims, "Today salvation has come to this house, because this man, too, is a son of Abraham. For the Son of Man came to seek and to save what was lost" (vv. 9-10). This is the same message as in 5:31-32. The stories of Levi the tax collector and Zacchaeus bracket the beginning and end of the central section of the Gospel. The message of repentance and salvation for sinners has been proclaimed from Levi to Zacchaeus and met with great success.

■ The Final Days in Jerusalem

While the Gospel of John records three visits to Jerusalem in Jesus' ministry, the Synoptic Gospels record only the last visit. The Gospel of Luke focuses on Jesus' journey toward Jerusalem in chapters 9—19 (see 9:51; 19:28). It is apparent from the moment Jesus enters the city that His visit will lead to violence. Peter expresses his willingness to go to prison or even die for Jesus in Jerusalem (Luke 22:33). Luke states specifically that there were plots to kill Jesus (19:48; 22:2-6).

The Triumphal Entry was the crowning moment of His long journey from Galilee to Jerusalem (19:29-48). Jesus entered the Temple and began to disrupt normal festival commerce, driving out those who were changing money and selling animals for sacrifice. Both the Temple leaders and Roman authorities alike would have viewed this action with extreme disapproval. It would likely have appeared as an act of political protest, even though we now understand Jesus' motive as a concern for the sanctity of the Temple precincts. His fate may have been sealed after having been in the city only a few hours.

Luke's Vision of Salvation for All

Luke records the last days of Jesus' life in a manner very similar to Mark. However, the conclusion of the Gospel once again focuses on the theme of salvation for all. The resurrected Jesus, before being taken up into heaven, gives the disciples the commission to preach repentance and forgiveness of sins to all nations (24:47).

As we have seen, Jesus welcomed all at table to eat and drink and share fellowship with the Son of Man. The universal scope of Jesus' message is clear: "People will come from east and west and north and south, and will take their places at the feast in the kingdom of God" (13:29).

The Gospel of John

Authorship and Date

The Gospel of John, often referred to as the Fourth Gospel by New Testament scholars, is part of **Johannine literature,** which also includes the three letters of John. The Book of Revelation, though included in this group by some, is most likely separate from it because of its language and literary genre.

Even though the Gospel of John does not identify its author, it became associated with the apostle John ever since Irenaeus late in the second century. The question of authorship of the Fourth Gospel is intertwined with the identity of **the beloved disciple,** who appears in the second half of the Gospel as "the disciple whom Jesus loved." Christian tradition has linked him with John the apostle. Many modern scholars have disputed the accuracy of this linkage.[2] The date of the writing of the Gospel is not clearly known. Those who identify the beloved disciple with John the apostle date the Gospel in the 80s or early 90s.

The Purpose of John

John has explicitly stated his purpose as follows: "Jesus did many other miraculous signs in the presence of his disciples, which are not recorded in this book. But these are written that you may believe that Jesus is the Christ, the Son of God, and that by believing you may have life in his name" (20:30-31).

Variants in the Greek manuscripts of verse 31 make it uncertain whether the verb should be translated "that you may come to believe" or "that you may continue to believe." If the former, the Gospel apparently targets outsiders in order to bring them to faith. If the latter, its target audience is people in the church, and John's purpose would be to instruct and strengthen them.

Since John contains so many debates between Jesus and the Jews, some have argued that John's purpose is to make a case for Jesus as the Messiah to Jewish audiences that had trouble with such Christian claims. It is equally possible that John is addressing the Christian community. In the words of Beutler, "The Fourth Gospel was written to deepen the faith of Christians in Jesus as Son of God and Giver of Life, but at the same time also to encourage them to confess this openly, even under circumstances in which this confession would endanger their social position or even their lives."[3]

Content

John's Gospel may be outlined as follows:

Prologue	1:1-18
Ministry of Jesus	1:19—12:50
Glorification of Jesus	13:1—20:31
Epilogue	21:1-25

Unique Features and Themes of John's Gospel

■ Jesus Christ—the Word Became Flesh

Unlike the Synoptic Gospels, John starts from "the beginning," an echo of Genesis 1:1, in which he asserts the preexistence and deity of Jesus Christ (1:1). However, John just as emphatically declares that Jesus was truly human (v. 14). The eternal Word *(Logos)* has become human in the historical person of Jesus **(Incarnation).** Some early Christians were so eager to underscore the deity of Jesus Christ that they denied His real humanity. John, in concert with mainstream Christianity, rejects this view as heretical.[4]

■ Long Discourses

Whereas parables, proverbs, and brief sayings of Jesus abound in the Synoptic Gospels, they are nearly absent from the Gospel of John. In John we find long discourses on a given topic on the lips of Jesus. The occasion for these discourses varies. Some discourses arise from a dialogue that Jesus has had with someone (see, for example, Jesus' conversation with Nicodemus and the discourse that follows in chapter 3).[5] In other cases, the discourse is occasioned by a miracle that Jesus had performed (see the healing of the sick man in chapter 5 and feeding of the multitude in chapter 6).[6] Still other discourses have their setting in an event in the life of Jesus. Regardless of the occasion, the discourses are theological reflections or commentary on what had transpired. John has so skillfully blended the original event with the discourse that it is often difficult to know where one ends and the other begins.

These discourses present a theological reflection on the significance of the person of Jesus as the Son of God. For example, in the discourse that follows the healing of the sick man at the pool (5:19-47), Jesus says, "For the very work that the Father has given me to finish, and which I am doing, testifies that the Father has sent me" (v. 36).

The setting of the **farewell discourse** and prayer (chaps. 13—17), the longest discourse of Jesus in John, is the Last Supper.[7] In this discourse, Jesus reassures His disciples that He will come back after He has prepared a place for them (14:3). He promises that He will not leave them as orphans, that He is coming to them, and that they will see Him (vv. 18-20). In these verses the coming of Jesus seems to mean that He will appear to them after His death and resurrection. Thus the future eschatological return of Jesus in the Synoptic Gospels and in Paul's writings takes on a different meaning in John. The return of Jesus in John becomes in large measure a present reality in the life and experience of the disciples through the work of the Holy Spir-

it. The farewell discourse ends with a prayer in which Jesus prays for himself (17:1-5), for His disciples (vv. 6-19), and for future generations of believers (vv. 20-26).

■ Unique Words

One way we can capture the most important themes in John is to note frequently used words in the Gospel, particularly when these same words are much less frequent in the other Gospels. The most significant of these, in descending order of frequency, are the following: *know, Father* (as a reference to God), *believe, world, life, testify* or *testimony, glorify* or *glory, Son* (as a reference to Jesus), *truth, light, Spirit.*

John states in the **prologue** that the Word, who is Jesus Christ, is the source of light that shines in the darkness. Although the world came into existence through Him, the world did not know Him. John the Baptist came to testify to the light so that all might believe. All those who believe in the name of Christ become children of God. The Word became flesh and lived among us, and we have seen His glory. In Him we find the grace and truth of God. Christ, the only Son, who is

Bethany beyond Jordan (see John 1:19-34).

close to the heart of God the Father, has made God known to us.

Two points of clarification are necessary for a proper understanding of John's theology reflected in these words. First, in keeping with an Old Testament perspective, the verb "know" in John denotes more than intellectual perception. The knowledge of God is a relationship with God mediated through Jesus Christ.[8] Jesus himself knows God because He is from God (7:29). He also knows those who belong to Him in the same sort of relationship as a shepherd knows the sheep and lays down his life for them (10:14-15). Likewise, the sheep know the shepherd and follow him (v. 4). Unlike the world, the disciples know the Holy Spirit, the Spirit of truth, "for he lives with you and will be in you" (14:17). In the prayer of John 17, eternal life is defined as knowing "you, the only true God, and Jesus Christ, whom you have sent" (v. 3). To know God and Jesus Christ is not merely a cognitive or a mystical experience, but a relationship of love and faithful discipleship.

Another word in John to be clarified is *world*. In some passages, the world appears in an adversarial relationship to God and Jesus. Jesus says in His prayer of John 17, "Righteous Father, though the world does not know you, I know you" (v. 25). To Pilate He says, "My kingdom is not of this world" (18:36). On the other hand, the world is not hopelessly abandoned. The world was after all created through the Word (1:10). Furthermore, God has demonstrated His love for the world through Christ who has given himself for the life of the world (3:15; 6:51). Jesus came not to judge the world but to save it (12:47). Yet the coming of Jesus does involve judgment: "Now is the time for judgment on this world; now the prince of this world will be driven out" (v. 31); "For judgment I have come into this world, so that the blind will see and those who see will become blind" (9:39). Salvation, which is God's purpose for Christ's coming, is at the same time a pronouncement of judgment on the sinful ways of the world. Salvation and judgment are two sides of the same act of God in Jesus.

■ Miracles as Signs

Another way to come to grips with Johannine theology is to

Cana—site of Jesus' first miracle.

look at these seven miracles of Jesus during His earthly ministry:

1. Turning water to wine at the wedding in Cana (2:1-11)
2. Healing of the official's son (4:46-54)
3. Healing of the sick man at the pool (5:1-9)
4. Feeding of the multitude (6:1-15)
5. Walking on water (6:16-21)
6. Healing of a man born blind (9:1-12)
7. Raising of Lazarus (11:1-44)

Five of these seven miracles are only in John. The two exceptions are the feeding of the multitude and walking on water. The feeding miracle is the only one in all four Gospels.

John presents these miracles from a theological understanding of how they are related to faith. In John, there are various levels of faith. Miracles can certainly function as a catalyst to bring a person to faith in Jesus. This is clear from the story of the healing of the royal official's son who is dying (4:46-54). When the official begs Jesus to come with him and heal his son, Jesus seems a bit irritated and says, "Unless you people see miraculous signs and wonders, . . . you will never believe" (v. 48). However, when the official persists in his urgent plea, Jesus pronounces healing on the child. When the official arrives home and finds that the son is well again, he believes along with his whole household.

In another context Jesus says, "Do not believe me unless I do what my Father does. But if I do it, even though you do not believe me, believe the miracles, that you may know and understand that the Father is in me, and I in the Father" (John 10:37-38). It is for this reason

that John calls the miracles of Jesus signs. A miracle is not an end in itself but is a sign that points to Jesus as the Son of God (20:30-31).

■ The Paraclete

The spiritual reality that John is concerned with can come about only through the ministry of the Spirit. Although there are many references to the Spirit throughout the Gospel, the farewell discourse is particularly significant in this regard. Here the Spirit is given the unique name **Paraclete,** which is the Anglicized form of the Greek *parakletos,* variously translated as *advocate, comforter, counselor, helper.* Although the exact meaning of the word has puzzled exegetes, the basic idea is that of "someone who offers assistance in a situation in which help is needed."[9] Jesus speaks of the work of the Paraclete in the following ways: being present with the disciples (14:16-17); teaching the disciples (v. 26; see also 16:12-14); bearing testimony to Jesus (15:26); convicting the world concerning Jesus (16:8-11).

■ "I Am" Sayings

In John, we find long discourses built around seven sayings of Jesus that begin with "I am." The

Seven "I Am" Sayings of Jesus in John

1. "I am the bread of life" (6:35).
2. "I am the light of the world" (8:12).
3. "I am the gate for the sheep" (10:7).
4. "I am the good shepherd" (10:11).
5. "I am the resurrection and the life" (11:25).
6. "I am the way and the truth and the life" (14:6).
7. "I am the true vine" (15:1).

predicates in the **"I am" sayings** are all familiar images for people in biblical times: bread, light, shepherd, vine, and so on. There are also several "I am" sayings without a predicate. In 8:58, for example, Jesus says, "I tell you the truth, . . . before Abraham was born, I am!"

In the Old Testament, we often find "I am" statements made by God in solemn declarations. God tells Moses that His name is "I AM WHO I AM" (Exodus 3:14), which in Hebrew is Yahweh. First-century hearers of the Gospel of John, familiar with the "I am" language of God in their Scriptures, would not miss the point: Jesus speaks with the same authority and dignity as God. It is no wonder that when Jesus said, "Before Abraham was born, I am," His hearers were about to stone Him for blasphemy.

■ Deity and Humanity of Jesus

John underscores the deity of Jesus in various other ways. Nearly 30 times the title "Son" or "Son of God" is used of Jesus. The Word, who is Christ, was in the beginning with God and was God (John 1:1). Jesus often speaks of God as Father. His statement, "I and the Father are one" (10:31), occasions another attempt to stone Him.

The sole purpose of the Gospel, as stated by the author himself, was "that you may believe that Jesus is the Christ, the Son of God, and that by believing you may have life in his name" (20:31). In spite of John's strong emphasis on the deity of Jesus, the Gospel just as seriously reckons with His humanity. "The Word became flesh and made his dwelling among us" (1:14). The humanity of Jesus is seen in various ways in John. He gets tired and thirsty and asks for a drink from a

Samaritan woman (4:6-7). When Jesus sees Mary and others weeping at the death of Lazarus, He is so disturbed and moved that He weeps (11:33-35). As Jesus approaches Jerusalem, acutely aware of the prospect of His own death, He says, "Now my heart is troubled" (12:27).

The theological sophistication and subtleties of the Gospel of John must not be underestimated. It is precisely in the limitations of human existence that Jesus lives out His divine Sonship, and only in this manner the revelation of God the Father becomes visible through Him.

■ Death of Jesus

John portrays the death of Jesus as His glorification. His glorification is not limited to the Resurrection and Ascension. As absurd as this may sound, Jesus is glorified on the Cross. Indeed, His whole life is the working out of the glory of God. "We have seen his glory," John says (1:14). When Jesus prays, "Father, the time has come. Glorify your Son, that your Son may glorify you" (17:1), the glory He has in mind includes the Cross. In 12:32 Jesus says, "But I, when I am lifted up from the earth, will draw all men to myself." How will Jesus be lifted up? The Greek word used here for "lifted up" is the same one that is most often translated "exalted" in other places in the New Testament. It refers to Christ's glorious exaltation to the right hand of God. John, however, has intentionally given the word double meaning: Jesus will be lifted up on a cross and He will be lifted up to the right hand of God through the Resurrection and Ascension. The Cross is clearly in view in 3:14

where Jesus says, "Just as Moses lifted up the snake in the desert, so the Son of Man must be lifted up."

John's Gospel presents the crucifixion of Jesus at the time when the Passover activities were starting, with the slaughter of the lambs at the Temple. John the Baptist had earlier pointed to Jesus as "the Lamb of God, who takes away the sin of the world" (1:29). The fact that the legs of Jesus are not broken (19:33) and the comment in verse 36 that this fulfilled Scripture may be a reminder of Old Testament regulations that the bones of Passover lambs were not to be broken (Exodus 12:46; Numbers 9:12). John seems to identify Jesus as the true Passover lamb that takes the place of the older Jewish practices.[10] This may well have been the early Christian tradition, since Paul also calls Jesus "our Passover lamb" (1 Corinthians 5:7).

John's understanding of the death of Jesus is that of a good shepherd who out of sheer love lays down His life for the sheep (John 10:11). "Greater love has no one than this, that he lay down his life for his friends" (15:13).

◼ Resurrection of Jesus

As with Matthew and Luke, so also John ends his Gospel with the resurrection of Jesus and His appearances to His disciples. However, John's uniqueness can be seen here as well. John does not simply make the Resurrection the last chapter or two of the story of Jesus. The theme of resurrection and life is splashed everywhere in his Gospel (see this theme in 1:4; 5:21-29; 6:25-40; 10:7-10). The best example of the resurrection of Jesus working itself back into His earthly ministry is the raising of Lazarus in chap-

Lazarus' tomb (interior).

ter 11. In His conversation with Martha, Jesus emphatically proclaims: "I am the resurrection and the life. He who believes in me will live, even though he dies, and whoever lives and believes in me will never die" (11:25-26).

It is worth noting that Martha, along with most Jewish people in the time of Jesus, believed that there would be a final resurrection for the people of God on the last day in the distant future.[11] However, Jesus brings Martha to a new understanding, namely, that He himself is the resurrection and the life. The final resurrection in the distant future has become a present reality in Jesus.[12] The resurrection life is already at work in the lives of those who believe in Jesus. Jesus relates to Martha that real life, eternal life, or abundant life is much more than physical existence. Martha's response shows that resurrection life is rooted in the faith affirmation, "I believe that you are the Christ, the Son of God" (v. 27).

We conclude with another observation about John's Resurrection narrative. Mary Magdalene is the first person to discover the empty tomb and later see the resurrected Jesus, who commissions her to go and announce to the disciples that He is ascending to the Father (20:17). Discipleship in John (and the other Gospels, for that matter) is not restricted to men. The Samaritan woman, Mary and Martha, and now Mary Magdalene all have significant roles in the life of Jesus and the ministry of the gospel.

The Resurrection narrative includes a final meeting of Jesus and Peter. Three times Jesus asks Peter if he loves Him "more than these" (21:15; see vv. 15-19), reminiscent of the three times that Peter denied the Lord (13:36-38; 18:17, 25-27). The risen Christ comes to Peter with His forgiving love and commissions him to his future ministry. Jesus also challenges him to follow in His footsteps, which means willingness to suffer martyrdom for the sake of the gospel.

The Gospel concludes with a statement about the trustworthiness of the testimony of the disciple who is the author of this narrative of the life of Jesus.

Summary Statements

- Infancy narratives that contain stories about Jesus' birth and early life are a special feature of the Gospel of Luke.
- Luke presents the early life and ministry of Jesus in the setting of the Jewish life and culture of the first century.
- Women play a prominent role in the Gospel of Luke.
- The central message of the Gospel of Luke is the salvation of sinners who respond to God through repentance.
- Luke presents Jesus as committed to His journey to Jerusalem.
- John emphasizes both the deity and humanity of Jesus.
- Long discourses are a unique feature of the Fourth Gospel. In John's Gospel, words such as *know, believe, life, light, glory, truth, world, Father, Son,* and *the Spirit* have special theological meaning.
- John repeatedly refers to the Resurrection to show that its power was already at work even before it took place.
- The purpose of the Gospel of John is to deepen the faith of the disciples of Jesus.

Questions for Reflection

1. Does your own faith journey sometimes present you with conflicting agendas and tensions? How do you work to reconcile them?
2. In what ways does Jesus' concern for the marginalized challenge you in your life of faith? Are there ways you can act to follow His example?
3. Why do people often ask God for a miracle?
4. What does it mean for you to lay down your life for others, particularly in a culture that values ambition and self-advancement?

Bible Study Assignment

Read Luke 15. What is the common theme that connects the three stories in this chapter? What do you think is the objective of the introduction in verses 1-2? Who, in your opinion, is the main human character in the story of "the lost son"? Explain why.

Read John 4:1-42 and answer the following questions:

1 Why did Jesus leave Judea? Refer to a map of Palestine and identify the locations of Judea, Samaria, and Galilee.
2. Jesus is engaged in a number of activities here that are unusual and out of step with the Jewish customs. Identify these actions and evaluate them to discover the portrait of Jesus that John is presenting to the reader of his Gospel.
3. What does this story teach us about the Samaritans and their customs and beliefs?
4. How does Jesus present himself to the Samaritan woman?
5. What is the significance of verse 42? How does this verse relate to the theological objective of the Gospel writer?
6. How do you relate this story to the Church's mission today?

Resources for Further Study

Brown, Raymond E. *The Community of the Beloved Disciple.* New York: Paulist, 1979.
Fitzmeyer, Joseph A. *The Gospel According to Luke,* in *The Anchor Bible,* 2 vols. New York: Doubleday and Co., Inc., 1985.
Green, Joel B. *The Gospel of Luke,* in *The New International Commentary on the New Testament.* Grand Rapids: Wm. B. Eerdmans, 1997.
Smith, D. Moody. *The Theology of the Gospel of John.* New York: Cambridge University Press, 1995.

22 The Growth and Expansion of the New Covenant Community: The Book of Acts

 bjectives:

Your study of this chapter should help you to:

- Narrate the story of the spread of the gospel from Jerusalem to Samaria and Northern Africa
- Describe the complexities of the social and religious barriers to the spread of the gospel
- Trace the spread of the gospel by Paul from Antioch to Rome
- Explore some of the issues the early Christians faced as the gospel spread through the Jewish communities of the Dispersion

Questions to consider as you read:

1. How does Acts' story deal with ethnic and religious prejudice?

2. What would have been some of the community experiences of the participants of the early Christian movement?

3. Where does Paul fit in Judaism in the days of the Early Church?

4. The spread of the gospel in the Mediterranean basin was somewhat chaotic and characterized by conflict. Why would the leading of the Holy Spirit result in such conditions for the early missionaries of the church?

Key Words to Understand

Luke
Theophilus
Pentecost
Sadducees
Hellenists
Stephen
Philip
Paul
Cornelius
Jerusalem Council
"We" sections

Authorship and Date

Acts is the continuation of the work begun in the Gospel of Luke. Our author, by tradition **Luke** the companion of Paul, wrote this work in the late 70s or early 80s A.D. The community for which he wrote favored the mission to the Gentiles and was probably very similar to, if not in fact, the church in Syrian Antioch, the church that commissioned Paul and Barnabas to go to the Gentiles. As in the Gospel, Luke writes to **Theophilus,** who perhaps sponsored the project.

Content

The story of Acts may be outlined as follows:

Origin of the Christian Movement	1:1—7:60
Gospel to Samaria and North Africa	8:1—10:48
From Antioch to Rome	11:1—28:31

The structure of Acts tells the story of Acts. The first seven chapters chronicle the establishment of the nascent movement in Jerusalem, probably over the period of a few years. Chapters 8—10 record the spread of the gospel to Samaria and North Africa and culminate with the conversion of the Gentile God-fearer Cornelius and his family. In the next section (chaps. 11—28), we find the story of the spread of Christianity from Syrian Antioch, across the Mediterranean basin, all the way to Rome.

The Inauguration of the Movement in Jerusalem

The first chapter describes the presence of the resurrected Jesus among His frightened followers, His ascension, and the selection of the replacement of Judas as apostle. Following the dramatic ascent of Jesus to heaven, the narrative turns to the first days of the new movement. The descent of the Holy Spirit on 120 people at **Pentecost,** a Jewish festival occurring 50 days after Passover, represents the birth of the Christian Church (Acts 2). This event is the shift from the age of Jesus to the age of the Holy Spirit in the

Chapel of Ascension, the traditional site of the ascension of Jesus.

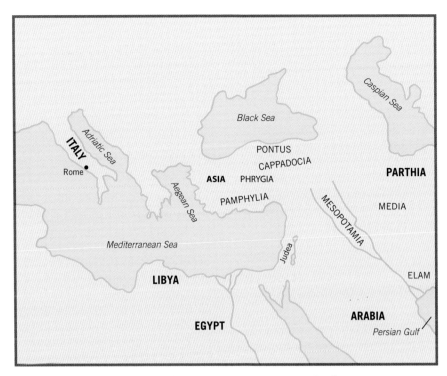

Geographical locations of the Jewish Diaspora in the first century A.D.

Church. Both literal and symbolic meaning can be found in the great rushing wind (symbol of empowerment), tongues of fire (symbol of purification), and the many languages (symbol of communication).

Some have suggested an allusion to the Genesis story of the Tower of Babel in Acts 2. In Genesis, God confounds the pride of the people by giving them different languages (11:1-9). This Pentecost event in Acts symbolically lifts that curse with praise for God being spoken in all the languages of the ancient Near East: Parthia, Media, Elam, Mesopotamia, Judea, Cappadocia, Pontus, Asia, Phrygia, Pamphylia, Egypt, Libya, and Rome (Acts 2:9-11). The order is significant in that it moves from the distant east of Parthia to the western city of Rome. These believers at Pente-

cost proclaimed the gospel to the known world, an event that could be understood as the beginning of the global mission of early Christianity.

Peter's inaugural Christian sermon (2:14-36) gives us an account of the content of early Christian preaching. The style of this sermon is unique. We find here an alternation between preaching and quotation from the Old Testament. Peter weaves together different Old Testament passages to answer four different questions: what age is this? (vv. 14-21); who is Jesus? (vv. 22-28); why was He raised from the dead? (vv. 29-36); what do we need to do now? (vv. 37-42). Peter clearly saw the death of Jesus inaugurating a new era of God's activity in history. Jesus is the fulfillment of Israel's hope in the coming of a Davidic messiah. God raised Jesus from the dead in accordance to His promise to David concerning the establishment of his kingdom as an eternal kingdom. The sermon concluded with a call for repentance and baptism to receive forgiveness of sins and the gift of the Holy Spirit. Three thousand were baptized in the coming months and, significantly, they continued to worship in the Temple daily, a reminder to us that these early believers were still a Jerusalem-based Jewish messianic sect.

The Community in Crisis

■ Religious Tensions

The unexpected growth of the Christian movement posed a theological challenge to traditional Judaism. The **Sadducees,** a hereditary class of prominent conservative Jews, disagreed with the doctrine of resurrection from the dead being promulgated by the Jesus movement (4:2). Traditional Judaism also rejected the Christian movement's radical reinterpretation of the messianic texts in the Hebrew Scriptures. After the healing of the man born lame, the very highest Jewish authorities met together to consider the case of these "unschooled, ordinary men" (v. 13). Though Peter

and John were arrested, they were released "because all the people were praising God for what had happened" (v. 21). The atmosphere became so charged with tension that few disciples dared to enter the Temple with Peter and John (5:13).

■ Tensions Within the Movement

Stephen, the first Christian martyr, is now introduced in the narrative of Acts. He is the leader of a group of **Hellenists** who are given responsibility for the daily distribution of food to the widows (chap. 6). In response to complaints of unfairness from the Hellenists, Peter appointed a team of seven individuals to manage the distribution. The seven all have Greek names, and most, but perhaps not all, would have been from outside of Israel. They all likely spoke Greek as their first language, as opposed to Aramaic and Hebrew for the locals, and would have been more tolerant of the ways of Greek culture, government, and leisure than the regional Jews. Hellenists seem to have been more open to the idea of spreading the messianic message beyond Jerusalem and even beyond Judaism. The first to take the gospel outside of Judea to Samaria was Philip, a Hellenist (8:5).

■ Stephen's Martyrdom

Luke tells us of a crucial dispute between **Stephen** and members of the Synagogue of the Freedmen that had a profound impact on the Jesus movement. Saul (later known as Paul), a native of Tarsus in Cilicia, was present during the dispute. When Stephen prevailed in the debate about Jesus, it was non-Christian Hellenists

T

The Christian Community in Acts

The Christian community in Acts was characterized by a close-knit fellowship. They shared not only times of rejoicing and praise at the victories being won (2:47) but even their possessions, food, and land (vv. 44-46; 4:32-37). The communal nature of the movement must have strengthened the believers to endure times of persecution and doubt as they sought to be obedient to the gospel.

Samaria—
columns of
Herod's palace.

who took offense at his arguments. These opponents brought charges of blasphemy against him and said he spoke about destroying the Temple and changing Jewish customs (6:11, 13-14).

When brought before the council on these charges, he defended his case for Jesus the Messiah by surveying the story of God's actions in Israel's history as the background for his argument. The resulting outcry led to a mob action, and Stephen was killed by stoning. This first martyrdom marked a turning point for Christian history.

■ The Movement Breaks Out of Jerusalem

In the wake of Stephen's death, both Christian Jews and the Hellenists fled the city for a time. The apostles refused to be uprooted, however, and the Jewish Christian heart of the Church remained centered in Jerusalem until the Great Revolt of the Jews against Rome in A.D. 66. **Philip** was a colleague of Stephen and one of the seven Hellenists appointed to look after the distribution of the

food (v. 5). He went to Samaria to proclaim the gospel there as the community's first evangelist (8:5). That Philip began his preaching

Samaria, Galilee, and Decapolis.

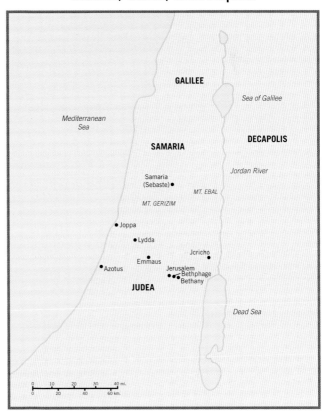

at Samaria, a place hated by the Jews, demonstrates the power of the gospel to bridge cultures and heal ethnic division. The gospel of Jesus Christ and His message of love for one's neighbor was preached first to Judah's neighbors, the hated Samaritans.

The Gospel Spreads to Northern Africa

The story of Philip's encounter with the Ethiopian eunuch is reminiscent of the Old Testament prophets (Acts 8:26-40). An angel directed Philip to the road to Gaza where he met the eunuch who was reading a manuscript of Isaiah 53:7-8. Philip interpreted Isaiah's portrayal of the servant as Jesus the crucified Messiah. The eunuch believed the message of the gospel and was baptized, and he continued on his way to Africa, taking the good news of Jesus with him. In a short period of time after the Dispersion from Jerusalem, the gospel was already taking root in Samaria and northern Africa.

Paul's Encounter with the Risen Jesus

In three places in Acts, Luke recounts the story of **Paul**'s life-altering encounter with Jesus on the road to Damascus (9:1-22; 22:4-16; 26:9-18; compare Galatians 1:13). The beginning point of Paul's preaching was often his personal experience of the risen Jesus. Students of Paul's life have debated the meaning of his so-called conversion on the road to Damascus. Yet *conversion* may not be the best word to describe his encounter since he did not cease to think of himself as Jewish. His profound experience that day convinced him that Jesus was

indeed the Messiah, an idea he had vigorously sought to suppress (9:1-2; 22:4-5). Paul's midlife reversal on this matter altered not only his own life but also the history of Christianity.

The Conversion of the First Gentiles

Chapter 10 narrates the story of the conversion of **Cornelius,** a God-fearing Gentile who lived in Caesarea by the sea. This story is the first conversion of a Gentile to the gospel of Jesus. Two visions provide the background of this story. In one vision, God bids Cornelius to send someone to Joppa for Peter. In another vision, God bids Peter not to call unclean what God has made clean. These two visions open the door to Gentile evangelism. Peter arrived at the house of Cornelius and preached the gospel that resulted in the conversion of Cornelius and his family. Not only that, but the Gentiles also received the Holy Spirit, which further indicated the truth that God showed no partiality on the matter of salvation.

The Spread of Christianity from Antioch to Rome

The theme of Acts 11—28 is the spread of the gospel among the Gentiles. The establishment of the church at Antioch on the Orontes in Syria further paved the way for the mission to the Gentiles (11:19-26). Barnabas, a native of Cyprus (see 4:36-37) who became a key leader in Jerusalem, came to Antioch and later introduced Paul to the believers there. Luke adds the historical fact that the disciples came to be known as "Christians" at Antioch (v. 26). Persecution of the Christians during the reign of Herod Agrippa I, grandson of

Herod the Great, and Peter's miraculous escape from jail are key events narrated in chapter 12. The rest of the book shows how ministry unfolds among the Gentiles through Paul's travels and preaching of the gospel.

■ Paul's Missionary Travels

Paul had an inveterate desire to take the gospel to places it had never been preached. This meant that his life as an evangelist was a life of travel and hardship. Three journeys are recorded in Acts. The first occurred in the mid to late 40s, the second in the late 40s and early 50s, and the third in the mid 50s. Paul and Barnabas were first commissioned to undertake a missionary journey by the church in Syrian Antioch, the largest and most energetic church outside of Judea at that time. The church was full of the Spirit and had an aggressive view about spreading the gospel throughout the cities of Asia Minor. The evangelists traveled from Antioch to Cyprus, and from there to Perga, Antioch of Pisidia, Iconium, Lystra, and

Ruins of Jerash, the best preserved city of the Decapolis, a confederation of 10 Roman cities dating from the first century B.C.

Derbe (13:1—14:28). John Mark also accompanied the evangelists, but he returned home when they reached Perga in Pamphylia. At Cyprus, they presented the gospel to the proconsul, Serqius Paulus, who became a believer, though a local magician attempted to turn the proconsul away from faith.

Paul initiated the second journey and selected Silas as his traveling companion. This journey took the evangelists through the regions of Cilicia and Galatia to the western seaport of Troas. Paul

Mars Hill.

Paul's First Missionary Journey.

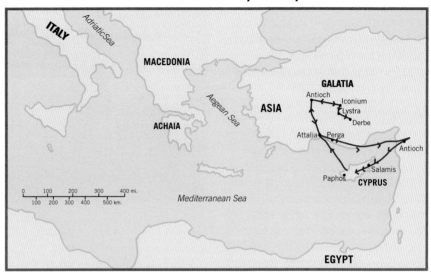

Paul's Second Missionary Journey.

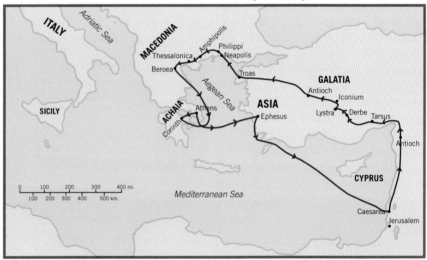

recruited Timothy to join the team while he was passing through Lystra. Luke reports that a vision of "a man of Macedonia" (16:9) that Paul saw while at Troas gave the evangelists the urgency to go over to the Macedonian province of Greece (vv. 6-10).

At Philippi, the evangelists met with some devout Jewish women, exorcised a demon-possessed fortune-teller, and were thrown in jail on charges of breaking the Roman law. A midnight vigil by the evangelists led to their miraculous escape from prison and the subsequent conversion of the jailer. The city magistrates urged them to leave the city without causing further trouble, and they went on to Thessalonica. Paul's preaching caused an uproar among the Jews in Thessalonica, which prompted the evangelist to leave town and go on to Beroea, where they found hospitality among the Jews. Paul had to leave the city again because of the opposition of the Jews who followed him from Thessalonica. He traveled from Beroea to Athens, where he met with Epicurean and Stoic philosophers and debated with them as a Christian philosopher. He addressed the Athenian crowd from Mars Hill (Areopagus) on the nature and existence of the one true living God.

From Athens, Paul traveled to Corinth, where he met with Aquila and Priscilla, a devout Jewish couple who were also tentmakers by trade. Paul spent 18 months preaching and teaching the gospel at Corinth. Luke also reports opposition to Paul's preaching at Corinth and the Jewish complaint before Gallio, proconsul of the region of Achaia. From Corinth, he returned to Antioch via Ephesus, Caesarea, and Jerusalem (16:1—18:22). The third journey took him to Ephesus, where he spent over two years, before making a final tour of the Macedonian and Corinthian churches and returning to Jerusalem (19:1—21:16).

◼ The Content of Paul's Preaching

Seven sermons of Paul are recorded in Acts. They are as follows: in Antioch Pisidia on the first missionary journey (13:16-41); in the Areopagus in Athens on the second journey (17:22-34); to the Ephesian elders on the third journey (20:18-36); to a mob in the Temple in Jerusalem (22:1-29); before the chief priests in Jerusalem (23:1-11); to Tertullus in Caesarea (24:10-21); and before Agrippa, again in Caesarea (26:1-29). In these sermons Paul emphasizes his conversion (three times), his faithfulness to Judaism, the resurrection of Jesus from the dead, the arguments from Scripture for the Messiah, and that his enemies in Jerusalem are persecuting him, not for subversion, but for declaring the doctrine of the resurrection of the dead. The sermons are a fascinating representation of Paul's message by Luke, and the gospel of Jesus is clearly sounded throughout.[1]

Paul's Third Missionary Journey.

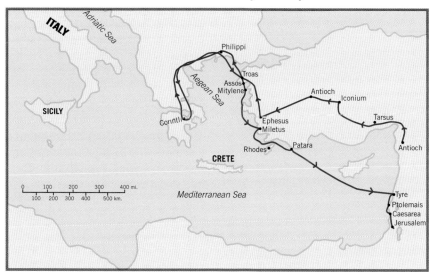

Paul's first sermon in Acts (13:16-41) was delivered in Antioch Pisidia during his first missionary journey. It bears considerable similarity to sermons by Peter and Stephen (Acts 2 and 8 respectively).

Both Paul and Peter focus on the promise of a Messiah in the line of David (2:29-31; 13:22-23)—not a characteristic Pauline theme but undoubtedly crucial to the early proclamation of Jesus as Messiah. Both find the proof of Jesus' identity as the Messiah in His resurrection from the dead (2:24-32; 13:30-37), which is familiar from Paul's letters. Both blame the Jewish leaders of Jerusalem for complicity in the death of the Messiah (2:23; 13:27-28). Paul and Stephen's sermons are similar in that they both start with a long recitation of Israelite history.[2]

A Chronology of Paul's Life

The details of Paul's life will always be debated, but the general dates are well documented and the following is intended as a guide for the reader.[3] In 10 years of intense activity from A.D. 47 to A.D. 56, Paul was able to establish churches in Galatia, Asia Minor, Macedonia, and Achaia. In his own thinking, he had exhausted the opportunities for evangelization in those areas and longed to travel to Rome to complete his work.[4]

10-15	Birth
34	Damascus Road Event
34-36	In Arabia—the Transjordan area (Galatians 1:17)
36-46	Cilicia
47-48	First Missionary Journey
48	Jerusalem Council
49-52	Second Missionary Journey
50-51	Corinth
52-56	Third Missionary Journey
56	Arrest in Jerusalem
56-58	Caesarea
59-61	Rome
61	Martyrdom

■ The Jerusalem Council

Some Jewish Christians strongly argued that the Gentile believers must be circumcised as a requirement for their salvation. Chapter 15 sums up the proceedings of the **Jerusalem Council,** sometimes called the Apostolic Council, which was convened to consider this debated issue and the question of the relationship of the Gentile believers to the Jewish customs and religious practices. This gathering included all the leaders of the new movement, including Peter, James, the brother of Jesus, and other local elders. In his speech to the council, Peter argued that circumcision should not be a requirement for Gentiles, and he thus opened the door to salvation based on faith alone (15:6-11)—after all, the Gentile Cornelius had been saved through Peter's preaching. James, the leader of the Jerusalem church, added his approval to the Gentile mission (vv. 13-21; 21:25). All agreed that everyone is saved "through the grace of our Lord Jesus" (15:11). A letter was sent by the council to the church at Antioch conveying this momentous decision for the church and for the ministry of Paul (vv. 23-29).

The seeming harmony in Luke's account does not mean the issue was permanently settled that day. In fact, the dispute continued for decades and is often evidenced in Paul's writings and later in Acts (Galatians 2:9 ff.; 5:12; Philippians 3:2; Acts 21). From a literary perspective, Luke's description of this great council sets the stage in Acts for the movement to proceed with a clear, two-pronged mission of salvation to both Jews and Gentiles. Paul became the head of the Gentile mission and

Peter and James the mission to the Jews. Immediately following this policy victory for the Gentile mission, Paul and his companions departed on the second evangelistic journey (15:36).

■ Appearance Before the Chief Priests

At the end of his third journey Paul went up to Jerusalem against the advice of coworkers and supporters. He had described himself to the Ephesian elders as "compelled by the Spirit" (20:22) and drawn to the city. On the advice of the local Jewish church leaders in Jerusalem, he joined some disciples fulfilling a seven-day temporary Nazirite vow (see Numbers 6:1-21). This time "Jews from the province of Asia" stirred the crowd into a riot (Acts 21:27 ff.), charging him with bringing Gentiles into the Temple precincts. Paul addressed the crowd (22:1-21) and was taken into custody by the tribune of the Antonia Fortress, the soldier barracks overlooking the Temple court (vv. 22-29).

■ Paul's Legal Battles and the Trip to Rome

Acts 23—28 contains the narrative of a lengthy series of legal proceedings. Various groups and authorities brought charges against Paul, accusing him of agitation against Rome, profanation of the Temple, and being a "ringleader of the Nazarene sect" (21:28; 24:5; 25:7). Paul vigorously and repeatedly defended himself in the presence of mobs, the Jewish authorities, Felix, the Roman governor of Judea, his successor Festus, and even Herod Agrippa II, the client king of northern Palestine (22:1—23:10; 24:10-21; 25:8; 26:1-29). The Roman authorities could not find

The "We" Sections of Acts

A notable feature of Acts is the **"we" sections,** the occasional change from third-person narrative ("they") to first-person narrative ("we"). This occurs in 16:10-17; 20:5-15; 21:1-18; 27:1—28:16. The change would seem to indicate that the author actually traveled with Paul during parts of his journeys. This creates a vivid and lively presence to the narrative, as well as supplying an intriguing connection between the world of the gospel literature and the world of the apostle Paul. It is remarkable to think that the author of the Gospel of Luke was actually a companion of Paul.

any chargeable offense and Paul was forced to appeal to the emperor's tribunal to avoid being returned to the jurisdiction of the council in Jerusalem (25:9-12). Ironically, it is Paul's Roman citizenship that saves him, since no citizen could be condemned without due process and all Roman citizens had access to a direct appeal to the emperor.

The final two chapters of Acts record Paul's journey to Rome and give a detailed account of his travels by ship from Caesarea to Rome. The perilous journey that included winter storms and shipwreck finally ended with Paul's safe arrival in Rome, where he was placed under house arrest (28:16, 30-31). Luke reports that Paul had considerable latitude to meet with his visitors and for two years he proclaimed the kingdom of God in Rome "boldly and without hindrance" (v. 30; see vv. 25-31). Luke's chronicle of the early history of the Christian movement ends here without resolution of Paul's legal situation. Tradition holds that Paul was martyred in Rome in the early A.D 60s.

Summary Statements

- The descent of the Holy Spirit on 120 believers at Pentecost is the birth of the Church.
- The resurrected Jesus was central to the preaching of Peter.
- The conversion of the Gentiles in Acts 10 marks the beginning of the Gentile mission.
- The spread of the gospel among the Gentiles is a key concern of Acts 11—28.
- Paul carried out three missionary journeys to take the gospel among the Gentiles.
- Jesus as Messiah is a central theme in the sermons of Paul in Acts.
- Paul taught that God saves the Gentiles without requiring their conversion to Judaism.
- Paul's legal battles led to his journey to Rome as a prisoner.

Questions for Reflection

1. The religious and racial barriers to the spread of the gospel were profound, yet God overcame these and even worked through them. How can religious and racial barriers be breached by the preaching of the gospel today?
2. What do conflict and persecution teach the Church about life in the Spirit?
3. What lessons do we learn about the life of the Church today from the examples of the courageous leaders of the Early Church?

Bible Study Assignment

Read Acts 15:6-11 and answer the following questions:

1. What is the historical, cultural, and religious setting of this passage?
2. Why did some people in the Early Church insist on the circumcision of the Gentile believers?
3. Why did this issue become divisive in the Early Church?
4. What was the response of the leadership to this issue? What was the message that Peter communicated through his speech to the council? What are the specific points that he made about the Gentiles and their conversion experience?
5. What is the ministry of the Holy Spirit, according to Peter (see v. 9)?
6. How do you define *salvation*, based on verse 11?
7. What are the cultural and social issues that cause division today? What are the contemporary applications of this text to the life and mission of the Church today?

Resources for Further Study

Bruce, F. F. *Commentary on the Book of Acts*. Grand Rapids: Wm. B. Eerdmans Publishing Co., 1976.

Conzelmann, Hans. *Acts of the Apostles*. Philadelphia: Fortress Press, 1987.

Hengel, Martin. *Acts and the History of Earliest Christianity*. Philadelphia: Fortress Press, 1980.

UNIT VII

PAUL: SPOKESPERSON OF THE NEW COVENANT COMMUNITY

Your study of this unit will help you to:

- Describe the life contribution of the apostle Paul to the Christian Church
- Identify the form and classification of the letters of Paul
- Discuss the various elements of Paul's core theology
- Describe the setting, content, and theological themes of Paul's letters preserved in the New Testament

■ Paul and His Letters

■ Paul's Letter to the Romans

■ 1 and 2 Corinthians and Galatians

■ Ephesians, Philippians, and Colossians

■ 1 and 2 Thessalonians

■ 1 and 2 Timothy, Titus, and Philemon

23 Paul and His Letters

O bjectives:

Your study of this chapter should help you to:

- Describe the significance of the apostle Paul to the Christian faith
- Discuss the religious and cultural background of Paul
- Understand the structure and classification of Paul's letters
- Evaluate the core theological concepts found in Paul's letters

Q uestions to consider as you read:

1. In what ways did Paul's background as a devout Jew as well as a Greco-Roman citizen shape his theological thinking as a Christian?

2. What are the similarities and differences between a typical Greek letter and the letters of Paul?

3. Why did Paul write his letters?

K ey Words to Understand

Tarsus
Saul
Gamaliel
Soteriological letters
Eschatological letters
Christological letters
Pastoral letters
Letters
Epistles
Salutation
Thanksgiving
Body
Paraenesis
Conclusion
Diatribe
Kyrios
Body of Christ

Paul's Background

In Paul's own words, he was a Jew, "from **Tarsus** in Cilicia, a citizen of no ordinary city" (Acts 21:39). Tarsus was a frontier city. To the west was the Hellenistic world of the Greco-Roman culture dominated by Rome; to the east lay the Hebrew world of Judaism. His parents were devout Jews who circumcised their son according to the Law on the eighth day (Philippians 3:3). He was from the tribe of Benjamin and was named after the first king of Israel, Saul, the most celebrated member of the tribe of Benjamin and a great hero of the nation who died in the battle against the Philistines. He adopted the Greek name Paul *(Paulos)* and seldom refers to himself by his Jewish name **Saul** in his letters. How Paul gained Roman citizenship is not known. This may have been a privilege gained by his father or grandfather for some outstanding service to Rome.[1] Paul also identifies himself as a Pharisee who was trained in Jerusalem in the Law of his ancestors under the great first-century teacher **Gamaliel** (Acts 22:3; 23:6; 26:5; Philippians 3:5). He was well versed in both the Hebrew Scriptures and the Greek Septuagint. He was also a student of Greco-Roman philosophy and a master debater skilled in both Greco-Roman rhetoric and the traditional Jewish Midrash.

Tarsus city under excavation.

Luke introduces Paul as a willing accomplice to the stoning of Stephen and a fierce opponent and persecutor of the followers of Jesus (Acts 7:57—8:3). His dramatic encounter with the resurrected Christ Jesus on the road to Damascus changed the course of his life. The zealous persecutor of Christians became the most forceful preacher of the gospel of the resurrected Christ and the pioneer missionary-evangelist to the Gentile world.

Paul's Letters

Paul apparently was a much more gifted writer than public speaker. The New Testament preserves 13 letters attributed to Paul. Some of these are letters that he wrote to the churches he established during his missionary travels. These letters show various aspects of Paul's theology—his understanding of sin, salvation, the end time, the work of Christ, the Christian life, the nature and mission of the Church, and so forth.

Paul's letters provide us with a great deal of information about the cultural, social, and religious context in which Christians lived in the first century A.D. Each letter contains profound and timeless truth combined with specific practical life application. Individually and collectively, Paul's letters make a major theological contribution to Christian thought.

Paul's Epistles are collected in the New Testament in two basic groups. The first group consists of nine letters to specific churches, with the longest letter first, followed by the shorter letters. The second group follows with four letters addressed to individuals,

Tarsus or Jerusalem?

Where did Paul receive his formal education and training? Was he educated at Tarsus, the capital city of the province of Cilicia, a cosmopolitan Hellenistic city known for its rich social, cultural, political, and intellectual heritage? Or as the son of pious and wealthy Jewish parents, was he trained at Jerusalem, away from the influences of his native city? Scholars are divided on this question and its answer. William Ramsay, toward the end of the 19th century, suggested that Paul's training and education at Tarsus prepared him well for his vision of a worldwide church. According to Ramsay, this Tarsus background also is seen in his "extraordinary versatility and adaptability . . . and his quickness to turn the resources of civilization to his use."[2] Some modern scholars continue this perspective and claim that Paul's training in the Septuagint (the Greek translation of the Old Testament) at Tarsus and the Greco-Roman cultural influence of his native city is evident in some of his letters.[3] There are others who seem to think that though Paul was a native of Tarsus, much of his education and training took place at Jerusalem. F. F. Bruce, by citing evidence from the Book of Acts and Paul's letters, holds the view that though Paul was born in the Greek-speaking city of Tarsus, he was brought up in a strict Jewish family in which Aramaic was the language spoken at home. Bruce also thinks that his parents would have sent Paul to Jerusalem at an early age to grow up in Jerusalem under the Jewish cultural influence and to attend the school of Gamaliel.[4] Though we cannot prove with certainty where Paul received much of his educational and cultural training, one thing is clear. His Jewish religious heritage and Greco-Roman cultural understanding made him a most suitable candidate to be an apostle to the Gentile world.

again with the longest letter first and shorter letters following thereafter. Chronologically, the order of the letters would be quite different. The Thessalonian letters and Galatians were probably written first. The Corinthian letters would have been written next, followed by Romans, Philippians, Colossians, and perhaps Philemon, followed by Ephesians. First and Second Timothy and Titus would likely be the last Pauline Epistles written.

Some scholars have used key theological themes found in these letters as a basis for classifying Paul's letters. Accordingly, Romans, 1 and 2 Corinthians, and Galatians are called **soteriological letters,** since salvation (Greek *soteria*) is a primary theme in these letters. The Second Coming and the end time (eschatology or the end time events) are key issues in

1 and 2 Thessalonians; therefore they are called **eschatological letters.** Ephesians, Philippians, Colossians, and Philemon emphasize the theme of the person and work of Jesus Christ (Christology); they are therefore called **Christological letters.** Duties and responsibilities of pastoral leaders is a key theme in the **pastoral letters** (1 and 2 Timothy and Titus).

Scholars also classify the letters of Paul based on their similarity to various types of Greco-Roman letters. Accordingly, 1 Thessalonians and 1 Corinthians are called *exhortational* or *paraenetic* letters, since these letters are mostly Paul's instructions or exhortations to his readers. Philemon could be an example of a *letter of recommendation,* since the apostle is requesting Philemon to welcome his runaway slave Onesimus as a

Christian brother. Second Corinthians is an example of *self-commendation* or Paul's defense of his apostolic authority. Galatians is an *apologetic letter* that follows the style of self-commendation. Philippians, though it is paraenetic in form, also follows the style of a *family letter,* with its reassurances about both the sender and the recipients. Romans may be consid-

L Letter Writing in the Greco-Roman World

The following two Greek papyrus letters show the pattern of letter writing in the Greco-Roman world. The first letter is dated to about A.D. 25, and the second letter comes from the second or the third century A.D.[5] Both letters show resemblance to the structure of the letters of Paul; the second letter in particular shows salutation, prayer, body, and final greetings—all found in Paul's letters.

Theon to the most honoured Tyrannus very many greetings. Heraclides, the bearer of this letter, is my brother, wherefore I entreat you with all my power to take him under your protection. I have also asked your brother Hermias by letter to inform you about him. You will do me the greatest favour if you let him win your approval. Before all else I pray that you may have health and the best of success, unharmed by the evil eye. Goodbye. [Addressed] To Tyrannus the dioecetes.

Irenaeus to Apollinarius his dearest brother many greetings. I pray continually for your health, and I myself am well. I wish you to know that I reached land on the sixth of the month Epeiph and we unloaded our cargo on the eighteenth of the same month. I went up to Rome, on the twenty-fifth of the same month, and the place welcomed us as the god willed, and we are daily expecting our discharge, it so being that up till today no body in the corn fleet has been released. Many salutations to your wife and to Serenus and to all who love you, each by name. Goodbye. Mesore 9. [Addressed] To Apollinarius from his brother Irenaeus.

ered an *ambassadorial letter,* since it was written in anticipation of his visit to Rome.[6]

■ Structure and Characteristics of Paul's Letters

We now turn to an examination of the structure and characteristics of these letters that are attributed to Paul in the New Testament.

The Pauline Epistles in the New Testament are occasional correspondence, written at a particular point in time to specific congregations or individuals to address distinct situations in their given historical context. Similarity to Greek papyrus letters has led some scholars to maintain the view that Paul's writings should be labeled as **letters** and not as **Epistles**, since the latter refers to intentionally created literary works for wider reading.[7] As occasional correspondence dealing with specific situations, one may call these writings letters. However, as Schreiner has shown, Paul's writings are much more than personal letters intended for a specific audience.[8] Though specific circumstances may have contributed to the writing of these letters, they demonstrate careful development of thought, use of language with precise meaning, and structure that are found in a well-planned literary composition. Thus the label Epistle can be rightfully applied to these writings. Moreover, these letters are presented as correspondence from an apostolic authority and hence were intended for public reading and circulation within the churches in a geographical region (see Colossians 4:16).

Paul's letters follow the pattern of letter writing in the ancient Greco-Roman world. A typical Greek papyrus letter begins with a salutation, which includes the name of the sender, recipients, and greetings. Occasionally one may find a thanksgiving as a part of the salutation. This is followed by the body of the letter, which contains the message being communicated by the sender. The letter usually closes with some final remarks and a formal conclusion. The conclusion contains a peace wish, final greetings, and farewell.

All Pauline Epistles generally follow a similar structural pattern consisting of five basic sections, and the exceptions are usually notable. The first section is the **salutation,** consisting of the sender, the recipient, and a brief greeting. Paul identifies himself as the sender of the letter with some qualifications or descriptions attached to his name, such as an "apostle" or "servant." Eight of the 13 letters (exceptions: Romans, Ephesians, 1 and 2 Timothy, and Titus) contain the names of some other individual or individuals along with Paul's name as the sender of the letter. The recipients are usually associated with the Christian communities to which they belonged (Rome, Corinth, Galatia, etc., with the exception of Timothy, Titus, and Philemon). The greeting utilizes both the traditional Greek and Hebrew forms of greeting. Grace *(charis)* is the Pauline adaptation of the traditional Greek *chairein* (meaning "greeting"). Peace (Greek *eirene*) is the equivalent of the Hebrew word *shalom.* The greeting tends to be longer and more detailed when Paul is writing to a congregation that he has not yet visited. The second section is the **thanksgiving** section, where Paul typically thanks God for the recipients and shares with

them his prayerful remembrances of their mutual faith. This section, not found in Galatians and Titus, often concludes with a doxological prayer of joy and thanksgiving. In some of the letters, the thanksgiving section alludes to the main concern expressed in the letter. The third section, usually the longest and most substantial, is the **body** of the letter. Here we find various elements, such as Paul's reasons for writing, his concerns for the recipients, responses to questions that have come to his attention, and major doctrinal and theological issues that need to be discussed with them. The theological concerns expressed in this section vary according to the particular needs of the recipients. This section usually begins with a request or disclosure or an expression of astonishment.[9] This section also often concludes with a doxological prayer. The fourth section, which may sometimes rival the third section in length, is technically called the *paraenesis.* The mode of the verb is the imperative, which presents an urgent challenge to respond in order to set things the way they ought to be. The material presented in this section includes ethical exhortations and practical considerations, often blended together. Some instructions are given as moral maxims; others as lists of virtues and vices; yet some others are in the form of a long exhortation or homily on certain topics.[10] The emphasis of this section is on application to life based upon information and reflection. The paraenetic material is concerned with the answer to the question: What, then, should we do and how, then, should we live in response to the truth that we have heard and believed? Some letters, such as

1 Thessalonians, 1 Corinthians, and Philippians, are either entirely or mostly in paraenetic form. The fifth section is the **conclusion,** which typically includes travel plans or other personal situations, a commendation of coworkers, a pronouncement of peace, personal greetings, some final instructions, and a benedictory prayer. Not all of these are found in every conclusion, and some are repeated or ordered differently in particular letters.

While Paul typically wrote in this manner, he frequently departed from it, adapting various forms to suit his needs. Paul worked dynamically within the letters, utilizing a broad, diverse variety of literary constructs to communicate his message. He includes within his letters formal and informal prayers and benedictions, domestic codes, slogans or unique views held by some of his readers, hymns and homilies, wisdom sayings and aphorisms, metaphors and similes, creedal and baptismal formulas. He passes along traditions that he had received, recites words of the Lord, quotes and paraphrases scripture passages, raises and answers rhetorical questions, and pronounces both blessings and judgment without equivocation. He is kind and gentle in dealing with young converts, yet at times caustic

Diatribe in Paul's Letters

Paul utilized a conversational method in some of his letters to communicate with his audience. In this method of communication, the writer anticipates a possible question or objection from the audience directed at what he or she intends to state as a primary argument. The writer then states that objection or question and then gives a response. Scholars label this method of communication **diatribe,** a literary feature in some Pauline letters. This is illustrated below:

Paul's statement

Romans 2:25-29: "Circumcision has value if you observe the law, but if you break the law, you have become as though you had not been circumcised. If those who are not circumcised keep the law's requirements, will they not be regarded as though they were circumcised? The one who is not circumcised physically and yet obeys the law will condemn you who, even though you have the written code and circumcision, are a lawbreaker. A man is not a Jew if he is only one outwardly, nor is circumcision merely outward and physical. No, a man is a Jew if he is one inwardly; and circumcision is circumcision of the heart, by the Spirit, not by the written code. Such a man's praise is not from men, but from God."

Question anticipated from the audience

3:1: "What advantage, then, is there in being a Jew, or what value is there in circumcision?"

See other such questions in Romans

3:9: "What shall we conclude then? Are we any better?"

4:1: "What then shall we say that Abraham, our forefather, discovered in this matter?"

6:1: "What shall we say, then? Shall we go on sinning so that grace may increase?"

6:15: "What then? Shall we sin because we are not under law but under grace?"

7:7: "What shall we say, then? Is the law sin?"

Paul found this conversational method to be an effective way of getting a message across to the readers. Scholars have recognized diatribe as a common teaching method in the classroom in the Greco-Roman world. Paul may have borrowed this method and adapted it to his particular need to give instruction to his audience.[11]

and sarcastic with veterans. He encourages, consoles, and comforts a struggling church, yet he also challenges, confronts, and commands that same congregation.

■ Key Theological Themes in Paul's Letters

When Paul's occasional letters are collected and read together within the larger Christian canon, two things become readily apparent. First, there is a coherent theological core or center that appears in some form in the majority of his letters. Paul did not state this theological core in any single place. Rather it must be discovered by investigating both the arguments and assumptions that are found in the letters. Second, the way Paul expressed and drew upon this theological core varied from letter to letter. How the apostle made use of the theological core was contingent on the specific goal he had for each letter. The variety in the way he applied the core has occasionally led to accusations of inconsistency on Paul's part. It is certainly possible that the apostle was not always consistent or that he changed his mind on some issues. However, careful study of his letters suggests that he had a strongly consistent core theology from which he drew in differing ways to meet the various needs of the churches and individuals to whom he wrote. The following key elements should be included in any discussion of Paul's theology.

The Old Testament Foundation

In his letters, Paul does not describe God in any abstract way. Rather, he begins from the basic understanding of God that was the shared heritage of Judaism and the Old Testament. God's holiness, mercy, power, and wisdom are often treated without introduction. He often refers to Old Testament events and persons and assumes that his readers would have knowledge of these matters.

Christology

With the earliest church Paul believed that Jesus was the long-awaited Messiah. Thus he understood that God had acted in history to fulfill the promises that He had made to His people Israel in the past. Paul also confessed Jesus as Lord (Romans 10:9; 1 Corinthians 12:3). The Greek word for "Lord" is **kyrios.** This title meant for Paul not only Jesus' right as master to own His Church and those who believe in Him but also His Lordship of the entire universe. Often he used the title to imply that Jesus is "Lord" in the same way the Old Testament spoke of Yahweh (translated as *kyrios* in the Septuagint), the God of Israel (see Romans 10:13). Scholars debate whether Paul ever actually called Jesus "God" in his letters. The Church developed a clear articulation of the doctrine of the deity of Christ a few centuries after Paul. However, regardless of whether the apostle used the actual word *God,* it is clear that he was thinking in the terms that would lead the Church to confess that Jesus was God.

Paul also understood Christ as a second Adam. This is especially clear in Romans 5:12-21 and 1 Corinthians 15:20-49. In these passages, he builds on the theological speculations of Jewish rabbis that described Adam as both a historical individual at the beginning of time and as the entirety of the human race throughout time. In Romans 5:12-21 Paul notes that Adam's disobedience brought death to the entire human race. In a similar fashion Christ's obedience brought life to a renewed or restored humanity. Thus Christ's obedience reversed the effects of Adam's disobedience and offered hope for God to restore human beings to the holy relationship with himself He had originally designed for them. In a symmetrical fashion Paul saw Adam and his disobedience bringing ruin upon the human race at the beginning of time, while Christ and His obedience brought restoration to the human race at the end of time. This Adam Christology may have been an original contribution to Christian theology by Paul.

Trinity

Neither Paul nor any other New Testament author ever used the word *Trinity* with reference to God. However, as was the case with the deity of Christ, one can find some of the "building blocks" of the doctrine of the Trinity in Paul's writings. One can say that Paul experienced God as Trinity even though he did not use the word *Trinity* to describe God.

Only in a few places in Paul's letters do we find the full title Son of

God (Romans 1:4; 2 Corinthians 1:19; Galatians 2:20; and Ephesians 4:13) for Jesus. However, there are frequent references to Christ as "his Son" or "the Son" in contexts where it is clear that God is the Father. These passages make clear the distinction in persons between the Father and the Son. For example, Romans 8:3 and Galatians 4:4 speak of God sending "his Son" into the world.

Many passages in Paul speak of Christ and the Holy Spirit, and sometimes these are brought into such proximity that it is difficult to determine if Paul really distinguished between the two. However, the distinction between the Son and the Spirit was clear for the apostle (see 1 Corinthians 6:11 for a clear distinction between the two). He never spoke of the Spirit being crucified or raised.

There are also a series of texts that refer to God (the Father), Christ (or the Son), and the Spirit in a way that identifies the three distinct persons of the Trinity. Romans 5:1-5; 8:14-17; 15:30; 1 Corinthians 2:7-16; 6:11; 12:4-6; 2 Corinthians 1:21-22; and 13:13— all suggest that Paul's experience of God was Trinitarian.

Salvation

The letters of Paul show little interest in the teachings or miracles of Jesus; the emphasis is on the death and resurrection of Christ. Through that death and resurrection God made possible the gift of salvation to all who by faith would receive it. Pauline letters show a broad array of metaphors that describe this saving result of Christ's death and/or resurrection. One of the common Pauline terms is *salvation* with the corresponding verb *to save*. The root idea of this word is rescue or deliverance

Beroea—Mosaic of Paul's call to Macedonia.

from danger. Some scholars trace Paul's use of the word *salvation* to the Old Testament passages that describe Yahweh saving Israel from her enemies. Others trace this word group to the Greco-Roman world where a number of deities are described as "saviors" for people in need.

Another common metaphor describing the results of Christ's death and resurrection is *justification* or *righteousness*. This word is derived from the language of law where it describes a person in right relationship with other persons. The Old Testament uses the word *just* or *righteous* to describe both God and persons in right relationship. Paul's justification language is found more often in Romans and Galatians where he declares that a person could be put into a right relationship with God through Jesus Christ. *Reconciliation* is another common Pauline metaphor that belongs to the language of interpersonal relationship. This term conveys the idea that sin causes a broken relationship with God and that through Christ's death and resurrection God has taken the initiative to restore that relationship. Other metaphors for salvation in Paul's letters include *sacrifice of atonement* taken from the practice of sacrifice, and *redeem* taken from the practice of slavery in the ancient world. These various metaphors have given the Church a key resource to describe in different ways the saving results of Christ's death and resurrection.

The Church

We find a variety of terms in Paul's letters for the Church. The common Greek word for church (*ekklēsia*) shows continuity with the Old Testament congregation of

Paul's ship stopped at Rhodes harbor (Acts 21:1).

Israel. Other Pauline terms such as *the people of God, the saints,* and *the elect* also show continuity with the Old Testament. The church is also the family of God and the fellowship (*koinōnia* in Greek) of the Spirit.

The **Body of Christ** is the most significant expression of the Church in Paul's letters. This expression conveys the idea that every believer participates in a meaningful way in the full reality of Christ incarnate through the Church. In Romans 12 and 1 Corinthians 12, the apostle uses this image of the Church as the Body of Christ to plead for both unity and diversity within the Church.

Eschatology

Paul's letters show that he shared the first-century Christians' understanding of last things—the final events of human history (eschatology). For both Paul and the first-century Christians, the eschatological issues were both present-tense and future-tense concerns. On the one hand, the last days had begun with the coming of Jesus the Messiah and "the fulfillment of the ages" had dawned upon the first-century believers (1 Corinthians 10:11). Paul also looked forward to the second coming of Christ and the final fulfillment of all the eschatological promises of God. He saw Christ and the Spirit as down payments or guarantees in the present that the end of time had both begun and would come to swift consummation. This "already-not yet" understanding of eschatology permeated Pauline theology. For him, Jesus was the long-awaited Messiah. He understood both salvation and the Church in the framework of the "already-not yet" fulfillment of God's final promises.

Paul's letters show various expressions of these core theological concerns. The particular circumstances of each local church and the changing circumstances of Paul's own life made every letter different from the others. We see in these letters Paul's attempt to contextualize these theological concerns to particular needs and circumstances. Thus Paul's letters are examples of practical theology, applying the truth of Christ to the real problems of people and churches.

Paul's statue in Rome at St. Paul's Outside the Walls, a basilica built over the apostle's tomb.

Summary Statements

- Paul was well versed in the traditions of Judaism.
- Paul's letters show influence of the Greco-Roman culture on his method of communication.
- Paul's letters were occasional in nature, written in response to specific need that existed in various churches he established.
- Paul's letters follow a five-part arrangement: salutation, thanksgiving, the body of the letter, paraenesis or instructions, and conclusion.
- The Old Testament foundation, Christology, Trinity, salvation, the Church, and eschatology are some of the key elements of Paul's core theology.
- Paul related his theology to the varying circumstances of his readers.

Questions for Reflection

1. In light of your understanding of Paul's conversion and his life and contributions as a Christian disciple, discuss the impact of conversion (its goal, intended result, etc.).
2. How is the Lordship of Jesus at work in your life?
3. What does it mean to be a member of the Body of Christ today?

Bible Study Assignment

Read the salutation section (1:1-2) in the letter to the Philippians. Compare and contrast this salutation with salutations in the rest of the letters of Paul. Identify the theological emphases in some salutations that are lacking in others.

Resources for Further Study

Bruce, F. F. *Paul: Apostle of the Heart Set Free*. Grand Rapids: Wm. B. Eerdmans, 1977.
Roetzel, Calvin J. *The Letters of Paul: Conversations in Context*. Louisville, Ky.: Westminster/John Knox Press, 1991.
Schreiner, Thomas. *Interpreting the Pauline Epistles*. Grand Rapids: Baker Book House, 1990.

24 Paul's Letter to the Romans

Objectives:

Your study of this chapter should help you to:

- Discuss the significance of the letter to the Romans to the Christian tradition
- Describe the context of Paul's letter to the Romans
- Summarize the major theological themes of Romans
- Evaluate Paul's ethical instructions and apply them to contemporary Christian life

Key Words to Understand

Martin Luther
Protestant Reformation
John Wesley
Augustine
Corinth
Phoebe
God's righteousness
Wrath of God
Justification by faith
Grace
Baptism
Circumcision of the heart
Sanctification
Adoption
Glorification

Questions to consider as you read:

1. What does Paul mean when he states, "All have sinned and fall short of the glory of God" (Romans 3:23)?

2. What is faith? What role does it play in one's salvation?

3. What are justification and sanctification?

Paul's letter to the church at Rome has been called "the Gospel in its purest form."[1] The richness and diversity of the profound theological expressions set forth in this letter have exerted great influence upon the Christian church for centuries. **Martin Luther**'s expositions of Romans that he began in November 1515 brought him to a clear understanding of Paul's emphasis on justification by faith, which later became a key principle of the **Protestant Reformation.** On May 24, 1738, **John Wesley** wrote in his journal the following words: "In the evening I went very unwillingly to a society in Aldersgate Street, where one was reading Luther's preface to the Epistle to the Romans. About a quarter before nine, while he was describing the change which God works in the heart through faith in Christ, I felt my heart strangely warmed. I felt I did trust in Christ, Christ alone for salvation. And an assurance was given me, that he had taken away my sins, even mine, and saved me from the law of sin and death."[2] Wesleyan scholars trace the beginning of the Evangelical Revival in the 18th century to this experience of John Wesley.

Setting and Date

Paul wrote this letter during the final days of his third missionary journey (A.D. 55-56). Some scholars date this book to A.D. 57 or even 58, depending on their reconstruction of the chronology of Paul. Toward the end of his third journey, he returned to the churches in the region of Macedonia and Corinth to receive a relief offering for the poor saints at Jerusalem (1 Corinthians 16:1-6; see also Acts 20:1-2). Paul's mention of this collection and his impending journey to Jerusalem to deliver this offering strongly suggests that he wrote this letter from **Corinth** (Romans 15:25-28). It is very likely that **Phoebe**, a member of the church at Cenchrea, near Corinth, carried the letter to the church at Rome (16:1-2).

The Christian church in Rome likely began very early, possibly with some Jewish believers that

Augustine and the Letter to the Romans

Augustine (A.D. 354-430), the greatest theologian of Western Christianity, was converted after reading Romans 13:13-14. Though he was raised by a devout mother, young Augustine pursued a life of worldly pleasures and evil. He recounts for us what happened one day when he sat in the garden of his friend and former student Alypius, deeply agonized over the power of evil upon his life.

I heard the voice as of a boy or a girl . . . coming from a neighboring house, chanting and oft repeating, "Take up and read; take up and read." . . . So, restraining the torrent of my tears, I rose up, interpreting it no other way than a command to me from Heaven to open the book, and to read the first chapter I should light upon . . . So quickly I returned to the place where . . . I put down the volume of the apostles . . . I grasped, opened, and in silence read that paragraph on which my eyes first fell,—"Not in rioting and drunkenness, not in chambering and wantonness, not in strife and envying; put ye on the Lord Jesus Christ, and make no provision for the flesh, to fulfill the lusts thereof." No further would I read, nor did I need; for instantly, as the sentence ended,—by a light, as it were, of security infused into my heart,—all the gloom of doubt vanished away."

This text from Romans 13:13-14 led him to his conversion at the age of 33.[3]

were present in Jerusalem during the Pentecost festival when God poured out His Spirit upon the believers in the Upper Room (see Acts 2). When these Jewish Christians returned to Rome, they would have continued to worship within the synagogues and eventually in the "house churches" in their community. In A.D. 49, the Roman emperor Claudius expelled all the Jewish community from Rome, and these Jewish Christians would have been among the Jews forced to leave the city. The only remaining Christian community in Rome would have been the remnant of Gentile God-fearers that had been attracted to the Jewish Messiah Jesus, who had previously worshiped with the Jewish Christians. With the death of Claudius in 52, many Jewish Christians legally returned to Rome over the next several years. However, the church they returned to was different from the church they had left behind at Rome. Gentiles had a much more prominent role than previously, and there was bound to be some friction in blending the congregations back together again. The Jews would have understood themselves to provide the primary leadership within the church, as they had from the very beginning. But the Gentiles, emboldened by the news of Paul's ministry among the Gentiles, and the nature of the gospel that he was preaching, were not willing to take a secondary or subordinate role in the church. The letter implies a sharp disagreement that existed between these two groups on the believers' relationship to certain aspects of the Mosaic Law (see 14:1—15:13). It is thus likely that Paul wrote the letter to deal

Bust of John Wesley.

with the Jewish-Gentile tension and to bring about healing to a divided congregation. However, as Douglas Moo points out, we cannot limit the purpose of this letter to this issue alone.[4] It is obvious that Paul needed this congregation's support of his plan to evangelize Spain (15:24). He also needed to defend his theological understanding of the gospel he was preaching among the Gentiles. Thus Paul may also have intended this letter as a statement of his faith to win the favor of the church and to clear up any misunderstanding caused by those who tried to slander him (see 3:8). William Greathouse describes this letter as "an ecumenical theology designed (1) to show and insure the *true meaning* of the Torah in light of God's final word in Christ, and (2) to liberate the message of Christ from its Jewish trappings in order 'to win obedience from the Gentiles' (15:18)."[5] Regardless of the reasons why he wrote this letter, this work is considered to be the most profound

Salutation and Thanksgiving

The letter opens with the longest salutation found in any of Paul's Epistles. The opening verses (1:1-6) give a detailed introduction of Paul as a servant and apostle of Jesus Christ. These verses also hint at a number of significant theological issues that Paul will discuss at length in the letter. Paul begins with a strong claim that God had called him to be an apostle and that he was "set apart for the gospel of God—the gospel he promised beforehand through his prophets in the holy Scriptures" (vv. 1-2). He also affirms that Jesus is the Messiah, born of the Davidic line, as well as the Son of God, raised up from the dead. Jesus Christ is also Lord, the one who provides grace to bring about the obedience of faith among all the nations for His name's sake. After a brief notation of the recipients and the standard "Grace and peace" greeting in verse 7, Paul moves quickly through a short thanksgiving section in verses 8-10 to the body of the Epistle.

Via Appia, the ancient road that Paul traveled in Rome.

theological treatment of Paul on the matter of sin and salvation.

Content

For the purpose of our study, we follow a simple outline, though the content may be divided into numerous subunits based on Paul's treatment of the relationship of the gospel to the Mosaic Law.

God's Righteousness

Most scholars agree that **God's righteousness** is the theme that Paul develops in the body section of the letter that runs from 1:11 to 11:36. This section begins with statements that convey Paul's longing and desire to visit the church in Rome in order to impart a spiritual gift to them, and to encourage and further establish them in their faith (1:11-13). The apostle also expresses here his conviction that he is under obligation to preach to both Greeks and barbarians, and the wise and the foolish. Paul emphatically states that he is "not ashamed of the gospel, because it is the power of God for the salvation of everyone who believes: first for the Jew, then for the Gentile" (v. 16). This motif that gives priority to the Jew but equal status to the Gentile will recur throughout the body section of Romans. The reason that Paul can so boldly declare this all-inclusive gospel is clearly disclosed in verse 17. This powerful gospel is the vehicle through which the righteousness of God is faithfully revealed "from faith to faith" (NASB). Paul draws support for this proclamation from the book of the prophet Habakkuk in the Old Testament scriptures where this principle is clearly stated: "The righteous will live by faith" (1:17; Habakkuk 2:4). This is the foundation upon which Paul builds his subsequent arguments.

Paul's focus then shifts immediately to the **wrath of God** against all ungodliness and unrighteousness. In careful rhetorical fashion, he argues that the primary human sin is idolatry, the intentional and deliberate suppression of true knowledge about the sovereign Creator God that has been available to all humanity from the beginning of creation. In the refusal to honor and acknowledge God as Creator, creatures set up alternative objects of worship, taking to and for themselves the role that rightly belongs to the sovereign God alone. What results from the creature's efforts to supplant the right and true with the "lie" of self-sovereignty is the shattering of "right-relatedness" with the sovereign Creator. When creatures inexcusably deny what can be known about God and re-

fuse to grant to Him the honor that He is due, then God gives them up to the darkness, lust, and depravity of their lies. The ultimate consequences of such actions are degradation, abandonment, and death (1:18-32).

In chapter 2, Paul reminds the church that judgment belongs to the One Lord God alone and that God's impartial judgment is righteous and as such will fall upon all who do evil, the Jew first and also the Greek. He subtly argues against the Jewish notion that since Jews have the Law, they will be exempt from the righteous judgment of God. On the contrary, having the Law puts them under the closer scrutiny demanded by that very Law. The essence of the Law would demand that the Jew first and foremost have no other gods before

T Righteousness of God

Throughout the Bible God is described as a righteous God. This attribute of God is essential to our understanding of God as a holy God. The Bible portrays God's righteousness revealed through His saving actions. H. Ray Dunning describes God's righteousness as "salvific"; that is, His actions to bring salvation to those who are oppressed or to "put things right."[6] God as a holy God comes to the aid of those who are weak and helpless by nature or by social condition and extends to them His help. Dunning connects this meaning of righteousness with the Pauline view of God's righteousness. He states: "The apostle makes use of the idea of the righteousness of God to refer to His justifying activity toward those who were undeserving, thus preserving the essentially salvific connotation of the idea from the Old Testament."[7] This understanding of righteousness as God's "free bestowal of mercy upon the believing sinner" is a significant contribution of Martin Luther to Christian theology.[8]

Wrath of God

We often hear people asking the question, "How can a loving God also be a God of wrath?" The Bible clearly expresses the view of God as a God of holy love. However, the Bible also describes the wrath of God. How can this be? It is important to note that the wrath of God is God's response to human sin. However, this cannot be understood as His anger toward sinful humanity. The Bible does not portray God as an angry God who expresses His angry attitude and emotion toward humanity. However, sinful humanity is subject to God's wrath, which is His holy response to sin and sinners. Willard H. Taylor describes God's wrath as "His steady, holy displeasure at sin." He further states that the goal of God's wrath is to "maintain the created order and to punish those who rebel against His providences and redemption and who persist in acting wickedly."[9] The good news of the gospel is that His wrath is not forever. Though Paul often speaks of God's wrath in Romans, he also speaks of the redemptive work of Christ on the Cross that brings deliverance and salvation from God's wrath. God's purpose is not to condemn sinners to their eternal judgment, rather to draw them toward himself and thus to enable them to be the object of His holy love.

God. So, to place themselves in the role of judge over the Gentiles is to replace their God with themselves. The only value of the Law for the Jew in relationship to righteousness before God comes when they in fact keep and maintain the "right-relatedness" with God that the Law was intended to provide. That would include above all else having no other gods before Yahweh. This kind of lawful obedience to the commandments of God requires not an external circumcision of the flesh in accordance to the Law, but rather an internal circumcision of heart through the Spirit. This is what brings praise from God and what it means to be truly Jewish. Paul also counterargues that when the Gentiles without the Law do what the Law requires in matters of the heart, their uncircumcision will be considered as circumcision by God, and that they will stand in judgment upon the physically circumcised but Law-breaking Jews.

In chapter 3, Paul declares that while the Jew has many advantages over the Gentile, they are alike in that both live under the power and influence of sin. "There is no one righteous, not even one" (3:10). Works of the Law cannot make a person righteous before God. However, now apart from Law, the righteousness of God has been revealed through the faithfulness of Jesus Christ for all who believe, Jew and Gentile alike. The God of Jews and Gentiles is One God, the Lord, who "justifies" or makes people righteous on the basis of faith in Jesus Christ, who has demonstrated God's faithful righteousness. This concept is illustrated further in chapter 4, where Paul reminds the Romans that Abraham was reckoned righteous by God on the basis of his faith prior to his circumcision, becoming thereby the father of all who would come to God by faith, the Jew first but also the Gentile.

Chapter 5 brings the first part of the body of the letter to a logical conclusion, yet also works as the foundation for the heart of the

Epistle, which is found in chapters 5—8. Chapter 5 further illustrates and amplifies the implications of **justification by faith.** Justification provides for sinners peace and reconciliation with God. They are no longer under the wrath and judgment of God. Moreover, they have the hope of sharing God's glory. They enjoy not only new life in Christ Jesus but also God's love that has been poured out into their hearts—love that God demonstrated for the sinful world through the death of Christ.

To further illustrate his gospel of justification by faith, Paul contrasts the disobedience of Adam with the obedience of Jesus Christ and shows how both have impacted the world (5:12-21). Sin entered the world through "one man" or Adam, bringing with it a universal infection and the ultimate consequence of death to all humanity. However, the good news of the gospel is that through "one man" Jesus Christ has come "the gift of righteousness" (v. 17). This is God's **grace,** an unmerited favor from God. Sinners can do nothing to merit the righteousness and the life that comes through this free gift. Moreover, God extends this grace to all humanity. Though sin continues to proliferate in the world, God continues to extend this grace without limit to sinful humanity. The goal of God's grace is to lead sinners under the dominion of death to "eternal life through Jesus Christ" (v. 21).

Though Paul's proclamation of justification by faith is really good news for both Jews and Gentiles, this gospel also raises some significant questions. In chapters 6—7, Paul addresses two significant questions, one from each side of the spectrum of the diverse Ro-

man congregation. He then pulls both sides into a climactic conclusion in chapter 8. In chapter 6, Paul addresses a question from the Gentile perspective with a carefully crafted rhetorical argument. If grace increases beyond the increase of sin (v. 20), why not continue in sin so that more grace might be extended to them (6:1)? Paul's answer is a resounding *no.* He reminds those who misunderstood the full implications of justification by faith that in their baptism they have died to sin.

Baptism is one's identification with the death of Jesus. Those who have been crucified with Him cannot go on living in sin, and they should no longer be

T Circumcision of the Heart

The ritual act of circumcision, which God established for Abraham and his descendants as an external sign of the covenant, receives a spiritual meaning in later biblical texts. Moses challenged the people of Israel to circumcise their "hearts" (Deuteronomy 10:16) and later promised that God will circumcise their "hearts" and the "hearts" of their descendants (30:6; see also Jeremiah 4:4; 9:26). Gerhard Von Rad sees in these texts in Deuteronomy the ideas of cleansing and one's commitment to live on God's terms.[10] The Wesleyan doctrine of entire sanctification finds its Old Testament pattern and promise in these passages.

In the New Testament, **circumcision of the heart** is a spiritual circumcision (Romans 2:29; Colossians 2:11-12; 3:14). Paul also equates true circumcision with the "circumcision of the heart" evident through faithful and obedient living (Romans 2:29). Spiritual circumcision is thus the circumcision of heart through which we receive deliverance and cleansing from our rebellious and disobedient nature. God's gracious work of cleansing our sinful hearts gives us a new disposition and a new commitment to live a life of wholehearted love for God and humanity.

slaves to sin. Christ died to sin once and for all; sin and death no longer have any power over Him. He was raised from the dead by the power of God unto life, and the life that He now lives is a life lived unto God. Therefore, those who are baptized into Christ also should consider themselves to be dead to sin but alive unto God in Christ Jesus (vv. 3-11). As a result, sin is no longer to reign and rule over their bodies in unrighteousness (vv. 12-14). Instead, they are to present themselves to God as "slaves to righteousness" (v. 19). Though Paul has spoken of righteousness in the previous chapters as right relationship with God, the call here is for moral and ethical conduct and behavior. The result of this decision to become servants of righteousness or "enslaved to God" (v. 22, NRSV) is **"sanctification"** (NRSV) or "holiness." Holiness is one's conformity to the character of God. The ultimate outcome of being slaves to righteousness is "eternal life in

Christ Jesus our Lord" (v. 23).

The primary question that Paul addresses in Romans 7 is a question that would have been of great concern to the Jewish Christians. What about the Law? The typical Jewish Christian may have had little interest in the case Paul had made previously about the sinfulness of humanity and the righteousness of God, since they believed that they already had an adequate way to deal with sin in the careful observance of the Torah/Law.

So what did Paul say to those who know the Torah? In 7:1, he states the well-known principle that the Law has jurisdiction over a person as long as that person lives. However, he explains further that death frees and releases an individual from the Law and enables that individual to be joined to another without violation of the Law. Thus a woman whose husband has died is free to be joined to another man without being adulterous. In the same way, those who are baptized into

Roman Colosseum, as seen from the Arch of Titus.

the death of Christ have died to the Law and are now free to belong to Christ. Those who are thus joined to Christ are free from the old covenant, which once held them captive. They are now in a new covenant relationship with Christ and are free to serve Him in the newness of the Spirit (vv. 1-6).

In verses 7-13, he illustrates the point by dealing with the Law in relationship with sin. Though the Law had been given to reveal sin or to make known what sin is, sin seized the holy, righteous, and good Law and perverted it into an instrument of death. He emphatically states that the Law is not sin (v. 7). Sin took advantage of the Law, contorted and twisted it into an instrument for its own purposes. In verses 14-25, Paul suggests that the result of sin's perversion of the Law of God creates an opposing law that sets itself against God. This "law of sin" is in diametric opposition to, even open warfare against, the Law of God. Working upon humanity through the flesh, it brings bondage and ultimately death to those captured under its dominion. The whole problem of this "anti-law" in conflict with the Law of God is brought to a climax in verses 24-25. The problem is that the Law is weak through the flesh (8:3), and in and of itself it is powerless to overthrow the law of sin. Yet 7:25a is a hymn of praise for deliverance that comes through Jesus Christ. He ends the whole section begun in chapter 5: "Thanks be to God—through Jesus Christ our Lord!" Thus chapter 7 not only explains the relationship of the Law to death and to sin but also points to God's gracious provision of the new life in the Spirit discussed in chapters 6 and 8.

Chapter 8 opens with a clear message. "Therefore, there is now no condemnation for those who are in Christ Jesus" (v. 1). Why? Because God has acted in the death and resurrection of Jesus to set them free from the law of sin and death. What is now at work in the life of those who are in Christ is the Spirit of God who dwells in them. Christ's death makes it possible for those who are in Him to live a life being led by the Spirit. This Spirit is a life-giving Spirit, and the ultimate outcome is peace that comes from God. Moreover, they no longer live in fear and bondage but rather live in the inner assurance that they are children of God, adopted by Him as His heirs and "co-heirs with Christ" (v. 17).

Paul reminds his readers that **adoption** as God's children does not mean that the Christian life will be free from suffering. God's plan is to liberate the whole creation from the decay brought upon it by human sin. What awaits the children of God is yet another "adoption," which is the final "redemption of our bodies" (v. 23) and sharing of the glory of God (v. 17). This restoration of humanity to their true destiny will also mean the restoration of the whole creation. Christians live with this hope in their future glory and release from all suffering (vv. 18-25). This life they live with the full awareness that the Spirit helps them in their "weakness." They are also confident in their faith that "all things work together for good for those who love God" (v. 28, NRSV). They know fully well that God's purpose for them is not only their justification but also their **glorification** (vv. 26-30).

Nothing in the whole creation can separate them from this hope they have in God and God's love they experience in their lives (vv. 31-39).

In chapter 9, Paul addresses his profound concern for his own people, Israel, and explains his understanding of the gospel to the Jew first and also to the Greek. Israel indeed is a blessed nation because of the covenant, the Law, and the promise to the patriarchs. God's word of promise to Abraham did not fail even if not all of Abraham's children have proven to be his true descendants. Some of Abraham's children have denied their calling and thus could not be considered true children of the promise (vv. 6-18). However, in Paul's thinking, both Jews and Gentiles, who are faithful to their calling from God, are indeed the children of the promise and thus the true heirs of Abraham (vv. 22-29). He concludes that Gentiles attained righteousness through faith in God's faithfulness, even though they were not striving for it. Israel, however, failed to achieve righteousness before God because they pursued it through the works of the Law and not through faith. More than that, in their intense pursuit of the Law, they stumbled over the "stone" (which is Christ) that God has placed in their path for their salvation (vv. 30-33).

Paul continues the theme of righteousness that comes from God in chapters 10—11. He affirms that Christ is the completion of the Law, providing righteousness unto salvation for everyone who believes, the Jew first but also the Gentile (10:1-13). Israel failed to embrace Jesus as Messiah. Though they did hear the word of Christ, they did not obey what they heard

(vv. 14-21). Yet chapter 11 makes it clear that Israel's rejection is neither total nor permanent. As there was a remnant during the time of Elijah, even so there remains a remnant of Israel (vv. 1-6). If they abandon their unbelief, they, too, will be saved, just as branches broken off can be grafted again to an olive tree. In their unbelief, they were broken off, but in their faith they will be grafted again as God's people (vv. 23-24). Paul ends the discussion with a beautiful vision of the ultimate salvation that will embrace all of the new true Israel, including Gentiles that have been called by faith to experience the mercy of God extended to all humanity (vv. 25-32). The hymn in verses 33-36 brings the entire body section of the Epistle to a close and makes an excellent transition to the paraenesis that follows.

■ Instructions

Chapter 12 begins with a powerful admonition to the Roman Christians, Jew and Gentile alike, to present their bodies as living, holy sacrifices unto God. They are not to be conformed to the world. But they are to be a renewed, transformed people whose very lives display God's good will completely (vv. 1-2). The practical implications of this life are spelled out in the remainder of the chapter. He reminds his readers that though they are diverse in their makeup, they are indeed "one body in Christ" (v. 5, NRSV). They are also recipients of a variety of gifts given to them by God's grace, and these gifts are to be used for the community. He concludes this chapter with an admonition that love must be the basis of all Christian conduct and relationships (vv. 3-21).

Chapter 13 continues the theme of love, extending it into the areas of civic duty and responsibility. Respect for civil authorities and paying taxes are all part of Christian civic duty. Paul reminds his audience that the essence of the commandments is love and that the one who loves thus fulfills the Law. Christians must live an honorable life, free from the deeds of evil and other sinful influences. Salvation has already dawned upon them, and the day of the Lord's coming is near. Therefore they must clothe themselves with the life that comes to them through Christ, a life in which there is no room for the desires of the flesh.

In chapter 14, Paul revisits the problem of judgment and judging within the Body, reminding Jewish and Gentile Christians alike that God alone is the ultimate and final Judge before whom all humanity will one day stand. He instructs the strong in faith to be patient with weaker brothers and sisters, and do nothing that would cause another to stumble.

In chapter 15, Paul urges harmony among all in the Christian fellowship with special praise to God for His good plan to bless all humanity beginning with the Jews and extending that blessing to include Gentiles as well (vv. 1-21). He ends chapter 15 with a summary of his travel itinerary, which includes his plan to visit Rome on his way to Spain (vv. 22-33). The final chapter includes his recommendation of "Phoebe, a servant of the church in Cenchrea" to the church at Rome and his greetings to several friends and coworkers. He concludes the letter with a benediction, an expression of praise to the eternal God, who in His wisdom revealed the mystery of Jesus Christ to the Gentiles "to bring about the obedience of faith" (16:26, NRSV).

Summary Statements

- Paul's letter to the Romans had profound influence on the lives of Augustine, Martin Luther, and John Wesley.
- Paul wrote this letter to the church at Rome to share the content of his preaching of the gospel of Jesus Christ.
- God's righteousness is a major theme in the letter to the Romans.
- Both Jews and Gentiles stand under the judgment of God.
- Trust/faith in the faithfulness of God demonstrated through Jesus Christ is necessary for one's right relationship with God.
- Justification is a free gift of God's grace that God extends to all humanity.
- Justification calls for one's commitment to live as servants of righteousness.
- God's provision for a justified believer is a new life in the Spirit, free from the power of sin and death.
- A justified believer can have hope in the sharing of God's glory.
- Christians must practice love in all areas of human relationships.

Questions for Reflection

1. What perspective do you gain about humanity in the early chapters of Romans?
2. What perspective do you gain about God and His attitude toward humanity, based on your reading of this Epistle?
3. What should be our proper response to God's demonstration of righteousness in our lives?
4. What are the ways by which you practice hospitality toward others?

Bible Study Assignment

Read Romans 5:6-11 and answer the following questions:

1. Read the entire chapter 5 and attempt to discover the thematic continuity of verses 6-11 to verses 1-5 and 12-21.
2. What is the human condition that Paul introduces in verses 6, 8, and 10?
3. What perspective about Jesus' death does Paul portray in verse 6?
4. Compare verses 7 and 8. What is the argument that Paul makes in verse 7?
5. What parallel ideas do you find in verses 6 and 8? What new thought does Paul introduce in verse 8 that is not found in verse 6?
6. What is the meaning of the words *justified, saved,* and *God's wrath* in verse 9?
7. What is the benefit of justification, according to verse 9?
8. What is the result of the death of Jesus, according to verse 10?
9. What is the meaning of the word *reconciliation* in verse 11?
10. What is Paul's overall objective that you recognize in this text?
11. What does this text say to us about humanity, sin, death, life, death of Jesus Christ, God's love, justification, reconciliation, God's wrath, and salvation?
12. How do you see yourself in light of this text? What does this text say about the mission of the Church today?

Resources for Further Study

Greathouse, William. *Wholeness in Christ: Toward a Biblical Theology of Holiness.* Kansas City: Beacon Hill Press of Kansas City, 1998.

Moo, Douglas. *Romans,* in *The NIV Application Commentary.* Grand Rapids: Zondervan, 2000.

Stulmacher, Peter. *Paul's Letter to the Romans.* Louisville, Ky.: Westminster/John Knox Press, 1994.

25 1 and 2 Corinthians and Galatians

O bjectives:

Your study of this chapter should help you to:

- Describe the context of Paul's letters to the Corinthians and Galatians
- Discuss Paul's relationship to the churches of Corinth and Galatia
- Describe the key theological issues in 1 and 2 Corinthians and Galatians
- Relate the meaning and message of 1 and 2 Corinthians and Galatians to the Christian Church today

Q uestions to consider as you read:

1. What are the problems that existed in the church at Corinth?
2. What does Paul say about unity and diversity in the church?
3. What is the relationship between Christian faith and the surrounding culture?
4. What is the relationship between the Law and the gospel in the letter to the Galatians?

K ey Words to Understand

Corinth
Achaia
Julius Caesar
Gallio
South Galatian theory
North Galatian theory
Judaizers
Justification

1 and 2 Corinthians

In Paul's day, **Corinth** was the capital of **Achaia**, the Roman province in the southern part of Greece, and the leading and the most prosperous city in Greece. The city that Paul visited was the Roman Corinth rebuilt under the order given by **Julius Caesar** before his death in 44 B.C. The city's population was primarily made up of Roman citizens who were retired members of the Roman army and other citizens who relocated to Corinth from Rome. The city also had a large number of Greeks, a significant Jewish population,[1] and many entrepreneurs from the Middle East. The Greek inhabitants who remained in and around the city were not counted as citizens and they did not have the same privileges held by the colonists. The government of the city was patterned after the Roman system of government. In architecture, the city's buildings were patterned after the Roman style, and it would have looked more like a typical Roman city.[2]

Religion played a significant role in the life of the Corinthian population. Romans at Corinth incorporated Greek gods and goddesses into their religious worship. Corinth had a large number of pagan temples and shrines to honor a variety of Greek and Roman deities. The temples in Corinth were centers of sacred prostitution and other sexual activities in connection with temple meals. The city also promoted the imperial cult in which the citizens played a prominent part since such activities helped them gain status in the society.

Paul at Corinth

Paul's first visit to Corinth took place during his second missionary journey (Acts 18:1-17). There he met a Jew named Aquila and his wife, Priscilla, who were forced to leave Rome around A.D. 50 under a decree given by the Roman Emperor Claudius.[3] Luke also reports that **Gallio,** who took office around A.D. 51, was proconsul of Achaia.[4] Paul's stay at Corinth for 18 months (v. 11) would have taken place around A.D. 50-52. After his arrival at Corinth, he joined with Aquila and Priscilla in the business of manufacturing tents (v. 3; see 1 Corinthians 4:12). He also attended the local synagogue every Sabbath and tried to persuade both Jews and Greeks to the Christian faith (Acts 18:4). His preaching of the gospel brought opposition, and the Jews brought charges against him before the tribunal, but Gallio dismissed the charges citing that they were complaints made on the basis of Jewish Law and not matters that concerned Roman law. After 18 months of stay at Corinth, Paul left the city accompanied by Aquila and Priscilla and crossed the Aegean Sea to Ephesus in Asia Minor, perhaps in late A.D.

The Corinthian Canal that connects the Gulf of Corinth with the Saronic Gulf.

51 or early 52. From there he traveled to Jerusalem and on to Antioch (vv. 12-23).

Setting and Date

During Paul's stay in Ephesus in A.D. 52-55 (his third missionary journey), he remained in frequent dialogue with the church at Corinth, writing them several times and returning for a brief visit as well. This ongoing communication provided unique opportunities for Paul to deal with some issues that were reported to him by members of the church (see 1 Corinthians 1:11; 5:1) as well as to respond to the questions the church asked him on various matters (7:1). These communications show that the church was divided on various issues, which in turn led to a real crisis in the life of the church. These letters also offer us personal, intimate insights into the stormy relationship that Paul had with this troubled and divided church.

Paul wrote an initial letter to the Corinthians from Ephesus to resolve the moral crisis in the church (see 1 Corinthians 5:9), but this letter is not preserved by the Christian tradition. First Corinthians in the New Testament is most likely his second letter to the church at Corinth. Paul sent Timothy to the church and later he himself went there to resolve some of the problems, but it was a failure and he returned to Ephesus in humiliation (2 Corinthians 2:1-2; 12:21). Paul then wrote a third letter, which is described as painful, written with a heavy heart (2:3-9; 7:8-12). This harsh letter has also been "lost," although some scholars have speculated that part of it may be included in 2 Corinthians 10—13.

Evidently Titus, who took this letter, met Paul in Macedonia with encouraging news about the church's response. Scholars believe that 2 Corinthians is Paul's fourth letter, which he wrote from the Macedonian region as a letter of reconciliation (A.D. 55/56). The rift between Paul and the church must have been healed, because Paul later returned to Corinth to receive an offering from the Gentiles for the poor of the Jewish Jerusalem church.

Acrocorinth (the acropolis of ancient Corinth), the site of several shrines, including a temple of Aphrodite.

1 Corinthians

Content

The structure of 1 Corinthians fits the standard model reasonably well. We outline the content of this letter as follows:

Salutation and Thanksgiving	1:1-9
Main Body of the Letter	1:10—4:21
Paraenesis Section	5:1—16:18

In the salutation Paul addresses the recipients as "those sanctified in Christ Jesus and called to be holy" (literally *holy ones*) (1:2). The thanksgiving (vv. 4-9) is typical, with some early hints of the major theological discussion to follow relating to themes of grace,

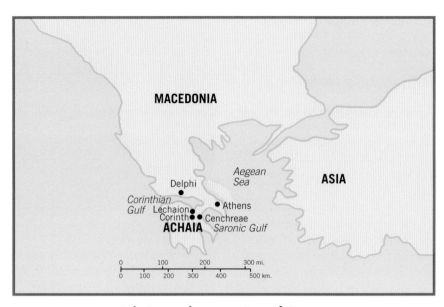

Achaia, southern province of Greece.

speech, knowledge, spiritual gifts, and ultimate confirmation as blameless at Christ's Parousia.

In the body of the letter that runs from verse 10 to 4:21, Paul contrasts knowledge and ignorance, wisdom and foolishness, power and weakness, the spiritual and the natural, holiness and sexual immorality, the "puffed up" and those who build up others. The focus of these chapters is on unity in the church. Though the church was divided into various groups, each claiming loyalty to different leaders, Paul contended that believers are all one, united into one new created order in Christ (1:10-16). He was commissioned by Christ to proclaim the gospel without the usual "words of human wisdom" (v. 17; see 2:4). The gospel of the Cross he preached at Corinth was foolishness to the wise and a scandalous stumbling block to the Jews who could not grasp the concept of a crucified Messiah (1:18, 23). However, he was determined to preach

the crucified Christ not with eloquent words but in "fear, and with much trembling" (2:3) and in the power of Spirit (vv. 1-5). Paul invites the Corinthians to follow his model by living their life in pursuit of the true wisdom of God, instead of following the wisdom of the world as "people of the flesh" (3:1, NRSV; see 2:6—3:15). He concludes with the reminder that the collective church body is the holy temple of God, which is marked by the presence of God's Spirit, and that this community of faith belongs to Christ and not to any human leaders (vv. 16-23).

In chapter 4, Paul contrasts arrogance with humility and considers the impact of these upon the Body. The arrogant are "puffed up," proud of the gifts they have received and contemptuous of others within the Body. Paul invites the arrogant members of the church to follow the model of the apostles who consider themselves as slaves and stewards of Christ, and he encourages them to use their gifts for building up and edifying the Body as a whole instead of being puffed up with self-pride.

The paraenesis section (instructions and exhortations) extends from 5:1 to 16:18, making it nearly three times the length of the body of the letter. Paul begins with a strong admonition not to associate with the immoral people in the church and not to take fellow believers to the public court system to settle disputes (chaps. 5—6). In 6:12-20, he stresses the importance of embodying the reality of their salvation as members of Christ. Paul reminds the Corinthians that their bodies are the temples of the holy God and the dwelling places of His Holy Spirit. They no longer belong to themselves but to the God who has redeemed them from the slavery of sin.

Chapters 7—14 seem to contain Paul's response to the questions from the Corinthians (see 7:1). He begins with a discussion on the sanctity of marriage and then gives instructions on various issues, including divorce, remarriage, and celibacy (vv. 1-40). Some of these instructions are personal perspectives, but some he attributes as instructions from the Lord. The question of whether a Christian should eat food offered to idols is discussed in chapter 8. He admonishes those who possess superior knowledge on this issue to be sensitive to the weak (those who find it offensive to eat food offered to idols) among them. What builds up the community is not one's knowledge but love for others. Giving up one's freedom and rights may be necessary for the building up of community. Paul illustrates this principle by his own conduct among the Corinthians (9:1-27). Though he was an apostle, he gave up his rights as an apostle and made himself "a slave to everyone" for the sake of the gospel (v. 19). He warns his readers to "flee from idolatry" (10:14) and denounces a believer's participation in pagan religious rites (vv. 6-22). He reminds them that while all things may now be lawful to him in Christ Jesus, not all things are profitable,

Temple of Apollo
at Corinth.

Remains of the Bema, the Roman tribune, where Paul stood before Gallio.

for the "body and blood of the Lord" (11:27; see vv. 17-34).

In chapters 12 and 14, Paul directly addresses the issue of spiritual gifts and graces within the Body of Christ. God is the giver of all gifts to individual members of the Body of Christ. Though members of the believing community may show evidence of a variety of gifts, they all proceed from one Spirit, one Lord, and one God (12:4-11). Paul implies that the unity within the three persons of the Godhead is a model for the Church, the recipient of diversity of spiritual gifts. He points out that Christ is the head of the Body, the Church, and that everything that flows out graciously from that head has one primary function—enhancing, sustaining, and nurturing the entire Body for the sake of the whole Body. Paul makes it clear that not all have the same specific gifts and that there is not any single gift that is shared by all within the Body, except for the more excellent way—the gift of love. It seems that some members of the Corinthian church may have promoted "special languages" and

and he will do everything within that freedom in Christ to the glory and honor of God (vv. 23-33). He concludes with a denunciation of their worship practices, especially in relation to the Lord's Supper. The sacred time of communal meal (the Lord's Supper) had become the context for gluttony and drunkenness for some in the church. Paul gives clear instructions on how the Lord's Supper should be properly observed, and he warns them of the consequences of eating the bread and drinking the cup without respect

T Prophecy and Tongues in 1 Corinthians 14

Paul's treatment of prophecy and tongues in 1 Corinthians 14 gives us insight into how Paul viewed these two spiritual gifts. Prophecy is a gift for all believers, since it is given for upbuilding, encouragement, and consolation of others. Prophecy is given in an intelligible language understood by all who hear it, whereas those who speak in tongues speak to God in a language others do not understand. Prophecy did not require interpretation whereas tongues needed someone to interpret the unknown things. Prophecy in Corinth seems to be a Spirit-inspired speech given spontaneously for the upbuilding of others. Paul also makes clear that tongues are a sign not for the believers but for the nonbelievers, "a sign of judgment that they are out of touch with God."[5] In contrast, prophecy is a sign for believers of "the gracious presence of God in the community in which it occurs."[6] We must also keep in mind Paul's treatment of the limited and temporary nature of these spiritual gifts (see 13:8-11). Paul's concluding instruction is that whatever spiritual gifts are exercised in the Christian community, they all must show evidence of peace and order because "God is not a God of disorder but of peace" (14:33).

frenetic worship as marks of their spirituality. Paul encourages thoughtful proclamation and order and community-building during public worship. He carefully places the great love chapter (chap. 13) between the chapters devoted to spiritual gifts (12 and 14). Nothing is more essential to the life and practice of the church than the gift of God's gracious love extended to and through His people. That love in action is the true mark of the presence of God's living Spirit among His people.

Chapter 15 provides significant autobiographical material about Paul, tied to a major theological treatise that deals with the resurrection of the dead. Verses 1-11 give the foundational core of Paul's gospel and the affirmation of his apostolic authority. In the retelling of the appearances of the risen Christ to His disciples, Paul includes the story of Christ's encounter with him, a persecutor of the Church, one who does not "even deserve to be called an apostle" (v. 9), as a sheer display of divine grace.

The remainder of chapter 15 is devoted to a discussion of the resurrection of Christ Jesus from the dead. Paul logically develops his argument that if resurrection from death is impossible, then Christ could not have been raised from the dead. He asserts that Christ has been raised as "the firstfruits of those who have fallen asleep" (v. 20). Christ's resurrection is the proof that God has commenced the activity in human history that will one day demonstrate His total sovereign rule over all creation. The resurrection of Christ further shows that the power of death has been conquered. Paul ends this chapter with a discourse on the nature of the resurrected body as spiritual, imperishable, and immortal.

The final chapter of 1 Corinthians includes some practical requests concerning the collection for the poor in Jerusalem, Paul's future travel plans, and final exhortations. He ends this letter with greetings, his personal signature, and with a benediction (16:19-24).

I Marriage and Celibacy

Paul's treatment of marriage and celibacy in 1 Corinthians 7 is best understood if we approach it from the context of marriage and family relationship in the Roman world. Roman marriages were mostly arranged and as such were nothing more than social and economic contracts between a man and a woman to live together in peace and harmony. Husbands, usually much older than wives, held power and authority and dominant position in the family.[7] First Corinthians 7 begins with a popular slogan of those who were ascetic ("It is good for a man not to marry"), which cannot be taken to mean that Paul is advocating celibacy for Christians. Though he prefers singleness for the sake of greater devotion to the Lord, he does not devalue marriage or consider sexual relations as sinful. Against the Roman view of the dominance of the husband over his wife, Paul teaches that just as the body of a wife belongs to her husband, so does the husband's body belong to his wife. His strongest argument against ascetics, who consider sexual relations as sinful, is his instruction that in a marital relationship sex should be abstained only by mutual agreement for a time of prayer.

2 Corinthians

As stated earlier, Paul wrote this letter of reconciliation from the Macedonian region around A.D. 55-56, after hearing encouraging news from Titus about the Corinthian church. The content of this letter is somewhat unorganized, and therefore it is difficult to follow the development of the apostle's thought. We give the following outline to the content of this letter:

Salutation and Blessings 1:1-11
Paul Defends His Ministry
                       1:12—7:16
Collection for the Church at
    Jerusalem   8:1—9:15
Paul Defends Himself
    and His Work   10:1—13:10
Final Greetings and
    Benediction   13:11-14
Second Corinthians begins in very typical epistolary fashion, al-

though the salutation (1:1-2) is quite brief. In place of the typical thanksgiving immediately following the salutation, Paul pronounces praise and adoration to God (vv. 3-11; "Praise be to the God . . ."). Paul uses the noun and verb form of the Greek word *parakaleo* (meaning "to comfort or to console") 10 times in verses 3-7 to emphasize God's provision of consolation or comfort for a people facing severe sufferings and trials. There has been suffering, both on Paul's part and in the life of the Corinthian congregation. Paul is confident, however, that those who share in the suffering of Christ will find comfort and consolation that comes through Christ. Chapter 2 begins with a reminder of his concern for the church and the pain and agony he felt when he wrote the

C

Paul's Letters to the Corinthians in Their Social and Cultural Setting

Witherington notes a number of possible connections between Paul's letters to the Corinthians and the social-cultural life of the Corinthian citizens. These include the following:

1. Civic and individual pride displayed in the inscriptions found at Corinth show that at Corinth people often sought public recognition of their accomplishments. Paul challenged the believers to take pride in their relationship with Christ (1 Corinthians 1:31).

2. Sexual activities were a part of the temple meal at Corinth. Paul warns the Christians not to indulge in this idolatrous way of life, which included eating, drinking, and dancing (1 Corinthians 10:7-8).

3. The sanctuary of Asklepios was a popular place for dining and exercise, and other forms of relaxation. First Corinthians 10:27-30 may be viewed as Paul's instructions to Christians who may be invited to eat food that had been offered to gods in the pagan temples.

4. Instructions in 1 Corinthians concerning marriage and divorce may be viewed as Paul's response to those who may have had questions concerning their previous sacred marriage relationship with Hera, a goddess of marriage and childbirth.

5. It is possible that 14:34-36 may be Paul's response to the problem of Corinthian church women interrupting male prophets with their questions, similar to the questions about childlessness, and the like, asked of the Delphi oracle.[8]

letter that brought them great sorrow and pain. Paul makes it clear in verse 17—3:18 that he is not a mere peddler of the gospel for the monetary gain that it could bring. In chapter 4, he reminds them that despite everything that has happened to him and to them, he does not lose heart. He recounts being afflicted, perplexed, and persecuted, but he also affirms that he has not been destroyed by the power of death. He does not lose heart because the inner humanity is being renewed day by day through the power of God's Holy Spirit, given as the pledge and guarantee of God's ultimate and final salvation for those who are in Christ (v. 16—5:10).

In verses 11-21, we find some of the most powerful, profound theology in the New Testament. Paul asserts that the love of Christ compels those who belong to Christ to "no longer live for themselves but for him who died for them and was raised again" (v. 15). If any person is in Christ Jesus, old things have passed away, new things have begun—a new creation comes into existence (v. 17). And all of this comes about directly through God's reconciling ministry of the entire world brought about through Christ, the One who was made sin on our behalf that in Him "we might become the righteousness of God" (v. 21; see vv. 19-21). In 6:1-10, Paul discusses the badge of true discipleship. Opposition and difficulties do not negate what God had accomplished through His word and power. Believers must remember that they are the temples of the living God, and therefore they must live in holiness and the sanctity of flesh

and spirit, "perfecting holiness out of reverence for God" (7:1).

Paul returns in verses 2-16 to the issue of the pain that his powerful letter had caused them. In chapters 8—9, he details the importance of the offering that he wanted to take to the poor in Jerusalem. He urges the predominantly Gentile churches to be generous in their giving to the poor saints in Jerusalem as an expression of their gratitude to God.

The tone changes dramatically in chapters 10—13, where he moves to a confrontation with his most vocal opponents. These so-called superapostles had mocked and defied Paul, ridiculing and deriding him for his strong letters but weak performance when he was present with them on the failed visit. Paul declares that he would boast only in the Lord and not according to the fleshly standard of his opponents. He is confident in the sufficiency of God's grace in the midst of the most trying times, and His power is made perfect in the midst of human weakness (12:9).

Paul concludes the letter with a challenge to the Corinthians to test if the power of God is at work in their lives. Those who are weak in God are indeed those who have the power of God at work in their lives. They will strive to build up the Body of Christ instead of tearing it down. That indeed is the true test of apostolicity.

Letter to the Galatians

Paul's letter to the Galatians is addressed to an audience that includes Gentiles who appear to be under heavy pressure to become Jewish in their belief, behavior, and practice. Apparently some Jewish Christians insisted that the Gentiles must obey the Law of Moses in order for them to be considered truly Christian. This letter seeks to address this issue with a bold claim of the Gentile believers' freedom from the Law of Moses. Paul reiterates in this letter his understanding of the gospel of Jesus Christ. Along with Romans, this letter also emphasizes the justification of a believer by faith and not by works of the Law. The letter is often referred to as the Magna Charta of Christian liberty because of its overriding emphasis on the freedom of Christians from the Law of Moses.

Setting and Date

Paul addresses the recipients of his letter as "the churches in Galatia" (1:1) and as "Galatians" (3:1). The location of the audience plays a role in determining the date of this letter. Those who locate the "churches in Galatia" in the southern part of the province of Galatia **(South Galatian theory)** propose a date either before the Jerusalem Council (see Acts 15) or a year or two after the council. This would place the letter around A.D. 48 or 50/51. Those who locate Galatia in north central Asia Minor **(North Galatian theory)** think that Paul wrote the letter from Ephesus around A.D. 53-55, during his third missionary journey.[9] The choice made concerning date and region has little effect on the message of Galatians.

Galatians clearly reflects a strong and powerful Jewish influence within the early Christian church. Apparently some preachers had come to the region after Paul had left and persuaded the churches that Gentile converts had to become completely Jewish to be truly Christian. These **Judaizers** undermined the message of the gospel of freedom that Paul had preached, and their perspective became dominant in the churches of Galatia. Paul, in this letter, responds to this distortion of the gospel message in an eloquent and powerful way, at times with expressions of his anger and frustration at those who have been misled by the Judaizers.

Content

Paul's tone and approach in Galatians clearly demonstrate his agitation with those who were preaching a radically different gospel. He skips the customary thanksgiving section and moves to defend his apostolic authority and then challenges the strange teaching that the Galatians had embraced. We give the following outline to the letter:

Introduction and Occasion of
the Letter   1:1-10
Defense of Paul's Apostolic
Authority   1:11—2:21
Justification by Faith   3:1—4:31
Christian Liberty   5:1—6:10
Conclusion and Benediction
     6:11-18

The opening statements make clear the context of Paul's letter to the Galatians. The recipients of this letter have deserted the "one who called you by the grace of Christ" and have turned to a "different gospel" (1:6). He rejects the notion of "another gospel" and pronounces a solemn curse (anathema) on those who create confusion among the Galatians by perverting "the gospel of Christ" (v. 7; see vv. 7-9).

In the next section, Paul establishes his authority as an apostle (v. 11—2:21). He declares that his gospel came directly from God and that his mandate to go to the Gentiles was not a mere human endeavor. Here he inserts a brief autobiographical sketch, which includes his former life as a zealous Jew who violently persecuted the Church in an attempt to destroy it. He reflects on his call and commission as part of God's sovereign plan for his life even before his birth (1:15-16; see also Jeremiah 1:4). God not only called him through a special revelation but also gave him the charge to proclaim Christ among the Gentiles. He reinforces the divine authority behind his mission by claiming that everything he did was a response to God's special revelation to him. He neither conferred with the Jerusalem leaders nor did they send him out on his ministry to the Gentiles. Eventually, when he met with the Jerusalem leaders and shared with them his calling to the Gentiles, they acknowledged "the grace given" to him by God to take the gospel to the Gentiles (Galatians 2:9; see vv. 1-10).

The major foundation of Paul's gospel is that a person is "not justified by observing the law, but by faith in Jesus Christ" (v. 16; see vv. 15-21). **Justification** is God's act of declaring and making persons righteous. This gracious divine act is possible because of the faithfulness of the crucified Messiah Jesus. Paul claims that his life is centered on the crucified Christ who loved him and gave himself for him as a demonstration of God's grace to sinners. He proclaims his solidarity with the crucified Christ ("I have been crucified with Christ" [v. 20]) and asks the Galatians to reconsider the implications of their demands upon Gentile converts.

Chapter 3 begins with Paul's rebuke of the Galatians who have become victims of the misguided teachings of those who pervert the gospel. He argues that Abraham had believed God and that faith was the basis of his being reckoned righteous by God, totally apart from any works of the Law. Thus Abraham was blessed and in Christ Jesus that same blessing has now been extended to Gentiles who receive the promise of the Spirit through faith (vv. 5-14). He contends that the Law served as a tutor to lead all to Christ, that they might be made righteous by faith in the new order that no longer consists of Jew and Gentile, slave and free, male and female. Instead, there is one new humanity in Christ Jesus, and all who believe are Abraham's true children (vv. 24-29). Jesus Christ came into this world to bring freedom to those who live under the Law and to bring them to a relationship with God as His children and His heirs (4:1-7). They are no longer bound as slaves to the flesh but are now free to serve God in the Spirit by faith working through love (v. 8—5:6). The argument concludes sharply with his cutting advice to those who would nullify the scandal of the Cross by submitting to circumcision of the flesh (vv. 10-12). After contrasting deeds of the flesh with the fruit of the Spirit in verses 19-23, Paul declares that those who live by the Spirit shall also walk by the Spirit, having crucified the flesh in Christ Jesus (vv. 24-25). The Law of Christ must be the guide for one's life in society (6:1-10).

Paul concludes his letter to the Galatians with a final reminder that the cross of Christ is the true mark of a Christian and that the scandal of the Cross cannot be avoided. What is crucial to the Christian life is the newness of life that comes neither through circumcision nor through uncircumcision, but through the cross of Christ. He describes the Cross as the "marks of Jesus branded on my body" (v. 17, NRSV). He ends the letter with a formal benediction (v. 18).

Summary Statements

- Paul wrote his letters to the Corinthians to deal with various issues that contributed to a crisis in the life of the church.
- Spiritual gifts should not become a source of pride, but in humility they must be used for the building up of the Body.
- Giving up of one's freedom may be necessary for the building up of community life.
- Paul celebrated his weakness in Christ, though he was confident in the power of God at work in his life through his weakness.
- Paul defended his apostolic authority in 2 Corinthians.
- Freedom of the Gentiles from the Law of Moses is a key issue in Galatians.
- Paul emphasized the doctrine of justification, God's act of declaring and making persons righteous by the faithfulness of Christ.
- Christians are called to live by the law of Christ, being guided and led by the Holy Spirit.

Questions for Reflection

1. What are different ways to promote unity within the Christian community today while celebrating diversity within the Church?
2. How do you distinguish between nonnegotiable matters of Christian faith and culturally conditioned practices that have no bearing on one's salvation experience?
3. What are various expressions of legalism today? What does it mean to live in freedom from the Law but in subjection to the law of Christ?

Bible Study Assignment

Read Galatians 3:6-9 and answer the following questions:
1. Read 3:1-29 and attempt to discover the continuity and connection of verses 6-9 to the rest of this chapter.
2. There are two Old Testament quotations in this text. Find out the book, chapter, and the context in which these verses are found in the Old Testament.
3. What is the argument that Paul is making in verse 7? Why does he make this argument? How does he relate the Old Testament text to the argument he is making in verse 7?

Bible Study Assignment, *cont.*

4. What is "scripture" for Paul in verse 8? How does scripture function, according to this verse? What particular understanding does scripture convey about God, according to Paul?

5. What is the argument that Paul is making in verse 8? Why does he make this argument? How does he relate the Old Testament text to the argument he is making in verse 8?

6. What is Paul's final conclusion, according to verse 9?

7. What role does Abraham have in the story and faith of the people of God, according to Paul? According to Paul, why did God call Abraham to follow him and why did God give him the promises?

8. What conclusion do you make about faith, based on these verses? How does faith work in your life? How do others see faith at work in your life?

Resources for Further Study

Barrett, C. K. *A Commentary on the First Epistle to the Corinthians.* New York: Harper and Row Publishers, 1968.

Guthrie, Donald. *Galatians.* Grand Rapids: Wm. B. Eerdmans, 1973.

Witherington, Ben, III. *Conflict and Community in Corinth: A Socio Rhetorical Commentary on 1 and 2 Corinthians.* Grand Rapids: Wm. B. Eerdmans, 1995.

_____. *Grace in Galatia: A Commentary on Paul's Letter to the Galatians.* Grand Rapids: Wm. B. Eerdmans, 1998.

26 Ephesians, Philippians, and Colossians

bjectives:

Your study of this chapter should help you to:
- Describe the context of Paul's letters to the Ephesians, Philippians, and Colossians
- Discuss the content and message of Ephesians, Philippians, and Colossians
- Describe the key theological themes of Ephesians, Philippians, and Colossians
- Relate the meaning and message of Ephesians, Philippians, and Colossians to the Christian Church today

ey Words to Understand

Christological Epistles
Prison Epistles
Ephesus
Rome
Tychicus
Philippi
Via Egnatia
Epaphroditus
Colossae
Kenosis hymn
Epaphras
Gnosticism

Questions to consider as you read:

1. What is the portrait of Christ and His Church that Paul presents in his letter to the Ephesians?

2. What is the source of joy and contentment to Paul while he wrote his letter to the Philippians?

3. What was the Colossian heresy? What instructions does Paul give to his readers at Colossae to help them overcome the influence of heretical teachings?

Christological Epistles is a term that may be applied to Paul's letters to the churches at Ephesus, Philippi, and Colossae. These short but powerful letters contain some of Paul's highest and finest expressions of Christology (i.e., his understanding of the nature and person of Jesus Christ). These letters are also called **prison Epistles** or captivity letters because Paul was in prison at the time of their writing. The Book of Acts indicates two lengthy imprisonments of Paul, one in Caesarea (Acts 23—26) and another in Rome while awaiting his trial before Caesar (chap. 28). In addition to these two instances, he may have been in prison at other locations for shorter periods, such as his overnight jail experience at Philippi (16:19-40; see 2 Corinthians 11:23). Some recent scholars think that one or two of these prison letters originated during Paul's imprisonment at **Ephesus.** Though Paul spent three years at Ephesus during his third missionary journey, there is no record of this imprisonment in Acts or in the Pauline writings. Most scholars think either Caesarea or Rome would have been the setting of these letters. If he wrote these letters from Caesarea, then we may assign A.D. 56-58 as the date of writing. The traditional view assigns **Rome** as the place of writing, which means the writing of these letters would have taken place around A.D. 59-62.[1]

The Letter to the Ephesians

Ephesus

Ephesus, located along the coastal region in the southwest part of Asia Minor, has a long history. Around 290 B.C. the city came under Greek rule, and later the city came under Roman rule in 133 B.C. As the capital of the province of Asia, Ephesus was a major political, commercial, and religious center for the entire region of Asia. The prosperity of the city continued through the reign of various Roman emperors until the late 2nd century A.D. In addition to the much-renowned temple dedicated to Artemis, one among the pantheon of pagan gods, the city also had its share of imperial temples, such as the temple of Roma and Julius Caesar, Domitian's temple, and the temple of Augustus. Though Ephesus was the primary cult center of the Ephesian Artemis, the city also became a leading center for Roman emperor worship in the first century. The city was also a center for many Gnostic religious groups and groups that practiced magic and astrology. Though Judaism was among the city's many religions, archaeology has not yet yielded any physical evidence of its Jewish population in the Greco-Roman period.[2] Acts 18:19 indicates that there was a Jewish synagogue in the city.

Paul at Ephesus

Based on the accounts in Acts 18—20, we may conclude that Paul was the earliest Christian leader to exert Christian influence in this city known for its pagan temples and imperial cult. Paul's first recorded visit to Ephesus took place during his second missionary journey (18:18-21). He stopped at Ephesus, preached in the synagogue, and had discussion with the Jews at the conclusion of his second journey (A.D. 52). After promising his audience that he would return to them, Paul left Ephesus and went on his way to Jerusalem. It is likely that Paul undertook his third journey to fulfill his promise to the Jews at Ephesus. He arrived in the city perhaps around A.D. 53, began to preach in the synagogue for three months, and then continued his ministry in the public marketplace for two years (19:1-20). Luke tells us that "all the Jews and Greeks who lived in the province of Asia" heard the gospel proclaimed by Paul (v. 10).

It is quite clear that Paul played a crucial role in the spread of Christianity at Ephesus. Tradition associates the apostle John also with Ephesus. The church's existence in the early second century is evident from the Epistle of Ignatius to the Ephesians. Our understanding of the nature of the Christian community at Ephesus comes from the content of Paul's letter to the Ephesians. Paul describes the community as formerly of the Gentile background. They were once "excluded from citizenship in Israel and foreigners to the covenants of the promise" (Ephesians 2:12); now they are no longer "foreigners and aliens, but fellow citizens with God's people and members of God's household" (v. 19; see vv. 11-22).

Context

The Epistle to the Ephesians contains one of the best portraits of the Church and life within that community that God has established through His Son Jesus Christ. Unlike some of the other letters in the Pauline corpus, the letter to the Ephesians does not show any clear evidence of the context that prompted the writing of this letter. There are no indications of heresy or other major problems in the church. The focus seems to be on the essential place of the Gentile believers as the people of God and the intimate relationship between the Church, the Body, to Christ who is the

Who Wrote Ephesians?

Scholars who question the authenticity of a number of Pauline Epistles place Ephesians among the deutero-Pauline collection of letters in the New Testament (other so-called deutero-Pauline letters are Colossians, 2 Thessalonians, 1 and 2 Timothy, and Titus). Though Ephesians bears a clear letter structure very similar to all other Pauline Epistles, the author may have composed it as a circular letter with a much wider audience in mind than a single congregation. There are some Greek manuscripts that lack the name of a specific recipient in 1:1, and not a single individual within the congregation at Ephesus is mentioned anywhere within the letter itself. This would seem most unusual in a letter addressed to the congregation that Paul pastored longer than any other, unless he intended this message to be given to multiple congregations in and around Ephesus as well as to the specific congregation within Ephesus itself. Scholars think that the author was someone other than Paul because of some apparent vocabulary and stylistic differences between Ephesians and other letters credited to Paul. The letter also bears a remarkable similarity in thought and language to the Epistle to the Colossians, so much so that some scholars have speculated that an anonymous author used the latter as a blueprint to write Ephesians. Yet Ephesians has numerous unique features and characteristics, typical of the diversity found within all of the Pauline letters. The similarity to Colossians may be due to the fact that both letters come from the same period of Paul's imprisonment either at Caesarea or at Rome. It is likely that **Tychicus** was the bearer of both Ephesians and Colossians to their respective recipients (6:21-22; see also Colossians 4:7; 2 Timothy 4:12).

Head of the Church. Does this mean that there was divisiveness or lack of unity between Jewish and Gentile Christians in the church at Ephesus? We do not have an answer to this question.

Content

The letter may be outlined as follows:

Salutation	1:1-2
Thanksgiving Section	1:3-23
Jews and Gentiles: Heirs to God's Promises	2:1—3:21
Exhortations	4:1—6:20
Conclusion and Benediction	6:21-24

The thanksgiving section sums up Paul's Christology (1:3-23). All blessings and redemption from God come through Christ. Christ unites all things in heaven and on earth. Through Christ believers have an inheritance with God. The Holy Spirit is the pledge of that inheritance of God's people. Christ who sits at the right hand of God in the heavens is the Head of the Church, which is His Body, and God has put all things under Him and has made Him the Head over all things.

In chapters 2 and 3, Paul provides his most comprehensive treatment of the nature of the Church. Christ has brought together two totally different and distinct entities, Jews and Gentiles, into one new, transformed people of God. Together they now constitute a new temple of God, built upon the foundation of prophets and apostles with Christ Jesus as the Capstone that holds this entire new structure together.

In the paraenetic section (chaps. 4—6), Paul instructs the Church to be united as "one body and one Spirit," proclaiming "one

hope . . . , one Lord, one faith, one baptism; one God and Father" (4:4; see vv. 1-6). The Church must exercise the variety of gifts given to her by Christ to promote unity, knowledge of Christ, and maturity and growth.

Paul's instructions also include the challenge to the believers to live no longer in the former ways of their life but in a new way of life characterized by righteousness and holiness in life (v. 17—5:20). In speech and actions the believer must strive to impart grace to others. In verses 1-20, Paul contrasts the walk of a holy people with the walk of those who are disobedient and unrighteous. He begins this section with a call to imitate God. In the Christian life there should be no place for sexual immorality, impurity, greed, filthiness, empty chatter, or any such inappropriate behavior. Christians should live as those who understand the will of the Lord, making the best use of the time, and with songs of praise and gratitude to God.

Paul's concluding admonitions include instructions for proper life and relationship within the faith community, addressed to wives, husbands, children, fathers, slaves, and masters (v. 21—6:9). Submission, sacrificial love, obedience, and discipline are essential to proper relationship within the community of faith. It is important to note that Paul introduces these instructions given to individuals of various family and social relationships with the keynote admonition, "Submit to one another out of reverence for Christ" (5:21). Ultimately, this mutual submission is the key to unity in the family of God.

Paul closes his final admonitions with the charge to put on

the whole armor of God so that God's people might be able to withstand the forces of evil and darkness arrayed against them (6:10-17). Truth, righteousness, faith, salvation, and the Word of God—these are the weapons and implements of defense that will enable the Church to prevail and prepare her to continue to proclaim the gospel that brings peace to humanity. The letter concludes with a typical benediction, which invokes God's peace, love, and grace for the community of faith (vv. 23-24).

Letter to the Philippians

Philippi

Philippi in northern Greece derived its name from Philip II of Macedon who brought this city under his kingdom in 356 B.C. Rome incorporated the Macedonian region as part of its empire in the second century B.C. Philippi was an outpost of the Roman province of Macedonia on the **Via Egnatia,** the ancient Roman road that connected the east with Rome. Latin was the official language of the city, and Roman law provided the basis of the city's judicial system. During Paul's time, this city was the principal city in the Roman province of Macedonia (see Acts 16:12).[3]

Philippi most likely had a sizable population of Roman citizens, which included the Roman colonists who settled there and those who gained full legal rights as citizens of Rome. These rights included exemption from scourging and illegal imprisonment and the right to appeal to the emperor.[4] The Book of Acts indicates that there was a small population of Jews in the city, not large enough to maintain a synagogue as the place of prayer. The city also had many Greeks as well as Orientals as part of its population.

Paul at Philippi

Luke traces Paul's arrival at Philippi to the Macedonian call during his second missionary journey (Acts 16:6-10). Paul's first convert at Philippi was Lydia, a dealer in purple dyed cloth; members of her house also were baptized, and they became the first Christian family at Philippi. Here Paul and Silas were imprisoned after Paul exorcised a slave girl possessed with the spirit of divination. Luke also narrates the miraculous events that led to the conversion of the jailer and his family. The city magistrates decided to release the evangelists and let them go free. After gaining an apology from the city magistrates for illegally imprisoning Paul, a Roman citizen, the evangelists left the city and went on to Thessalonica (vv. 11-40). Acts 20:1-6 indicates that Paul returned to Philippi twice during his third missionary journey.

Traditional site of the river where Paul met his first converts at Philippi.

Via Egnatia in Philippi.

The Church at Philippi

Based on Luke's narrative, we may conclude that Paul established the church at Philippi around A.D. 49-50. From the standpoint of Early Church history, this was an important event, since the congregation he established here was the first recorded Christian church on European soil. Many scholars think that Paul and Silas left Luke in charge of this fledgling congregation (the "we" section in Acts that begins in 16:10 ends at the end of this chapter). Despite a difficult beginning for the church, the congregation grew and became a strong church in the Macedonian region.

Context

Why did Paul write this letter to the church at Philippi? A cursory reading of this letter shows that this is more like a personal note from the apostle to the congregation at Philippi. Paul describes this church as an exemplary partner with him and a source of financial support for the traveling apostle (Philippians 4:15-16). He had received gifts from the church several times before, and most recently the church had sent a gift through **Epaphroditus,** which Paul de-

scribes as "a fragrant offering, an acceptable sacrifice, pleasing to God" (v. 18). This letter, then, is most likely a thank-you note from the apostle to one of his most beloved congregations for its faithful partnership and support of his ministry (see Paul's description of the church "whom I love . . . , my joy and crown" in v. 1). Epaphroditus was the carrier of this letter to the church at Philippi (2:25-29).

However, this letter is more than a personal thank-you letter. The content of this letter shows that Paul wrote this letter also to deal with some problems that existed in the church. Evidently the Christian community at Philippi was not free from opposition to the preaching of the gospel (1:28). It is also likely that there was division within the church. Paul urges the church more than once to be of one spirit and mind (v. 27; 2:2). This lack of unity is also reflected in his appeal to Euodia and Syntyche "to agree with each other in the Lord" (4:2). Evidence also seems to indicate that those who preached the necessity of circumcision for one's salvation (Judaizers) have had some influence on the Christians at Philippi (3:2 ff.). Paul may have heard about these issues through Epaphroditus, and the letter contains his instructions to the church on these matters.

Content

This brief letter may be outlined as follows:

Salutation and Thanksgiving
1:1-11
Paraenetic Section   1:12—4:9
Expression of Gratitude for the
Gift   4:10-20
Doxology and Final
Greetings   4:21-23

Following the customary salutation, the thanksgiving section begins with Paul's profound sense of joy and affection for the Philippians (1:3-11). Paul is grateful because the Philippians stood with him as his fellow workers and partners in the gospel enterprise "from the first day until now" (v. 5). This section concludes with Paul's confidence that the God who began the good work in them through the gospel would bring it to completion through Christ Jesus.

The next section of the letter can rightly be called a paraenetic body, extending from 1:12 through 4:9. Paul begins this section with a statement of his confidence in the power of the gospel and his desire to exalt Christ. Though his desire is to die and to be with Christ, for the sake of the Church, he would rather live and continue to labor for Christ. He concludes this section with an admonition to the Philippians to be united together for the cause of Christ and in their struggle against those who are their opponents (1:12-30).

In chapter 2, Paul's Christology reaches its highest peak as he exhorts the church to set their minds upon the will and word of God following the servant example of Christ Jesus. Though Christ was "in very nature God," He exemplified humility by emptying himself to become fully human, a servant obedient to the point of death upon the Cross. God raised Him up from the dead and gave Him a name above every name and made Him the object of worship by the whole creation. It is this faith in the exalted Christ that compels Paul to press on toward the higher calling of God and the ultimate reward that is found only in Him (3:7-14). He does not put any confidence in attaining righteousness through the traditions he kept as a zealous Jew and a Pharisee. He is, howev-

The traditional site of Paul's imprisonment at Philippi.

Remains of the Byzantine Basilica at Philippi.

believers can experience "the peace of God, which transcends all understanding" (v. 7) in the midst of their anxiety-filled life. This peace (shalom) will stand as a guard, a soldier on duty, over the hearts and minds of believers.

He concludes the letter with commendation and gratitude to the Philippians for their gifts and offering to him, the customary final greetings, and benediction (vv. 15-23). The Philippians have fully rewarded him for his faithful service among them. Their gifts that he received from them is a "fragrant offering" to God (v. 18). He expresses his wish that just as the Philippians "satisfied" the apostle, God would "satisfy every need" (v. 19, NRSV) of his beloved congregation.

er, confident in the righteousness that comes through faith and through his knowledge of Christ and the power of His resurrection.

Paul calls upon the Philippians to recognize that they are now citizens of the new heavenly kingdom. Therefore, they must live lives worthy of that Kingdom and walk in a manner that reflects the One who called them (1:27; 2:1-4, 12-15; 3:20—4:1). Paul urges the Philippians to live in harmony and unity with the mind-set of Christ as the standard. He also encourages them to discover the ultimate contentment of a life that is completely committed to the Lordship of Christ (vv. 1-14). He is confident that through prayer the

Letter to the Colossians

Colossae

The town of **Colossae**, located about 120 miles east of Ephesus, was a small market town during the days of Paul and far less significant than many of the other places where Paul had established churches during his missionary

---

T

Kenosis Hymn

Many scholars consider that 2:6-11 is an early Christian hymn. This text is called the **kenosis hymn** because Jesus, according to Paul, "emptied himself" (NRSV) (Greek *ekenōsen*) to take the form of a servant. Paul describes this *emptying (kenosis)* of Jesus as the example in his exhortation to the Philippians for unity and oneness of mind through humility. The primary focus of this text is on humility, which in Paul's thinking is a Christian virtue. This self-emptying does not mean that at any time in His earthly life Christ ceased to be God or relinquished His divine attributes. Hooker states, "It is in his [Christ's] self-emptying and his humiliation that he reveals what God is like and it is through his taking the form of a slave that we see 'the form of God.'"[5] God is love, and this is the nature of God that we see in the person of Jesus Christ. Paul makes very clear in this hymn that the Cross is the greatest display of the self-emptying of Christ.

journeys. In the fifth and fourth centuries before the Christian era, Colossae was a great and prosperous city. The city seems to have lost its significance in the Roman period. The coins from Colossae indicate that the Gentile population here worshiped a number of deities, among whom the Ephesian Artemis and the Laodicean Zeus were the most prominent. The city was most likely destroyed by an earthquake around A.D. 60 or 64.[6]

The Church at Colossae

The origin of the Christian community in Colossae may be traced to the work of Christians who were once a part of the communities that Paul had established in larger cities of Asia Minor.[7] Most scholars think that the church at Colossae was established by **Epaphras,** who is "working hard" for the Colossians as well as for the believers in Laodicea and Hierapolis (4:12-13). Colossae was the home of both Philemon and his runaway slave Onesimus (Colossians 4:9; Philemon 10).

The congregation was made up mostly of Gentiles despite the fact that there was a notable Jewish population in the city. Paul makes reference to their heathen past in Colossians 1:21 and 2:13 He also describes the Colossians as those who hold their faith in Christ and love all the saints (1:4). They are a people among whom the gospel has been "bearing fruit" (v. 6).

Context

Paul wrote the letter to caution and give warning to the Colossians concerning false teachers and their deceptive teachings. This warning is clearly seen in 2:8. It seems that these false

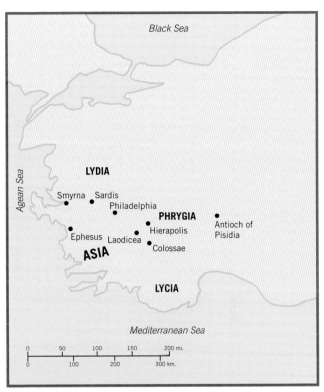

Locations of churches in western Asia Minor.

teachers who promoted their teachings through "hollow and deceptive philosophy" were adherents of some kind of **Gnosticism.** The strange combination of Gnostic elements with Jewish rituals suggests a unique kind of heresy that confronted the Colossians (vv. 16-23). Scholars are still uncertain as to the precise make-up of the opponents of the gospel. However, it is clear that Paul responds to this heresy with the strong affirmation of Christ as Lord over the world and as the Head of the Church (1:15-20).

Content

The letter to the Colossians may be outlined as follows:

Salutation	1:1-2
Thanksgiving	1:3-8
Body of the Letter	1:9—4:6

Final Greetings and
  Instructions   4:7-18

Following the salutation and thanksgiving, Paul begins the body section with a prayer that the Colossian community would be filled with the knowledge of God's will and that they would live a life pleasing to God (1:9). The high Christological language of verses 15-20 has led some scholars to conclude that these verses were taken from an early Christian hymn.[8] In this hymnic section, Paul speaks of Christ as the image of the invisible God, the firstborn of all creation, and as the Head of the Church. The Christ hymn is followed by a challenge to the Colossians that they must stand firm in the faith so that Christ might present them as a holy people before God (vv. 21-23).

Paul describes in the body section of the letter three essential components of the Christian life. They are: (1) living a life worthy of God; (2) increasing in love for God and for all humanity; and (3) living a holy life. Paul's prayer in verses 9-14 centers on his desire for the Colossians to live in a manner worthy of the Lord. As a people redeemed from the dominion of darkness, their lives are to reflect the reality of God. Paul also instructs the Colossians to live in Christ, firmly rooted in Him and established in their faith in Him (2:6-7). Believers must also conduct themselves in such a way that they would be a witness to those who are outside of the community of faith (4:5).

Closely related to this instruction for a Christian life worthy of God is the idea of the Christian life characterized by ever-increasing love (3:12-17). Loving God means entering into and maintaining a dynamic love relationship with God. Paul suggests several things that Christians should put on as fitting to those who are holy and beloved of God. Beyond all other things, they should put on love, which is the perfect bond of unity (v. 14). Love is the culmination, the most significant binding and uniting aspect of their experience as new creatures in Christ.

Paul's instructions on living a holy life focus on living a life in the Spirit, a new way of living that is in striking contrast to the former way of life. The major metaphor that Paul uses to depict living the new life in Christ is that of putting off the "old self" or humanity and putting on the "new self" or humanity. Paul draws a sharp contrast between these two radically different kinds of humanity in verses 1-17. The old humanity is characterized by earthiness, sexual immorality, impurity, passion, evil desire, greed, idolatry, anger, wrath, malice, abusive speech, lies, and bigotry, whereas the new humanity is marked by compassion, kindness, humility, gentleness, patience, forbearance, forgiveness, love, peace, and thanksgiving. Paul's instructions on the new life concludes with admonitions to wives, husbands, children, slaves, and masters (v. 18—4:6). In all of these family and social relationships, Paul urges the Christian community to conduct themselves as members of the new humanity that God has created through Jesus Christ.

The formal conclusion of the letter includes personal messages and greetings and some final instructions (vv. 7-18). The letter ends with Paul's personal signature and with a request to remember him, a prisoner for Christ.

Summary Statements

- Paul wrote Ephesians, Philippians, and Colossians while he was a prisoner either at Caesarea or at Rome.
- The letter to the Ephesians describes the church as the Body of Christ made up of both Jews and Gentiles that God has brought together as His people.
- Unity in the Church is a key theme in Ephesians.
- Believers must live a new way of life that is distinctly different from their old ways of life.
- Paul states in Philippians that Jesus, though He was in the form of God, emptied himself and became fully human, a servant obedient to the point of death on the Cross.
- Paul called the Philippians to seek contentment in life through complete commitment to Christ.
- Colossians is a letter written to warn the church at Colossae about false teachers and deceptive teachings.
- In Colossians, Paul declares that all things in creation are held together in Christ, who is the image of the invisible God.

Questions for Reflection

1. What are the areas in our social life where humanity continues to erect walls of separation? What does it say to you about the mission of the Church today?
2. What actions do you need to take in your life to follow Christ completely?
3. Compare and contrast contentment that Paul advocates in his letter to the Philippians with the type of contentment that our culture promotes through consumerism and the possession of wealth.

Bible Study Assignment

Read Philippians 4:10-13 and answer the following questions:
1. According to Paul, where was he when he wrote the letter to the Philippians?
2. What is the specific context of Paul's letter to the Philippians?
3. Read 4:14-20. How does this text help us understand verse 10?
4. What does Paul say about himself and his state of mind in verses 11-12?
5. Based on verses 10-12, what do you think Paul means by "I can do everything"?
6. What is the secret of Paul's contentment, based on verse 13?
7. How content are you in life? What brings contentment to your life? What lesson do you learn from Paul about contentment?
8. How do you apply Paul's "I can do everything" in your personal life today?

Resources for Further Study

Barth, Markus. *Ephesians: Introduction, Translation, and Commentary,* 2 vols. New York: Doubleday, 1974.

Hooker, Morna D. *Philippians,* vol. 11 of *The New Interpreter's Bible.* Leander E. Keck, ed. Nashville: Abingdon Press, 2000.

Lohse, Eduard. *Colossians and Philemon,* trans. William R. Poehlmann and Robert J. Karris, in *Hermeneia: A Critical and Historical Commentary on the Bible.* Philadelphia: Fortress Press, 1971.

27 | 1 and 2 Thessalonians

Objectives:

Your study of this chapter should help you to:
- Describe the context of Paul's letters to the Thessalonians
- Identify the key theological concerns found in 1 and 2 Thessalonians
- Relate the message of Paul found in 1 and 2 Thessalonians to the life of the Christian Church today

Key Words to Understand

Parousia
Thessalonica
Corinth
Silas
Timothy
Sanctification
Day of the Lord
The rebellion
The lawless one

Questions to consider as you read:

1. How does Paul describe the church at Thessalonica? What are some of the characteristics and qualities of the Thessalonian church?

2. What is sanctification and its relation to sexual purity, according to Paul?

3. What does Paul say about the second coming of Jesus Christ? How should Christians conduct themselves while waiting for the Second Coming?

The Thessalonian letters are addressed to a predominantly Gentile audience where Paul gives a clear answer to the question: How shall Christians live until the **Parousia**—the second coming of Christ? These letters reflect Paul's pastoral concerns for the congregation at Thessalonica. Paul's primary concern for them was the strength of their faith under persecution and the quality of character that they should display in their lives until the coming of the Lord Jesus Christ. In these two letters, Paul instructs the believers at Thessalonica to live, work, and walk in a manner worthy of their calling, in holiness and sanctity as befitting the Lord Jesus Christ so that they would be ready for His arrival and presence.

Thessalonica

The city of **Thessalonica**, located about 90 miles west of Philippi, was founded in 316 B.C. by Cassander, who named it in honor of his wife, Thessalonike, a stepsister of Alexander the Great. Romans gained control of the Macedonian kingdom around 168 B.C. and made Thessalonica the capital of the province of Macedonia in 146 B.C. Thessalonica was a "free city" with the government in the hands of an assembly of people. In the first century, the city of

Arch of Galerius at Thessalonica.

Thessalonica was a large, prosperous community. The city's proximity to the Via Egnatia and its natural harbor and seaport on the Aegean Sea facilitated its commercial prosperity. The city was also the seat of much ancient culture. The city's population in the first century A.D. included mainly Greeks, but there was also a large Roman and Oriental presence, including a colony of Diaspora Jews. The Book of Acts indicates that there was a Jewish synagogue in the city (Acts 17:1).[1]

Paul at Thessalonica

The church in Thessalonica was the second church established in Macedonia by Paul. He came to this city, after leaving Philippi, during his second missionary journey. He carried out his preaching and teaching ministry in the Jewish synagogue for three weeks. The focus of his teaching was the suffering, death, and resurrection of Jesus the Messiah. Those who believed the message of Paul were mostly Greeks, including some leading women. Because of the Jewish opposition to Paul's preaching, Paul left the city and went on to Beroea. It appears that Paul had to leave before he was able to fully establish the new church (vv. 1-15).

Context

Paul was concerned about the young church's ability to withstand affliction and persecution. So when he went on to Athens, he left behind Silas and Timothy to oversee the work in the Thessalonica-Beroea area (vv. 14-15). Later when Paul was at **Corinth,** Timothy joined the apostle from Thessalonica. It is likely that Paul wrote his first letter from Corinth as a response to "the good news" that Timothy had brought from Thessalonica (1 Thessalonians 3:6). At the time of writing 1 Thessalonians, both **Silas** and **Timothy** were with Paul (see 1:1). Traditional dating places 1 Thessalonians around A.D. 50-51. Second Thessalonians may have followed shortly thereafter, also from Corinth.

Paul's first letter to the Thessalonians makes it clear that the church had remained true and faithful to the gospel, but this new congregation did have some major questions that Paul needed to address. The church needed instructions on holy living, sexual conduct, moral and ethical responsibility, and issues related to the Second Coming. The second letter clarifies more fully Paul's perspectives on the Second Coming and the question of how to conduct oneself while waiting for the "coming" of the Lord Jesus Christ.

Content

The Thessalonian letters may be outlined as follows:

Agora in ancient Thessalonica.

Paul begins the first letter by the usual epistolary introduction, which includes a detailed thanksgiving section. In his thanksgiving, Paul describes the Thessalonians as a people who have not only received the gospel in the midst of persecution but also imitated the apostle by their participation in the work of evangelism. In chapter 2, Paul reminds the congregation of the example he has set before them. He recalls how he worked "night and day" so that he would not be a burden to others (v. 9; see vv. 1-12).

Verses 13-16 resemble a thanksgiving section, often found in the beginning of Paul's letters. Paul's longing to see the Thessalonians face-to-face is vividly expressed in verses 17-20. Though the apostle wanted to visit the church at Thessalonica, he was unable to fulfill his desire. Paul views obstacles to his travel plans as the work of Satan.

In chapter 3, Paul explains that he sent Timothy to "strengthen and encourage" the believers at Thessalonica to remain faithful during their persecution (vv. 1-5). Timothy's return from Thessalonica and his good report about the faith he witnessed there revived

Holiness and Sexual Purity

Contemporary views on sexuality and sexual behavior promote a lifestyle contrary to the biblical ideals of holy living. There is indeed a "holiness code" in the Bible that calls the community of faith to pursue a life of moral and ethical integrity in the area of sexual conduct. The "holiness code" that Paul promotes in 1 Thessalonians 4:1-8 calls for purity of motive and sacrificial love as the basis of human relationships. Holy conduct involves abstinence from all immoral activities. Paul makes it clear that without holiness in life, it is difficult to maintain integrity in sexual conduct.

the apostle's spirit and his desire to see them again (vv. 6-10). The closing prayer in chapter 3, which echoes the thanksgiving in chapter 1, expresses Paul's desire for the church to increase in her love for others (3:11-13). This prayer also serves as a good transition to the paraenesis that follows in chapters 4 and 5. He prays that God would establish their hearts "in holiness" and that they may be "blameless" before Him at the Parousia.

The paraenesis section combines several commands and admonitions. These instructions are authoritative because they are given in the name of the Lord Jesus (4:1). The goal of his instructions is to teach the Thessalonians the manner of life that is pleasing to God. He begins his instructions with an explicit affirmation that **sanctification** is God's will for His people (v. 3). Therefore, they are to abstain from all manner of sexual immorality. Moreover, they must honor and sanctify their marriage relationships and conduct all personal relationships with godly love. Paul concludes his instruction on holiness and sexual purity with the warning that those who reject this instruction indeed reject God who gives His Holy Spirit to the believers to live a holy life (vv. 1-12).

Instructions on holy living set the stage for Paul's discussion of the

Parousia (v. 13—5:11). Paul comforts his readers with the declaration that no one who dies before Christ's return will miss that glorious event. The language of 4:16-17 contains apocalyptic imagery. These verses also reflect the Old Testament theophany narratives, which describe God's coming to meet with His people (see Exodus 19:16-20). The text affirms the certainty of the Second Coming; however, the symbolic language of the text cannot be interpreted literally.

Though Paul confidently expresses his faith in the Second Coming, he stops short of giving a specific timetable of this event. This event will occur suddenly, without warning. God's people do not live in darkness but in the light of God's revelation shining through the gospel of Jesus Christ. Therefore, when the day of the Lord comes, it will not be a surprise to them. Paul urges the believers to continue living and walking as children of the day, because the dawning **Day of the Lord** lies just ahead (1 Thessalonians 5:1-11).

Paul closes the letter with a prayer that sums up his desire for the church at Thessalonica. "May God himself, the God of peace, sanctify you through and through. May your whole spirit, soul and body be kept blameless at the coming of our Lord Jesus

Christ. The one who calls you is faithful and he will do it" (vv. 23-24). The letter concludes with the typical Pauline greetings and benediction (vv. 25-28).

2 Thessalonians

Second Thessalonians reflects many of the same concerns and issues found in 1 Thessalonians. It is likely that Paul wrote this letter to address three specific issues. The opening chapter makes reference to intense persecution of believers. Chapter 2 indicates that there was a mistaken view among some in the church at Thessalonica that the day of the Lord had already come. Chapter 3 contains a strong admonition to those who were living in idleness, not doing any work. As mentioned earlier, Paul may have written this letter from Corinth not too much longer after his first letter to the Thessalonians.

Questions about the Parousia persisted at Thessalonica. Paul responds to these questions in 2:1-12. It is likely that the Thessalonians had misunderstood or misinterpreted Paul's previous letter or his teaching while he was at Thessalonica (v. 2). It is also possible that the source of their misunderstanding was a prophetic word from some other individuals or a letter attributed to Paul. The primary concern that Paul deals with is the mistaken view that the day of the Lord has already come. He assures his readers that that day has not come. Certain things such as **the rebellion** (literally, the apostasy) and the appearance of **the lawless one** (v. 9) (or "man of lawlessness" [v. 3]) must precede the coming of the Lord. The word *rebellion* perhaps indicates a large-scale increase in ungodliness and immorality in the world. "The law-

> # T Entire Sanctification
>
> "May God himself, the God of peace, sanctify you through and through. May your whole spirit, soul and body be kept blameless at the coming of our Lord Jesus Christ" (1 Thessalonians 5:23). This prayer is parallel to Paul's prayer in 3:13 ("May he strengthen your hearts so that you will be blameless and holy in the presence of our God and Father when our Lord Jesus Christ comes with all his holy ones"). Ernest Best notes: "'May God sanctify you' (v. 23) balances 'sanctify yourselves'" (4:3a). Though the Thessalonians "need to strive for holiness (4:3) God alone can produce holiness in them."[2]
>
> In the Wesleyan tradition, this text (5:23) has been understood as the classic New Testament passage that provides the biblical foundation for the phrase "entire sanctification."[3] Sanctify you "entirely" means sanctify you "through and through," "completely," or "wholly." H. Ray Dunning describes 5:23 as "the climactic statement of a series of exhortations designed to emphasize the sanctity of the whole of life. It emphasizes the whole person's involvement in the holy life."[4] The phrase "spirit, soul and body" does not mean three distinct components of a human person, as in the Greek thinking. Paul is referring here to the whole person. Sanctification in the Bible, on the one hand, is one's separation from the world and complete belonging to God. Equally important is the idea of one's conformity to the character and likeness of God. This ethical transformation within a believer, which involves one's whole being, is the prayer wish that Paul expresses in 5:23. The apostle is confident that the God who calls us to belong to Him is also faithful to accomplish this work of salvation in us (v. 24).

Second Coming and the Signs of the Time

In Christian history, there has been a great deal of interest in the Second Coming and events that might occur in the end time. Paul's letters to the Thessalonians clearly show that the believers at Thessalonica were concerned about the timing of the Parousia. At the center of this concern is the question: How could we be prepared for an event if we do not know when it is going to take place? In the Thessalonian letters Paul invites us to live our lives daily in the hope of the Second Coming, so that regardless of the timing, we will be found ready for that glorious day. A preoccupation with the signs of the time may lead us to unnecessary worry and concern. It may even lead us to think that that day is far away in the future, a thinking that might lead us to become slack in our Christian commitment. Paul challenges us to be ready at all times.

less one" (or "the man of sin" in some manuscripts) seems to refer to a human being. Obviously Paul had given some previous instructions on "the lawless one" to the Thessalonians (vv. 5-6). It is thus possible that the readers had some understanding of what Paul meant by this label. Interpreters have taken this label to mean the Roman Empire with its demand for emperor worship or a supernatural power or Satan. In the absence of a specific identity, we may think of this as a reference to the power of evil that is already at work in the world, a power that will appear in its full force in the end time.[5] God will bring His judgment upon this power and on all who refuse "to love the truth" that leads to salvation (v. 10).

The power of evil cannot nullify the reality of God's gracious work of salvation and sanctification for those who stand firm in the faith and hold fast to the teaching of the gospel (vv. 13-15). Paul expresses his gratitude to God for the Thessalonians for their salvation "through the sanctifying work of the Spirit and through belief in the truth" (v. 13).

Chapter 3 includes Paul's closing appeals and final exhortations. He reminds the church that preoccupation with last things should not become a hindrance to living a meaningful, productive life in the present. The best way to prepare for Christ's return is to live, walk, and work in the manner that is worthy of the One who has created the new people of God in His own image. The letter concludes with the typical Pauline greetings and benediction (vv. 16-18).

Summary Statements

- Paul instructs the Thessalonians to remain faithful in the midst of their suffering for Christ.
- Sanctification is God's will for His people.
- Holiness calls for moral and ethical integrity in the area of one's sexual conduct.
- God's gracious plan for His people is to transform our whole being—body, soul, and spirit—to His character and likeness that is made known to us through Jesus Christ.
- Christians should be prepared for the Second Coming.

Questions for Reflection

1. How does faith, hope, and love work in your personal life?
2. What are your concerns about the Second Coming? What answers do you find in Paul's instructions to the Thessalonians?
3. What does it mean to live a holy life in your cultural context today?

Bible Study Assignment

Read 1 Thessalonians 1:2-10 and answer the following questions:
1. What part of the typical Pauline letter does this text belong to, and what function does it serve?
2. What does Paul convey to the Thessalonians in verse 2?
3. How did the Thessalonians demonstrate faith, hope, and love (v. 3)?
4. How did Paul preach the gospel to the people of Thessalonica?
5. How did the Thessalonians respond to the preaching of the gospel by Paul (v. 6)?
6. What does Paul say about the Thessalonian church in verses 7 and 8?
7. What do verses 9 and 10 say about the believers at Thessalonica?
8. What is the Christian faith that is expressed in verse 10?
9. Based on this text, describe the qualities of a true church of Jesus Christ.
10. What challenges does this text place before the contemporary Christian Church?

Resources for Further Study

Best, Ernest. *A Commentary on the First and Second Epistles to the Thessalonians.* New York: Harper and Row, 1972.

Marshall, I. Howard. *1 and 2 Thessalonians: The New Century Bible Commentary.* Grand Rapids: Wm. B. Eerdmans, 1983.

Wanamaker, C. A. *The Epistles to the Thessalonians.* Grand Rapids/Exeter: Wm. B. Eerdmans/Paternoster, 1990.

28 1 and 2 Timothy, Titus, and Philemon

O bjectives:

Your study of this chapter should help you to:

- Describe the context of Paul's letters to Timothy, Titus, and Philemon
- Discuss the content and message of Paul's letters to Timothy, Titus, and Philemon
- Summarize the key theological themes of 1 and 2 Timothy, Titus, and Philemon
- Relate the message of 1 and 2 Timothy, Titus, and Philemon to contemporary Christian life

K ey Words to Understand

Pastoral Epistles
Crete
Ephesus
Nicopolis
Jewish Gnosticism
Overseers
Bishops
The First Epistle of Clement
Onesimus

Q uestions to consider as you read:

1. What are the responsibilities of a faithful church leader?
2. What is sound doctrine?
3. How does Paul model true Christian leadership to his younger pastors?
4. How did Paul view the master-servant relationship?

In the final four Pauline Epistles in the New Testament, Paul addresses individuals rather than congregations, with specific, personal letters. These letters share some common structural features with the previous letters and with each other; however, they also show some characteristic features that are unique to each letter. In this chapter, we will examine each letter to study the contributions it makes to the New Testament and the Christian faith.

The two letters to Timothy and the letter to Titus are often grouped together under the designation **Pastoral Epistles.**[1] These letters include Paul's pastoral concerns for Timothy and Titus; they also address issues related to congregational life within the churches where these men were serving as leaders. However, that designation should not obscure the reality that each letter has its own context and setting, which are important considerations for the interpretation of these letters. The shortest Pauline letter, the Epistle to Philemon, which belongs to the prison Epistles, will be examined last even though it may well have been written prior to the Pastoral Epistles.

Context

We encounter several critical issues when we try to determine the time and historical setting of each of the Pastoral Epistles. All three are internally attributed to Paul as the sender. However, the historical setting reflected in these letters is difficult to fit into all of the details that we know about Paul's life and ministry as recorded in Acts and corroborated in Paul's other letters. Many scholars in the last two centuries have argued that the content of these letters reflect a second-century context with an established hierarchy of leadership in the Church. They have also noted language and style differences from other Pauline letters and have concluded that the Pastoral Epistles belong to a period decades later than Paul's lifetime and that the writer(s) of these letters attributed the authorship to Paul.[2]

Scholars who prefer to see the Pastoral Epistles as the work of Paul argue for the possibility that these letters reflect Paul's changed perspective that would be consistent with a later Roman imprisonment of the apostle near the end of his life in the mid A.D. 60s. According to some scholars, Paul was released from his house arrest in Rome and later returned to areas where he had previously established churches. They think that he left Titus in **Crete** (Titus 1:5) and Timothy at **Ephesus** (1 Timothy 1:3) as overseers of the work at these places, and then went on to Macedonia. Scholars speculate that Paul wrote Titus and 1 Timothy during his travels in the Macedonian region, possibly from **Nicopolis.** At some point in Paul's travels, he was arrested again (A.D. 65-66), this time as a Christian under indictment for treason. This reconstruction of the final days of Paul would thus place him back at Rome, from where he composed 2 Timothy, shortly before his martyrdom during the reign of Nero.

What is more important than the actual time of writing is the life setting of the Pastoral Epistles. These letters reflect the setting of intense persecution and the imprisonment of key leaders (2 Timothy 4:6-8) and the rise of false doctrines promoted by false leaders who twisted and distorted the truth of the gospel. These letters are addressed to younger leaders charged with the responsibility of setting in order the Christian church in and around Ephesus (Timothy) and Crete (Titus). They are given instruction concerning their own personal work and character as ministers and guidelines for developing a Christian community that truly reflects the gospel of Christ. Encouragement, comfort, and hope—which are characteristics of the Pauline letters—are prominent in the Pastoral Epistles.

1 Timothy

First Timothy contains elements of a personal paraenetic letter. Paul is the model to be followed, and Timothy is to be a similar model to the church. Paul gives instructions concerning Timothy's actions and sets them as opposite to the actions of those who are the opponents of Paul. These instructions give this Epistle its distinctive character.

Content

First Timothy could be outlined as follows:

Salutation and Greeting   1:1-2
Instructions to Church
   Leaders   1:3—6:21

The brief salutation and greeting is followed by a lengthy discussion of the duties of the church and church leaders. The first charge given to church leaders is to instruct the false teachers to discontinue their teaching of strange doctrines and "myths and endless genealogies" (1:4; see vv. 3-4, 6-7). It seems that the church at Ephesus was under the influence of false teachers who promoted elements of **Jewish Gnosticism**.[3] The sound doctrine focuses on the truth of the gospel that Christ came to the world to save sinners. Paul illustrates this truth using his own story as an example of how

Remains of the ancient city of Ephesus.

God's grace, mercy, and forgiveness came to him though he was the foremost of sinners (vv. 12-17).

Chapter 2 contains miscellaneous instructions including instructions on intercessory prayer (vv. 1-7). Christian duty is to pray for the salvation of all humanity because God's desire is for all to come to the knowledge of the truth. Paul affirms that Jesus, who gave His life as a ransom to save all, is the only Mediator between God and humanity. Verses 9-15 reflect a domestic code for women.[4] Interpretation of verses 11-15 is difficult, and there is no consensus among scholars. Some who hold the Pauline authorship of the Pastorals think that these verses are a later insertion to the letter. Chapter 3 explicitly details appropriate conduct for those who are leaders in the church. **Overseers** and **bishops** must be above reproach and people with excellent reputations inside and outside the church family. Deacons must be faithful in all things entrusted to them.

Paul returns to the issue of false teaching in the church in chapter 4. He connects here the false teaching and other problems in the church with the work of Satan. Verse 3 may be a reference to Gnostic teachings, which promoted abstinence from marriage and certain foods. Chapter 5 contains a good deal of practical advice on dealing with church matters with wisdom. Christian leaders should treat older and younger members, men and women alike, with respect and purity of heart. Concern for the care and conduct of widows is the focus of verses 3-16. Paul also instructs the church to hold in high esteem and respect the elders who are involved in preaching and teaching. The chapter ends with a charge to the minister to maintain purity and upright conduct, avoiding sin of every kind.

Chapter 6 begins with instructions for the conduct of Christian slaves toward their masters. This is followed by final instructions to teach and defend the Christian faith against false and conceited teachers who associate their godliness with material gain. The final challenge to Timothy is to pursue the righteous life that is consistent with the true faith, and guard the instructions that have been given to him.

2 Timothy

The content of 2 Timothy may be outlined as follows:

Salutation and Thanksgiving
1:1-5
Exhortation to Timothy
1:6—2:13
Sound Doctrine and False Teaching   2:14—4:8
Final Instructions and Greetings   4:9-22

Second Timothy bears the structure of a personal paraenetic letter. Paul presents himself as a father to Timothy, evoking in his memory the model that he can and should imitate. The theme of remembering dominates the

Celsus library in Ephesus, built in A.D. 135.

Women and Ministry in Paul's Letters

Some Christians have taken 1 Timothy 2:11-15 along with 1 Corinthians 14:34-35 as the biblical basis for their opposition to the preaching, teaching, and leadership position of women in the church. First Timothy 2:11-15 calls for women to be silent and have no authority over men. What makes the text difficult is the reason for this prohibition given in verses 13-14. These verses suggest that Adam was formed first and that the culpability of sin in the garden belongs only to Eve, and not to both Adam and Eve. Verse 15 then states that childbearing is a necessary means for a woman to experience salvation. First Corinthians 14:34-35 is also a prohibition against women speaking in churches.

How do we understand these texts? If we take these texts at their face value without looking at the context, culture, Paul's overall theological perspectives on equality and freedom of all Christians, mutuality of genders, and his endorsement of women who were his trusted coworkers, then we might be tempted to agree with those who deny women any place of ministry in the Christian church. We cannot support this perspective without violating all the rules of biblical interpretation.

In dealing with these difficult passages, one must look at the overall evidence in Scripture. Even in the Old Testament God called women to leadership positions (examples: Miriam, Deborah the judge, Huldah the prophetess, etc.). Joel the prophet anticipated the outpouring of God's Spirit on all people and both "sons and daughters" becoming the vehicle through which God would speak His words (Joel 2:28). Women have played a significant role in the life of Jesus and in the history of the Early Church. In Paul's letters, he mentions three women as leaders of house churches (see Chloe in 1 Corinthians 1:11; Nympha in Colossians 4:15; Apphia in Philemon 2). He also mentions Mary, Tryphena, Tryphosa, and Persis (Romans 16:6, 12) as those who worked very hard for the gospel. Priscilla and Aquila were trusted coworkers of Paul (vv. 3-4). In Philippians 4:2-3, Euodia and Syntyche are grouped with Clement and the rest of Paul's fellow workers. Phoebe was a key leader in the church in Cenchrea and most likely the one who carried Paul's letter to Rome (vv. 1-2). Paul's statement in 1 Corinthians 11:5 suggests that prophecy and praying were activities women carried out in the Corinthian church. And most importantly, Paul emphatically claimed and taught the freedom of all believers in Christ. Paul's statement, "There is neither Jew nor Greek, slave nor free, male nor female, for you are all one in Christ Jesus" (Galatians 3:28), should be our primary hermeneutical guideline with which we understand his perspective on women in ministry.

opening and middle sections of 2 Timothy (1:3-6, 13-14; 2:1, 8, 14), and this connects well with the theme of 1 Timothy. Timothy is charged to remember, hold on to firmly, guard the faith, and never to compromise with those who are opponents of the true faith.

In his thanksgiving, Paul recalls Timothy's faith heritage, faith that was evident in the life of his grandmother Lois and his mother Eunice. His instructions begin with the charge to Timothy to keep alive that gift of faith that is in him through the help of the Spirit. He also challenges Timothy to embrace suffering, which awaits all who have responded to the "holy calling" that comes from God to preach the gospel. He must "hold to the standard of sound teaching" (v. 13, NRSV) and with the help of the Holy Spirit guard the gospel that has been entrusted to him.

Chapter 2 begins with instruction to Timothy to pass along to faithful people what he has re-

Clement on the Order of Ministers

"The apostles have preached the gospel to us from the Lord Jesus Christ; Jesus Christ [has done so] from God. Christ therefore was sent forth by God, and the apostles by Christ. Both these appointments, then, were made in an orderly way, according to the will of God. Having therefore received their orders, and being fully assured by the resurrection of our Lord Jesus Christ, and established in the word of God, with full assurance of the Holy Ghost, they went forth proclaiming that the kingdom of God was at hand. And thus preaching through countries and cities, they appointed the first-fruits [of their labours], having first proved them by the Spirit, to be bishops and deacons of those who should afterwards believe. Nor was this any new thing, since indeed many ages before it was written concerning bishops and deacons. For thus saith the scripture in a certain place, 'I will appoint their bishops in righteousness, and their deacons in faith'" (**The First Epistle of Clement** to the Corinthians, chapter 42, ca. A.D. 96).[5]

"I have fought the good fight, I have finished the race, I have kept the faith" (2 Timothy 4:7).

ceived from Paul, so that they may in turn teach others what they have learned from Timothy. Though teachers do not comprise an order of ministry established in the Early Church, we find here the ministry

of teaching as one of the key functions of Christian leaders. Using the metaphors of a faithful soldier, a dedicated athlete, and a hard-working farmer, Paul challenges Timothy to be a faithful and loyal servant of Christ by correctly handling the Word, reproving those in error, and living a life useful to the Master in every aspect.

The third chapter vividly describes the challenges that will come from evil persons who are bent on undermining the gospel that had been preached. Although these false teachers will succeed in leading some away from the true faith, such difficult realities will not negate the effect of the gospel so long as those who are faithful to the truth will stand firm and remain loyal and committed to the faith they have received. Paul challenges Timothy to be ready and well prepared to proclaim and explain the true faith in the midst of difficult times. The final instructions to Timothy run from 4:9 to 4:18 and include a warning against those who opposed Paul's teaching. The letter closes with personal greetings to many of their mutual friends and a gracious benediction.

Titus

Titus, the recipient of this letter, is known to us a trusted companion of Paul, whom the apostle addresses as "my true son in our common faith" (1:4). Some have attempted to identify him with Titius Justus mentioned in Acts 18:7. He was a Gentile and most of our knowledge of this individual comes from Galatians and 2 Corinthians. Titus accompanied Paul when the latter went to Jerusalem after his conversion (Galatians 2:1-10). Though Judaizers insisted that Titus the Gentile Christian be circumcised, neither Paul nor the Jerusalem leadership yielded to their demand. According to 2 Corinthians, Paul sent Titus twice to bring about a peaceful resolution to the problems at Corinth (2 Corinthians 7:6-7, 13-14; 8:6, 16-17). We do not have any clear indication in the Book of Acts or at any other place except in Titus 1:5 that Paul and Titus had made a journey to Crete. Second Timothy 4:10 indicates that Titus traveled to Dalmatia, in the southern part of Illyricum, on the eastern side of the Adriatic Sea.

The Epistle to Titus has many similarities to the letters addressed to Timothy and seems closest in historical context and structure to 1 Timothy, even though the church in Crete appears to be at a significantly different stage of development than the church in Ephesus at this time. Titus is told to appoint leaders in the various cities, which suggests that Paul is dealing with a much more rudimentary Christian community than that which had been established in Ephesus. The opponents seem to have much stronger Jewish roots and they appear to be making significant inroads into the primitive Christian community in Crete.

Content

Titus may be outlined as follows:

The introductory greeting section is followed by a discussion of the qualifications of church leaders. Paul left Titus at Crete primarily to "straighten out what was left unfinished and appoint elders in every town" (1:5). These leaders were to be above reproach, monogamous, good managers of their households and families, moderate in lifestyle, and even-tempered. They were to be models of discipline that would be worthy of discipleship and were expected to hold fast the faithful word according to the teaching and sound doctrine that Paul had established among them previously. Their responsibility included the exhortation and encouragement of fellow believers as well as the repudiation of those who contradicted the message of the gospel.

Chapter 2 spells out in detail what constitutes acceptable behavior for all age-groups within the Body. Characteristics and qualities of Christian life include patience, prudence, faith, love, self-control, submission to authority, respect for others, sound speech, and similar virtues. Paul concludes this chapter with a bold proclamation of the universality of salvation—God's grace at work in all humanity that leads us to reject the world-centered life and embrace a godly life (vv. 11-14). Christ is not only the Redeemer of the Church but also the One who sanctifies her to do good work for Him.

In the final chapter, there is additional exhortation to be submissive and obedient to those who rule and govern. All people, even those outside the community of faith, are to be treated with consideration and respect. Paul emphasizes that salvation is based solely upon the grace and mercy of God made known in Jesus Christ. On the basis of this, he challenges God's people to be engaged in good deeds and live a productive, righteous lifestyle. General exhortations in 3:1-7 give way to specific exhortations concerning heretics in verses 8-11, followed by a brief conclusion in verses 12-15.

Philemon

Setting and Date

The last letter placed in the collection of Pauline letters in the New Testament is often referred to as a personal letter of Paul to a Christian by the name of Philemon. Philemon is believed to have been an influential and wealthy person at Colossae. It is likely that he became a Christian through the ministry of Paul (see v. 19). However, the addressees include others as well, including Apphia, Archippus, and the church that met in Philemon's house (v. 2). Though scholars have attempted to establish the identity of Apphia and Archippus, they remain to us as unknown individuals, most likely close friends and coworkers of Paul.

This letter is also commonly grouped together with Colossians since **Onesimus,** a key character in Philippians, is said to have returned to Colossae with Tychicus, the courier of Paul's letter to the church at Colossae (Colossians 4:7-9). Evidence seems to support Colossae as the location of Philemon and the house church mentioned in verse 2. It is also likely that both Colossians and Philemon were written from the same place and at the same time. We place Philemon along with Paul's other letters from prison, written most likely from Rome between A.D. 59 and 62. There is no reason to doubt the authenticity of this letter.

Onesimus, once a slave owned by Philemon, freed himself and left Colossae. Why he left Philemon is not clear. The suggestion that he ran away after a theft is not clear, though some see an implied reference to it in verse 18. The circumstance of Onesimus's meeting with Paul during his imprisonment is also not clear. Onesimus became a Christian through his contact with Paul. Though Paul would have preferred to keep his new convert with him for his own service, the apostle decided to send him back to Philemon, perhaps because of the latter's legal claim over his runaway slave. He wrote the letter to urge Philemon to take Onesimus back and treat him as a "dear brother" (v. 16). Onesimus himself would have been the bearer of this letter.

Content

This brief Epistle has the following outline:

Salutation, Greeting, and
    Thanksgiving   1-7
Appeal on Behalf of
    Onesimus   8-21

Final Greetings and
  Benediction   22-25

Paul begins this letter with a prayer of thanksgiving for Philemon's love for "all the saints" (v. 4)—those who have membership in the community of faith. He is thankful also for this Christian's faith in Christ and for his life, which has been a source of strength and encouragement to many others.

It is clear that Paul makes his appeal on behalf of Onesimus on the basis of these qualities that he finds in Philemon. Paul appeals to Philemon to let his faith and love work in his relationship with Onesimus, his runaway slave. It is important to note that he is not making this appeal on the basis of his apostolic authority (vv. 8-9). Though he has his rights as an apostle to direct a Christian follower to obey his apostolic command, Paul demonstrates love as the principle of his relations with Philemon and leaves the decision to his free choice.

Paul concludes the letter with an anticipation of a visit to Philemon's house. The letter ends with greetings from a number of coworkers and with a typical benediction (vv. 22-25).

Christianity and Social and Legal Customs

Paul worked within the context of the social and legal customs of his day. He would have preferred to keep Onesimus for his service, but he returned him to his master. For Paul, it would be a violation of Philemon's rights to keep Onesimus for his service during his imprisonment. He sees this opportunity, however, to make clear the point that the slave who is coming back to his master should be treated with forgiveness and Christian love. Both the master and the slave have one Lord, and they share the same faith. The master should therefore treat the slave as a brother who is useful not only to him but also to the Lord. Both are recipients of the same divine love (agape), and that love must be evident in human relations within the church. Paul thus sets forth in this letter a principle for conduct within the life of the church. He takes a social issue (slavery) and places it in the context of the life of the church and instructs both the master and the slave to deal with this issue on the basis of the transforming power of divine love. Love thus liberates the slave from bondage. The master is no longer an oppressive power but a brother in Christ. It is this liberating power of love at work in the church that gives him the theological legitimacy to speak the words: "There is neither slave nor free . . . you are all one in Christ Jesus" (Galatians 3:28). It is this gospel that challenges us to be agents of change in the world, which continues to oppress and exploit the powerless in society.

Summary Statements

- The Pastoral Epistles reflect the context of false doctrines and false teachers in the Early Church.
- Sound doctrine is a key emphasis in the Pastoral Epistles.
- Overseers or bishops of the church should maintain exemplary character and thus be models of piety and godliness in the community to their congregation.
- In the letter to Titus, Paul proclaims the universality of the grace of God.
- Philemon calls for Christian love as the basis of all social relationships.

Questions for Reflection

1. What criteria would you use to distinguish between sound doctrine and false teaching?
2. Why is it necessary for a believer to be firmly grounded in the sound doctrines of the Bible?
3. In what ways should the Church be involved in bringing about social change in the culture in which you live today?

Bible Study Assignment

Read Titus 2:11-14 and answer the following questions:

1. Read 2:1-15 and discuss the literary and thematic relationship of verses 11-14 to the preceding and following verses.
2. What does the phrase "the grace of God that brings salvation has appeared" (Titus 2:11) mean? Consult a commentary to discover what Paul means by this phrase.
3. What is Paul's understanding of the scope of salvation?
4. Describe what Paul says about the instructional ministry of the grace of God in verse 12. What instructions are given in this verse about Christian life?
5. Discuss the relationship of verse 13 to verse 12. What is the future hope expressed in verse 13? How does this hope relate to life lived in the present age?
6. What particular understanding of Jesus Christ is found in verses 13 and 14?
7. What is the relationship between Christ and His Church, and the task of the Church, according to verse 14?

Resources for Further Study

Hanson, A. T. The Pastoral Epistles: The New Century Bible Commentary. Grand Rapids: Eerdmans, 1982.
Martin, Ralph P. Colossians and Philemon: New Century Bible Commentary. Grand Rapids: Eerdmans, 1981.

UNIT VIII

TRIALS AND TRIUMPHS OF THE NEW COVENANT COMMUNITY

Your study of this unit will help you to:

- Recognize the difficulties and tensions that developed within the early Christian community
- Describe the steps taken by the Church to maintain faith while it encountered opposition and heretical teachings
- Identify the key themes of the general/catholic letters
- Discuss the occasion and purpose of the Book of Revelation

29 The Letter to the Hebrews

Objectives:

Your study of this chapter should help you to:

- Describe the authorship problem of the letter to the Hebrews
- Discuss the background of the original audience of the letter to the Hebrews
- Identify the historical and theological issues relative to the Book of Hebrews
- Evaluate the significance of the Christological emphasis in Hebrews

Key Words to Understand

General/catholic
Clement of Rome
Paul
High Priest
Apostasy
Covenant
Faith
Discipline
Holiness

Questions to consider as you read:

1. What Old Testament symbols does the author use for Christ? How is Christ different from these symbols?

2. What dangers did the original readers of this book face? How does the author address those issues?

3. Why is the suffering of Christ important for the author?

4. How does the author define faith? What is its importance?

Hebrews; James; 1 and 2 Peter; 1, 2, and 3 John; and Jude are commonly designated as **general** or **catholic** (meaning "universal") Epistles. This designation goes back to the days of the Early Church fathers.[1] However, most of these fathers placed Hebrews with the Pauline Epistles. These letters are called "general" or "catholic" because they (except for 2 and 3 John) were written to a wider audience than to one particular church or person. The early Christian writers do not mention most of these Epistles until almost A.D. 200, although **Clement of Rome** seems to draw from the thoughts of Hebrews in a letter to the Corinthian church around A.D. 96.[2]

Although early Christian tradition ascribes the authorship of Hebrews to Paul, the earliest manuscript of the New Testament shows only the audience designation, "to the Hebrews."[3] The authorship of Hebrews is one of the most disputed issues in New Testament studies; the debate has been going on from before the days of Origen, a third-century Christian scholar. The churches in the eastern part of the Roman Empire have usually regarded **Paul** as the author of Hebrews. The western churches, however, doubted that Paul wrote Hebrews and even excluded it from the canon at first. Other suggested names for the author of this letter include the following: Barnabas, companion of Paul; Luke because of the good style of Greek; Clement of Rome; Apollos, an Alexandrian Jew associated with the churches at Corinth and Ephesus; Sylvanus, companion of Paul; Philip, apostle and missionary to Samaria; and Priscilla, coworker of Paul and teacher of Apollos. It seems probable that the Epistle was written by someone closely associated with Paul, perhaps a student of Paul's, an idea first suggested by Origen. A cursory reading of the book shows that the author was thoroughly trained in the Hebrew Scriptures and a strong proponent of the superiority of the Christian faith to the Tabernacle ritual of Judaism.

Setting and Date

The letter is addressed to the Hebrews. We do not know the precise identity of this audience. Some scholars think that the letter addresses the first-century Jewish Christians while others think that both Gentile and Jewish Christians are included in the designation "to the Hebrews." Because we do not know for sure the identity of the author or the audience, it is impossible to date the letter with any certainty. Most scholars prefer a setting anywhere between A.D. 60 and 90. However, some argue for a period as early as A.D. 40 and some for a date later than A.D. 100. Some scholars prefer a date before the destruction of the Jerusalem Temple in A.D. 70. They call attention to the fact that the book contains no reference to the destruction of the Temple and the cessation of sacrifices.

There are several considerations in favor of a period between A.D. 60 and 90 as the possible setting of the writing of Hebrews. The Jewish revolt that broke out in the Palestine area against Rome in A.D. 66 culminated in the destruction of the city of Jerusalem and the Temple by the army of Titus in A.D. 70. This period would have been a difficult time for the Jewish Christians who were still strongly loyal to their Jewish traditions and customs. For the Jewish Christians, the tension between loyalty to their parental religion and loyalty to the Christian faith continued through the next two decades or more.

Model of Herod's Temple that was standing until its destruction in A.D. 70.

During the second half of the first century A.D., Jewish Christians also encountered hostility from Judaism. These Christians were no longer welcome in the synagogue services. This was one more wedge between the Jews who did not believe in Christ and the Jewish Christians. They were living in a world where they had to choose between their Jewish heritage and their Christian religion. If they renounced Christianity, they could go back to their Jewish families and friends and enjoy protection against Roman persecution. If they renounced Judaism, they were cut off from family, friends, and traditions, and faced deadly persecution. Though we are uncertain about the precise date of the setting of Hebrews, its message seems to address the Jewish Christians who lived under the difficult times of A.D. 60-90.

Content

All scholars agree that the Book of Hebrews has been carefully constructed, but very few agree on *how* it was constructed or on an outline of the book. The difficulty is due to the alternate mixing of doctrinal teaching and moral application. The following is a broad outline of the content of the book:

Jesus the Son of God   1:1—4:13
Jesus the Eternal High
   Priest   4:14—10:31
Importance of Faith
                 10:32—12:29
Practical Advice Conclusion
                     13:1-25

Hebrews examines two main roles of Christ: Christ as the divine Son of God and Christ as the heavenly **High Priest** who both presides over the sacrifice and is the sacrifice itself. Its main purpose is to show the superiority of Christianity over the ancient traditions of Judaism as an antidote to **apostasy** (falling away from one's former beliefs) in the face of difficult circumstances.

■ Jesus—the Son of God

The author begins this sermon by establishing Jesus Christ, the Son of God, as the perfect One to

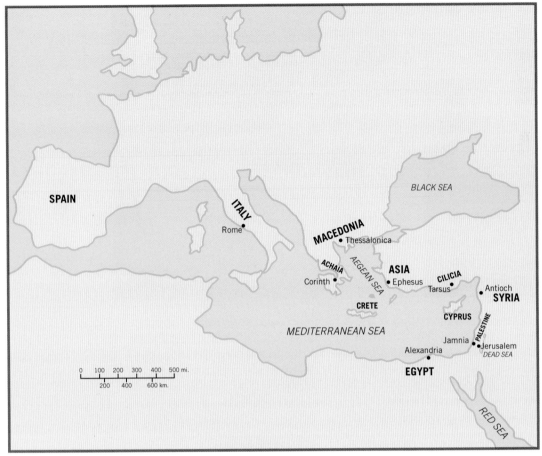

Roman Empire A.D. 70.

communicate God's word to His people. The detailed description of the nature of Christ is followed by a warning to pay careful attention to His message. If the message delivered by angels and prophets was binding—how much more important is the message delivered by Christ and testified to by God's signs and miracles (2:1-4).

The author portrays Jesus as greater than Moses because although Moses was faithful as a servant, Jesus was faithful as a Son. As a result of Jesus' relationship to the Father, believers are also children of "God's house" and not just servants (3:1-6). The author concludes this section with a warning that those who reject God's word in the post-Pentecost era will suffer greater punishment than those who rebelled against Moses in the wilderness.

▪ Jesus—the Eternal High Priest

This section is the main body of the sermon. The author presents Jesus as the great heavenly High Priest and then instructs the readers to hold firmly to their faith. In contrast to the practice of the selection of the high priest in the first century by the Roman government, the author says that no one can be a high priest unless God calls him. The high priest's task is to represent the people before God and to offer gifts and sacrifices for sins, and he must be able to deal gently with the ignorant and wayward (4:14—5:10).

In the next section, the author encourages the readers to go on to maturity and perfection (5:11—6:20). They are babies in the faith and need to mature to the point of eating solid food. They should have been teachers by now but have remained immature, unable to distinguish between good and evil. The author goes on to state that there is no forgiveness of sins for those who have once known the salvation of God but live a life denying Christ (6:4-6). In the first-century context Jewish Christians had to choose between following Christ and their loyalty to Judaism. To leave the Christian faith and return to Judaism was a denial of Christ and His salvation.

After this stern warning against apostasy, the author then reminds readers of the certainty of God's promise. God is unchanging and He does not lie. This certain hope is the anchor of their souls, and it enables them to enter the inner sanctuary where Jesus has gone before them as their eternal High Priest, "in the order of Melchizedek" (v. 20).

In chapter 7, the author recounts a Jewish tradition about Melchizedek that he was not born and did not die but remains a priest forever. Jesus is of the same lineage and as such is superior to the earthly and time-bound priesthood of Levi. The author also states that when there is a change of priesthood, there must be a change of law (v. 12). This means that the old law is set aside because it was weak and useless (i.e., it was not able to bring one to perfection).

Because Jesus lives forever and has a permanent priesthood, He is able to save us completely. Jesus is "holy, blameless, pure, set apart from sinners, exalted above the heavens" (v. 26). In contrast to other high priests, "he does not need to offer sacrifices day after day, first for his own sins, and then for the sins of the people" (v. 27a). Furthermore, Jesus sacrificed for our sins "once for all when he offered himself" (v. 27b).

Jerusalem Temple layout.

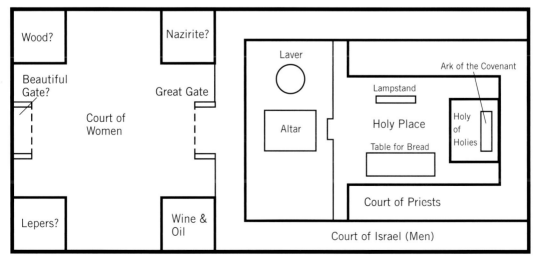

Court of the Gentiles

Hebrews and the Wrath of God

Hebrews 10:31 states: "It is a dreadful thing to fall into the hands of the living God." Discussion or warning about hell and the wrath of God is not a popular topic today. However, in the first century and especially for the Jewish Christians who were very familiar with the Old Testament, the wrath of God was a reality and an important balance to the love and grace of God.

Although the love and sacrifice of God through Jesus Christ is enough to encourage one to a God-pleasing life, the reality of punishment for sin must neither be forgotten nor ignored. If taken seriously, it will encourage one's daily walk and evangelism efforts. The author of Hebrews comes back to this reality of punishment again and again throughout the Epistle.

Hebrews relates to the suffering and afflictions of the faithful people of the Old Testament.

The author then claims that if the first **covenant** (promise or agreement) had been faultless, then God would not have offered a new covenant. He quotes Jeremiah 31:31-34 to support the assertion of the necessity of a new covenant. The new covenant has made the old covenant "obsolete," some-thing that will "soon disappear" (Hebrews 8:13).

In 9:1-8 the author describes briefly the regulations for earthly worship and the arrangement of the earthly sanctuary. While the earthly sanctuary and priesthood mediated the old covenant, Jesus has come as High Priest of the great and more perfect heavenly tabernacle. Jesus is the Mediator of the new covenant. The shedding of earthly blood was necessary for the old earthly covenant. But a better sacrifice was needed for the new heavenly covenant. So, Christ offered himself as a sacrifice to take away the sins of humanity (vv. 15-25). In chapter 10, the author emphasizes another aspect of Jesus' death. The sacrifice of Jesus Christ once for all offers not only forgiveness but also sanctification of the believer (v. 10).

The author then inserts another section of exhortations and warnings (vv. 19-39). Since believers have confidence to enter the holy of holies through the blood of Christ and a great High Priest, they must persevere, encourage one another, maintain hope, and attend their regular meetings. This is followed by another specific warning against apostasy and the fact that a person cannot be saved

while continuing to sin. The author sternly warns that because of the tremendous grace the readers have received in the blood of the new covenant, their punishment will be much greater than those of the old covenant, if they reject it.

▪ Importance of Faith

In transitioning to the topic of **faith,** the author of Hebrews reminds his readers of their past. They suffered persecution, stood side by side with those who were persecuted, sympathized with those in prison because of their faith, and joyfully accepted the confiscation of their property.

Chapter 11 begins with a definition of faith followed by several examples of faith from the Old Testament Scriptures. These people were insulted, flogged, chained, imprisoned, tortured, stoned, sawed in two, killed by the sword, and destitute, but they never gave up their vision of the real, heavenly world—they never gave up their faith!

Chapter 12 begins with the exhortation to "run with perseverance the race marked out for" the believer (v. 1). The capstone of the

Faith Defined

Hebrews 11:1 is the only place in the Bible where faith is defined. Other biblical authors describe or illustrate faith, but the author of Hebrews defines it: "Now faith is being sure of what we hope for and certain of what we do not see." The author does so within the framework of the platonic system of two parallel worlds—the seen and the unseen, the earthly and the heavenly. Faith gives us access to the heavenly or truly *real* world.

The author defines faith in terms of hope and certainty. What is hoped for will certainly happen. This hope is hope in the things that are eternal—the promise of salvation that God offers to us. This hope is more than wishful thinking; it is a matter of certainty. This hope is founded on a conviction that God is faithful. We are certain of our salvation, because by faith we believe that the One who promises salvation will be faithful to deliver His promises.

argument is a description of what Jesus endured so that the readers will not "grow weary and lose heart" (v. 3). Quoting Proverbs 3:11-12, the author challenges them to consider their suffering as **discipline** from God. Their present trials are an illustration of God's love for them.

The author of Hebrews challenged his readers to run the race with perseverance.

T Hebrews' Faith Hall of Fame

Hebrews' Faith Hall of Fame includes the names of ordinary people—some with no reputation, including a prostitute and an illegitimate person. Abel, Enoch, and Noah belong to the pre-Israelite history. Their stories exemplify simple faith, an earnest desire to walk in fellowship with God. Abraham, Isaac, and Jacob are Israel's patriarchal figures. Against all odds, they trusted in the covenant promises of God. Joseph held the firm belief that God was with him even in the most difficult circumstances of life. Moses' parents defied the royal decree, and Moses challenged Egypt's capacity to challenge the authority of Yahweh, Israel's God. The Israelites saw God at work both at the Sea of Reeds and at the walls of Jericho. Rahab the prostitute, though a Canaanite woman, believed in the God of Israel, who brought His people to His land. Gideon, Barak, Samson, Jephthah, Samuel, and David—all fought heroic battles against overpowering enemies. The prophets, though they were ostracized by the nation, refused to surrender to the will of the people.

Here we have a list of people who put tremendous trust in God. Often they were lonely, rejected, and despised by their own people. All of them were confident, however, that God was on their side. This hall of fame contains the names of heroes who "chose to be in God's minority rather than with earth's majority."[4]

Chapter 12 ends with the exhortation to pursue peace with everyone and holiness. The writer presents **holiness** not as an abstract idea but rather as a way of life essential to one's seeing of God (v. 14). This is a call to live Christlike lives, free from bitterness, godlessness, and immorality. Holiness is God's requirement for those who expect to have fellowship with God under the terms of the new covenant.

■ Practical Advice and Conclusion

Chapter 13 concludes Hebrews with advice on everyday living, intimate and public relationships, money, and church traditions. The readers must not drift into heresy, especially the teachings of the Judaizers who claim that salvation comes through the keeping of Jewish ceremonial laws. The suffering and sacrifice of Jesus makes His people holy, and it is through Jesus that Christians "continually offer to God a sacrifice of praise" (v. 15).

After a short request for prayer, the letter ends with a benediction and final greetings.

Summary Statements

- Hebrews is classified as part of the general (catholic) Epistles.
- The identity of the author of Hebrews is not clearly known.
- It is possible that Jewish Christians of the second half of the first century may have been the targeted audience of the letter to the Hebrews.
- The main purpose of Hebrews is to show the superiority of Christianity over the ancient traditions of Judaism as an antidote to apostasy.
- Hebrews 11:1 defines faith as "being sure of what we hope for and certain of what we do not see."

Questions for Reflection

1. Based on your understanding of Hebrews, discuss some of the challenges that young converts into the Christian faith might face in the 21st century.
2. If faith is "being sure of what we hope for and certain of what we do not see," how do we know that we "have faith"?
3. How would the author of Hebrews address those Christians today who want to return to the comforts of relativism or historical certainty for their salvation?

Bible Study Assignment

Read Hebrews 12:18-29 and answer the following questions:

1. Identify the verses that can be labeled as exhortation and the verses that can be labeled as warning in this section.
2. What is the Old Testament story/event that is reflected in verses 18-21? What particular religious and theological perspectives are introduced in these verses?
3. What is being described in verses 22-24? What theological ideas are introduced here by the writer?
4. How does the writer compare and contrast Mount Sinai with Mount Zion? What significant differences does he make between the two?
5. Why do you think Mount Zion is a better option for the readers, according to the writer?
6. What is the warning and concluding exhortation?
7. What insights do you gain from this text about worship in the Old Testament and the New Testament?
8. How do you relate the message of this text to your life today?

Resources for Further Study

Attridge, Harold W. *The Epistle to the Hebrews.* Philadelphia: Fortress Press, 1989.
Bruce, F. F. *The Epistle to the Hebrews,* rev. ed. Grand Rapids: William B. Eerdmans Publishing Company, 1990.
Hagner, Donald A. *Encountering the Book of Hebrews.* Grand Rapids: Baker Academic, 2002.

30 The Letters of James, Peter, and Jude

bjectives:

Your study of this chapter should help you to:
- Identify the primary suggested authors for the letters of James, Peter, and Jude
- Describe the nature of the audience to whom these letters were written
- Discuss historical and theological issues relative to these books

ey Words to Understand

James
Synagogue
True religion
Silas
Resident aliens
Testament
False teachers
Day of the Lord
Jude

Questions to consider as you read:

1. What are the literary forms of these letters and why are they in the New Testament?
2. What are the Jewish Christian contributions to the theology of the Early Church?
3. What dangers did the original audience of these letters face? How do these letters address those issues?
4. Why is suffering important for the authors?

James

The Book of James, five chapters in length, is full of advice on Christian living. However, the thought world of James is thoroughly Jewish in character. The book reflects the Jewish emphasis on good deeds as an important part of the Christian life. James's emphasis on good deeds seems to contradict Paul's theology of grace and faith. This may be one of the reasons why it was one of the last books to be placed in the New Testament canon.

The Book of James begins with an identification of the author as **James**, "a servant of God and of the Lord Jesus Christ" (1:1). James, "the Lord's brother" (Galatians 1:19), was a prominent authority figure in the early Christian church. The Book of Acts portrays James as a mediator of the Jerusalem Council and as head of the Jerusalem Church (15:13-21; 21:18-26). James, the brother of Jesus, seems to be a good candidate for the authorship of this letter.

The text of James indicates that the writer was fluent in Greek. The author was also deeply influenced by Jewish wisdom writings, which promote proper moral and ethical conduct. Many modern scholars think that an anonymous Christian wrote this letter and presented it as James's letter. Ralph Martin suggests that a Hellenistic Jewish editor in Antioch reworked James's original text and this would account for the good Greek grammar and style.[1]

Jewish Christians of the first century seem to be the recipients of this letter ("twelve tribes" of the Diaspora). The assembly of worshipers in James is a **synagogue** (2:2) rather than a church (ekklēsia) found elsewhere in the New Testament. Elders lead the community (5:14), a custom of the Jewish community life.

Setting and Date

According to some traditions, James the brother of Jesus was martyred in A.D. 62. Some scholars place his death in A.D. 69 or 70. This would place the date of this book prior to A.D. 70. It is very likely that the book belongs to a period between A.D. 40 and 62, when James was the head of the church in Jerusalem. The book reflects a later period when the Christian community failed to maintain the community life that characterized the Church in the early 30s.

The letter of James is too general and the salutation is too vague for us to conclude with certainty the location of James's original audience. It is possible that they lived in Jerusalem where the author himself lived. It is more probable that they lived in large Roman cities in Syria and Asia Minor.

The book is in the form of exhortation or instruction (paraenesis). The author does not offer the readers anything new but encourages them to follow what they have been taught and to keep that faith pure. It resembles a compilation of Jewish wisdom literature topics that revolve around a "pure and faultless" religion (1:27).

Content

Because of the proverbial nature of James, there is rarely an agreement on an outline. The following outline attempts to group the numerous exhortations into three main categories:

Salutation and Greeting	1:1
True Religion	1:2-27
True Faith	2:1—3:12
True Wisdom	3:13—5:18
Closing Admonition	5:19-20

■ True Religion

James begins his letter with instructions on the qualities and characteristics of those who practice **true religion.** He instructs his readers to face trials that will result in the development of character, maturity, and faith. The author also distinguishes between trials of faith and temptations that originate in evil desires. Overcoming trials of faith will lead us to receive the "crown of life," whereas yielding to temptation will lead to sin and eternal death. There is no place for anger in the life of righteous believers; they get rid of all wickedness. They are not only hearers of the word but also doers of the word. Chapter 1 concludes with a definition of religion. For James, true religion has practical implications. This includes caring for the orphans and widows in their need and avoiding the immoral influences of the world (1:27).

■ True Faith

True faith is evident in the lives of those who treat everyone the same without showing partiality to the rich, just as God is not partial to the rich. They keep the royal law by maintaining a proper relationship with God and their neighbor (2:1-13).

James reminds his readers that true faith is manifested in works. He claims that faith without works is "dead" (v. 17). One cannot claim to have faith and refuse to pay attention to the physical needs of a brother or a sister. Faith is manifested not only by works but also by the ability to control one's speech. James says that no one can tame the tongue. It takes a change of nature that only God can bring about.

■ True Wisdom

True Christian life is also marked by true wisdom, which is a gift that comes from above (3:13-18). In contrast to worldly wisdom, wisdom from above is meek, pure, peace-loving, gentle, and open to reason. James reminds his readers that "friendship with the world is hatred toward God" (4:4). The truly wise do not "boast" about tomorrow, for they know that their future is totally in the hands of God (vv. 13-17).

In chapter 5, James warns against those who oppress and refuse to show charity to the poor (vv. 1-6). The focus of verses 7-12 is on patience, a quality essential to the Christian life. James closes his letter with a series of instructions, including prayer for the sick by anointing with oil. The sick person will not only be healed but, if a sinner, also be forgiven. James's final words are those of love and reconciliation. The community is to care for the sinner and gently bring him or her back to God.

1 and 2 Peter

The letters of Peter also share James's concern on matters of proper behavior, social discrimination, and the need for patience in trials. But these letters are very different from James in writing style.

Both the text and Church tradition cite Peter, also known as Simon Peter and Cephas, an apostle of Jesus Christ, as the author for 1 and 2 Peter. The author refers to **Silas** as his amanuensis or scribe (1 Peter 5:12). The authorship of 2 Peter is more problematic. The book makes no mention of an

Resident Aliens

The term **resident aliens,** which is translated "strangers" in KJV and the NIV, is a specific word that identified them as noncitizens, permanently living in a foreign province. This term and its synonyms are used by Peter to indicate not only geographical dislocation but also political, legal, social, and religious limitations and separation.

Ancient literature indicates that these resident aliens included "slaves, serfs, . . . homeless strangers who lacked citizenship either in their previous homeland or where they currently resided. Although the cities had their share of such *paroikoi* [resident aliens], the far greater number was found among the rural populace of tenant, farmer, slaves and local artisans . . . who provided the work force and economic basis of the community."[2]

tians. Second Peter is written to "those who through the righteousness of our God and Savior Jesus Christ have received a faith as precious as ours" (2 Peter 1:1). This addresses a very broad, general audience, which again includes both Jewish and Gentile Christians.

Setting and Date

Those who view the apostle Peter as the author regard a period before A.D. 68 as the date of the writing of these two books. Scholars who reject the Petrine authorship of these Epistles prefer a late first century and early second century date (A.D. 90-150).

The time between A.D. 64 and 70 was extremely volatile between Jews and Romans. The Roman Emperor Nero blamed the Christians as the culprits of the fire that broke out in Rome in A.D. 64. Many Christians and their leaders were arrested and put to death during this period.

Meanwhile Jewish riots broke out in Palestine against the Roman occupation in A.D. 66 with repercussions all over the empire. Since Christianity was still considered a

amanuensis. Due to its brevity and lack of citations in the Early Church literature, many modern scholars doubt that it was written by Peter the apostle.

Peter describes his first Epistle readers as "strangers" or resident aliens who live in Pontus, Galatia, Cappadocia, Asia, and Bithynia. It is very likely that 1 Peter is directed to both Jewish and Gentile Chris-

Remains of an ancient house at Derbe in Asia Minor.

Circus Maximus in Rome, the large oval track where chariot races took place.

sect of the Jews during this time, both Jewish and Gentile Christians became subject to Roman retaliation. These events would have increased the Christians' anxiety as "resident aliens" in the Roman world. They would have faced the temptation to blend in with society especially in the Roman-controlled coastal areas.

First Peter 5:12 states the purpose: "I have written to you briefly, encouraging you and testifying that this is the true grace of God." The letter's rhetorical style is paraenesis or exhortation. The author does not present any new teaching but rather encourages his readers to stand in the "true grace of God."

Second Peter is a letter of instruction that resembles the **testament** genre of the Old Testament. It appears to be Peter's farewell speech before his death.

Content

The following outlines help us understand the literary structure of these two books.

■ Exhortations on Christian Living

First Peter begins with a celebration of the Christian hope, an "inheritance" in heaven (1:3-4). Therefore, Christians are to keep their eyes on eternal salvation and not on the temporary persecutions (vv. 6-12). Quoting Leviticus 11:44, he charges them to live a holy life in the midst of their trials because God who has called them is a holy God (1 Peter 1:13-16).

In chapter 2, the author reminds the readers that they are a special people, "a chosen people, a royal priesthood, a holy nation,

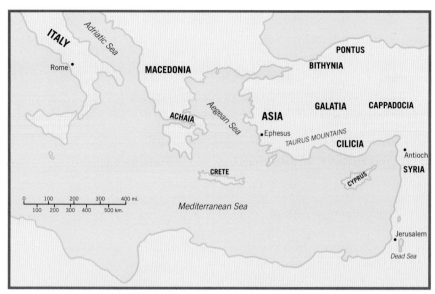

Spread of Christianity in the Roman Empire (see 1 Peter 1:1).

[and] a people belonging to God" (v. 9). The Christian community inherited the same privileges and blessing that God extended to Israel at Mount Sinai (see Exodus 19:5-6). Therefore they have a responsibility to live as a people of God, a testimony to God's grace and mercy among the pagans around them (1 Peter 2:13—3:7).

Peter urges his readers to show "good behavior in Christ" (v. 16) in their everyday life. Christ's suffering is a model for Christians to follow (vv. 8-22). Christians also have an obligation to live "for the will of God" (4:2) a lifestyle that is free from sinful behavior (vv. 1-6). One's good behavior in Christ also includes hospitality and sharing God's grace with others—all for the glory of God (vv. 7-11). The author returns to the theme of suffering in verses 12-19. A Christian's suffering is, in reality, participation in the suffering of Christ, for which one should be thankful.

First Peter closes with final exhortations to elders and young people (5:1-11). Elders must serve as shepherds of God's flock. Their reward waits for them at the Second Coming. Young people

Household Code of 1 Peter

Peter's "household code" (2:13—3:7) contains typical Greco-Roman hierarchical values for submission to authorities, especially submission of slaves to their masters and wives to their husbands. Giving proper respect to authorities within the first-century A.D. cultural setting was necessary for the Christians to avoid undue persecution.

The surprising element in light of the contemporary literature is Peter's exhortation to the husbands to be considerate of their wives and treat them with respect, and as "heirs" with them of "the gracious gift of life" (3:7). This emphasis on equality of respect and participation in life radically differed from the commonly accepted values of the Greco-Roman world. Paul also echoes this theme: "Submit to one another out of reverence for Christ" (Ephesians 5:21). When the Body of Christ submits to one another and allows equal participation in the life of the community, then it can extend the kingdom of God most efficiently and powerfully.

should live in submission to their elders. Christians should resist the devil who "like a roaring lion . . . prowls around" (v. 8, NRSV) looking for its prey. The letter ends with greetings from fellow Christians in Rome and from Mark.

Grow in Grace

Second Peter encourages Christians to grow in grace. The virtues that promote growth are goodness, knowledge, self-control, perseverance, godliness, brotherly kindness, and love (1:3-11). The author reminds the readers that the stories about Jesus are not "cleverly invented stories" (v. 16) but eyewitness accounts. Believers can have confidence in the Scriptures because those who wrote them were inspired ("moved by the Holy Spirit" [v. 21, NRSV]) by God (vv. 12-21).

False Teachers

Chapter 2 contains stern warnings about false teachers and their teachings (vv. 1-22). **False teachers** will always be around and will be known by their actions. They are bold and arrogant and do not recognize their ignorance and lack of understanding of spiritual things. Their judgment is certain.

Second Coming

He concludes with an exhortation on the **day of the Lord** and explains why Jesus had not returned (3:1-18). The delay in the Second Coming does not mean that God has broken His promise. Indeed the day will come "like a thief" (v. 10). The delay is nothing but a demonstration of God's patience and His will to save all who repent. The book ends with a challenge to the readers to remain blameless and at peace with God, and to be on guard against false teachers.

Jude

Jude is probably the most neglected book of the New Testament. Much of Jude is found in 2 Peter, and the discussions continue over whether Peter used Jude or Jude excerpted part of 2 Peter, or whether they both used an earlier source.

The main purpose of Jude is to encourage Christians to be faithful to the earliest Christian teach-

False Teachings

The letters of Peter and Jude include serious warnings about heresies and heretical teachers. A heresy is a false teaching or a distorted understanding of truth. Christians of the first and second centuries were especially victims of such teachings promoted by teachers who were influenced by pagan religions or philosophical ideas. The Christian Church has never been exempt from the influence of heresies. This tragedy continues to occur even in our present-day world.

How do we know what teaching is a distortion of biblical truth? Truth about God and His way of salvation are clearly described in the Bible. Therefore, it is important for a Christian to daily meditate on God's Word and seek the daily guidance of the Holy Spirit. When a new teaching is presented to us, we should examine and evaluate it in light of the clear testimony of God's Word. Studying the Scriptures diligently will save us from becoming victims of false teachings today.

ing. Jude warns of godless people who have slipped into the church. They serve only themselves and do not have the Spirit. Whereas 2 Peter refers to these people as "false teachers," Jude calls them godless people.

The writer of **Jude** describes himself as "a servant of Jesus Christ and a brother of James" (v. 1). Tradition connects James and Jude as half-brothers of Jesus. We think the writer was most likely a Jewish Christian based on the references to the history of the Jewish people. The book also draws from 1 Enoch, a Jewish apocalyptic writing (v. 14), and from a Jewish legend about Moses and the archangel Michael (v. 9). Many recent scholars believe Jude is a pseudonymous writing.

Jude is addressed to "those who have been called, who are loved by God the Father and kept by Jesus Christ" (v. 1). Although this is a "general" address, the writer is writing a personal letter most likely to Jewish Christians of his time.

Setting and Date

There is no reference in the book that guides us to date this letter with any precision. Our major considerations come from the identity of the author. If we regard the author as the brother of Jesus, then the best date would be between A.D. 55 and 80. Those who consider the work to be pseudonymous date the letter between A.D. 100 and 125.

The text of Jude does not give any clues as to where the author was when he wrote the book, nor where the readers resided. Jude may have written from Palestine since tradition places him there between 60 and 80. There are no real historical events indicated in the book. The author seems to be

Jewish apocryphal books like 1 Enoch were found among the Dead Sea Scrolls discovered in the ruins of Qumran.

addressing a situation in which there was apostasy—the problem of believers drifting away from the gospel, perverting it and no longer acting like Christians.

Content

Jude encourages his readers to stay true to the gospel of Christ. The author refers to those who have turned away from the gospel and as a result are empty and barren spiritually. The following outline shows the development of this theme in this letter.

Greeting	1-2
Description of Godless People	3-16
Encouragement to Continue in Faith	17-23
Doxology	24-25

Following the greeting, the author reviews the history of God's deliverance, including the destruction of those who chose to rebel against Him. Jude describes these godless people as arrogant, rebellious, and selfish. Some of them are selfish leaders (shepherds) who grumble, boast about themselves, and flatter others to get what they want. Jude assures his readers that God will destroy these people. The history Jude recounts comes from Jewish traditions with direct quotes coming from Jewish apocryphal books (vv. 9, 14b-15) and the prophecies of the apostles (v. 18).

Jude urges his readers not to give in but to build each other up and pray in the Holy Spirit. He also challenges them to keep themselves in God's love, be merciful to the doubting, and do everything they can to convert or reclaim those who are not following the faith.

Jude concludes his letter with a beautiful doxology. The author reminds his readers that no matter how strong the temptation is to turn away from the faith, God is able to keep them from falling and to present them "before his glorious presence without fault and with great joy" (v. 24).

Summary Statements

- James, 1 and 2 Peter, and Jude were written primarily to Jewish Christians in the Diaspora.
- The Book of James is a sermon, or exposition, on early Jewish Christian piety, giving practical advice on how to live a life that is pleasing to God.
- James reminds his readers that faith without works is "dead."
- First Peter encourages the readers to stand in the "true grace of God."
- Both 2 Peter and Jude address the issue of false teachers who will always be around and can be known by their actions.

Questions for Reflection

1. How does James define true religion? Does it contradict the gospel of Paul? Why or why not?
2. What kinds of suffering does 1 Peter talk about? Which kind(s) should Christians expect and praise God for? Why?
3. According to Jude and 2 Peter, why should hypocrisy (false teachers/godless people) not be tolerated?

Bible Study Assignment

Read James 1:2-8 and answer the following questions:
1. What should be the Christians' response when they face trials?
2. What kinds of trials does James refer to? Why does James think it is possible for a believer to have deep joy in the midst of adversities of life?
3. What is the difference between testing of faith and temptation that leads to sin?
4. How can perseverance be developed in the life of a Christian, according to James? Why is perseverance needed in the life of a Christian?
5. What is the mark of Christian maturity, according to James?
6. What is wisdom? Where does one find wisdom, and what should a person do to gain wisdom?
7. What do you think James means by "he must believe"? What is the difference between honest doubt and doubt that is a hindrance to faith?
8. What is double-minded behavior? How does James's analogy help to understand the word *double-minded*?
9. How do you respond to trials in life?
10. How do you relate James's words to your life today?

Resources for Further Study

Buckham, Richard J. *Jude, 2 Peter*, in *Word Biblical Commentary*. Waco, Tex.: Word, 1983.
Martin, Ralph. *James*, vol. 48 in *Word Biblical Commentary*. Waco, Tex.: Word Books, 1988.
Perkins, Pheme. *First and Second Peter, James and Jude*. Interpretation. Louisville, Ky.: John Knox Press, 1995.

31 The Letters of John

bjectives:

Your study of this chapter should help you to:

- Understand the authorship issues of the letters of John
- Discuss the background of the original readers of the letters of John
- Identify the historical and theological issues relative to the letters of John
- Evaluate the significance of 1 John's emphasis on the humanity of Jesus

ey Words to Understand

Ephesus
Chosen lady
Gaius
Domitian
Diotrephes
Teleios
Docetism
World
Sarx
Antichrist
Hospitality
Demetrius

Questions to consider as you read:

1. What seems to be the problem or crisis in the Johannine churches?

2. Why was division in the Christian community a problem for the author of these letters?

3. John talks about two kinds of sin in 1 John. What are they and how are they forgiven?

4. Who are the readers of 2 John and how do they relate to the issues in 1 John?

5. What seems to be the specific problem in 3 John and how does it relate to 1 John?

The three letters of John are among the most beautiful and simply written books of the New Testament. First John, especially, is often the first book of the New Testament recommended to a new Christian to read. And yet, it contains some of the most profound and important theological principles found in the Bible. First John is the longest of the three letters and includes the main message of the writer. Second and Third John confirm this message and add to our understanding of the readers.

None of the letters claim to have been written by the apostle John, or any John for that matter. First John is really not a letter but a sermon or tract, so does not have a salutation. Second and Third John are personal letters where the writer refers to himself as "the elder." Although most scholars agree that the same person wrote all three letters, they do not agree on who that person is.

Early Christian traditions maintain John the apostle as the writer of these letters. It is likely that the apostle moved to **Ephesus** during the Jewish revolt (A.D. 66-70). Tradition associates him with ministry in that area in the final years of his life. Carson, Moo, and Morris suggest that John was "the elder" in this area who held special authority as an apostle.[1] Many scholars, however, believe that there was a "school" of teachers in the Johannine churches who were disciples of the apostle John. They think that the author of these letters was a member of this school.[2]

First John has no greeting and no specific address of his readers, other than calling them "my dear children" (2:1, 12, 13, 18, 28; 3:7; 4:4; 5:21) or "dear friends" (NRSV, "beloved") (2:7; 3:2, 21; 4:1, 7, 11). Second John is written to "the **chosen lady** and her children." The meaning of this phrase is not clear. Though the phrase plainly refers to a highborn woman or patroness and her children, most interpreters since the fourth century have taken it to mean a local church and its members.[3] It is entirely possible that the letter was addressed to a woman pastor or patroness in whose house the church met and the church itself. Third John is written to "my dear

John and his brother were fishermen who would have used a fishing boat like this model boat.

Ephesian street and civic agora.

friend **Gaius**" (v. 1), who may have been a prominent Christian in Asia Minor. None of the Epistles of John indicate where the readers lived. It is likely that all three were written to people in the churches of Ephesus and the surrounding area.

Setting and Date

These letters belong to the last decade of the first century or the first two decades of the second century. Scholars who view these letters as the work of John the apostle prefer the former date, while those who reject the traditional view follow the latter date.

It is likely that the letters belong to the last decade of the first century, when **Domitian** enforced emperor worship in the Roman Empire. Christians were faced with severe persecution during this period. They were living as aliens in a foreign land and were in need of community and identity. In addition to this external threat, the Church also faced the danger of syncretism, a prevalent practice borrowing religious ideas from pagan religions in the area of Ephesus. First and 2 John contain several references to a heresy that denied the humanity of Jesus. These letters also indicate division in their community. Third John reveals an internal church problem of a different kind. Here we encounter **Diotrephes,** "who loves to be first, will have nothing to do with us" (v. 9). This leader is ambitious, selfish, gossiping, and inhospitable to traveling teachers and evangelists.

1 John

First John does not have the regular features of a letter. There is no salutation indicating the author or the readers, there is no thanksgiving section at the beginning of the letter, and there is no closing—not even a benediction. But it is more than a tract written to Christians everywhere, for

St. John's Church in Ephesus.

John addresses his audience as "dear children" and as "dear friends" or "beloved ones." He also addresses specific issues. Lack of clear structure makes it hard to categorize as a tract or sermon. It is a letter of encouragement or exhortation *(paraenesis)*. John is not telling them anything new but is reminding them of what they already know so that they will not be led astray (see 1 John 1:1-5; 2:7, 26).

Content

Although there is no consensus on the structure of 1 John, most scholars would outline the Epistle into at least these four main sections:

Prologue   1:1-4
Walking in the Light   1:5—2:29
The Love of God   3:1—5:12
Conclusion   5:13-21

The prologue of 1 John has some similarities to the prologue of the Gospel of John. Both the Gospel and the Epistle emphasize "beginning," use the term *Word* for Jesus Christ, and refer to hearing, seeing, and touching Jesus. The humanity and deity of Jesus are key concerns in both writings.

■ Walking in the Light

John begins the body of his letter declaring that there are two lifestyles, one that walks in the light with God, because God is light, and one that walks in the darkness. Those who walk in the light have fellowship with God and with each other. The blood of Jesus purifies them from all sin if they confess their sin, because all have sinned.

Those who walk in darkness claim to have fellowship with God, hate their brother or sister, and love the "world." They claim to be without sin and so have deceived themselves. Walking in the light is not just a matter of saying so, but a matter of behaving as Jesus did. So if someone says that he or she is walking in the light but his or her actions don't testify to this, then he or she is walking in darkness.

John also refers to those who walk in darkness as "antichrists" (2:18). These antichrists deny that Jesus is the Christ, the Messiah (v. 22). The issue is not just that Jesus is denied as the Messiah but that because Jesus is the Son of God, they are also denying the Father. Moreover, those who deny that Jesus was the Son of God, by saying that a spiritual being came down at Jesus' baptism and left before He died on the Cross, deny Jesus as the Christ as well.

■ The Love of God

John begins the second half of the body of this Epistle by exclaiming, "How great is the love the Father has lavished on us, that we should be called children of God!" (3:1). In this section he also explains that there are two ways of living, but this time he uses the metaphor of love instead of light. Those who break the Law commit sin and do not do what is right. They hate their brother or sister. They have material possessions but do not share with those in need, and above all do not love. They do not know God and are not children of God.

Love for John is defined by God (4:16) and by what Jesus did in laying down His life for us. Love comes from God and is made possible in our lives only because we live in God and God lives in us. John tells his readers "we ought to lay down our lives for our brothers" (3:16). He goes on to emphasize this action-based love when he says, "Dear children, let us not love with words or tongue but with actions and in truth" (v. 18). Thus his readers can tell who is from God and who is not, by whether their actions are loving actions or hateful ones.

Since God is love, and love originates with God, John tells his reader that by living in God and God living in the individual, love is made complete, mature, or "perfect" (in Greek, *teleios*). This "perfect" does not mean that a person never makes any mistakes or sins, but that his or her motivations are godly and come out of the love that God gives. Those who are "perfect" or complete in love do not fear judgment (4:18). This is not because they never sin again but because their motivation is to love; so when the Holy Spirit convicts them of an unloving action or motivation, the children of God quickly confess that sin and are immediately restored to a right relationship with God.

The conclusion of the letter shows that the writer's purpose was to make sure that the readers

---

T Docetism and the Johannine Community

Gnosticism as a full-blown heresy does not appear until later in the second century A.D., but incipient forms of this belief system are known to have existed in the first century. One form of this is **Docetism,** which came from the platonic worldview that everything was divided between matter and spirit. Christians who followed this heresy promoted the view that Jesus only appeared or seemed to have a human form (docetic from the Greek word *dokeō*, meaning "to seem") but He was not truly human and did not have a material body. John rejects the claims of the Docetic Christians and asserts that he is an eyewitness to the physical life of Jesus (1:1-2).

The Meaning of *World* in 1 John

The author of 1 John uses the word ***world*** (Greek, *kosmos*) to mean several different things. In 4:9 and 17 it refers to the created universe or planet earth. In 2:2, "the whole world" means the whole human race. But in most of 1 John "the world" refers to a way of life that opposes God. The world opposes and is opposite of the children of God. The world is sinful and transient—the place where deceivers and the Deceiver live. Those who are of the world are heard by the world and the world hates the children of God. This way of life is described in verse 16 as one that chases the desires of the body (flesh; Greek, ***sarx***), gives in to the lusts of the eyes, and trusts (boastfully) in earthly things.

knew they had eternal life so that they could live confident Christian lives.

2 John

Second John follows the classical form of a first-century letter. The author, "the elder," is identified first; then the readers are described as "the chosen lady and her children, whom I love in the truth" (v. 1). This salutation is followed by a prayer or wish for "Grace, mercy and peace from God" (v. 3). The body of the letter concludes with greetings from "the children of your chosen sister" (v. 13).

This brief letter is a letter of exhortation or strong encouragement *(paraenesis)* to continue in truth and in the teaching of Christ. Verse 12, "I hope to visit you and talk with you face to face," indicates this is a letter of friendship even though the reader's name is not given. It also gives advice on what to do if deceivers should come to her house.

Content

Second John is a very brief letter that covers the topics of truth, love, and obedience in just a few lines. Some of the chosen lady's children are "walking in the truth" (v. 4), and John reminds her that the command from the beginning was to "love one another" (v. 5). Here John defines love as walking in "obedience to his [God's] commands" (v. 6).

Second John echoes the antidocetic concern about "deceivers, who do not acknowledge Jesus Christ as coming in the flesh" (v. 7). He calls them "antichrists" and

The Sin That Leads to Death

First John 5:16 deals with two kinds of sin: one that leads to death and one that does not. Now according to John, "all wrongdoing is sin" (v. 17) and needs God's forgiveness to give life to the sinner. So how does one know which sin is forgivable and which is not? John does not go into much explanation; perhaps he is assuming that his readers know what he is writing about.

The overall teaching of the Bible is that there is no forgiveness for those who have known the truth but have made a conscious choice to live in continual rebellion against God. Those who recognize their sinful way of life can always find life through repentance and forgiveness that comes from God. However, Scripture warns those who choose to continually rebel against God that they have no other recourse for salvation. Even then, we must recognize the truth that God is love and that He is a merciful and compassionate God. Ultimately, this is the hope for even the most defiant sinner.

advises the chosen lady not to take them into her house or even welcome them.

3 John

Third John also follows the classical letter form. Again the author is identified as "the elder," but this letter is written to "my dear friend Gaius." A typical prayer for the reader's good health and success follows the salutation. The body of the letter closes with a prayer for peace and greetings from friends.

This letter is also a letter of personal friendship that uses praise and blame (*epideictic*) to make clear to the reader what behavior is considered proper in the

John and the Antichrist

John acknowledges in 1 John 2:18 that the **Antichrist** will come in the last hour and since there are many antichrists, it must be the last hour. What is important for John is the spirit of the Antichrist that is a "spirit of opposition to Christ, denying that Jesus is the Christ and denying the Father-Son relationship. It is more than failure to believe: it is deliberate, reasoned rebellion."[4]

church. John also gives specific advice to Gaius on how to treat visiting teachers.

Content

Following the salutation and prayer for Gaius's health and suc-

Hospitality in the Early Church

Hospitality was a highly regarded virtue and a necessary gift for the advancement of the Early Church. Most respected people stayed with family or friends when they traveled. Staying in a roadside inn was only a last resort. It was considered dangerous, since one did not know the innkeeper or the people staying there.

Those who did not have family or friends in a city they needed to stay in would ask their friends for letters of introduction so that they could stay in a private home rather than a public inn. Anyone who rejected someone with a letter of introduction without cause was considered to be an impolite and uncivilized person.

It was through traveling missionaries like Paul and the "brothers" or teachers referred to here in 3 John that the gospel spread quickly across the Roman Empire. The following excerpt from the *Didache* (also known as *Teaching of the Twelve Apostles,* dated to the end of the first century A.D.) shows the guidelines for hospitality established by the Christians so that guests would not become a burden to their hosts.

12:1 Let every one that cometh in the name of the Lord be received, but afterwards ye shall examine him and know his character, for ye have knowledge both of good and evil.

12:2 If the person who cometh be a wayfarer, assist him so far as ye are able; but he will not remain with you more than two or three days, unless there be a necessity.

12:3 But if he wish to settle with you, being a craftsman, let him work, and so eat;

12:4 but if he know not any craft, provide ye according to your own discretion, that a Christian may not live idle among you;

12:5 but if he be not willing to do so, he is a trafficker in Christ. From such keep aloof (*Didache*, chapter 12).

cess, John tells of his joy in finding out that Gaius has been faithful to the truth. He praises Gaius for receiving the teachers of the truth, even though they were strangers to him. John advises him to send them on to the next church with plenty of food and money since they need it, and they are teaching the truth (vv. 7-8).

He follows this praise of and advice to Gaius with criticism (blame) of Diotrephes, who was not hospitable to these teachers. This individual loved to be first, spread evil words against John, and actually tried to stop other churches or leaders from extending **hospitality** to the traveling teachers.

John then gives advice in light of these examples of how to live, and he encourages Gaius to do good and not evil. Those who do good are from God, and those who do evil have not seen God (v. 11).

Third John closes with a recommendation of **Demetrius,** who may have been the one who carried the letter to Gaius. He also wants to talk more with Gaius but does not want to write his thoughts; instead he hopes to see him soon and talk face-to-face.

Summary Statements

- The Christian tradition ascribes the authorship of 1, 2, and 3 John to John the apostle.
- First John does not follow the style of a typical ancient letter.
- First John contrasts two lifestyles: those who walk in the light with God and love others, and those who walk in the darkness and hate their fellow human beings.
- First John emphasizes the truth that God is love.
- All three letters of John promote correct belief and loving actions as important characteristics of the true children of God.

Questions for Reflection

1. Can a person love God and hate his or her brother or sister? Why or why not?
2. The Scriptures say that perfect love casts out fear. Does that mean that if we have fears and worries, we do not love God with all our heart? Why or why not?
3. Is hospitality a virtue today? Is hospitality defined the same way today as it was in the first century?

Bible Study Assignment

Read 1 John 2:12-14 and answer the following questions:

1. Who are the three groups of people addressed in these verses?
2. What is distinctive about each group and what does John say to each group?
3. What conclusion may be drawn about the spiritual maturity of each group?
4. What might be the hidden challenge that John is placing before each group about their relationship with God?
5. Using these three groups as a model, what conclusion can be made about the various stages of spiritual development in an individual's life?
6. What contemporary applications do you find in this text for your personal life?

Resources for Further Study

Bruce, F. F. *The Epistles of John.* Grand Rapids: Wm. B. Eerdmans Publishing Co., 1970.

Marshall, I. Howard. *The Epistles of John.* Grand Rapids: Wm. B. Eerdmans Publishing Co., 1978.

Yamauchi, Edwin M. *Pre-Christian Gnosticism: A Survey of the Proposed Evidences,* 2nd ed. Grand Rapids: Baker Book House, 1983.

32 The Book of Revelation

Objectives:

Your study of this chapter should help you to:
- Gain an understanding of Jewish and Christian apocalyptic literature
- Describe the historical and theological issues relative to the writing of the Book of Revelation
- Evaluate the practical and theological importance of the Book of Revelation
- Describe the different types of interpretation of Revelation

Key Words to Understand

Patmos
Apocalypticism
Dualism
Domitian
Literal interpretation
Montanists
Idealist view
Preterist view
Historicist view
Futurist view
Eschatology

Questions to consider as you read:

1. What are some of the similarities and differences between Revelation and Jewish apocalyptic literature?
2. Why was Revelation written in apocalyptic style?
3. What do we learn about the nature of God and His relationship to His creation from Revelation?

Revelation is one of the most talked about but least understood books of the New Testament. Three factors contribute to one's misunderstanding of this book: (1) Its literary style is not familiar to the modern reader. (2) Its historical context is drastically different from the modern context. (3) The original readers may have understood the meaning of many of the symbols in the book, but they remain unclear to its modern readers. In spite of these difficulties, it is possible to grasp the main message of hope the book gives to its ancient audience as well as its modern readers.

"Revelation" is the traditional translation of the Greek word *apokalypsis,* the first word in the Book of Revelation. It means an uncovering or unveiling of something that was originally covered. An apocalypse reports things that were formerly hidden or secret, especially spiritual realities and future events. Revelation is the only book in the New Testament written entirely in an apocalyptic style. It is similar in literary form (genre) to the Book of Daniel, an apocalyptic book in the Old Testament.

The early Christian tradition regarded the apostle John as the author of Revelation. This view is attested by ancient Christian writers such as Papias, Irenaeus, Tertullian, Hippolytus, and Origen. Some scholars conclude that no New Testament book has a "stronger or earlier tradition about its authorship than does Revelation."[1] Many scholars today doubt that the apostle John wrote this book. They point out that the author does not claim to be an apostle but a brother and cosharer in the suffering of his readers. They also cite that there are significant theological and linguistic differences between the Gospel of John and Revelation.

In this study we follow the traditional perspective on the authorship of Revelation. According to tradition, John ministered in Jerusalem from A.D. 30 to 68 and in Ephesus from A.D. 68 to 98, where he died. Part of this time he was in exile on the island of **Patmos,** the location of the visions of Revelation (1:9). It is possible that an editor may have been responsible for the final form of the book, as suggested by the reference to John in the third person (vv. 1-3). However, the content and the visions most likely belong to John the apostle.

Apocalypticism

Jewish apocalyptic literature flourished throughout the intertestamental period and in the first and second centuries A.D. The Jesus movement in the first century A.D. as well as the Early Church developed in a culture influenced by Jewish apocalyptic tradition and symbolism.

The characteristics of Jewish and Christian **apocalypticism** include the use of celestial and supernatural symbols or images. The prophecies of deliverance are clothed in the language of symbol. Apocalyptic literature is also characterized by the idea that evil will continue to grow and will lead to a cosmic catastrophe and universal judgment. Apocalyptic writers divide time into the present evil time and the future perfect time. The writers also subscribe to the idea of cosmic **dualism,** or the existence of material and spiritual worlds. Humanity is also sharply divided between good and evil people. A call to total commitment to God is also a key feature of this type of literature.

Revelation is addressed to "the seven churches in the province of Asia" (v. 4): Ephesus, Smyrna, Pergamum, Thyatira, Sardis, Philadelphia, and Laodicea. The individual letters written to these churches indicate that there were a variety of issues that needed to be addressed in these Christian congregations. Some of these include apostasy, impending persecution and imprisonment, toleration of heresy, spiritual deadness, spiritual apathy, and encouragement for those who are patiently enduring persecution.

Setting and Date

The common historical setting of all apocalyptic writings is that of oppression with no hope of liberation by earthly leaders. For the apocalyptic writer and his readers, only God breaking into history could change their situation. Since the writer uses symbolic language familiar only to his readers to communicate his message of hope and deliverance, there is little fear of retaliation by authorities.

Although the visions of John may have occurred earlier, most scholars date Revelation around A.D. 95-96, during the reign of Emperor **Domitian** (81-96). Domitian, who was worshiped as a god in different parts of the empire, carried out an empire-wide and intense persecution of those who did not worship him, especially Christians.

John reports that he received his visions on the island of Patmos, just off the coast of Asia Minor near Ephesus. But the visions were probably written down in Ephesus where John spent the last part of his life. Ephesus was an important center of Christianity in the late first century.

Emperor Domitian.

The readers were located in Asia Minor along a circuit of seven important cities. They are addressed in the natural order that a messenger would take: From Ephesus, north to Smyrna and Pergamum and then east to Thyatira, then south to Sardis, Philadelphia, and Laodicea.

Content

The first line of Revelation is *Apocalypsis Iēsou Christou*—A Revelation of Jesus Christ—which indicates to us that the purpose of the writer is not to predict the future events but to proclaim Christ and His message. Many books have been written on Revelation predicting the conditions and dates of the Second Coming but have missed the essential message of this book.

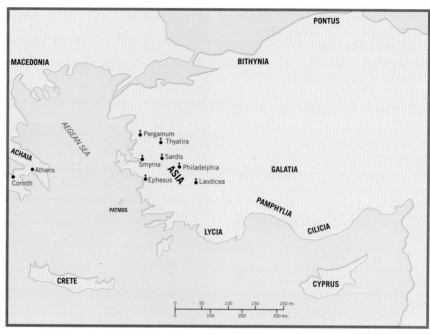

Seven churches in the Province of Asia.

The content of Revelation can be outlined as follows:

Prologue	1:1-8
Letters to the Seven Churches	1:9—3:22
Visions of the Throne of God and Seven Seals	4:1—8:1
Visions of the Seven Trumpets	8:2—11:19
Visions of the Woman, Dragon, and Beast	12:1—14:20
Visions of the Seven Bowls of Wrath	15:1—16:21
Visions of the Great Whore, the Fall of Babylon, and the Return of Christ	17:1—19:21
Visions of Christ's Millennial Reign and the New Heaven and New Earth	20:1—22:5
Epilogue	22:6-21

The introduction (1:1-2) presents the content of the book as "the revelation of Jesus Christ" from God, which an angel communicated to John. The book begins with a pronouncement of blessing to its readers and a formal greeting (vv. 3-5). This is followed by an announcement of the coming of Christ and the identification of God as "the Alpha and the Omega"—the beginning and the end of all things (v. 8). The writer identifies himself as a believer exiled to Patmos because of his faith and testimony. The visions came to him on the "Lord's day." He received the command to write in a book the content of the visions and send it to the seven churches (vv. 9-11).

Church of St. John.

For each church, there is a specific message. Each church is also given a commendation or a condemnation, and a concluding exhortation and promise. The first church, Ephesus, receives the commendation as a church that endured hardships for the sake of Christ. Yet it has forsaken its first love (2:1-7). The second church, Smyrna, receives commendation as a church that experienced afflictions and poverty (vv. 8-11). The third church, Pergamum, receives the commendation for its faithfulness even in the midst of persecution and martyrdom of its members. However, there are some in the church that follow false teachers and their teaching. They are called to repent or face the consequence of judgment (vv. 12-17).

The fourth church, Thyatira, receives commendation for its love, faith, and service; yet the church also tolerates false teachers (vv. 18-29). The fifth church, Sardis, receives a stern warning to wake up. Though they seem to be alive, they are on the verge of death. Only a few in the church have remained faithful (3:1-6). The sixth church, Philadelphia, receives commendation for its faithfulness and patience (vv. 7-13). The seventh church, Laodicea, receives condemnation for its lukewarm condition. The message urges the church to repent and enter into fellowship with Christ (vv. 14-22).

Chapter 4 describes the vision of God seated on His throne in heaven, surrounded by songs of praise and adoration of 24 elders and four living creatures. Chapter 5 contains the vision of the Lamb that was slain for the salvation of humankind. The four living creatures, the 24 elders, and all in heaven sing praise to the Lamb

St. John's cell.

who is worthy to open the scroll sealed with seven seals. The opening of the first six seals is described in chapter 6. The opening of the first four seals announced destruction of various kinds, brought about by riders of four horses—white, red, black, and pale horses respectively.

The two visions in chapter 7 announce protection to 144,000 from the 12 tribes of Israel during tribulation (7:1-8) and salvation to "a great multitude . . . from every nation, tribe, people and language" (v. 9; see vv. 9-17). The opening of the seventh seal led to a fearful silence, anticipating the severe judgment that followed (8:1). The author recounts the sounding of seven trumpets by seven angels and the consequences that fol-

Aqueduct and bathhouse ruins of Laodicea.

The Meaning of Numbers in Revelation

The use of numbers in apocalyptic literature is quite common and is related to the ancient study of astronomy. In fact, ancient astronomers were called "mathematicians." Numbers were used not only to convey how many but also to describe quality.

The number 12 symbolizes completeness. Twenty-four (12 plus 12) elders seated on thrones before God, 12 gates in New Jerusalem, 12 different kinds of fruit from the Tree of Life, 12 foundations that are made of 12 different gemstones—all indicate completeness in Revelation.

Number 7, the number of perfection, is especially prominent in Revelation. The text is divided into seven sections, there are seven churches of the apocalypse, seven seals, seven trumpet blasts, and seven angels with seven plagues or bowls of wrath.

The number 6 has several interpretations. Most prominent is that of imperfection, since it is one less than seven. In Revelation, the best-known number is 666, the number of the beast (13:18). John tells us that this is a number of a human being. However, it is futile to try to determine the identity of this person.

The number 4 is related to the four corners of the earth and the directions from which come the four major winds. It also represents completeness or the "whole" of something specific on earth.

Three (three angels in chapter 14) perhaps reflects three parts of the universe: the sky of fixed stars, the sky of planets, and the fixed earth. Three is more related to the cosmic whole or the essence of being.[2]

lowed each trumpet sound in verse 6—11:19. The first four trumpets brought hail, fire, blood, water pollution, and darkness. The fifth trumpet brought the plague of fearsome locusts. The sixth trumpet unleashed a powerful cavalry to kill one-third of the human population. Before the seventh trumpet, the author sees two visions. In the first vision, the visionary was asked to eat a scroll (10:1-11). The second vision focuses on the prophesying activity, martyrdom, and resurrection of two prophetic witnesses in the holy city (11:1-13). The seventh trumpet announces that "the kingdom of the world has become the kingdom of our Lord and of his Christ, and he will reign for ever and ever" (v. 15).

Chapter 12 narrates the vision of "a woman clothed with the sun," a monstrous red dragon, and a male child that was born to the woman.

A war broke out in heaven, and Michael, the archangel, with his angels defeated the dragon and his angels, who were thrown out of heaven. Two beasts occupy the center of the visions in chapter 13. The dragon gave authority to a beast that came out of the sea, and it became the object of worship of the whole earth. Another beast that came out of the earth deceived and forced the people to worship the first beast. All were forced to put a mark of the beast on their hand or forehead, showing their allegiance to the beast.

Chapter 14 contains a series of visions that give assurance to the faithful of their ultimate vindication by God. The visions also include the judgment of those who worshiped the beast and the defeat of Babylon (Rome).

Judgment of the earth is the key theme of the visions in chapters 15 and 16. Various kinds of judgments take place as seven angels pour out on earth "seven bowls of God's wrath" (16:1). Visions in chapters 17 and 18 report the fall of Babylon (Rome). Chapter 19 narrates the victory celebration of Christ and the "wedding supper of the Lamb" (v. 9). Chapter 20 describes the temporary imprisonment of Satan, his release, the final conflict, the final overthrow of Satan, and the final judgment. The book closes with visions of the new Jerusalem (chaps. 21 and 22). God creates a new heaven and a new earth. He makes His dwelling on earth. The Lord God will be light and life for His people and they will "reign for ever and ever" (22:5).

■ Theology of Revelation

Although Revelation is fundamentally different in style from the rest of the New Testament books, its theology remains the same. God the Creator of the universe guides the course of history. He will overcome evil and bring an end to the suffering of His people. He is "the Alpha and the Omega," the One "who is, and who was, and who is to come" (1:8). The hymns in Revelation proclaim the majesty, greatness, and glory of God. He is holy and worthy to be worshiped because He "created all things" (4:11). He is the "living God" and author of salvation (7:2, 10). "Praise and glory and wisdom and thanks and honor and power and strength" belong to God (v. 12). The kingdoms of the world belong to Him (11:15). His judgments are "true and just" (16:7). He reigns over the earth (19:6). He will create a new heaven and a new earth and establish His dwelling with humanity (21:1-4).

Jesus is the "faithful witness, the firstborn of the dead, and the ruler of the kings of the earth" (1:5). He is "the Alpha and the Omega" (v. 8) and holds the "keys of death and Hades" (v. 18). He is the "Son of God" (2:18) "who holds the seven Spirits of God" (3:1). He is "holy and true" and holds "the key of David" (v. 7). He is "the Lion of the tribe of Judah" and "the Root of David" (5:5). He is the "KING OF KINGS AND LORD OF LORDS" (19:16). He is the "lamb" or the One sacrificed for the sins of the world but is also divine and has the same nature as God, the Father (5:6; 22:12-13).

I Interpretations of Revelation

Literal interpretation is the oldest known interpretation of Revelation. This method was popular among the second- and third-century **Montanists** who announced that the heavenly Jerusalem would descend near a certain village. The movement began in Phrygia, just east of the seven cities of the apocalypse.

Today, there are four classical views of the interpretation of Revelation. The **idealist view** interprets Revelation as a symbolic description of the ongoing struggle between God and the forces of evil. It emphasizes the final triumph of God over evil. The **preterist view** sees Revelation as a message of hope for those being persecuted in the Roman Empire during the late first century. The city called Babylon is a code name for Rome, and the events represented symbolically were contemporary and not predictions of the future.

The **historicist view** builds on both the idealist and the preterist views and sees Revelation as a symbolic description of the Church's history from its beginning to the return of Christ. The symbolic accounts are prophetic representations of past, present, and future events.

The **futurist view** interprets Revelation as a prophecy of future events. These events include a great tribulation lasting seven years, followed by Christ's second coming and the final Judgment.

The people of God will experience the ultimate joy of God's salvation. They are servants or slaves of God, a kingdom, priests, saints, the blameless, the redeemed, and the bride of the Lamb. They are to continue believing in Jesus as the Word of God, being alert to perversions and deception, keeping God's commands, being holy, and doing the work God has assigned them to do.

Revelation is one of the main sources for **eschatology** or the study of the end times. And its eschatology is consistent with the rest of the New Testament. Every believer can have the certainty of life after death. Christians also can be sure of their personal resurrection and reward for righteous living. The second coming of Christ will affect all of creation. Each person will be assigned to his or her eternal reward or punishment. And there will be the creation of a new heaven and a new earth. In the new Jerusalem, God will dwell with His people. They will be forever free from all suffering, mourning, crying, pain, and death.

This book holds no particular view on the interpretation of Revelation, except that it is the inspired Word of God communicated in apocalyptic language. Committed, born-again Christians have held all of the views discussed in this chapter. It is important to realize that the primary message of Revelation is about the *hope* we have in Jesus. What we do know for sure is expressed not only in Revelation but also in the rest of the New Testament: Jesus is coming again soon. He will come at an unexpected time like a thief in the night. God will triumph over all. God's people will dwell with Him for ever and ever. So, with the author of Revelation, we also pray, "Come, Lord Jesus" (22:20).

Summary Statements

- Revelation is an apocalyptic book that utilizes symbolic language and other literary features of Jewish apocalyptic literature.
- The Christian tradition ascribes the book to John the apostle.
- The original readers of Revelation were seven churches in the province of Asia.
- Most scholars date Revelation to A.D. 95-96 during the reign of Emperor Domitian.
- Revelation presents itself as a "prophecy" but is in the form of a letter.
- The number seven, symbolizing perfection, is prominent in Revelation.
- The primary message of Revelation concerns eschatology, or the study of the end times.
- Revelation proclaims Jesus Christ as the hope of the Christian believer.

Questions for Reflection

1. What do you think is the primary message of Revelation? Why?
2. In what ways is the message of Revelation relevant to the 21st century?
3. Does Revelation make a difference in how we live our lives daily, or is it just for the future? Why? Or why not?

Bible Study Assignment

Read Revelation 3:14-22 and answer the following questions:

1. What is the literary form (genre) of this text? Who are the addressees? Who is the speaker? What is significant about John's description of the speaker?
2. What does the author mean by "the angel of the church"?
3. Where was Laodicea located? What was its historical significance?
4. Consult a commentary and discover the source of the metaphor "cold nor hot."
5. In what sense was the church rich? In what sense was it poor?
6. What should the church do to be rich and healthy, in spite of its claim of wealth?
7. What is the challenge and invitation in verses 19 and 20?
8. What is the reward for those who overcome the enemy?
9. What are the key theological lessons of this letter to Laodicea?
10. What descriptions of John will you use to describe your spiritual life? What specific applications do you find in this text for your personal and community life today?

Resources for Further Study

Metzger, Bruce. *Breaking the Code: Understanding the Book of Revelation.* Nashville: Abingdon Press, 1993.

Mounce, Robert H. *The Book of Revelation. The New International Commentary on the New Testament.* Grand Rapids: William B. Eerdmans Publishing Company, 1977.

Epilogue

We have come to the end of our discovery of the Bible. This journey has taken us through the writings of the Old Testament and the New Testament, which together make up the Christian Scriptures. In this journey, we have discovered an intrinsic connection between these two Testaments. Within these Scriptures we see two communities of faith, though not all alike in their makeup and belief system, coming into existence as God's people. The narratives of these two faith communities make up the history of God's people in the Bible. The narrative of the people of Israel is centered on their conviction that their destiny was to be a source of blessing to all humanity. It was for this purpose that God had called them and made a covenant with them at Sinai. That narrative, however, also contains their tragic failure to become a "light to the Gentiles." It is precisely at this point that the narrative of the Christian community finds its connecting link with the story of Israel. The early Christian community was formed around the simple, yet profound, teachings of Jesus of Nazareth, the true Israel, who indeed fulfilled all the hopes and expectations of His nation Israel. The Christian narrative contains the profound truth about the identity of Jesus as God's Son, the Christ who is the Savior of all humanity. It is this narrative of Jesus

that not only brought the community of Christians together but also energized them to become a powerful religious movement in the first-century Roman world.

Biblical story and faith do not end with the pages of the Bible. They continue in the faith traditions of modern-day Judaism and Christianity. Though these two faith communities maintain their own particular and unique theological perspectives, they share a common heritage and history found in the pages of the Hebrew Scriptures. Most importantly these communities share a common faith in one true God, "the Maker of heaven and earth." The unity of this faith is something that calls for celebration and dialogue on interfaith issues that are of common concern to both Judaism and Christianity. In the same way, the common faith in Christ calls the various Christian communities not only to celebrate their differences but also to celebrate unity as members of the Body of Christ.

The biblical faith communities are nurturing communities. It is within the community of faith that faith is developed and nurtured in the individual. In ancient Israel as well as in modern Judaism, an individual's life is shaped by the nation's narrative of God's great and mighty acts in Israel's history. The early Christians shaped their life and faith by the narrative of Jesus of Nazareth, which outlined for them the essential principles of community life. Biblical stories thus inform us that one's spiritual life is not a solitary affair, but a life to be shaped and nurtured by and lived out in the community. As the community shapes and nurtures the individual, the individual participates in the life of the community, its mission, and the purpose for its existence. This act of receiving and giving is significant to faith development. It is through this act of receiving and giving that individuals move out into the arena of faith as participants in the Christian life. The nurtured in turn become the nurturing ones, and faith is transmitted to the next generation.

Discovering the Bible was written to enable and initiate our readers to enter into a journey of faith and become part of the ongoing history of God's people. This journey requires one to interact with the Bible—read and study God's Word—on a regular basis. This book has provided the essential background to understand the history, geography, culture, and religious ideas found in the pages of the Bible. Our hope and prayer is that your discovery of the Bible through this volume has already initiated you into a journey of faith, a life that is lived out in a Christian community. We also trust that as you have entered into the narrative of God's people, you find yourself being surrounded and nurtured by a "cloud of witnesses," those who are "saints" and exemplary models of Christian living.

Notes

Chapter 4

1. The classic expression of the composite nature of the Pentateuch is found in Julius Wellhausen's *Die Komposition des Hexateuchs,* 1877. Critical scholars label the primary sources of the Pentateuch as Yahwistic (J), Elohistic (E), Priestly (P), and Deuteronomic (D).

2. See "Akkadian Myths and Epics," translated by E. A. Speiser in James B. Pritchard, *Ancient Near Eastern Texts Relating to the Old Testament,* 3rd ed. (Princeton, N.J.: Princeton University Press, 1969), 68.

3. For a survey of the various views on the week of creation, see Henri Blocher, *In the Beginning: The Opening Chapters of Genesis* (Downers Grove, Ill.: InterVarsity Press, 1984), 39-59.

4. For a theological understanding of the image of God, see H. Ray Dunning, *Grace, Faith, and Holiness* (Kansas City: Beacon Hill Press of Kansas City, 1988), 150-61.

5. See the full text of this epic in Pritchard, *Ancient Near Eastern Texts,* 72-99.

Chapter 5

1. See Brevard Childs, *Exodus: Old Testament Library* (Philadelphia: Westminster, 1974), 232-37, for an excellent summary of the history of interpretation of the Exodus-Crossing of the Sea in the Christian and Jewish writings.

2. Scholars are divided on the issue of the parallels between the Sinai covenant and the ancient Hittite treaties. See D. J. McCarthy, *Treaty and Covenant* (Rome: Biblical Institute, 1963), for a survey of the debate.

3. See Victor Hamilton, *Handbook on the Pentateuch* (Grand Rapids: Baker Book House, 1982), 213-21, for an analysis of the laws of the covenant code and the nonbiblical legal codes.

Chapter 6

1. Yehezkel Kaufmann, *The Religion of Israel* (Chicago: University of Chicago Press, 1960) and J. Milgrom, *The Anchor Bible: Leviticus 1—16* (New York: Doubleday, 1991) are among the advocates of the early seventh century B.C. origin of the Book of Leviticus.

2. Jacob Milgrom presents 26 strong reasons and 23 supportive ones for his assignment that the priestly materials in the book belong to a period much earlier than the postexilic period. See *The JPS Torah Commentary: Numbers* (Philadelphia: Jewish Publication Society, 1989), xxxii-xxxv.

3. For a detailed discussion in support of a date much earlier than the seventh century B.C., see P. C. Craigie, *The Book of Deuteronomy: The New International Commentary on the Old Testament* (Grand Rapids: William B. Eerdmans Publishing Company, 1976), 24-32.

Chapter 7

1. For a full text of this *Hymn of Victory of Mer-ne-Ptah* (also known as the "Israel Stela"), see Pritchard, *Ancient Near Eastern Texts,* 376-78.

2. See John Day, "Canaan, Religion of," in vol. 1 of *Anchor Bible Dictionary* (New York: Doubleday, 1992), 831-37.

Chapter 9

1. According to 1 Kings 9:16, Pharaoh of Egypt gave Gezer as a wedding gift to his daughter whom he gave as a wife to Solomon. Bright thinks that Pharaoh was attempting to make Solomon an ally by this unusual marriage relation, since Egyptian Pharaohs were not known for giving their daughters in marriage to foreign kings. See John Bright, *A History of Israel,* 4th ed. (Louisville, Ky.: John Knox Press, 2000), 212.

2. This chronology is based on John Bright's reconstruction of Israel's history. See Bright's Chronological Charts in his *History of Israel* cited above. Other chronological schemes present the division of the kingdom at 930 B.C. See Edwin R. Thiele, *The Mysterious Numbers of the Hebrew Kings: A Reconstruction of the Chronology of the Kingdoms of Israel and Judah* (Grand Rapids: William B. Eerdmans Publishing Company, 1965).

3. See Bright's Chronological Charts in the appendix of *A History of Israel.*

Chapter 10

1. See Pritchard, *Ancient Near Eastern Texts,* 316.

2. See R. K. Harrison, *Introduction to the Old Testament* (Grand Rapids: William B. Eerdmans Publishing Company, 1969), 1153-57, for a detailed discussion of the authorship and date of Chronicles.

3. For a survey of Old Testament genealogies, see Robert R. Wilson, "Genealogy, Genealogies," in vol. 2 of *Anchor Bible Dictionary* (New York: Doubleday, 1992), 929-33.

4. See Harrison, *Introduction to the Old Testament,* 1145-49, for a detailed study of the date of the ministry of Ezra and Nehemiah.

5. See ibid., 1087-90, for a detailed discussion of the problems of dating and authorship of Esther.

Chapter 11

1. See the full text of the *Instructions of Amen-em-opet* in Pritchard, *Ancient Near Eastern Texts,* 421-24.

2. See *The Babylonian Theodicy,* a poem on human suffering in the form of a dialogue be-

tween the suffering individual and a friend in Pritchard, *Ancient Near Eastern Texts,* 601-4.

3. For a discussion of the date and authorship of Job, see Robert Gordis, *The Book of God and Man: A Study of Job* (Chicago: University of Chicago Press, 1965), 209-18.

4. See the full text of *The Admonitions of Ipuwer* in Pritchard, *Ancient Near Eastern Texts,* 441-44.

5. See Pritchard, *Ancient Near Eastern Texts,* 434-37.

6. See ibid., 601-4.

7. See John Hartley's excellent introductory work on literary genre and parallels in his commentary, *The Book of Job: New International Commentary on the Old Testament* (Grand Rapids: William B. Eerdmans Publishing Company, 1988).

8. See Elizabeth R. Achtemeier, "Righteousness in the OT," in vol. 4 of *Interpreter's Dictionary of the Bible* (Nashville: Abingdon Press, 1962), 80-85.

9. This book represents, according to most scholars, the latest Hebrew in the Bible. Robert Gordis, citing the relationship of the apocryphal book Wisdom of Ben Sirach (Ecclesiasticus) to Qoheleth, proposed a time around 250 B.C. as the date of Qoheleth's composition. Robert Gordis, *Koheleth—The Man and His World* (New York: Schocken Books, 1968), 67.

Chapter 12

1. For a detailed survey of the history of the interpretation of Song of Songs see Marvin H. Pope, *Song of Songs: A New Translation with Introduction and Commentary,* in *The Anchor Bible* (New York: Doubleday, 1977), 89-229.

2. Ibid., 210.

3. See the lament texts from ancient Mesopotamia in Pritchard, *Ancient Near Eastern Texts,* 458.

Chapter 13

1. For an excellent study of the various forms of prophetic speech, see Claus Westermann, *Basic Forms of Prophetic Speech* (Philadelphia: Westminster Press, 1967).

2. Christopher R. Seitz gives a good analysis of the theological structure of these chapters in his *Isaiah 1—39: Interpretation* (Louisville, Ky.: John Knox Press, 1993), 15-18.

3. See Paul D. Hanson, *Isaiah 40—66: Interpretation* (Louisville, Ky.: John Knox Press, 1995), 1-4, 185-92, for an overview of the possible historical setting and the relation of Isaiah 56—66 to Isaiah 40—55.

Chapter 14

1. See various interpretations of these symbolic acts in Ralph H. Alexander, *Ezekiel: Expositor's Bible Commentary,* vol. 6 (Grand Rapids: Zondervan Publishing House, 1986), 769-71; John B. Taylor, *Ezekiel: Tyndale Old Testament Commentaries* (Downers Grove, Ill.: InterVarsity Press, 1969), 74-85; Walther Eichrodt, *Ezekiel: A Commentary,* trans. Cosslett Quin (Philadelphia: Westminster Press, 1970), 80-91.

2. See a discussion on the various points of contact between Ezekiel 38—48 and Revelation 19—22, and on the interpretation of Ezekiel 40—48 in Alexander, *Ezekiel,* 937-52.

Chapter 15

1. See this view expressed by James L. Mays, *Hosea: A Commentary* (Philadelphia: Westminster Press, 1969), 24-25.

2. See James L. Mays, *Amos: A Commentary* (Philadelphia: Westminster Press, 1974), 2.

3. See Samuel Pagan, *The Book of Obadiah: The New Interpreter's Bible,* vol. 7 (Nashville: Abingdon Press, 1996), 436.

4. See Phyllis Trible, *The Book Jonah: The New Interpreter's Bible,* vol. 7 (Nashville: Abingdon Press, 1996), 466, footnote 8, for bibliographic references to various dates for Jonah proposed by scholars.

Chapter 16

1. See O. Palmer Robertson, *The Books of Nahum, Habakkuk, and Zephaniah: The New International Commentary on the Old Testament* (Grand Rapids: William B. Eerdmans Publishing Company, 1990), 32, and Ralph L. Smith, *Micah-Malachi: Word Biblical Commentary* (Waco, Tex.: Word Books, 1984), 63, for various views on the home of Nahum.

2. See Smith, *Micah-Malachi,* 93, for a summary of various legends and views on the identity of Habakkuk.

3. Theodore Hiebert, *The Book of Habakkuk: The New Interpreter's Bible,* vol. 7 (Nashville: Abingdon Press, 1996), 654.

4. See Robertson, *Books of Nahum, Habakkuk, and Zephaniah,* 39.

5. See Smith, *Micah-Malachi,* 121, for this view proposed by Donald L. Williams in *Journal of Biblical Literature* 82 (1963), 85-88.

6. See ibid., 121-23, for an extensive analysis of various proposals for the date of Zephaniah's ministry. He prefers a date around 627 B.C.

Chapter 17

1. See Leo Oppenheim, *The Interpretation of Dreams in the Ancient Near East* (Philadelphia: American Philosophical Society, 1956), for examples.

Chapter 18

1. This historical overview is taken from Bright, *History of Israel,* 417-27.

2. For a detailed summary of the history of the Jews, see Flavius Josephus, *Wars of the Jews,* in *The Works of Josephus,* trans. William Whiston (Lynn, Mass.: Hendrickson, 1980), 429-605.

3. The following survey is taken from Merrill C. Tenney, *New Testament Survey* (Grand Rapids: William B. Eerdmans Publishing Company, 1961), 66-68. Robert H. Gundry, *A Survey of the New Testament* (Grand Rapids: Zondervan, 1981), 35-37.

4. Flavius Josephus, *Antiquities of the Jews,* Book XIII, Chapter X in *Works of Josephus,* 281.

5. Howard C. Kee, Franklin W. Young, Karl-fried Froehlich, *Understanding the New Testa-*

ment (Englewood Cliffs, N.J.: Prentice-Hall, 1965), 39.

6. Josephus, *Works of Josephus,* 281.

7 Helmut Koester, *Introduction to the New Testament: History, Culture, and Religion of the Hellenistic Age,* vol. 1 (New York: Walter de Gruyter, 1982), 241.

8. Ibid., 235.

9. Ibid., 235-36.

Chapter 19

1. Several other early Christian writings outside the New Testament have "Gospel" in their titles as well, such as the Gospel of Thomas, the Gospel of Peter, and so forth. (See Bart D. Ehrman, *The New Testament and Other Early Christian Writings: A Reader,* 2nd ed. [New York: Oxford University Press, 2004], 116-42.)

2. Dennis C. Duling, *The New Testament* (Belmont, Calif.: Wadsworth, 2003), 294; cf. Craig A. Evans, Mark 8:27—16:20, in *Word Biblical Commentary,* vol. 35b (Nashville: Thomas Nelson, 2001), lxxxii-lxxxiii.

3. Raymond E. Brown, *An Introduction to the New Testament* (New York: Doubleday, 1997), 102-3; John Drane, *Introducing the New Testament* (Minneapolis: Fortress, 2001), 169-71.

4. Brevard S. Childs, *Biblical Theology of the Old and New Testaments* (Minneapolis: Fortress, 1993), 225-27; James H. Charlesworth and Walter P. Weaver, *The Old and New Testaments* (Valley Forge, Pa.: Trinity Press International, 1993); Fredrick C. Holmgren, *The Old Testament and the Significance of Jesus* (Grand Rapids: William B. Eerdmans Publishing Company, 1999).

5. Brown, *Introduction to the New Testament,* 114.

6. Ibid., 365.

7. Johnnie Godwin, "Baptism," in *Holman Bible Dictionary* (Nashville: Holman Bible Publishers, 1991), 150.

8. Bernard Brandon Scott, *Hear Then the Parable* (Minneapolis: Fortress, 1989), viii-ix.

9. For a useful introductory text on the parables of Jesus, see Robert H. Stein, *An Introduction to the Parables of Jesus* (Philadelphia: Westminster, 1981).

10. Pheme Perkins, "Messiah," in *Harper's Bible Dictionary* (San Francisco: Harper and Row, 1985), 630.

11. Jouette M. Bassler, "Cross," in ibid., 194.

Chapter 20

1. Donald Senior, *The Gospel of Matthew* (Nashville: Abingdon, 1997), 20.

2. Brevard S. Childs, *The New Testament as Canon: An Introduction* (Philadelphia: Fortress, 1984), 69.

3. Ibid., 78.

4. Donald Guthrie, *New Testament Introduction* (Downers Grove, Ill.: InterVarsity Press, 1970), 32.

5. Ulrich Luz, *Matthew 1—7* (Minneapolis: Augsburg, 1989), 156-64.

6. Senior, *Gospel of Matthew,* 160-64.

7. For a brief discussion of this discourse see "Jesus' Olivet Discourse," in H. Ray Dunning, ed., *The Second Coming* (Kansas City: Beacon Hill Press of Kansas City, 1995), 55-77.

8. John R. Donahue and Daniel J. Harrington, *The Gospel of Mark,* vol. 2 of the Sacra Pagina Series (Collegeville, Md.: Liturgical Press, 2002), 38-39.

9. Brown, *Introduction to the New Testament,* 161-64.

10. Robert A. Guelich, *Mark 1—8:26,* in *Word Biblical Commentary,* vol. 34a (Dallas: Word Books, 1989), xli.

11. R. T. France, *The Gospel of Mark* in *The New International Greek Testament Commentary* (Grand Rapids: William B. Eerdmans Publishing Company, 2002), 11-14.

12. Bruce M. Metzger, *A Textual Commentary on the Greek New Testament* (New York: United Bible Societies, 1975), 122-28.

Chapter 21

1. For New Testament Apocrypha see Willis Branstone, ed., *The Other Bible* (New York: HarperSanFrancisco, 1984). See also, E. Hennecke, *New Testament Apocrypha: Gospels and Related Writings* (London: Lutterworth Press, 1963).

2. George R. Beasley-Murray, *John, Word Biblical Commentary,* vol. 36 (Waco, Tex.: Word Books, 1987), lxvi-lxxv; Brown, *Introduction to the New Testament,* 368-69.

3. Johannes Beutler, S.J., "Faith and Confession: The Purpose of John," in *Word, Theology, and Community in John,* ed. John Painter, R. Alan Culpepper, and Fernando F. Segovia (St. Louis: Chalice, 2002), 19-31.

4. Leon Morris, *Jesus Is the Christ: Studies in the Theology of John* (Grand Rapids: William B. Eerdmans Publishing Company, 1989), 43-67.

5. The discourse address to Nicodemus changes from singular "you" to plural "you," which indicates that the addressees of this speech have been shifted from a single person to a group of people, most likely the Jewish community that refuses to recognize Jesus as Messiah. See Ernst Haenchen, *John I: A Commentary on the Gospel of John, Chapters 1—6 (Hermeneia: A Critical and Historical Commentary on the Bible)* (Philadelphia: Fortress, 1984), 202.

6. For other examples of the relation between miracle and discourse see Morris, *Jesus Is the Christ,* 20-42.

7. The farewell discourse in John seems to be a substitute for the eschatological discourse of Jesus in the Synoptics (Mark 13, Matthew 24—25, Luke 21). See C. K. Barrett, *The Gospel According to St. John,* 2nd ed. (Philadelphia: Westminster, 1978), 68.

8. Barrett, *Gospel According to St. John,* 85.

9. Herman Ridderbos, *The Gospel of John: A Theological Commentary* (Grand Rapids: William B. Eerdmans Publishing Company, 1997), 503.

10. Barrett, *Gospel According to St. John,* 175-77, 545, 558.

11. N. T. Wright, *The Resurrection of the Son of God* (Minneapolis: Fortress, 2003), 200-206.

12. John F. O'Grady, *According to John: The Witness of the Beloved Disciple* (New York: Paulist, 1999), 124-25.

Chapter 22

1. Hans Conzelmann, *Acts of the Apostles* (Philadelphia: Fortress Press, 1987), xliii-xlv.

2. E. Keck and J. L. Martyn, *Studies in Luke-Acts* (Philadelphia: Fortress Press, 1980), 208-16.

3. Edgar J. Goodspeed, *Paul: A Biography Drawn from the Evidence in the Apostle's Writing* (Nashville: Abingdon Press, 1947), 222. The dates here are Goodspeed's, with some adjustments.

4. F. F. Bruce, *The Book of Acts* (Grand Rapids: William B. Eerdmans Publishing Company, 1976), 26.

Chapter 23

1. F. F. Bruce, *Paul: Apostle of the Heart Set Free* (Grand Rapids: William B. Eerdmans Publishing Company, 1977), 38. Some modern scholars are skeptical of the historical authenticity of Paul's Roman citizenship. See Calvin J. Roetzel, *Paul: The Man and the Myth* (Columbia: University of South Carolina Press, 1998), 19-22.

2. William M. Ramsay, *St. Paul the Traveler and the Roman Citizen* (London: Hodder and Stoughton, 1897. Reprint. Grand Rapids: Baker Books, 1962), 34.

3. See, for example, Calvin J. Roetzel, *The Letters of Paul: Conversations in Context* (Louisville, Ky.: Westminster/John Knox Press, 1991), 19-25.

4. Bruce, *Paul: Apostle of the Heart Set Free*, 41-44.

5. See both of these letters in C. K. Barrett, *New Testament Background: Selected Documents* (Reprint. New York: Harper and Row, 1961), 28-29.

6. See descriptions of these various types and classifying letters using rhetorical critical method in William Klein, Craig Blomberg, and Robert Hubbard, *Introduction to Biblical Interpretation* (Dallas: Word Publishing, 1993), 355-58.

7. A view introduced by Adolph Deissmann in the early part of the 20th century in his *Light from the Ancient East: The New Testament Illustrated by Recently Discovered Texts of the Greco-Roman World* (London: Hodder and Stoughton, 1927), 228-41. This view is cited in Thomas Schreiner, *Interpreting the Pauline Epistles* (Grand Rapids: Baker Book House, 1990), 24.

8. Schreiner, *Interpreting the Pauline Epistles*, 24.

9. See ibid., 31, where Schreiner lists various introductory formulas found in the beginning of the body section, taken from J. L. White, "Introductory Formulae in the Body of the Pauline Letter," *Journal of Biblical Literature* 90 (1971): 91-97.

10. Roetzel, *Letters of Paul*, 65-66.

11. See S. K. Stowers, *The Diatribe and Paul's Letter to the Romans* (Chico, Calif.: Scholars Press, 1981).

Chapter 24

1. This description does not minimize the significance of the Gospels as the authentic records of the life of Jesus Christ. Rather, this phrase conveys the idea that the Epistle to the Romans gives the most profound explanation of the content of the gospel message—the "good news" of what God has accomplished through His Son Jesus Christ.

2. John Wesley, *The Works of John Wesley* (Kansas City: Nazarene Publishing House, n.d.), 1:103.

3. J. G. Pilkington, trans. *The Confessions of St. Augustine.* Book VIII, Chapter XII. Philip Schaff, ed. *Nicene and Post-Nicene Fathers* (Peabody, Mass.: Hendrickson Publishers, 1995), 1:127.

4. For an excellent survey of the many reasons why Paul wrote the letter to the Romans, see Douglas Moo, *Romans*, in *The NIV Application Commentary* (Grand Rapids: Zondervan, 200), 21-24.

5. William Greathouse, *Wholeness in Christ: Toward a Biblical Theology of Holiness* (Kansas City: Beacon Hill Press of Kansas City, 1998), 85.

6. Dunning, *Grace, Faith, and Holiness,* 205.

7. Ibid., 206.

8. Ibid.

9. Willard H. Taylor, "Wrath" in *Beacon Dictionary of Theology,* Richard S. Taylor, ed. (Kansas City: Beacon Hill Press of Kansas City, 1983), 552.

10. Gerhard Von Rad, *Deuteronomy: A Commentary,* trans. Dorothea Barton (Philadelphia: Westminster, 1966), 84.

Chapter 25

1. Otto F. A. Meinardus, *St. Paul in Greece* (New York: Caratzas, 1979), 61.

2. See Ben Witherington III, *Conflict and Community in Corinth* (Grand Rapids: William B. Eerdmans Publishing Company, 1995), 5-19, for a detailed survey of the Roman Corinth.

3. Meinardus, *St. Paul in Greece,* 66.

4. Ibid., 66-67.

5. Witherington, *Conflict and Community in Corinth,* 285.

6. C. K. Barrett, *A Commentary on the First Epistle to the Corinthians* (New York: Harper and Row Publishers, 1968), 324.

7. Witherington, *Conflict and Community in Corinth,* 170-71.

8. Ibid., 5-19.

9. For an excellent survey of the discussion of these two theories, see Werner Georg Kümmel, *Introduction to the New Testament,* trans. A. J. Mattill Jr. (Nashville: Abingdon, 1966), 191-93; and Donald Guthrie, *New Testament Introduction* (Downers Grove, Ill.: InterVarsity Press, 1970), 450-57.

Chapter 26

1. For an excellent survey of the place and time of the writing of the letter to the Philippians, see Kümmel, *Introduction to the New Testament,* 229-35.

2. Richard E. Oster Jr. "Ephesus," in *Anchor Bible Dictionary,* David Noel Freedman, ed. (New York: Doubleday, 1992), 2:542-48.

3. For a detailed survey of Philippi, its history, culture, and religion, see Holland L. Hendrix, "Philippi," in *Anchor Bible Dictionary,* 5:313-17.

4. Meinardus, *St. Paul in Greece,* 10.

5. Morna D. Hooker, *Philippians,* vol. 11 in *The New Interpreter's Bible,* Leander E. Keck, ed. (Nashville: Abingdon Press, 2000), 508.

6. See the article on "Colossae" by Clinton E. Arnold, *Anchor Bible Dictionary,* 1:1089. Also, Eduard Lohse, *Colossians and Philemon,* trans. William R. Poehlmann and Robert J. Karris, in *Hermeneia: A Critical and Historical Commentary on the Bible* (Philadelphia: Fortress Press, 1971), 8-9.

7. Lohse, *Colossians and Philemon,* 2.

8. Lohse calls it "The Christ-Hymn." See ibid., 41.

Chapter 27

1. See the history and culture of Thessalonica in Holland L. Hendrix, "Thessalonica," in *Anchor Bible Dictionary,* 6:523-27.

2. Ernest Best, *A Commentary on the First and Second Epistles to the Thessalonians* (New York: Harper and Row Publishers, 1972), 242.

3. See W. T. Purkiser, *Exploring Christian Holiness,* vol. 1: *The Biblical Foundations* (Kansas City: Beacon Hill Press of Kansas City, 1983), 188.

4. Dunning, *Grace, Faith, and Holiness,* 350.

5. See I. Howard Marshall's excellent treatment of verses 6 and 7 in his commentary on *1 and 2 Thessalonians: The New Century Bible Commentary* (Grand Rapids: William B. Eerdmans Publishing Company, 1983), 193-200.

Chapter 28

1. The name Pastoral Epistles was attached to these letters for the first time in the 18th century. See Kümmel, *Introduction to the New Testament,* 259.

2. For a detailed discussion of the authorship and the problem of dating and other historical elements, see A. T. Hanson, *The Pastoral Epistles: The New Century Bible Commentary* (Grand Rapids: William B. Eerdmans Publishing Company, 1982), 2-51. Hanson is a strong advocate of a second-century date and the non-Pauline authorship of these letters.

3. Hanson, *Pastoral Epistles,* 57.

4. Ibid., 71.

5. A. Cleveland Coxe, "The First Epistle of Clement to the Corinthians" in *The Apostolic Fathers,* American ed., 2nd printing (Peabody, Mass.: Hendrickson Publishers, 1995), 16.

Chapter 29

1. Clement of Alexandria, Origen, and Dionysius applied the term *catholic* to all or a part of these seven Epistles and since the time of Eusebius this has become the common designation. http://www.ccel.org/fathers2/NPNF2-01/Npnf2-01-07.htm#P938_461218

2. There are a number of parallels between I Clement and the letter to the Hebrews. The following is a list of some of these parallel passages: I Clement 36:2-5 and Hebrews 1:3-12; I Clement 17:7 and Hebrews 11:37; I Clement 17:5 and Hebrew 3:5.

3. Papyrus 46, from the 2nd-3rd century A.D. This manuscript contains only the Pauline Epistles and Hebrews comes immediately after Romans. See Bruce M. Metzger, *A Textual Commentary on the Greek New Testament,* 2nd ed. (New York: United Bible Societies, 1994), 591.

4. William Barclay, *The Letter to the Hebrews,* in *The Daily Bible Study Series* (Philadelphia: Westminster Press, 1957), 186.

Chapter 30

1. Ralph Martin, *James,* vol. 48 in *Word Biblical Commentary* (Waco, Tex.: Word Books, 1988), lxiii-lxix.

2. John Elliot, *A Home for the Homeless: A Sociological Exegesis of 1 Peter, Its Situation and Strategy* (Philadelphia: Fortress Press, 1981), 68.

Chapter 31

1. D. A. Carson, Douglas J. Moo, and Leon Morris, *An Introduction to the New Testament* (Grand Rapids: Zondervan, 1992), 449.

2. Pheme Perkins, *Reading the New Testament,* 2nd ed. (New York: Paulist Press, 1988), 304.

3. F. F. Bruce, *The Epistles of John* (Grand Rapids: William B. Eerdmans Publishing Company, 1970), 137.

4. Ralph Earle, Harvey J. S. Blaney, Carl Hanson, *Exploring the New Testament* (Kansas City: Beacon Hill Press, 1955), 418.

Chapter 32

1. Carson, Moo, and Morris, *Introduction to the New Testament,* 468, citing Gerhard Maier, *Die Johannesoffenbarung und die Kirche,* WUNT 25 (Tubingen: Mohr, 1981), 1-69.

2. See Bruce J. Malina and John J. Pilch, *Social-Science Commentary on the Book of Revelation* (Minneapolis: Fortress Press, 2000), for more detailed information on the use of numbers in Revelation and the ancient first-century cultures.

Subject Index